HMO PROPERTY SET UP

Essential Advice And Guidance

To Ensure Your Success

By

James Blake

© 2023 by James Blake

All rights reserved. No part of this book may be reproduced in any form without the express written permission in writing by the author.

Disclaimer

The contents of this book are not to be taken as personalised legal, financial or investment advice. The author is not a financial advisor or licenced professional. The ideas provided in this book are for informative purposes only. The views expressed in this book are those of the author alone and should not be taken as expert instruction or commands. Readers should seek professional advice regarding such matters as interpretation of the law, financial planning and taxation prior to proceeding with any property investments.

To the maximum extent permitted by law, the author disclaims any and all liability in the event that any information, commentary, analysis, opinions, advice and/or recommendations contained in this book provide to be inaccurate, incomplete or unreliable or result in any investment or other losses. Although every precaution has been taken in the preparation of this book, the author assumes no responsibility for errors or omissions. Any perceived slight of any individual or organisation is purely unintentional.

ISBN 9798376789001

This book is dedicated to my wife, Hazel, for her love, support and encouragement and to our son, Rupert, who makes me so proud, motivates me and is an inspiration to me every day.

Preface

"Sharing knowledge occurs when people are genuinely interested in helping one another develop new capacities for action; it is about creating learning processes."

- Peter Senge

Congratulations and thank you for purchasing my book - I truly hope you enjoy reading it and that it proves to be useful tool for you in your HMO property development journey.

I wrote this book to help people who are seeking to change their lives through property development in the form of professional Houses in Multiple Occupation (HMOs) and who know there are many benefits associated with this type of asset, but who may be unsure of where to start. I initially had the idea for this book at the start of the second Covid-19 'lockdown' of 2020. I had some spare time after work and nowhere else to be! As I started to write down my ideas, the book evolved into a bigger project, covering a broader range of topics which I considered to be most relevant to setting up a professional HMO.

There are, of course, a myriad of other books out there on property development, HMOs and other investment strategies, but, if like me, you have read a number of these books, you may have found yourself becoming frustrated with the information contained in these books and wanting *more* when you come to the end. I've often thought that some of the 'helpful' tips and advice do not provide enough detail to allow you to confidently know what actions you need to take next.

This is where I hope you'll find this book differs from others. I have written it to include more detail on the crucial points of finding areas to invest in, how to comply with HMO licensing and planning legislation and the differences between the two, relevant building regulations and the associated additional legislation and considerations you will need to comply with as HMO property developers and landlords.

Please note, there are a number of recommendations for useful websites, products and services referenced throughout this book. I am not affiliated with any of these and they are included simply as personal recommendations to assist you.

Part I introduces you to the world of HMOs, if you are not already familiar and how HMO developments can be approached. It also covers your reasons for wanting to get started in HMO property development and how to make sure you can finance and have the right people around you to support your property development journey.

Part II is the more technical side of the book, discussing how to find where to invest, the relevant, HMO licensing, Planning and Building Control legislation you will have to consider, as well as other important legislation, guidance and considerations.

Part III covers the basics of being a landlord and how to stay on the right side of the law, legislation on data protection and property and tenant management systems.

In essence, this book aims to provide you with guidance on everything you should consider to enable you to confidently set up as a successful HMO property developer and take advantage of the opportunities available to you as a HMO landlord.

If you are already aware of HMOs, you may be thinking to yourself that the HMO market is already over-saturated and that you might have 'missed the boat' with all the changes in relation to the private rental sector (PRS). However, with the UK Government's continued failures to address the current housing crisis, coupled with a cost-of-living crisis – and the increased fluidity and transience of the population regarding employment - a fundamental need continues to exist for good quality, flexible housing options.

As someone who has worked as a professional Planning Consultant for a number of years, I have been privileged to be able to guide and advise numerous property developers and clients on how to professionally set up HMOs in England as well as provide bespoke planning advice. I now wish to share my knowledge and experience with a wider audience and help enable you to reach your own personal and financial goals.

Property, in any shape or form, is not a 'get rich quick' strategy. These do not exist. I would advise on steering well clear of anyone telling you they do. The reality is that property development can be risky. It takes time and patience to set up a HMO property development business correctly. Whilst the journey can sometimes be tricky to navigate, the important point to remember is that with the knowledge contained in this book, you will be able to enter the world of HMO property development confidently and competently.

I challenge you to take those first steps and work toward changing your life for the better.

Your journey starts over the page... so, let's begin!

Acknowledgements

Thanking all the people individually who have been involved in and helped to contribute to my knowledge over the years – and ultimately to this book would be a difficult task. I'll simply say a big THANK YOU to you all – you know who you are and I am very grateful for your help, support and guidance. I wouldn't have been able to do this without you!

About The Author

James is a Chartered Town Planner, who has worked in the property and construction industry for over a decade, first as a Design Engineer and Estimator for a nationwide flat roofing supplier and bespoke aluminium coping fabricator and secondly as a Planning Consultant for the world's first property investment franchise, which is one of the most well-known and highly respected property franchise companies in England, specialising in helping its franchise partners set up and run high-quality HMO properties for working professionals. He is currently based in the south of England, working on a diverse range of residential and commercial planning projects at a private planning practice.

James has long held an interest in planning and development, construction, investment and wealth creation. Using the knowledge gained from his experience, he has put together this book filled with useful steps and advice to guide you through the complex and often ever-changing world of HMO property development.

Outside of property and development, James enjoys reading and going on walks in the countryside or along the coast with his young family and their dog. He also has a keen interest in watersports. In particular, powerboating, sailing and motor cruising and holds an RYA Day Skipper licence. When time allows, he can quite often be found somewhere along the Dorset and Hampshire coastlines, building experience and working towards gaining his next RYA certification.

Table Of Contents

Preface	4
Acknowledgements	8
About The Author	9
Table Of Contents	10
List Of Figures	16
List Of Tables	20
Part I	23
Introduction	24
i. What Is A House In Multiple Occupation?	24
ii. Why Do HMOs Make Good Investments?	26
iii. Different Types Of HMOs And Tenant Profiles	35
iv. What This Book Covers	39
v. Other Property Development Strategies	41
Summary	42
Section I: Principles Of Property Development	43
1. Your Goals And Objectives	45
2. Property Development Key Terms	51
3. Devising A Business Plan	58
4. Business Structure And Exit Strategies	61
5. Financing Your Development Project	77

6. HMO Mortgages	95
7. Project Management	103
8. Your Power Team	106
Summary	110
Part II	111
Section II: Finding Your Investment Location	112
9. Where Do You Start?	113
10. Supply Vs Demand And Competition	118
11. HMO Licensing And Planning Legislation	125
12. Assessing The Location	128
13. Assessing The Suitability Of Properties	133
14. Development Costs	145
15. Arranging And Conducting Viewings	150
16. Acquiring Property	156
Summary	172
Section III: HMO Licensing And Standards	173
17. Introduction To HMO Licensing	174
18. Mandatory Licensing	176
19. Additional Licensing	178
20. Selective Licensing	180
21. Management Requirements	182
22. HMO Licensing Reforms 2018	184
23. National Minimum Standards	186

24. Locally Adopted Standards	188
25. Fire Safety And Risk Assessment	197
26. Housing Health And Safety Rating System	201
27. The Licence Application Process	206
28. Accreditation Schemes For Landlords	212
29. HMO Officer Relationships	214
30. Enforcement	217
Summary	219
Section IV: The Planning System And HMOs	220
31. Introduction To The Planning System	221
32. National Planning Policy	227
33. Local Planning Policy	230
34. Introduction To Permitted Development Rights	233
35. Use Classes	235
36. Householder PD rights	242
37. Adding Value And Fallback Positions	285
38. When To Carry Out Works Using PD Rights	289
39. Removal/Reduction Of PD Rights And Other Common HMO Planning Obstacles	291
40. Checking For PD Rights And Pre-application Advice	315
41. Planning Permission: Different Types Of Permission And Application Documents	322
42. Applying For Planning Permission, The Planning Process And Timescales	355

43. Planning Committee	362
44. The Planning Decision	364
45. The Appeal Process	369
46. Planning Enforcement	377
Summary	384
Section V: Building Regulations	385
47. Introduction To Building Regulations	386
48. Why Are Building Regulations Important For HMOs?	387
49. Approved Documents	389
50. Who Has The Responsibility For Building Regulations Compliance?	392
51. The Building Control Process	394
52. What Works Require Signoff?	397
53. The Signoff Process And Obtaining Building Regulations Approval	399
54. Competent Person Schemes	407
55. Contravention Of Building Regulations And Enforcement Action	408
56. Regularisation	411
Summary	413
Section VI: Additional Legislation And Considerations	414
57. Introduction	415
58. Party Walls	416
59. Restrictive Covenants	429

60. Vehicle Parking Standards, Bicycle Storage And Dropping A Kerb	436
61. Construction Design Management (CDM)	443
62. Joint Contracts Tribunal (JCT) Contracts	449
63. Council Tax: Re-banding And Valuations	454
64. HMO Insurance	466
65. Drainage, Water Supply And Build Over Agreements	475
66. Asbestos	484
67. Speaking To Neighbours	488
68. Reduced VAT	495
69. Sustainability And Energy Efficiency In HMOs	499
70. Refurbishment	509
71. Designing, Decorating and Furnishing HMOs	514
Summary	520
Part III	522
Section VII: Being A Landlord	523
72. Introduction To Being A Landlord	524
73. Certificates, Checks And Compliance	527
74. General Data Protection Regulations	559
75. Property And Tenant Management Software	563
76. Keeping Up To Date	569
Summary	572
Conclusion And Final Thoughts	573

List Of Figures

Figures	Page No.
Figure iii.i: Different types of HMOs	35
Figure 7.1: Time, Cost, Quality project circle	104
Figure 13.1: Property Deal Analyser example	138
Figure 36.1: Birds eye view of a detached dwelling and its curtilage	243
Figure 36.2.1: Side-on view of dormer extension to rear elevation of roof space	246
Figure 36.2.2: Front-on view of dormer extension to rear elevation of roof space	246
Figure 36.3.1: Birds eye view of roof lights/skylights installed on front elevation of roof space	247
Figure 36.3.2: Side-on view of roof lights/skylights installed on front elevation of roof space	248
Figure 36.4: Birds eye view of Principal Elevation and extensions	250
Figure 36.5: Birds eye view of a single storey rear extension across the full width of a detached dwelling, with skylights	251
Figure 36.6.1: Birds eye view of a single storey 3m deep rear extension across the full width of a semi-detached dwelling	252
Figure 36.6.2: Birds eye view of a single storey 4m deep rear extension across the full width of a detached dwelling, with skylights	253
Figure 36.6.3: Side-on view of an extension with a flat roof	253
Figure 36.6.4: Side-on view of an extension with a mono-pitched roof	254
Figure 36.7.1: Birds eye view of a single storey 8m deep Prior Approval rear extension with pitched roof to a detached dwelling	256

Figure 36.7.2: Birds eye view of a single storey 6m deep Prior Approval rear extension to a semi-detached dwelling, with skylights	257
Figure 36.8: Side-on view of a rear extension greater than one storey in height	258
Figure 36.9: Birds eye view of a single storey flat roof side extension	260
Figure 36.10.1: Birds eye view of a single storey side and rear extension combination to a semi-detached dwelling	261
Figure 36.10.2: Birds eye view of a single storey side and rear extension combination to a semi-detached dwelling	262
Figure 36.10.3: Birds eye view of a single storey side and rear extension combination to a detached dwelling	263
Figure 36.10.4: Birds eye view of a single storey side and rear extension combination to a semi-detached dwelling	264
Figure 36.10.5: Birds eye view of a single storey side and rear extension combination to a semi-detached dwelling	265
Figure 36.11.1: Birds eye view of separate single storey side and rear extension combinations to a semi-detached dwelling	266
Figure 36.11.2: Birds eye view of separate single storey side and rear extension combinations to a semi-detached dwelling	267
Figure 36.12: Birds eye view of conservatory to rear of semi-detached dwelling	268
Figure 36.13: Front and side view of doors and windows	269
Figure 36.14: Front view of integral garage conversion	271
Figure 36.15: Front view of side extension and detached garage conversion	272
Figure 36.16: Conversions to separate accommodation	274

Figure 36.17: Birds eye view of basement conversion	275
Figure 36.18: Birds eye view of paving a front garden	276
Figure 36.19: Birds eye view of patio and driveway alterations (to a detached dwelling with side access to rear garden)	277
Figure 36.20: Fences, gates and garden wall alterations	278
Figure 36.21: Birds eye view of outbuilding examples	284
Figure 39.1: Birds eye view of previous PD work by others to a detached dwelling and options for remaining PD rights for a rear extension	292
Figure 39.2: Birds eye view of previous works under PD to create a dormer extension	293
Figure 39.3: Birds eye view of PD rights for a dormer extension/loft conversion on a detached dwelling, where full PD allowance is utilised	293
Figure 39.4: Birds eye view of maximising your remaining PD rights on a detached dwelling	294
Figure 39.5: Birds eye view of dwellings on corner plots and applicable PD rights	313
Figure 41.1: Birds eye view of approved and proposed alterations to dormer extension for Variation of Conditions application to change approved plans	342
Figure 41.2: Rear elevation view of approved and proposed alterations to a single storey rear extension for a NMA application	346
Figure 41.3: Birds eye view of the 45° 'rule', demonstrated on a terraced dwelling	351
Figure 41.4: Rear elevation view of single storey rear extension to a terraced dwelling, taking account of the 45° rule	354
Figure 42.1: Planning Process Flowchart	355
Figure 51.1: Basic Building Control Process Flowchart	395

Figure 58.1: A typical Party Wall forming part of one building	417
Figure 58.2: A typical Party Wall between two (or more) buildings	417
Figure 58.3: Front view and birds eye view of a typical Party Fence Wall astride of two boundaries	418
Figure 58.4: A typical Party Wall between adjoining owners, separating two buildings, where construction has taken place up to an original wall	419
Figure 58.5: Typical Party Structures between adjoining owners	420

List Of Tables

Tables	Page No.
Table 1.1: Goal Setting Template	47
Table 3.1: Key Performance Indicators	60
Table 5.1: Good Debt vs. Bad Debt	78
Table 8.1: Power Team members for procurement and property development	107
Table 8.2: Power Team members for property marketing and ongoing maintenance	108
Table 13.1: Indicative standard and high-end back-to-brick HMO conversion Costs (m^2)	134
Table 14.1: Indicative extension and conversion costs	147
Table 14.2: Indicative other costs	148
Table 14.3: Indicative fixtures and fittings costs	148
Table 14.4: Indicative kitchen item costs	149
Table 15.1: Property viewing kit basics	151
Table 23.1: Minimum sleeping room floor areas (m^2)	186
Table 23.2: Indicative minimum kitchen provisions	187
Table 24.1: Indicative minimum kitchen sizes (m^2)	189
Table 24.2: Indicative dining room and kitchen sizes (m^2)	190
Table 24.3: Indicative living room or dining room sizes (m^2)	190
Table 24.4: Indicative kitchen facilities for up to five occupants	191
Table 24.5: Indicative kitchen facilities for between six and ten occupants	191
Table 24.6: Indicative washing facilities by occupant numbers	192
Table 24.7: Indicative toilet facilities by occupant numbers	193
Table 24.8: Indicative provision of electrical and USB sockets	195

Table 27.1: Indicative documents and certificates required when applying for a HMO Licence	207
Table 35.1: Former Use Classes by building type	235
Table 35.2: Updated uses now falling within Use Class E	236
Table 35.3: Definitions of a C3 dwellinghouse	237
Table 35.4: Use Class E uses to Use Class C3 uses	240
Table 39.1: Article 2(3) Designated Land	299
Table 39.2: Graded Listings	303
Table 41.1: Different types of planning applications relevant to HMOs	322
Table 41.2: Supporting technical reports or statements for planning applications	329
Table 41.3: Typical application requirements for Full Planning Permission	330
Table 41.4: Typical application requirements for Householder Planning Permission	331
Table 41.5: Typical application requirements for CLEUD applications for physical works	334
Table 41.6: Typical application requirements for CLEUD applications for existing uses	336
Table 41.7: Typical application requirements for Lawful Development Certificates – other submission requirements	337
Table 41.8: Typical application requirements for Approval of Details Reserved by Conditions applications	340
Table 41.9: Typical application requirements for Removal or Variation of a Condition applications	343
Table 41.10: Non-Material Amendment examples	345
Table 41.11: Typical application requirements for a Non-Material Amendment application	347
Table 41.12: Typical application requirements for Prior Approval for a larger single storey rear extension application	348
Table 41.13: The 45° 'rule' and design considerations	352
Table 45.1: Types of planning appeal procedure	372
Table 45.2: Typical appeal Statement of Case format	373

Table 45.3: Typical appeal documents for submission	373
Table 46.1: Summary of enforcement powers	382
Table 49.1: Approved Documents typically relevant to HMO projects	391
Table 58.1: Common works where a Party Wall Notice is required	421
Table 62.1: Standard Joint Contracts Tribunal (JCT) Contract Part One	452
Table 62.2: Standard Joint Contracts Tribunal (JCT) Contact Part Two	452
Table 63.1: Council Tax re-banding exceptions for combined bands	460
Table 63.2: HMO identification methods for Council Tax re-banding	462
Table 65.1: Self-certified Build Over Agreement criteria	479
Table 65.2: Approved Build Over Agreement criteria	481
Table 65.3: Circumstances where Build Over Agreements are prohibited	482
Table 71.1: Indicative items to be provided in a furnished HMO	518
Table 73.1: Typical House Manual content guidance	545

Part I

Introduction

i. What Is A House In Multiple Occupation?

I am in no doubt you will have heard of Houses in Multiple Occupation (HMOs) at some point; be that in the local news, through your own research – or you may even have lived in one at some point. But what actually is one?

The official definition of a HMO is provided in the Housing Act 2004[1]. Generally, a property is considered to be a HMO where it consists of one or more units of living accommodation which are not a self-contained flat (or flats) and there are at least three unrelated people living there as their only or main residence, forming more than one household, and who share one or more basic amenities, such as a toilet, bathroom or kitchen facilities with other people.

Another type of HMO is known as a 'Section 257 HMO' under the Housing Act 2004. These are typically converted blocks of flats whereby the standard of the construction fails to meet the relevant building standards and fewer than two-thirds of the flats are owner-occupied. These types of HMOs can be complicated to licence as the whole building may require a HMO licence, as well as any flats rented to three or more people forming two or more households[2].

Ok, so that's a helpful definition – but you may now be asking what defines a 'household'? This has been clarified by the

---

[1] Paragraph 254, Part 7 (https://www.legislation.gov.uk/ukpga/2004/34/part/7).
[2] The scope of this book does not extend to Section 257 HMO.

Government as either a single person, or members of the same family, living together. A family includes people who are married or living together, relatives, or half relatives and step parents and step children[3]. HMOs generally provide individual rooms for one person or a couple forming a household, as part of shared accommodation within a property for a group of people who are not necessarily related to one another but live at the same address and who share toilet, bathroom or kitchen facilities with one another.

Great – now we have a rough idea of what a HMO actually is. Your next questions may well be *"why are they so popular with landlords and property investors?"* and *"why should I be interested in them?"*

Well, I'll aim to answer both these questions (and more) in the following sections!

---

[3]https://www.gov.uk/private-renting/houses-in-multiple-occupation#:~:text=A%20household%20is%20either%20a,grandparents%2C%20aunts%2C%20uncles%2C%20siblings.

ii. Why Do HMOs Make Good Investments?

Geographically, the UK is an island with limited space, constrained by development pressures and protective legislation which restricts how and where housing can be built. This means demand is high and property costs, coupled with the rising costs of living, results in people typically not being able to afford to buy a place of their own.

In England, there is an ongoing shortage of homes at affordable prices for people to live in. The Government had set itself the ambitious target of achieving 300,000 new homes for people annually by the mid-2020s as part of its 2019 election manifesto. However, in 2020/2021, only 216,000 new homes were supplied[4] (albeit this figure was impacted by the Covid-19 pandemic). This target rate of new build homes is not expected to be met until at least 2032 – some eight years later than planned[5]. The housing crisis could be worsened still following an announcement by the Housing and Levelling Up Secretary in December 2022 that the national housing target was to be more 'advisory[6]' than 'mandatory', causing a number of local planning authorities (LPAs) across the country to either pause or scale back their housing plans. As a result, developers are warning this could result in 77,000 fewer homes being built each year, with the fewest homes being built in areas with the greatest demand[7]. Research by

---

[4] https://www.gov.uk/government/statistics/housing-supply-net-additional-dwellings-england-2020-to-202.1.
[5] https://www.independent.co.uk/news/uk/politics/government-housing-target-300000-b1784575.html.
[6] Which could also be construed as 'non-binding'.
[7] https://www.telegraph.co.uk/property/news/councils-scrap-building-targets-housing-crisis-worse/.

Rightmove has also identified that the average asking price for a typical first time buyer has hit a record high of £224,963[8], whilst in quarter one of 2023, the average price for a rental property in the UK was £1,190 per calendar month (outside London). This issue is compounded further with rental supplies very much constrained and tenant demand being four percent higher than in quarter one of 2022 and 48% higher than in 2019[9]. People are therefore still in desperate need of somewhere affordable to live.

As a result, there is a supply and demand issue with housing, which, in reality, will likely always remain. Indeed, in the 30 years to 2021, three million fewer properties were built than in the previous 20 years, whilst the population has increased by more than nine million people[10]. HMOs can help to contribute towards improving the housing affordability crisis by providing people with much needed accommodation, which is not only affordable, but can also be high quality. Surprisingly (or maybe not) most tenants are often able to save more of their hard-earned money quicker for their own future property purchase than if they were renting on their own. This is because most HMOs are usually marketed as being *all bills included* accommodation and their costs are typically fixed for the duration of their tenancy agreement. HMOs also provide a flexible way of living for tenants who are happy to move around for personal or work reasons. Additionally, HMOs provide plenty of social opportunities for people to mix with other tenants, which can be great for those moving into a new area.

---

[8] https://www.rightmove.co.uk/news/house-price-index/.
[9] https://hub.rightmove.co.uk/rental-trends-tracker-q1-2023/.
[10] https://www.bbc.co.uk/news/uk-58747051.

Simultaneously, HMOs can benefit you as a business owner and landlord by providing a consistent and secure financial income, as well as a lifestyle you may not otherwise be able to attain, provided you know what you are doing. HMOs are known to regularly and consistently make good investments because they are one of the best ways to maximise rental income whilst holding onto an appreciating asset[11]. This is why developing a HMO property portfolio can make such a difference to yours – and your tenant's lives.

Let's take a look at a quick example:

Ben and Amy both have around £65,000 each. They've decided that putting the money into savings or other investments isn't for them and want to invest their money into property instead. They've done their research and both understand property investment and development can be a good wealth creation vehicle.

Ben is a cautious investor. His research identified that a buy to let property rented out to a single family would be a safe bet. He's looked at the local market, found a house which needs almost no refurbishment work and then discussed renting the property out to a single family with a few estate agents, who tell him he could achieve a rental income of around £1,500 per month. Ben is very happy with this and goes ahead with the purchase, taking out a standard buy-to-let mortgage. With minimal work to upgrade the property, on completion of the sale Ben is quickly able to let his property to a family and awaits his £1,500 rental payment.

---

[11] An appreciating asset is any type of asset which increases in value.

Amy also knows that property is a good investment and whilst she is cautious, she decides that having carried out her own research, letting out an entire property to one family won't provide her with the kind of returns she is looking for. Instead, she checks out the local market and notices there is a demand for high quality HMOs in the same area as Ben. Amy buys an almost identical house on a nearby street to Ben's property and begins working to convert it into a six-bedroom HMO. Let's say a few months pass whilst refurbishment works take place. Once near completion, Amy begins marketing each of the six rooms at £500 per month. All the rooms end up being filled before the property is even finished, thanks to a strong marketing campaign. Amy's property will now achieve double the rental income of Ben's property.

Now let's say a year goes by for Amy and Ben. Ben's tenants decided they needed to move because the house is no longer suitable for their growing family. Ben hasn't been able to find another family to rent the property to yet, despite lowering the rental fee, as some prospective tenants were put off by the tired-looking interior.

Let's move on another few more months. Ben has had no income from his investment property for almost three months and has had to dip into his own savings to cover the mortgage payments. The reality of void periods is beginning to concern Ben and he's now having to spend some of his own money to update the house in the hope of attracting new tenants. Amy's property, on the other hand, is doing well. Out of the original six tenants, five are still there, having extended their tenancy agreements. One tenant left because she was offered a new job in another part of the country but was able to recommend the property to a former colleague who was looking for a new place to live. Amy was able to fill the empty room within days of her previous tenant leaving and as only one room was vacant for a short period of time, the loss of rental income was minimal because the other five tenants continued to pay. This meant Amy didn't have to worry about covering the mortgage payments herself.

With more people living in her property, Amy budgeted for higher associated costs with running and maintaining it, but she is happy knowing that the increase in yield[12] certainly makes up for that additional effort! In addition, the house has now been revalued and is worth much more than Ben's because of the refurbishment works Amy carried out and the income being produced due to tenanting the property. Amy is now able to recycle some of that money into setting up a second HMO property in the area as demand remains high for the high quality accommodation she is offering. Unfortunately for Ben, all of his original investment is still tied up in his one property, which has only seen a modest growth in value and will not allow him to take money out to fund another purchase.

As you can see from the above (albeit simplistic) example, HMOs make powerful wealth creation tools when set up properly, not only from the increase in the capital value of the property over time, but from the income generated by letting the individual rooms of a property. When fully occupied and managed correctly, the income generated is typically more than enough to cover all the bills, maintenance and other costs, with enough left for a tidy profit to be made each month. For this reason, HMOs remain very popular with

---

[12] This is the income returned on an investment.

landlords and property investors who want their money to go further, as they offer a dependable way to build wealth quickly through rental income, as well as over long term through the capital appreciation of the properties they own – even through times of nationwide financial hardship.

But there's more to setting up a HMO than many people realise – and plenty which can go wrong if you don't know how to approach HMOs correctly! This is why I created this book; to help guide you through the set-up process so you too can build wealth by investing in and setting up HMO properties the right way.

Are HMOs Still Viable And Worth Investing In?

The short answer is yes, absolutely!

The long answer is still yes; the trick here though is to think of investing in HMOs as long-term strategy to help secure your financial future. Property is a tangible asset and is therefore much more stable as an investment vehicle than say stocks and shares, which can be susceptible to the whims of short-lived market fluctuations. Naturally, there is often a certain amount of anxiety about investing in property, but strategically, residential property values and property in general are one of the few assets which almost always rebound in the long-term, even if short-term drop in value occurs during periods of economic downturn, hence the saying 'as safe as houses'.

HMOs differ from other property investment methods in that they are not a passive business model and need to be manage properly. You will need to be aware of the market and adapt your business model using an *investor mindset* to enable your portfolio to maintain its profitability, whilst providing a good service to your tenants. You can do this by learning to control the elements of investment as far as is reasonably practical by reducing the risks to your investment and by protecting your assets. Treat your investments as a business. It should be optimised as such so you can confidently grow your portfolio and make your investments resilient to short term market instabilities. This approach includes streamlining your business to run efficiently, helping you to improve on and control costs. Once you have achieved this, no matter where the market is going, your HMO investment portfolio will be able to weather most, if not all, storms and remain viable.

Most importantly, you will need to keep an eye on current market trends. Consider and respond to them accordingly but focus on what you want to achieve over the long term. Don't get 'bogged down' in the reporting of the 'latest threat to property investing'. There will always be something, but as with all things, the hype often passes relatively quickly.

Adaptive Investing Practices

The Private Rental Sector (PRS) has changed significantly over the past 20 years. Previously, whilst tenants may have been willing to accept lower quality bedsit-type accommodation, they are now in-part driving the demand for better quality accommodation with high-speed broadband, larger rooms, ensuites and quality furnishings and are willing to pay for good quality.

Legislative intervention has also evolved, seeking to ensure tenants have access to fairer tenancy agreements, better standards of accommodation and safer properties.

Throughout these changes, HMOs have remained one of the preferred options for young professionals to live in, although growth among other tenant profiles is now emerging as a result of the Covid-19 pandemic, the increase in working from home and changes to individual's personal circumstances. This includes both tenants and employers wanting more flexibility, with tenants wishing to have somewhere comfortable to stay that isn't in a hotel or Airbnb, perhaps only for a few nights a week, within commuting distance of city offices for in-person meetings and employers embracing new working practices.

The growth of working from home and remote working practices has also seen tenants having greater choice over where they want to live, rather than having to be located close to their place of work. Changing personal circumstances, such as martial divisions, have also seen people turning to HMOs as a more affordable way to live, rather than renting individual flats or apartments, where properties are often unfurnished, costs are typically higher and suitable accommodation is in short supply.

In light of the Covid-19 pandemic, the social aspect of living in a HMO has become increasingly attractive to people as well, particularly if they are new to an area, having recently moved, or wish to live with a group of friends. Consequently, an adaptive strategy towards HMO property development is essential.

In the context of the above and the rising costs of living, coupled with a housing shortfall, demand remains strong for quality shared accommodation across the country. HMOs typically costs less for tenants to rent a room in an *all bills included* HMO than it would do if they were to rent a flat or apartment individually, they don't have the hassle of trying to arrange utilities and they have more certainty over their monthly costs.

The Professional HMO Business Model

The professional HMO business model is therefore both a resilient and robust one, when set up correctly. Purchase costs, refurbishment costs, running costs and rental returns must be kept in check, but HMO property developers can typically excel in comparison to the returns achieved from a typical buy-to-let landlord. Running costs and maintenance are naturally higher than a standard buy-to-let rental, but because of the number of rooms in a typical HMO, this will usually enable a landlord to maintain a profit, even with up to one or two unoccupied rooms after all other costs are factored in, enabling landlords to weather most storms.

In summary, the supply and demand dynamic continues to grow, whilst new tenant pools are emerging in response to rises in the cost of living and changes to personal housing preferences. Because of this, I predict that demand for high-quality shared accommodation will only increase and so HMOs are here to stay.

iii. Different Types Of HMOs And Tenant Profiles

Before we get any further, it is important to clarify that there are different types of HMOs out there, catering to the different demands and needs of the tenants who occupy them. Each tenant profile comes with positives and negatives, so it is worth carefully considering the type of tenants you wish to let your HMO property to, as this will have some impact on your development strategy. Typically, there are three types of HMOs with very different tenant profiles. These are shown in Figure iii.i

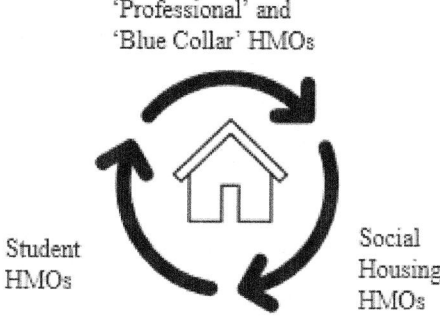

Figure iii.i: Different types of HMOs.

This book is primarily aimed at setting up 'professional' and 'blue collar' types of HMOs. However, the key principles of setting up a HMO still remain relevant for all other HMO types, regardless of the intended occupier.

Social Housing

Starting with social housing HMOs, these are typically occupied by people placed by the local council or local housing association. They could also be described as being more akin to hostels/bedsits or emergency accommodation for people who are in urgent need of somewhere to stay.

Some HMO developers can typically be nervous about renting their properties to this type of tenant and may seek to avoid them because they believe the tenants may not be able to afford the rent, could damage the property and/or not look after fixtures and fitting or may be (but not necessarily always) harder to manage. However, they can prove to be a shrewd investment option as the social housing provider will often rent the property for a fixed term, which is typically a five-year period. The provider will often cover utility bills, any void periods and rental arrears during that time giving the landlord certainty over occupancy and income for the period.

Once the fixed term ends, they will then either seek to return the property to the landlord in the same condition, taking account of 'fair wear and tear' or request an extension to the fixed term.

Student HMOs

When it comes to HMOs, the typical image which comes to most people's minds is unfortunately one of an 'unkempt' looking student house.

It is true student HMOs do tend to suffer a greater level of wear and tear, but students are often less likely to request high end facilities and amenities, as they generally only stay for a short period of time before moving out once their academic year finishes, so you can typically afford to set one up on a tighter budget, provided you are still meeting minimum standards.

The nature of student occupancy however can result in a predictable 'cycle' of occupancy and voids. Although the void periods do present an opportunity to undertake repairs and maintenance, as necessary, before new tenants move in for the start of the next academic year. The upshot of this cycle is that whilst the property will bring in rental income during term time, void periods can last for months outside of this[13]. However, once tenants are in the property, they'll usually be on one joint contract, so if one student decides to move on or drop out, the remaining tenants are required by their agreement to cover the rent. The tenant who leaves or drops out may even be required to find their replacement, depending on the terms of the tenancy agreement.

Traditional student HMOs are coming under increasing pressure from universities, who are rapidly adding new purpose-built student accommodation (PBSA) blocks, attracting students to high-spec, well-located flats with lots of facilities included, at a premium price of course.

In some areas, this has meant landlords are finding it difficult to let to some groups of students with bigger budget/funding. This could result in a 'race to the bottom' in terms of rental rates for this type of accommodation as supply outstrips demand. However, do bear in mind that not all tenants will be

---

[13] Although renting out the property as an Airbnb during these 'empty' periods could help to make sure your property remains profitable throughout the year.

able to afford PBSA and so demand for traditional student HMOs which meet standards is still likely to remain strong.

'Professional' And 'Blue Collar' HMOs

The third tenant type is the professional, *white collar*, *blue collar* or *key worker* tenant, working in the local area or commuting to towns and cities nearby. Many HMO developers and landlords prefer to let their properties to professional tenants and key workers because they are perceived to be easier to manage, more responsible and more likely to make rental payments.

These types of tenants will typically expect higher quality accommodation for the amount they are willing to pay, so you may need to spend more on refurbishments to make sure the property meets those high expectations, along with the associated maintenance costs. As tenants' expectations continue to rise, alongside the tightening of legislation, many developers are seeking to provide fully furnished large bedrooms with double beds, modern ensuites, high spec kitchens with bright, comfortable and homely communal and work-from-home areas, all with high-speed broadband throughout.

From personal experience, I've known the best results have been achieved by HMO developers who have set up high-quality HMOs for young professionals, blue collar and key workers. Changing working practices and employment flexibility have meant that tenants can range in age from 18 into their 50's and 60's, so catering to this broad age range can prove to be lucrative, provided you get the mix of tenants right.

iv. What This Book Covers

HMOs are naturally more costly to set up and more intensive to run and manage than a typically buy-to-let property. This is due to there being more stringent legislation, more people to deal with and increased administration and maintenance as a result. But the effort you put in can certainly make it financially worthwhile, as our earlier example with Ben and Amy demonstrated!

This book aims to give you the knowledge, understanding and HMO property developer perspective you need to make those first few steps on your HMO journey. If you are already familiar with HMOs and property development, it will also help serve as a reminder of some essentials you may have forgotten or may not be familiar with since you started. I have tried to make this book as accessible and 'jargon-free' as possible so it is as easy as possible to digest. Hopefully it will enable you to apply the knowledge contained throughout to your HMOs projects. This book is packed with detailed advice and guidance on relevant and up-to-date legislation for HMOs in England, although it is not meant to be a definitive *how-to* or *step-by-step* guide. That would need to be a far larger and much more technical book!

When starting out in HMO property development, it is most likely you will be taking on an active 'Project Manager' role. This means you'll be looking to source, purchase, refurbish and get your property rental-ready yourself – with the assistance of a specialised team of professionals to help you do so. I have therefore combined this book with other, perhaps less obvious, legislation and considerations which may crop up throughout the HMO set up process, such as dealing with the Party Wall Act or build over agreements, for example, which you may need to engage with as the project manager.

Property development is first and foremost a people-business and in addition to being a property developer, HMOs (and many other property development strategies where you intend to let out property) require you to be a landlord. Some people often seem to overlook the fact that once a HMO property or any rental property is set up, there is a long-term commitment to managing that property professionally, dealing with new and existing tenants and maintaining the standard of accommodation expected.

Being a landlord comes with many responsibilities which you must comply with to stay on the right side of the law and any changes in legislation. I have included some of the key responsibilities for landlords in Section VII. Please note that not everyone can (or should) be a landlord – so be honest with yourself at the very start and make sure you know what you are getting yourself into, unless you simply wish to set up the property and have a letting agent do all the 'heavy lifting' with tenants and maintenance (and take a reasonable chunk on your income for doing so).

The topics covered in this book will help enable you to confidently set up your HMO property portfolio successfully and professionally. However, please bear in mind that there are lots of moving parts within property development and this book cannot practically (nor is it intended to) cover all aspects or provide personalised legal, financial or investment advice.

v. Other Property Development Strategies

HMOs are one of many property development strategies out there. There are many more options to choose from, including property flipping, serviced accommodation, multi-lets, commercial property, rent-to-rent, commercial to residential, lease options and holiday lets to name just a few!

Each development strategy requires a different level of input, a different commitment in terms of time, money, discipline and a different approach. Some may be more passive, whilst others may require you to be more 'hands on' and take them on in a full-time capacity. HMOs typically fall into this category. Whilst each strategy is different, what you'll find is that they all involve similar 'set-up' steps, most of which are covered in this book, although I would stress it is always important to carry out proper due diligence to understand both the rewards – and risks associated with the property development strategy you wish to pursue.

Therefore, please feel free to take what you will learn from this book and apply the relevant parts of it to other property development strategies you may be interested in.

Summary

In this introductory chapter, I have outlined what a HMO is with you and why they should be of interest to you as a wealth building tool.

I have also discussed the various tenant profiles and summarised some of the pros and cons of providing accommodation for each tenant type.

Thirdly, I have set out what the purpose and scope of this book is and how the information within can be applied to setting up a HMO property portfolio, as well as to other types of property development projects.

Section I: Principles Of Property Development

In this section, I'll go over key elements of property development and how you should approach a development project to ensure you are likely to succeed. I'll start with discussing what you want to achieve from property development in the first place and how to orientate your goals and attention towards doing so.

I'll then go through business plans, business structure and importantly exit strategies before moving onto how you can go about financing your HMO development projects, project management principles and which professionals you'll need around you to assist you in your journey.

"Real estate investing, even on a very small scale, remains a tried-and-true means of building an individual's cash flow and wealth."

– Robert Kiyosaki

Property Development

Understanding what property development is and what it involves can mean the difference between making great gains or finding yourself with great losses. There are both positives and negatives associated with different types of property development strategies.

Property development is a broad term and can mean many things to different people. For example, an existing property being given a light refurbishment by adding some new carpets and redecorating throughout can be considered 'property development' at one end of the scale, albeit a very 'light touch'. At the other end of the scale, it could mean demolishing an existing dwelling and rebuilding new houses in its place or starting completely from scratch on a vacant plot of land and going through the whole process of planning permission to building out and/or selling on, renting out or occupying. Property development can also relate to changing the use of a property or building through conversion.

In this instance, HMO Property Setup focuses on property development in the form of converting existing residential dwellings into HMOs. Property development in this form is happening daily all over the country and as there is a sustained demand for housing, so too is there a demand for high-quality shared accommodation.

1. Your Goals And Objectives

Property development does not suit everyone for a number of reasons and there are many considerations to take account of before commencing. Before you start you need to be clear on your goals and objectives, what you are seeking to achieve and crucially, when you want to achieve them by. I cannot stress the importance of having clarity over your goals and your motivations before embarking on any form of development, be that in a personal capacity or for any other purpose. A lack of vision and no clear goals usually results in no progress.

Looking at the property market, it is well known that despite the cyclical nature of the property market[14], property is thought of as one of the greatest investments you can make to create wealth. This naturally attracts a wide range of people from all walks of life who are looking to change their lives. However, it isn't good enough to just dive straight in because you know you could make a profit. You need to take the time to look at what you want to get out of it and when you want to achieve this by; the term 'look before you leap' is very apt in this situation!

So, I would strongly encourage any potential developer - or an already experienced developer looking to diversify into HMOs - to sit down and really consider what your goals and objectives are, not just financially, but from a lifestyle point of view as well:

---

[14] Typically known as the '18-year property cycle', first recognised by British real estate economist Fred Harrison.

- Are you seeking to achieve 'financial freedom'? If so, what does that look like to you? Can you describe what you'd need to do to feel like you've achieved it?

- Are you seeking to make extra money to supplement your main income or are you looking to leave your main job altogether and go into property development on a full-time basis?

- Are you aiming to build a legacy business for your family or simply create a healthy pension pot so you can enjoy later life?

Take a few minutes now to think about what your goals are and write them down. You should then look to work out how to make your goals realistic and achievable. You've probably heard of 'SMART' goals, right? Well, using this technique can really help to focus your mind on what you wish to achieve. SMART stands for:

- Specific – what do you want to accomplish?

- Measurable – how will you know when you've achieved it?

- Achievable – how will you accomplish the goal, how realistic is it?

- Relevant – is it worthwhile; it is the right time; is it applicable to your circumstances?

- Time bound – when will you seek to achieve your goal by? What can you do today, in six months, a year or five years?

SMART is an effective place to start when working out your approach to property development. It provides clarity, concentration and commitment to help achieve your goals. It does this by encouraging you to define what you want to do and when it should be completed by. I have included an example goal setting template for you to use to help with this exercise.

Personal Goals	Goal 1	Goal 2	Goal 3
What			
Why			
How			
Target Achievement Date			
Review Date			

Professional Goals	Goal 1	Goal 2	Goal 3
What			
Why			
How			
Target Achievement Date			
Review Date			

Table 1.1: Goal Setting Template.

It doesn't matter if your goals and objectives change over time as you progress - they are meant to be regularly reviewed and updated. Once you have an idea of where you want to be and when you want to be there by, this will help you make appropriate choices in your property development and/or personal journey, including what you'll do when you reach your goals.

Setting yourself short-term goals with well-defined, achievable results means you can steadily 'chip away' at the larger overall goal whilst working towards the smaller goals at a manageable pace. These short-term goals effectively act as 'signposts' toward reaching your overall goal(s). For example, if your overall goal is to become financially free in eight years, with a portfolio of eight professional HMO properties, then you might set yourself a goal of completing one HMO conversion project annually to ensure you keep on track.

Using SMART, write down your goals and put them somewhere they will be readily visible. This will remind you of what you are working towards frequently, especially on days when you may feel stuck or have lost some enthusiasm and motivation. Don't forget to evaluate your goals regularly though and reflect on what you have achieved, what you still need to work on and whether your 'end goals' are still relevant. I would advise doing this at least every six months to a year.

Do You Have The Time?

A key priority of property development is ensuring you can commit enough time to invest in and grow your HMO portfolio, as well as manage the ongoing commitment of being a landlord, managing tenants, staying compliant and keeping on top of property maintenance. As I mentioned in the introduction, property is not a 'get rich quick' scheme and HMOs are certainly one of the most time intensive strategies. HMO property development requires you to dedicate time, money, discipline and effort to it. If you are unable to commit to actively working on your goals, you may find that, unfortunately, you don't achieve what you set out to.

When considering your goals, make sure to factor in enough time to achieve them. Keep a diary of how you spend your time for a few weeks and then identify blocks of time where you may otherwise be watching the TV, for example, to dedicate to achieving your goals and objectives. Perhaps try getting up a little earlier and putting aside an hour or so to work on small targets. These will act as stepping stones toward your main goals and objectives. Remember, it is not a race and any action, no matter how small, is a step in the right direction.

Is There A Good Time To Get Started?

You may have been thinking about starting a HMO property development business for a long time. You might have even been carrying out your own research to predict when the best time for you to make a 'real' start will be. Some people find starting is actually the hardest obstacle to overcome because of this.

Let me tell you this – there is never a 'perfect time' to get started in property – or any investment strategy of any sort. You could spend years waiting for the perfect conditions and always find a reason why 'now is not the time for you'. If you take that stance, there will always be something which causes you to be hesitant, whether that be impending legislative changes, rising mortgage interest rates, tax band changes, external market factors or a combination of these and other issues.

At this stage, the most important thing to do is acknowledge these concerns but not get too hung up on them. Otherwise you may find yourself always ready with an excuse not to get started, or you find yourself perpetually 'waiting to see what happens in the market'; by which time it may be too late for you to act – and you'll have missed your window of opportunity. Yes, the details are important, but too much analysis prevents you from progressing. I guarantee that once you've made a meaningful start you'll find the concerns holding you back are not as significant as you first thought they'd be – you may even question why they held you back for so long! Remember, as this popular Chinese proverb states:

"The best time to plant a tree was 20 years ago, the second-best time is now."

The message behind this is clear: if you want to see success and growth in the future, the best time to act to ensure it has a chance of flourishing is now.

2. Property Development Key Terms

Before we get too caried away, here's a good place to talk about some key terms in property development. There's been a few already discussed in the above chapters, but for those of you who may be unfamiliar, here are explanations of a common few:

Leverage

If you already own property, you will likely have a mortgage on it. Most people will also have several personal credit cards, a phone contract and maybe even have cars on finance. These are all forms of debt, but they are seen as standard forms of debt. As a result, debt has become a widely accepted modern way of living. As a property developer, you will need to become comfortable with the idea of using debt as an investment tool to help purchase property through leverage, or 'gearing', as it is also known by.

Leverage is the ratio between debt and equity (see page 60) and uses borrowed capital (debt) to increase the potential return of an investment. It is one of the best ways to fund the growth of a property development portfolio. Leverage can, however, be a bit of a double-edged sword. It works to your advantage during a buoyant market when property prices are rising and demand for buy-to-let property is strong. This is because it enables you to involve less of your own money and improves your returns. But it can also lead to losses if values decline. This can leave you at best unable to break even - and at worst out of pocket and in debt.

In this example, let's assume our HMO property developer, Amy, has £150,000 to invest in property. On top of her original purchase, she finds another house for £140,000 which she could buy outright, but that wouldn't result in a very good return on investment for her. Instead, she decides to put down a deposit of £37,500 on the property, which equates to 25%. She then takes out a mortgage at 75% loan to value (LTV – page 60), enabling her money to go much further by achieving a multiple of four times her original equity.

In essence, Amy could now buy three other £150,000 properties, each with a 25% deposit. Amy would then have assets worth £600,000. Say the property market rises by ten percent, Amy would make £60,000, which is an impressive figure, as she won't simply profit from the growth on her own money, but on the growth of the bank's money too!

By turning each property into a HMO, Amy can protect herself to a greater degree. This is because HMOs are widely recognised as high-income development strategies, although it should be noted that whilst this is a resilient strategy, it does not guarantee Amy won't fall foul of an interest rate hike or a significant drop in the housing market.

Loan-To-Value (LTV)

This term is often associated with mortgages and relates to the amount you are borrowing as a proportion of the value of the property you are buying. It is usually expressed as a percentage. The LTV ratio is calculated by dividing the amount borrowed by the appraised value[15] of the property.

For example, if you buy a property valued at £250,000 and put down a deposit of £75,000, this equates to 30% of the property purchase price. A lender would then offer to lend

---

[15] A professional judgement of a property's worth.

you the remaining £175,000 to fund the purchase, resulting in a LTV ratio of 70%.

Equity

Equity is defined as the value of how much of a property you own, less the amount you owe on a mortgage. If you have a mortgage balance on a property which is £250,000 and the property is worth £350,000, you have £100,000 equity in the property. Simply put, it's the amount of money you would receive after paying off the mortgage, should you sell the property.

The equity is made up of the deposit you paid towards the purchase of the property and any of the mortgage you have paid off. Assuming you purchased the property with a 70% LTV mortgage, you would have put in £75,000 (30%).

If you were to buy the property outright using your own cash or pay off the entire mortgage, you would have 100% equity in the property.

Gross And Net Profit

Gross profit is a useful measure of the overall profitability of your business. It is also a way of understanding the costs needed to generate revenue. Gross profit is the profit generated by a business and the costs of producing a product or service, minus the costs of producing it (cost of goods sold (COGS)). For a service-based business which does not manufacture 'goods', such as a property business, gross profit is calculated by subtracting the costs of providing the services you sell (the rooms for rent). The profits being calculated should only include the profits from the sale of services.

Net profit is another important way to help determine the financial wellbeing of your business and is the amount of money your business earns after deducting all operating, interest and tax costs incurred over a specific period of time (say over the course of a year). This can include expenses, such as interest of any loans or mortgages, depreciation of equipment (furniture/fixtures/fittings), administration costs, utilities and running costs, COGS and one-off or ongoing maintenance costs, for example.

If the value of net profit is not positive, this means your business will be running at a loss. Knowing what the net profit is can help you make important decisions about how your business is functioning and work out whether it is operating healthily or whether you need to try and reduce costs. Knowing what the net profit for your business is not only beneficial for your business, but is also beneficial if you are seeking to attract investors to help fund other HMO or property development projects. Investors will typically review gross and net profit figures carefully before deciding whether it is worthwhile investing.

In summary, gross profit is a measure of how much profit is left over when you subtract COGS, whilst net profit is a measure of all the profit made by the business after all expenses are accounted for.

Yield

When carrying out property development, achieving a good rental return is very important. If your income fails to meet your expenditure, you will lose money and if you have not left any room for contingencies, such as a boiler packing up, you could find you lose money even quicker.

A key factor to bear in mind is yield. Gross yield tells you the income return on an investment before expenses are deduced. This is calculated by working out the annual rental income divided by the value of the property, multiplied by 100 to get the percentage.

Net yield is slightly different as this is the rental return of a property, taking account of the costs involved in buying, owning and maintaining the property.

Net yield is sometimes more difficult to calculate because it depends on what costs and expenses are included. For example, you may decide to include a lettings agent or managing agents fee, but not bother to include the cost of replacing a broken lamp or maybe a minor maintenance job. If you are using either gross or net yield to help assess how different properties stack up against each other, make sure you calculate them using the same criteria.

Yield = Annual Income / Value of the property

From the earlier example, let's assume that Ben's property cost £250,000 and the annual rental amount was £18,000 (as a single by to let property rented for £1,500 per calendar month, with no void periods), the gross yield would be 7.2 percent.

Amy's property, which let's assume also costs £250,000 and has an annual rental amount of £60,060 (as a multi-let property with seven tenants paying an average of £715 each per calendar month (£5,005)), the gross yield would be 24%, significantly higher than the standard buy-to-let model produces.

Return On Investment (ROI)

This is a measure of how much a property costs and how much money it makes. It allows you to see it as a percentage of profit or loss:

ROI = (Profit from investment / Cost of investment) x 100

Knowing what your ROI is enables you (and any potential investors you might be hoping to work with) to assess whether putting money into a particular development scheme is going to be profitable or not.

Before you purchase a property, it is essential you estimate your costs and expenses as accurately as possible, as well as your rental income. Knowing this will give you the opportunity to compare it with other similar properties. ROI is typically calculated using the monthly income, monthly expenditure, the value of the property and the cash invested into it. In our earlier example, Amy's property cost £250,000 to purchase (this will be the property's value). The monthly income achieved is £5,005 and the monthly expenditure calculated could be £3,300. If Amy put in £75,000 of her own money down for the deposit (30%), the mortgage loan would be £175,000. Amy could also spend an extra £40,000 on refurbishment of the property. This total cash investment would equal £115,000.

These figures will enable you to work out the annual ROI by working out the annual profit (£5,005 minus £3,300, multiplied by 12) which equates to £20,460. This figure is then divided by the cash investment of £115,000 and multiplied by 100 to get an annual ROI of 17.79%.

Once you have a clear idea about what kind of ROI you wish to achieve, you can discount any properties which would not either meet or exceed your required ROI. Unfortunately, it is difficult to determine what a 'good' ROI is as it is often comes down to a personal judgement and can depend on your development strategy, but a 'bad' ROI would certainly be any one which results in a negative number as it would mean you will lose money!

In general, most single buy-to-let properties will produce a ROI of between five percent and seven percent. This is likely to be enough to covering the running costs, mortgage payments and other maintenance fees, but potentially not enough to generate any worthwhile profits - and may only result in breaking even. However, because HMOs typically have a far higher yield than single by-to-let properties, this means their ROI is often much higher – usually in the region of 11% to 18%. This is another reason why HMOs make sense as a development strategy because whilst you have to put in more effort, the returns are better as HMOs enable your money to work harder for you, providing you with a more profit and increased cash flow for other investments or lifestyle choices.

I expect you've probably had enough of reading about key terms now, so let's move onto the business side of things!

3. Devising A Business Plan

A business plan is an essential part of starting a business and should link in with your goals by setting out what you want to achieve, how you'll go about doing it and when you want to achieve it by, so are important tools which require some 'forward thinking'. I'm not going to say what your business plan should look like; that is personal to you and depends entirely on what you are setting out to achieve and how you intend to go about it.

Typically though, it should clarify your business idea/proposal, highlight opportunities and any potential issues, set out your goals and provide a way to measure your progress. Business plans can also be used to help secure investments or loans as it shows a potential investor or lender you have thought about what your business will do and how it will get there. You'll want to create a business plan to cover at least the next five to ten years. This enables you to define the market, your competition and what your business will look like – and whether you have the capabilities and resources to meet your goals. Its best to start with an overarching vision. For example:

"I want to achieve financial freedom through HMO property development within the next eight to ten years."

Your vision can then be broken down into steps to help work out what that means for you annually and what level of income would provide you with financial freedom.

Next, you'll want to create a list of goals to act as long-term aims for your business. These will provide your focus and can relate to:

- Profitability – what profit should your property portfolio be generating?

- Growth – how many properties are you seeking to purchase in the next twelve months? Two years? Five years etc.?

- Efficiency – can you improve the way you find new properties and tenants?

- Setbacks – what could happen to stunt your goals and what kind of contingency would you use to overcome it?

Setting yourself short-term targets based on your long-term goals helps make them more achievable. For example, your target could be to achieve a certain figure of income per month. When you achieve this, you know you are on track. If you don't, you know you need to make changes.

It is useful to review your business plan annually as it offers the opportunity to reflect on your achievements, refocus your long-term goals and implement any corrective measures to stay on track. To aid with this, set yourself key performance indicators (KPIs) to help you understand your business and how you can improve its performance to achieve its potential. A few KPIs could include:

Key Performance Indicators
Value of any property purchased
Costs of purchasing any property
Costs of refurbishing each property
Deposit required for any property
Mortgageable amount borrowed
Mortgage interest rate
Monthly mortgage payments
Monthly property maintenance
Other ongoing property expenditure and running costs
Number of HMO rooms
Gross monthly rental income per HMO
Occupancy levels
Net income per property
Return on investment
Return on capital employed

Table 3.1: Key Performance Indicators.

This information, when combined with your goals and targets, is a powerful steering tool that helps provide you with the motivation to continue, as well direction and clarity to keep you on track as you progress towards your vision. If you are not sure where to start, a useful guide to writing a business plan is available from Start Up Donut[16], whilst a business plan template can be downloaded from Start Up Loans[17].

---

[16] https://www.startupdonut.co.uk/business-planning/write-a-business-plan/essential-guide-to-writing-a-business-plan.
[17] https://www.startuploans.co.uk/business-plan-template/.

4. Business Structure And Exit Strategies

HMO property development is first and foremost a business. Knowing and understanding how you intend to operate your business and the way in which you buy and hold property can make a huge difference to the way in which you operate your HMO property portfolio. In turn, this will determine the profitability, the amount of tax you pay and even your eventual exit strategy. It is therefore vitally important to seek advice from an appropriate property taxation specialist or financial advisor at the very beginning of your HMO property development journey. The smartest way to approach your HMO property business is to start with the end in mind, including your overall goals and objectives and then work backwards from there to where you are now.

As with all property development strategies, there are financial implications to consider. Seeking professional advice early on will allow you to understand whether buying property as an individual or through a company is the most appropriate approach for you. This will of course depend on your personal circumstances, financial position, what you wish to achieve and when you wish to achieve it by. Setting up your strategy correctly from the beginning can help save you from having to make costly alterations further down the line and loosing significant amounts to tax in one form or another.

Property Held In Individual Personal Ownership And Section 24

For property held in individual personal ownership, the Section 24 amendment to UK tax laws[18] can make a big difference to the profitability of your portfolio. The amendment was announced back in 2015 by the then chancellor, George Osborne, due to concerns over a 'property bubble' developing. The amendment affects income received on residential rental properties, influencing the amount of tax relief landlords can receive. This means landlords are no longer able to off-set finance costs against gross profit when tax liability is determined, resulting in landlords paying more tax. Any mortgage administration or arrangement fees can no longer be deducted from costs either, so are taxed accordingly. Other costs which are no longer able to be claimed include penalties associated with settling a mortgage early and interest payable on loans taken out to refurbish and renovate properties.

The changes were introduced as control measures to 'cool' the private rental market (making it less favourable to be a landlord), increase the amount of housing stock available for first time buyers and to stop higher earners from claiming back larger amounts of tax relief. From a phased inception from April 2017, the amendment came into full force in April 2020, meaning tax now needs to be paid on all the rental income and earnings received from a property. Mortgage interest costs can be claimed back, but only up to 20%. This change means landlords who currently own properties under personal ownership now pay more tax up front. If a salary is

---

[18] Section 24 of the Finance (no.2) Act 2015.

also received from another job, this can result in landlord's being pushed up into the next tax bracket, further increasing their tax liabilities!

For landlords continuing to purchase properties to run as HMOs in their own name, this means taking home a significantly smaller portion of their income as the profits made from renting out their properties are added to their other earnings and taxed as income tax. For existing landlords with small portfolios held in their own names, the tax implications are somewhat minimal, but for landlords with larger portfolios already, or those who have aspirations of owning a large portfolio, where there may be a mix of several buy-to-let or HMO mortgages to pay, the tax implications do become quite significant.

There are several ways to mitigate the effects of Section 24. These can include re-mortgaging onto more competitive products, reviewing a portfolio's operating costs to reduce outgoings and overheads, increase rental rates to help cover the additional tax payments, reducing the size of an existing portfolio, transferring properties to a lower-income spouse or partner, or selling up and leaving the sector altogether. Another option would be to become a limited company and selling your properties to the limited company, as Section 24 does not (currently) apply to these structures. All of these options, however, require the input of a specialist tax adviser.

What If I Already Own Property As A Private Landlord?

If you already own properties as a private landlord, transferring them into limited company ownership can be done. However, this would have to be treated as a sale at market value to the company. An independent valuation would be needed for stamp duty purposes. This means Stamp Duty Land Tax (SDLT) at the higher rate will likely be payable on the purchase of the property/portfolio by the limited company. Capital Gains Tax (CGT) may also be triggered when selling the property to a limited company if the value of your property has risen since the original purchase date. If the property is mortgaged, this transfer will also need the lender's consent. You may even have to pay Early Repayment Charges (ERC) if you are still tied into an existing buy to let mortgage.

Other financial costs may be incurred as a result of the company taking out a new mortgage, as well as additional legal and valuation fees. This may mean if you are seriously looking in this as an option, it's usually better to transfer the property when the mortgage reaches the end of a fixed term, although this may not be practical in all circumstances. I would therefore strongly recommend seeking the advice of professionals over whether it is financially worthwhile to move a property or portfolio from personal ownership into company ownership. However, in general, the advice of professionals is to retain existing properties in personal ownership and seek to buy any future properties through a limited company.

Limited Company Structures Of Ownership

A limited company is a type of business structure which is incorporated into a legally distinct body from the individual(s) setting up the company. The company can own assets, including property and will have separate finances from the individual(s) setting up the company. In recent years, property investors and developers have increasingly brought rental properties through corporate structures. In total, 47,400 new buy-to-let companies were incorporated in the UK last few years, a rise of 14% since 2020[19]. In 2021, there were 260,862 companies set up to hold buy-to-let properties. This has since risen to 302,404 as of September 2022[20]. This is instead of individuals holding their buy-to-let assets personally. Estimates suggest that 40% of new buy-to-let purchases are now made through a corporation.

This growth in incorporation rates has happened for many reasons, but particularly because the amount of tax payable by a company can often be much lower (around half that of the higher rate of income tax) than for an individual.

Having property in a corporate structure means income produced from renting a property is not in the hands of an individual, but the company instead. What this means is that rental income and capital gains (profits) are subject to corporation tax, after expenses, but with full deduction available for interest. Holding property in a company can therefore be a more profitable option due to taxation and the ability to claim mortgage interest back as an operating expense, which should be a particular consideration for higher-rate taxpayers.

His Majesty's Revenue and Customs (HMRC) requires a company to declare all gross income, but you can claim back money through business expenses incurred. This means the set up and running costs of the business can be included,

---

[19] https://www.simplybusiness.co.uk/knowledge/articles/2022/01/huge-rise-in-buy-to-let-property-companies/.

[20] https://www.mortgagestrategy.co.uk/news/buy-to-let-company-count-doubles-in-five-years-hamptons/.

provided they are justifiable. Records of all costs and how they are paid are needed. Examples of other expenses which can be claimed back include: property insurance, landlord service charges, utilities, property upkeep (gardening and cleaning), staff costs (including wages, expenses and pension contributions), travel and accommodation costs for business trips (such as property viewings), property repairs and renovations, advertising and marketing, interest and finance charges and other direct costs, such as stationery, phone bills, marketing and advertising and any relevant association memberships. Speak with your accountant about how these expenses can be applied.

For most people seeking to carry out HMO property development, where you intend to create a medium to large portfolio of properties, rather than simply purchasing an individual property, buying and holding properties through a limited company is currently the preferred option, especially since the Section 24 tax changes came into effect[21].

April 2023 Corporation Tax Changes

Changes to the amount of corporation tax which UK companies and foreign companies with UK offices pay came into effect on 1st April 2023. The rise in corporation tax was initially proposed in March 2021 by then chancellor, Rishi Sunak, but was subsequently scrapped by chancellor Kwasi Kwarteng in September 2022 as part of his 'mini budget', before being reinstated again by Prime Minister Liz Truss in October 2022 (in, out, in, out, shake it all about…). These changes now see corporation tax rise from 19% to 25%, which will mainly hit rental profits made by limited company

---

[21] Although this may be subject to change in the future following further legislative alterations.

landlords with larger property portfolios, or those generating big profits. However, companies with annual profits of less than £50,000 will see the tax rate held at 19%, whilst the rate will rise up to 25% for those with profits of more than £250,000.

Whilst each landlord's circumstances will be different, incorporation still remains beneficial for most landlords, particularly for those who are higher rate taxpayers, as even with the rise to 25%, most company owners are likely to pay less tax on their earnings than if their property portfolios were held in their personal names.

How Do You Access Profit From A Limited Company?

While buying property through a limited company can be more tax efficient, there are other factors affecting how much you take home, as well as how you access your money. As a landlord who has personal ownership of a property, you can access money from your HMO properties directly as soon as it hits your bank account. You are then free to spent it as you wish. However, for a limited company, accessing your money can be a little more complex.

For landlords holding property in companies, all UK companies are required to have at least one shareholder. Shareholders can only take money out as dividend payments, or as a salary, both of which are taxable (unless the salary is less than your taxable allowance). Money can also be taken out by director loan repayments or as pension contributions.

Dividends

Dividend payments are payments made by the company to its shareholders. Payments are transfers of profit from the company account to a personal account and can be made regularly, provided the company has accumulated sufficient profit to do so. Dividend payments are an effective way to release cash as, if you are a UK resident, you receive a tax-free dividend allowance for the first £2,000 each year, regardless of your income.

Company profits can be shared between multiple shareholders, meaning you can take advantage of using multiple individual tax allowances. For example, you and your spouse or children (if over the age of 18) can each use as much of your income tax allowance as you want. This allows for a degree of flexibility as you don't have to take the same amount of profit as each other. You can even change the frequency of sharing out the profits. However, if you simply decide to leave the profits in the company account, you can use the accumulated profits to purchase another HMO property for your portfolio.

Director Loan Repayments

Another option to extract profit from your company is to use Director Loan repayments. This is an agreement between the company and yourself, as an investor in your company, that the company owes you money, because you invested in it. Therefore, the company, controlled by you, will repay its loan to you over time. As the repayment is a debt, it is not considered as income, so is not subject to income tax.

Pension Contributions

The third option of extracting profits from your company is through pension contributions. As the company Director, you can make pension contributions from the company to your personal pension pot.

Whilst you may not benefit from the profits now, they will certainly help your future self. Pension payments can be treated as an expense and are deductible from your gross income. This also has the added benefit of reducing the profits on which corporation tax is calculated.

Other Ways To Release Cash From A Limited Company

As discussed previously, business expense claims can be submitted to HMRC, meaning that paid reimbursements can also be withdrawn from a limited company. The sale of shares can also release cash, subject to capital gains tax.

Company Obligations

Owning and running a company as a director comes with a number of obligations which you must be aware of and understand. It is your legal responsibility to run the company and make sure necessary information is provided to Companies House in a timely manner, or you could risk fines and other penalties. Part of being a director requires you to always act accordingly and in the interests of your company to promote its success, rather than in your own interests.

The obligations also extend to registering with HMRC, keeping accurate company records, filing annual tax returns and confirmation statements, keeping accurate company accounts, paying corporation tax when it is due and updating Companies House of any changes which affect your business, such as a change of company address or the registration of charges, such as a mortgage.

Setting Up A Limited Company

Setting up a limited company is typically a straightforward process which can take minutes to do online, although you can ask your accountant or a company formation agent to help set up your business for a fee, if you would prefer.

To set it up yourself, you will need to think of a suitable name for your company and register it with Companies House. Your company must have at least one director and at least one shareholder, but these can be the same person. You will need to carefully consider whether you wish to be the only shareholder, or if you want to include a partner or spouse, for example. There is no limit to the number of shareholders you can have. You can assign any number of shares to yourself and other shareholders. For example, eight ordinary shares (equating to one 'vote' each), split between yourself and a business partner/spouse/children could mean you own six shares, whilst your partner owns the remaining two shares. You will own 75% of the company and your partner the remaining 25%.

Do think carefully about the structure of your company and whether it is appropriate for you and your long-term goals. Early tax planning is key and if you wish to end up with a limited company with many properties held within it and want to pass it onto your children, for example, structuring it properly from day one is key to mitigate against capital gains tax and inheritance tax. By including other family members at the point of creation means that the company can be structured to have different classes of shares and different ownership of shares, as well as how much you own in comparison to other owners.

If, or when, you come to sell the properties in the company, spreading the ownership means that the capital gain is spread amongst the family and can held with inheritance tax mitigation. For example, if a property was bought through a limited company today and the shares pasted onto a family member in 20 years' time, even though no money was transferred, a capital gain would still be created and a liability would exist as the value would be based on the market value of the shares. Therefore, if you brought a family member on board when the capital gain is at a lower rate or zero, this mitigates the impact of making that change in 20 years' time.

Next, you will need a company address. A UK company is required to have a registered office address in the UK. This is so that any company related mail or documents can be sent to company directors. The address can be your home or office address, or you can use your accountant's office address (with their permission), if you have one. Some company formation services allow you to register your business and use their office address too. They will even deal with the post for you, for a fee. You will need to register your company as an employer with HMRC, even if you are only paying yourself as a director.

You will also need to make sure you select the correct Standard Industrial Classification (SIC) codes. These provide Companies House with a description of your company's nature of business. For property companies, you will need to select the code which is appropriate for buying and holding a property and renting it out, although other codes may be appropriate depending on what else your company may do.

A 'Memorandum' and 'Articles of Association' are required as part of your company's formation. These set out how the company is administered and run, the powers of the director(s) and their responsibilities, including any Director Loan and Shareholder Agreements. There are standard formats you can use which are available from Companies House. However, you can create bespoke versions to suit you and your business's needs. Once you have applied to form your company, you will receive the paperwork confirming this within a few days or weeks. You will then need to set up a dedicated business bank account for your company, separate from your own personal finances. This will also help with obtaining a mortgage through your company.

To do this, you will need proof of identification, proof of address, your business address and contact details and Companies House registration number. In some cases, you may need to prove your own financial situation and produce a business plan or details of estimated annual turnover. Once your company and bank account are set up, pass these details onto your accountant and solicitor so they have them when you are ready to start purchasing properties. They can also register your company with HMRC.

Exit Strategies

Before getting too carried away though, we need to discuss 'exit strategies'. Your business needs to start with the end – or 'exit' in mind. But firstly - what is an 'exit strategy' and why are they so important? Well, an exit strategy is simply the point at which you will have (hopefully) achieved your goals as a business owner and maybe no longer wish to be an active investor. Your exit strategy may see you wanting to reduce or sell you portfolio for a profit, or transfer it to your spouse, business partner or children.

Finding an exit strategy that is right for you very much comes down to your personal circumstances and aspirations. In a lot of cases, the answer will probably be 'it depends on...'. Exit strategies, however, all include tax implications. These need to be factored into discussions with your tax or financial advisor. Discussions should be held at the very beginning of your HMO property development journey as the way in which you buy and hold property can made a big difference to the amount of profit you retain and are able to enjoy.

On the assumption that you will not be buying your HMO portfolio in cash, you will more than likely have mortgages (and in particular, interest-only mortgages) to think about too.

Liquidate Your Entire Portfolio

So, first option, - let's start with liquidation. You may decide after having spent time building your property portfolio that you have achieved your goals and now no longer wish to have any involvement in property or being a landlord whatsoever. You could look to liquidate your company and sell off all your properties to an investor or partner and then invest the proceeds somewhere else or spend, spend, spend!

However, whilst this may be a fairly quick way to offload your assets, it is not a very tax efficient exit strategy as the capital gains tax would most likely be quite significant, wiping out a large chunk of any profits accrued over the years.

Time Or Capital Based Exit

Another option would be to exit on a time or capital value-based exit strategy, where you split or streamline your existing portfolio after a given number of years, or when the value of your portfolio reaches a particular capital value (your end goal). This would require you to sell off enough of your assets to leave you in a comfortable position to pay off any debts accrued on the rest (including any mortgages), leaving you debt free with only properties you own outright, along with a 'safe' source of income each month (taking account of any voids).

If you have not refinanced, the value of the properties in your portfolio should have increased, whilst the debt will have remained the same, so you may find that you only need to sell one or two properties to pay off the debt on the others. You will need to consider the impact of capital gains tax where your properties have increased in value over time, but this can be minimised by the way you sell your properties and the personal allowances you have available to you.

Holding Onto Your Portfolio

Alternatively, you could seek to hold onto your portfolio. If you have no mortgages, you can simply hold onto the properties in your portfolio for income and then pass them over to a partner or relative, although there may be significant inheritance tax implications associated with this option. However, with people living increasingly longer, non-residential mortgages are now available to people over 60. As a result, you could be eligible to take out loans which don't need to be repaid until you are in your 70's or 80's. Where you do have a mortgage, if the property is held in a company, provided there is another director, they will be able to keep the mortgages going after you exit the business.

The main risk to you associated with this strategy is a change in either your circumstances or market circumstances occurring once you have made your exit. For example, your retirement fund could take a serious hit if future changes in taxation or interest rates occur.

Restructuring Your Portfolio

Another option could be to restructure your portfolio. This would involve a mix of all three of the above options. You may decide you want to raise some cash for other investments by selling a small amount of your portfolio to place into stocks, shares or bonds as a way of diversifying your assets.

Selling some of your properties could also help to reduce your loan-to-value rate. Restructuring could allow you to only keep the properties in your portfolio which have very low mortgages for income. This obviously all depends on your current and future income needs, your tolerance to risk and your lifestyle.

If you are reliant on having a regular income, then focus on keeping properties which produce a strong yield and sell the ones which may not be performing so well. If you have any leasehold properties, consider selling these over freehold properties as the last thing you want to be doing when looking to exit is being concerned about leases running out!

Legacy Businesses

If your properties are owned by a company and that company is intended to be a legacy business, you may be able to transfer/gift shares to your family by adding them as shareholders. As already discussed, careful planning is needed around this to ensure things are set up correctly. It also depends on whether you want to retain any interest in the company, whether you want to release any capital from the company and how ownership will be shared, including the transfer of shares or assets in a tax efficient way and the future management of the company.

Sensible and early planning can also help to mitigate inheritance tax (IHT) and reduce capital gains tax, which can optimise the value of your property portfolio and protect the future income of your family. Whatever option you choose as an exit strategy, a tax advisor or financial planner should be able to advise and confirm which of the above options would be suitable for your circumstances, your property portfolio and how they are held, taking account of what you wish to achieve.

5. Financing Your Development Project

It should come as no surprise that financing your HMO property development business will not be without financial cost. Unless you are a cash buyer, there's little point in going out to look at properties without firstly making sure you can borrow what you need to finance the purchase and the project.

But, even if you are a cash buyer, it can make sense to borrow money to fund your investment. You would use a lender's money as leverage, rather than putting all your own money into a property, which could leave you with no cashflow to do anything else! Being asset rich but cash poor does not present favourable conditions for growing a property portfolio – I am sure you will have heard the phrase 'cashflow is king'; so try not to tie all your money up in one property. Having accessible cashflow gives you flexibility and the option to move quickly, as and when you need to.

Using leverage ('gearing') will mean you need to be comfortable with the idea of debt and that it can be used as an effective tool for your property business, when understood and applied correctly. Put simply, 'good' debt increases your ability to generate income. Good debts can be assets; something that you can create an income stream from by taking it on. A HMO property should be seen as an asset which, if set up correctly, covers the cost of its debts, such as mortgage payments and other bills associated with running it. Contrary to this, 'bad' debts naturally reduce your ability to generate income. A bad debt is a liability. This can be something like buying a new car, which starts depreciating in value as soon as you drive off the forecourt, purchasing clothes you don't need or spending extra money on a flashy new phone just because it's the latest model.

You'll likely pay for these items either by using your own money, reducing your ability to invest it in wealth creation or by using a credit card, or buy on finance, which requires you to pay that money back, plus interest, each month until the debt is cleared, reducing your cash flow further. Taking on an 'investor mindset' may therefore help you to see what represents 'positive' purchasing options and 'negative' purchasing options and change your spending habits.

'Good' Debts	'Bad' Debts
Business Loans	Car and Car Loans
Mortgages	Credit Cards
Investing	The latest mobile phone
Real Estate	Payday/Consumer Loans
Education	Buying 'luxuries' you don't need

Table 5.1: Good Debt vs. Bad Debt.

Bridging Finance

One of the most effective ways of gaining funding quickly for a HMO project is to use 'bridging finance'. This can be used effectively as a short-term finance tool when purchasing a property and carrying out refurbishment works to convert into a HMO, until a more permanent financing solution is achieved.

It is an efficient way of gaining access to finance fast and can work well when a borrower is able to re-mortgage quickly to release an uplift in value when refurbishment works are completed. Once the property is in its final refurbished condition, it can be refinanced onto a HMO mortgage. The value of the property will have likely been increased because of the refurbishment works.

Whilst bridging is generally expensive, it can be arranged quickly, sometimes in as little as a few days, but usually within two to three weeks. This can enable you to effectively compete with cash buyers, although depending on the complexity of the deal, it can take up to (and over) eight weeks in some circumstances. When considering whether bridging finance is the right option for you, a few good points to think about include:

- Are there suitable profits to be had from the project to justify the costs of using HMO bridging?

- Are you looking for the best terms or the best rates?

- Do you have at least one suitable exit strategy to avoid getting stuck on bridging finance?

- What exit strategy will you use if the project does not go to plan?

Like any mortgage, the HMO bridging lender will instruct a chosen Royal Institute of Chartered Surveyors (RICS) qualified surveyor to inspect the property and determine its market value. The amount which can be borrowed is generally based on the market value of a property, although different lenders look at that value in different ways, as well as the borrower. This can either complicate or create opportunities for HMO developers. Decisions on lending finance for bridging purposes are often based on:

- The borrowers experience of undertaking HMO projects;

- How the loan will be repaid;

- How the borrower will seek to exit the bridging loan;

- Whether the borrower has any assets that could be used if the borrower defaults; and

- What income the borrower has.

Lenders may also provide a choice as to how interest payments are made on the amount loaned, which include:

- Rolling up at the start, where the lender withholds interest, deducting it from the gross loan advance at the start;

- Rolling up at the end, where the borrow is able to pay interest in one lump sum at the end of the loan; or

- Paying monthly in advance or arrears, where the borrow services the interest by making a payment each month.

There is no 'right' or 'wrong' option here. It simply depends on your circumstances, how much you wish to borrow and what your financial goals are. However, interest payments can make a significant difference to the amount you repay, so it is worthwhile doing your research and speaking with a suitably qualified broker.

Property Development Finance

This is a particularly broad term which covers specialist loans for established property development companies, as well as loans that cover heavy refurbishment.

If you were to approach a bank for a loan, they can often offer very versatile forms of finance and provide a degree of flexibility for your business, although they are not typically utilised for the funding of property transactions, but instead as working capital for redevelopment. This type of lending is typically targeted at experienced developers as it often involves the largest lending amounts. Most lenders will consider loans on a case-by-case basis, but some lenders may only accept applications from companies rather than individuals. A proven track record may also be necessary, so finding yourself someone experienced to partner with may be key to help unlock this source of financing. A thorough and well-prepared business plan will be necessary. This will be carefully reviewed by a lender who will need to be satisfied the business/project is viable before agreeing to any funding.

Personal Loans

If you already own the property in question and want to undertake some refurbishment work, you may want to think about taking out a personal loan, which can be the easiest way to access smaller levels of finance. Having a good credit rating and a regular income will go a long way to demonstrating to a lender that you will be able to make any repayments.

Private Investment, Other People's Money And Alternative Options

It is possible to fund your HMO property development business using private investment, other people's money (OPM) and some alternative options such as purchase lease options (PLO) and rent-to-rent (R2R) agreements, but there are pros and cons for these either way. Potential sources of private funds could also include joint ventures with professional investors and high net worth (HNW) individuals, pension funds (using a small, self-administered pension scheme (SSAS) or a self-invested personal pension (SIPP)), and peer-to-peer lending platforms. I'll cover a few of these below.

Joint Ventures (JVs)

One option would be to enter into a joint venture with an investor, where you put together the deal and an investor will then finance all or part of it, for a fixed return on their investment. JV's work when both parties add value to the deal. The investor could provide the capital and you may provide the service or vice versa. For example, finding the property, organising and overseeing its refurbishment and undertaking the management of the property once it is a HMO. This model, if carried out correctly, should see a profit for both parties; once you refinance, the investor get their money back, plus interest, whilst you are able to hold onto the profits and rent out the property, creating a revenue producing asset.

The downside of JV's is that you and your JV partner may have disagreements over what you want to achieve if your goals, objectives and timelines do not align. Communication issues can also crop up and your JV partner may not be as reliable as you first thought. This could make it difficult to continue a partnership if you fall out, especially if you have a contract in place for a fixed period. Any agreements when entering into JVs should be carefully drafted and reviewed by a suitably qualified solicitor. This will ensure you and your partner are covered, legally, over what each other's duties and responsibility are, in the event of a dispute arising.

Pension Funds

Using pensions funds to contribute to your property business could be another avenue worth exploring, depending on your circumstances. There are two types of pension fund which can be used to invest in property – a SIPP and a SASS.

A SIPP is a pension plan designed for people who are not company directors that enables them to choose and manage their investment, providing a greater choice over what their money is invested into, for example, a high yielding property portfolio.

A SIPP attracts tax relief on contributions from a member, but it can also be used to borrow against its own value to increase the scope of investment. A SIPP can borrow up to a maximum of 50% of its value, so if a SIPP has assets and cash worth £80,000, it could borrow a further £40,000. A SIPP does however require you to have a particular status and investment experience to qualify. Status is often determined by assets owned, income and previous investment experience.

It is worth noting that SIPPs should not be used to fund HMOs directly as they hold the same residential status as a traditional buy-to-let property and direct investment into residential property can result in a tax charge of at least 55%, plus further tax on any additional gains made.

SIPPs can be used to buy and hold property instead, however there are again specific restrictions and rules for buying residential property which are much stricter than for buying commercial property or land through a SIPP. Land or buildings that are being developed or converted into residential property (such as offices to HMOs) are not usually classified as residential property until they are ready for habitation.

If you wished to buy a residential property using a SIPP you can use a mortgage for the purchase, but the amount you can borrow will be restricted as a percentage of the property's value. Your SIPP can buy properties through mortgage financing and can buy shares of a property that owns properties in a SIPP in conjunction with other SIPPs, although you will only be able to borrow up to 50% of a property's value.

The other type of pension fund is a SASS, which is exclusively for company directors. It is a flexible property scheme created under legislation for company directors in the UK and provides access to every type of investment available to SASS investors. You can make any permitted investment at any age and do not need to be 55 to take control of the money in your pension.

As with a SIPP, you are only able to directly invest in or hold commercial property, however indirectly, you can invest in residential property through property loans, bonds, crowdfunding and loans to third-party property developers and other methods. Importantly, there is the ability to loan to a company using the SASS 'loanback' facility, allowing you to invest in property and grow your business. The structure allows you to transfer 50% of the value of any pension you have contributed to into your company for use in your business. This money can then be used for indirect residential property investment and property development purposes. You can also pool your pensions with other company directors (including family members), providing a larger pool of funds for investments.

If you are interested in using either a SIPP or a SASS for investment purposes, speak to a suitably qualified expert who will be able to advise you further based on your specific circumstances and what you wish to achieve.

Peer-To-Peer Lending

Another financing option is Peer-to-Peer (P2P) lending. Platforms, such as CrowdProperty[22], which has been operating since 2014, can be used to secure a range of loans for bridging finance, refurbishment and development finance, paid for by investors pledging money to your project as an investment. CrowdProperty is Financial Conduct Authority (FCA)-authorised and specialises in raising finance for development projects which have been thoroughly vetted, appraised and meet key performance factors.

CrowdProperty can help to finance various different projects. These include new builds, self-build, commercial to residential conversions, HMOs, served accommodation conversions, extensions and refurbishments, bridging purchases and auction purchases, amongst others. There is,

---

[22] www.crowdproperty.com.

however, a minimum borrowing amount of £100,000, so do factor this in if you are interested in P2P lending.

Borrowers, or contractors/developers they have partnered with, must have a proven track record of experience to qualify for any loans offered. If this is your first HMO project, partnering with an experienced HMO developer for example may help to secure funding, unless you have other relevant experience which would help you qualify. Interest is typically charged at 8.5 to ten percent per annum, alongside a fee of one to four percent depending on the scale of the project. Borrowers will also pay any legal fees and survey costs during the project if drawdowns are necessary. Loans terms are typically for a minimum of six months up to a maximum of 24 months.

Once a project has been accepted, a charge on the project is secured (meaning that if you as the borrower were to default, the company could take ownership of your property and the project). Investors can then view the project details, the terms of the loan and loan length and can decide whether to pledge money to fund it, raising the finance you need. Investors are incentivised with excellent returns on the capital which they choose to invest into your projects, so the more detail you can provide about your proposal, the more attractive it will be. Once your project has been funded, the amount borrowed, plus interest, is then paid back by you, as the developer, to the investors at the end of the loan term and on completion of the project. You can even repay the loan early and will not be charged for early repayment.

If, for whatever reason you cannot pay the loan back, whilst CrowdProperty has a first legal charge over the property, this measure will typically only be used as a last resort and

CrowdProperty will work with you to find acceptable repayment methods. This method of finance generation enables you, as a small-to-medium sized property businesses, to connect with investors and access the finance you may need for development project that might not be available to you by more conventional means.

Purchase Lease Options

Another option would be to set up your HMO business using Purchase Lease Options (PLOs). These are legal agreements allowing you to control a property and generate income from it with the right, but not the obligation, to buy it at a later date. PLOs can be complicated to implement, so need to be structured by experienced solicitors who are well-versed in the mechanics of putting together these intricate deals. It is worth bearing in mind that most property owners or landlords considering this option wouldn't usually do so, unless they were in negative equity, or needed to offload their property quickly.

This means they either owe more on their mortgage than they can sell the property for, or need to move or sell the property, usually due to unfortunate personal circumstances, such as the death of a relative, divorces, unemployment and needing to relocate, or landlords who no longer wish to manage their property, or whom are in financial difficulties. These types of owners are typically referred to as 'motivated sellers[23]'.

---

[23] A property owner who has a strong need to sell their property, which can motivate them to accept a lower offer price, discount or flexible financing terms.

The basic principle is to make a profit from managing a property for an agreed length of time by renting it out. As an example, say a four-bedroom property is worth £200,000 today and you have the option to purchase it in five years' time for £212,000. The option period is therefore five years. As the investor, you could pay the property owner/landlord an option fee to secure the property and a fee of say £500 per month to cover their ongoing mortgage payments. You could rent the four-bedrooms out to individual tenants at £500 per room and then keep a £1,500 of the rental income, less any expense for property maintenance and upkeep, as profit for yourself. At the end of the option period, the property could only be worth £205,000. You may therefore decide not to purchase the property, so would not exercise the option and simply return it to the owner. You could, however, seek to renegotiate a new option term.

Another scenario is that the property is now worth £220,000. If you needed to raise finance for a property involved in a PLO, you would typically need to do so via bridging finance to buy the property and then refinance onto a specialist HMO mortgage. If finance is made available to you, you could then purchase the property yourself at the agreed £212,000 and will have bought the property at a discount, whilst making an income through the option period. A further option would be to introduce a third-party purchaser to the owner who would buy the property for the agreed amount. Using carefully worded clauses, you could benefit from the uplift between the agreed purchase price under the option and the purchase price paid by the third-party.

PLOs mean you don't need to take out a mortgage yourself and enable you to invest very little cash upfront; just the option fee to the owner, which can be for a bare minimum sum in some (rare) cases. However, as the ownership of the property and the mortgage payments remain in the name of the property owner/landlord, PLOs only work with the permission of the mortgage lender.

For an investor, the downsides of this strategy are that the property owner is likely to be in an unstable financial position in the first place and may fail to pay the mortgage on the property, which could lead to repossession. If you have invested your money into the property to refurbish it to a standard suitable for attracting tenants, this could wipe out any value you may have added. Refurbishment costs could also wipe out any profit made in the short term, whilst ongoing maintenance costs to keep the property in a rentable condition could be high. Additionally, at the end of the option term the owner may refuse to let you exercise the option, which could force you to take legal action. Therefore, as with any financial strategy, it is essential to do your research and obtain professional advice to ensure you are investing your time, effort and cash in the most appropriate way for you.

Rent-To-Rent HMOs

A final option to consider is the rent-to-rent model, which can be a more affordable and accessible way to get into HMO property development than the traditional purchase of a long-term asset to refurbish and rent out. Rent-to-rent is a strategy whereby you rent a property from an existing landlord and run it as a HMO. The landlord retains ownership of the property, but you rent it from them and pay them rent. You then rent the property to tenants on a per room basis.

This model is based on two key matters: firstly, finding an existing landlord who is willing to enter into an agreement and is happy for you to rent out their property as a HMO and who will allow you to undertake works to their property to do so; and secondly, understanding how to set up the property efficiently and effectively.

Essentially, under the rent-to-rent model you are taking control of the property and the role of a manager of a HMO, rather than the owner. You will therefore need to obtain the appropriate licences and permissions to operate the property. You may also be responsible for payment of utilities and council tax, depending on your arrangement with the landlord.

Landlords may be open to the idea of renting out their existing property to you to operate as a HMO if their circumstances have changed, for example they may want a more passive role, want to improve their return without the extra hassle, may not have the time to administer a HMO themselves, or perhaps have moved and are no longer in the area but don't want to sell their property. Guaranteed rent, with no gaps in tenancies, little input into maintenance and virtually no effort required on their part are also attractive reasons for a landlord to consider entering into a rent-to-rent agreement.

For you as an investor, it represents a great opportunity to gain experience in operating a HMO without needing to come up with the investment/finance to purchase a property yourself. There's no need for a mortgage or to pay Stamp Duty as you aren't buying the property and you'll likely only need to provide a deposit to secure the agreement. There are also minimal legal costs involved to prepare the agreement, but this will be much less than you'd pay for conveyancing. Agreements can often be put together quickly, meaning you can get deals together in a matter of days, rather than waiting weeks or months to complete on a purchase.

You may come across a landlord who is renting out an existing HMO, perhaps one that is underperforming, not fully let, one set up for students that is currently vacant, or one which is a bit tired and in need of some light refurbishment. Alternatively, you could come across a standard rental property which has the potential to be easily turned into a profitable HMO.

In each case, depending on the willingness of the owner, you could approach them to rent and operate the property and undertake renovations yourself. This is, of course, provided you have their permission to do so and you give them appropriate notice of works proposed.

The landlord would only then be renting to you (less hassle for them) and you would be responsible for finding tenants and dealing with the day-to-day maintenance and running of the HMO (more work, but equally, more profit for you). Therefore, finding a property in a good location with good tenant demand is essential as any void periods can quickly eat into your profits.

Often, deals will be arranged for a fixed term (the longer the better for you) and an agreement will need to be reached over the amount of guaranteed rent to be paid to the landlord. This will likely need to cover, as a minimum, the landlords' mortgage (if they have one) and any other profits/costs they wish to cover. You will therefore need to make sure you will be making enough in rent to cover your own costs (for example, payments to the landlord and any refurbishment and maintenance works etc. required) to be able to create a profit for yourself.

You will also need to reach an agreement over the extent of the landlords' involvement on maintenance issues. For example, if the heating system or windows were to need replacing, whether they would cover this, or whether you are expected to. Any agreements should be drafted and reviewed by a qualified person, preferably a solicitor, to make sure they are lawful and fair. Often management agreement or commercial leases are used, but this depends largely on the individual circumstances of the agreement being made.

By the end of the fixed term, you can either choose to renew your agreement with the landlord, or if it is not working as you expected, hand the property back to the landlord in the same or better condition than you took the property on as. If you choose to renew, make sure you are still happy with the terms as you may be able to renegotiate with the landlord if the property is performing better (or worse) than both parties expected. Any works you undertake to physically improve the property are likely to add value to the landlords' property, so make sure to factor this into your negotiations.

There are of course, a few downsides. Firstly, if you struggle to get rent from your tenants, you still need to honour your agreement to pay the landlord their guaranteed rent every month. You also have a responsibility to deal with day-to-day tenant issues, maintenance issues, utility and council tax bills as well as dealing with other administrative tasks associated with HMOs, such as ensuring certificates are up-to-date and complying with General Date Protection Regulations (GDPR[24]).

In addition, as you won't own the property, you don't benefit from any capital growth over time so as the property's value increases over time, only the landlord is set to benefit. In addition to this, you have no control over the property. If the landlord therefore fails to make their own mortgage payments or changes their mind about the agreement before it ends, you may find yourself out of pocket, having invested in refurbishing the property and having to try and resolve a difficult situation with your tenants, as their rental agreements will be with you, not the landlord. Further, if going from a single buy-to-let property to a HMO, you'll need to make sure the landlord's mortgage provider is aware as it may breach the lender's terms if let to multiple tenants.

The property must also comply with HMO licensing standards (which could be costly to introduce if a new kitchen and internal reconfigurations are necessary) and mean the costs to convert the property effectively wipe out any profits generated initially. Planning permission and building regulations signoff may also be required, depending on what alterations are proposed, all of which add to your costs.

In summary, the rent-to-rent HMO model offers an exciting and affordable way to get into HMO properties and can allow you to get started quickly. However, it is not easy and agreements must be carefully put together to protect both you and the landlord. Profits are highly dependent on a good deal

---

[24] See Chapter 74.

being reached with the landlord, being able to keep the property occupied and managing it correctly.

6. HMO Mortgages

If you are purchasing a property using a mortgage, you must ensure you have the correct mortgage in place for the use of the property as a HMO as these are different mortgages from your standard mortgage to buy a house to live in or a mortgage for buy-to-let purchases. Harsh consequences are in place for those who do not, including the lender having the right to recall the mortgage, risking your credit rating and finding yourself being unable to borrow from a lender in the future.

This is because HMO mortgages are seen by regulators as 'specialist business loans'. Investors are treated as having a greater understanding of the commitments they are entering into than a regular person, who may just take out a mortgage to purchase their own residence. As a result of this 'specialist' nature, not all lenders include them in their products. However, where they do, HMO mortgages have been specifically designed to cater for them and the terms and conditions of the mortgage allow properties to be let under multiple tenancies. Lenders often require applicants to have experience in letting property to be eligible. The perceived risks mean higher deposits and arrangement fees may often be required too. Having prior experience as a HMO landlord will therefore give you access to more options, although this is not essential and for those of you just starting out, it shouldn't be a hurdle which cannot be overcome. A growing number of lenders are now considering new landlords with little or no experience, but you can expect their rates will often be higher than average.

HMO mortgages are generally offered through qualified mortgage brokers, rather than directly to landlords as the application process is comprehensive. Therefore, find yourself a good mortgage broker to work with who specialises in HMOs. They should have existing and direct relationships with lenders and are best placed to find exactly what you need, according to your requirements. Some, but not all lenders, will offer the following HMO mortgages:

1. HMO Refurbishment Mortgages, for light to extensive refurbishment projects, such as renovation or extensions and loft conversions. These are typically used for existing HMOs or residential properties yet to be converted to HMOs;

2. HMO Development Loans, for major build and significant construction projects; and

3. HMO Mortgages and Re-mortgages, for existing HMOs.

Different lenders operate using slightly different criteria, but will typically request a lot of upfront information from borrowers to gauge their experience, suitability and needs, including:

- The experience you have as a landlord (if any);

- Whether the mortgage will be a personal one or for a limited company;

- What Loan to Value (LTV) you are looking for;

- Where is the HMO will be located;

- How many rooms will be for rent in the HMO;

- Whether the HMO be managed by a letting agent or the landlord;

- Whether the HMO has (if existing) or needs a licence (if new);

- Whether there will be individual AST[25] agreements for each room/tenant;

- What is the proposed/actual rental income is; and

- What type of tenants live/will live in the HMO.

Lenders and brokers will also undertake standard mortgage affordability assessments, taking account of current incomes, credit scores, the amount you wish to borrow and the type of rate you would prefer.

For mortgage valuation purposes, although almost all valuations are carried out by RICS surveyors, what usually determines the value of a HMO is its size and type and the method of valuation used by different lenders. The most common valuations are based on traditional 'Bricks and Mortar' or residential value valuations, with inspections in combination with comparisons of 'like-for-like' properties in the same area. Factors such as size, number of bedrooms and square footage, condition and residential use classes are typically used. Where there are no HMOs in the area, valuations are based on the price achieved as if the property were a single household. This method doesn't account for the extra income HMOs generate through having multiple tenants and can therefore restrict the amount you are able to borrow.

Other lenders will use an investment/yield based or commercial valuation instead, which takes account of how much income the property will generate. These are more

---

[25] Assured Shorthold Tenancy.

commonly used for larger Sui Generis HMO valuations. Values using this method are more difficult to predict, but can result in better valuations, although surveyors will often err on the side of caution. Factors taken into account by surveyors include nearby comparables and the density of HMOs in the area, the size of the property, number of bedrooms and square footage, any area wide planning constraints, condition and how the property is managed.

Valuation Packs

For both types of valuation, a well-prepared valuation pack provided to your surveyor ahead of them visiting your property can really go a long way to improving the valuation price. A valuation pack is simply an information pack which informs and helps the surveyor understand the property better, what your future intensions are for the property and your experience in developing and operating it. The aim is to achieve as high a valuation figure as possible so you are then able to recycle and re-invest your cash into another project. Information to include in a valuation pack will typically comprise:

- The property address and a brief description of the property;

- A brief description of your company (if relevant) and its aims;

- High level numbers such as purchase price, legal costs, development costs, rental income figures, running costs;

- Existing and current floorplans to show how the property has changed since purchasing it;

- A description of the refurbishment and renovation works and their costs;

- Any planning permissions, building control signoff and licensing information;

- High quality (professional) pictures of the property;

- Local comparisons (the more recent and similar to your property, the better); and

- AST agreements (with redacted details for GDPR[26]) to prove rental income.

Your valuation pack should then be presented to the surveyor in a simple, clear and professional document with your company brand (if relevant).

How Long Does It Take To Process A HMO Mortgage?

HMO mortgages are typically processed in a similar timeframe to buy to let mortgages and follow the same pattern of progression:

1. Application;

2. Valuation;

3. Underwriting;

4. Approval; and

5. Release of Funds.

---

[26] General Data Protection Regulations.

If the property is in need of a HMO licence, but does not yet have one in place, most lenders will apply a condition to the mortgage stating that one must be applied for within a certain time period and that the borrower and/or their agent must be deemed as a 'fit and proper person' to manage the property.

When determining what type of HMO mortgage product to go for, a few key considerations should be made clear with your broker, such as:

- Speed – how quickly do you need the lender to process your application;

- Interest rate – depending on the loan-to-value and borrower, this can vary quite significantly;

- Loan-to-value – interest rates will usually be higher if the loan-to-value is higher; and

- Valuation – what type will be used – bricks and mortar or a multiple of the rent.

A compromise may likely be needed as lenders will not typically be able to offer a mortgage product which satisfies each consideration. Once a product is chosen, HMO mortgages are, on average, completed within four-six weeks. Subject to having all the necessary documents available, drawdowns can be completed in as little as one week, particularly for HMOs being re-mortgaged.

Interest-Only Vs Repayment Mortgages

As a landlord and property developer, you should know cashflow is key to running and maintaining an effective and competitive business. Having the option to retain as much cash to hand as possible is typically of benefit in case you need to cover unexpected repairs, for example.

Interest only mortgages are therefore often more attractive to landlords and property developers as the monthly payments (overheads) are lower than capital repayment mortgages would be – and reduce your risk of not being able to meet monthly payments. This could enable you to borrow more than you would otherwise be able to afford, depending on your circumstances. Conversely, a capital repayment mortgage increases the risks for you as a landlord, especially where void periods or maintenance costs could eat into your monthly profits.

Interest only mortgages should typically allow for a cashflow surplus to accumulate. This can be used to cover any future mortgage payments, used for further investments, or to pay off lump sums of the mortgage where penalties don't apply. Taking a sensible approach to your mortgage payments will enable you to manage your cash flow effectively, as well as the total debt outstanding. Over the long term, your property is likely to appreciate, whilst inflation will have had a positive effect on rental income and capital values. The outstanding loan amount on an interest only mortgage will therefore remain the same as the day it was taken out. For example, if you borrow £150,000 on a 25-year interest only mortgage, at the end of the 25-year period, you'd still owe the original £150,000. As a result of inflation however, this will have reduced the real value of the loan.

The downside of an interest only mortgage is that at the end of the mortgage term, you still owe 100% of the money you've borrowed and the amount of interest you end up paying will be greater than if you had a capital-repayment mortgage.

However, as the property will most likely be re-mortgaged at the end of the mortgage term or sold on at some point to someone else (depending on your exit strategy) for a profit, this would repay the mortgage and hopefully leave you with a tidy sum!

Property investment and development relies on positive cashflow and the management of liquidity. There is therefore little to be gained from putting unnecessary strain on your current cashflow by opting for a capital repayment mortgage and making higher repayments when you are seeking to expand your portfolio. You may need that extra cashflow saved to enable your portfolio's further growth. Additionally, when thinking about paying back mortgage loans, ask yourself this – in the event of a crisis, such as an urgent need for cash, would you prefer to have a slightly lower mortgage remaining or extra cash available to help get you out of a difficult situation? This question is largely why interest only mortgages remain popular with landlords and property developers.

7. Project Management

Project management is an essential part of property development. Being able to carry out this role effectively is a key skill, enabling projects to be delivered largely on time and within budget. Without it, there is a danger projects would fail to progress, or could be severely delayed, with budgets overrun. Unless you are happy to pay for a Project Manager, the 'small-scale' nature of a HMO project means you are likely to play that role yourself and will therefore need to oversee the organisation of people, trades and finance to progress the project and bring it to completion. Having a range of skills including patience, leadership, people-management, teamworking and communication skills is therefore crucial.

Project management typically revolves around a 'project circle', made up of time, cost and quality. Focusing on one element specifically may mean another may suffer. For example, if building to minimum costs, time and quality suffer, but building to the highest quality means the project takes longer and costs more. Finding a 'balance' or the 'sweet spot' in the centre between these three components is key, although this will likely result in reaching a compromise.

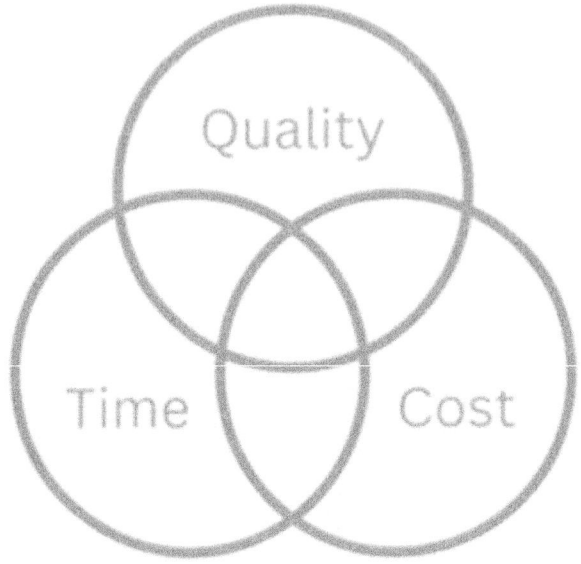

Figure 7.1: Time, Cost, Quality project circle.

Project management also requires suitable planning, including working out costs and allocating funds, making schedules and being clear on your goals and the actions needed to take place from the beginning.

It is likely you will not be familiar with all areas of a project, particularly when just starting out, so having a Power Team in place with specialists who are able to advise on certain 'expert' aspects, such as obtaining planning permission and building control details is not only useful to keep projects on track, but necessary.

Before starting any HMO development, it is very important to agree a plan with your Power Team, which includes detailed information on all stages of construction and a schedule for completion. This will enable the different stages of development to flow smoothly from one stage to the next, avoiding interruption and delays which could become costly. Once the project has commenced, being on site regularly during the development/refurbishment phase is useful as you will be able to see progress and answer your teams' queries quickly.

8. Your Power Team

Whilst understanding how the property development process works from start to finish can be useful, it is multi-faceted and multi-disciplined undertaking, calling upon numerous skills, experience and expertise. You can't be expected to be able to take on every role yourself - you'd never be able to make much progress if you spent all your time learning how each part of the puzzle fits together before acting; you'd never be able to make any meaningful progress!

Therefore, you need a specialist network of trusted people around you to help achieve your property development goals effectively. A 'Power Team' is an important addition to any HMO property developer's arsenal. This is made up of your professional team of advisors and contractors who will help guide and support you through the twists and turns of a development project, with their combined wealth of expert knowledge and experience.

Choosing the right Power Team members is essential to your success. You want people around you with relevant experience, who know what they are doing and how to go about doing it. Typically, your Power Team should consist of the following members at the procurement and property development stage:

Procurement and Property Development
Estate Agents
Solicitor
Accountant/Tax Advisor
Financial Planner/Advisor
Mortgage Broker
Insurance Broker
Planning Consultant
Architect/Architectural Technician[27]
Builders/Tradespeople/Contractors
Property Mentor/HMO Advisor

Table 8.1: Power Team members for procurement and property development.

Once up and running, you'll need a secondary Power Team of external parties to help manage your property and any growing portfolio. Depending on the skills you may already have and the extent of what you are prepared to get involved in as a landlord, this can be made up of the following:

---

[27] For accurate scaled plans/drawings.

Property Marketing and Ongoing Maintenance
Lettings Agent
Professional Photographer/Staging Agent
Cleaner
Gardener
Handyperson
Plumber
Gas Engineer
Electrician
Painter/Decorator
Bookkeeper
Property Manager

Table 8.2: Power Team members for property marketing and ongoing maintenance.

Some landlords find it easier to ask for referrals in their network, whilst others prefer to do their own research, checking out portfolios of work, the professionalism of websites, wording used and how services are explained.

Remember though; relationships are built on more than just one-off jobs. Make sure you built trust with your Power Team members as they are primarily there to help you! If you want to be able to rely on them for good service, you need them to understand what you are trying to do and encourage them to 'buy into' that vision. Once you have found good businesses or people to work with, communicate clearly with them, trust them with the work you have hired them to do, pay them promptly and try to be understanding if they have other clients to service. You want them to make themselves available when you need them – but always have a backup as well! By following these recommendations, it is more likely your Power Team members will want to pick up the phone to you, find time for you and treat you, your properties and tenants with respect.

Summary

In Section I, I have discussed the key principles of property development, starting with why it is essential to your HMO property development journey to have realistic goals and objectives set out to guide you and to clarify what you want to achieve and when you want to have achieved this by.

I have gone over some key terms within property development which you will need to become familiar with if you aren't already and have explained why they are relevant to you.

I have set out the key reasons why goal setting and developing a business plan is helpful to ensuring your success and how you should go about setting up the structure of your business to suit your personal circumstances, as well as discussing the need for a clear exit strategy.

This section has also discussed several ways in which you can finance your HMO development project and the fundamentals of project management. Finally, I have discussed the importance of project management and having a good Power Team around you to help ensure your success.

Part II

Section II: Finding Your Investment Location

In this section, I will discuss what to look for when working out your investment location and the factors you will need to consider to enable you to choose a suitable area to invest in.

"Risk comes from not knowing what you're doing."

– Warren Buffett

9. Where Do You Start?

With your vision, goals and targets clarified and your business plan in place, the next step is to decide where you want to set up your HMO property portfolio. This can be one of the more difficult parts about getting started and you may feel some pressure to get it right. As with any property strategy, becoming an HMO property developer comes with a level of risk that is important to acknowledge. Knowing what to do and where to look is therefore key to your success.

If you end up rushing at this stage, it could result in making regretful decisions; you could purchase the wrong house or invest in the wrong area - or even take on a project which doesn't align with your overall goals and objectives. This could result in losing your momentum, projected returns and wasting your time. Worse still, you may even find yourself in debt. However, with the right due diligence, research, preparation and knowledge, you will be able to minimise the risks and increase your chances of becoming a successful HMO property developer – and take enjoyment from the process whilst doing so!

To start, I would recommend creating a search area which is no more than one-hours' drive from where you live. If you are seeking to create a portfolio of properties, I would also recommend setting them up in either the same town or city, or somewhere in the same geographic area as your other properties. This is because when you factor in travel time and ongoing management, you won't appreciate having to travel for an hour (or more) in one direction to liaise with a builder on site during refurbishment at one property and then have to travel in the opposite direction to meet with a prospective

HMO Property Set Up

tenant at another property, for example. Additionally, by investing somewhere close to home, you will likely have some local knowledge of that area. This can help build up a local network of contacts for your Power Team. It surprising how many people you might know locally who'd be able to offer you their services when you think about it! You can then work on creating and building professional relationships with the people who are already in your network.

Local Estate Agents, Networks And Property Portals

Local estate agents are a mine of useful information and can help advise you on a number of matters such as tenant demands and profiles, rental rates, voids, demographics, the time taken to fill rooms, the type of properties which are most sought after and the best areas to invest in, as well as any areas to avoid!

If you're not sure who operates in your local area, carry out a Google search for local estate agents and get in touch with them, preferably by arranging a face-to-face meeting to establish a personal relationship. You are far more likely to be remembered when meeting in person than as just another caller on the phone or email in their inbox. Guide the conversation by letting them know you are a serious property developer wanting to develop a portfolio in the area. Tell them exactly what you are looking for so that if anything of interest comes their way, they know to contact you first, rather than someone else. If you mention you are looking for an agent to help manage your properties, they may also be more inclined to advise you as it would be in their interest to foster a long-term relationship. Local agents may even be able to put you in touch with a landlord seeking to sell an existing HMO

HMO Property Set Up

property or portfolio, which can be an easier way of getting a foot in the door, so to speak.

Another way to use find out more about a potential investment area is by joining local landlord groups, property groups and attending relevant local business meetings and events. Go along to these events and speak with other landlords, business people and developers in the area, get to know what issues they are facing and whether there are opportunities for what you wish to provide – they may even be able to provide you with their own contacts to help built your Power Team.

Most local authorities have their own landlord groups[28] too, so a simple search on their website will provide the contact and registration details, whilst property and business groups can be found easily enough through social media.

Property portals, such as Rightmove[29], Zoopla[30], On The Market[31] and even less conventional platforms like Facebook Marketplace, LinkedIn and Gumtree can be used effectively as property sourcing tools and are often a great place to start when seeking to narrow down an area of search. They also help you to identify what kind of properties are available in your area of interest, their condition and what those properties are currently on the market for.

Property Auctions

Property auctions are another great way to source properties within your area of search, often with a wide choice of

---

[28] See Section III, Chapter 28.
[29] https://www.rightmove.co.uk/.
[30] https://www.zoopla.co.uk/.
[31] https://www.onthemarket.com/.

HMO Property Set Up

properties available, a quick buying process and the chance to pick up a great bargain – provided you have done your due diligence first!

As with any property purchasing process, being prepared is vital when buying a property at auction, whether you are looking at a standard property to convert into a HMO, or an existing tenanted HMO. If you aren't aware of any auction houses near you, using an online property portal can be a good place to start to look for properties available at upcoming auctions. Alternatively, once you have decided on an area you are interested in, you can search for auction houses in that area and ask for catalogues or subscribe to mailing lists. Other websites, such as UK Auction List[32] or Essential Information Group[33] are great places to start, although you will have to register to view upcoming lots and pay a small fee for access. If you don't wish to sign up, you can always search on Rightmove or other property portals for properties being sold at upcoming auctions. By clicking on the adverts, you will see the auction house and can go direct their website to find out more information and to register to bid.

There are a few different auction methods that can take place at a property auction – the 'traditional' method and the 'modern method'. The traditional method is where you will usually attend an auction in person (but can also usually participate online or on the phone) and if you are successful, you'll exchange contracts and pay a deposit immediately after the auction finishes and will have 28 days in which to complete.

---

[32] https://www.ukauctionlist.com.
[33] https://www.eigpropertyauctions.co.uk.

HMO Property Set Up

The modern method allows you to delay completing contracts straight away. Instead you will pay a non-refundable reserve fee on the property, should you pull out. The cost is variable but is typically a percentage of your bid. Following this, a 56 day exchange window opens to exchange contracts and complete the purchase within.

Online auctions are increasingly popular ways of sourcing property, particularly since the Covid-19 pandemic, as more properties are being sold this way. Online auctions mean you can bid on property in real time, with auctions open for bids until a prescribed end period. Pre-auction offers can also be accepted. Online auctions enable you to view images of a property, bid on it and buy it, all from the comfort of your screen. You can bid live, or use proxy bidding, where you can't bid in real time. This is where you enter a maximum bid and the online system makes incremental bids for you, up to that value. If no-one else bids higher, you hold the winning bid.

I'll come back to auction properties in Chapter 16, as there are a few other important matters to consider first before raising your hand in front of the auctioneer!

10. Supply Vs Demand And Competition

Whether you are considering a new area of investment or are looking to invest where you may already have properties, location analysis is essential. Once you have settled on a place to invest, the whole process becomes much clearer and easier.

Supply and demand are key factors to be confident about before investing in a property. There's little point spending your time and money creating a beautiful property to rent out, only to find you cannot attract tenants because the local market is oversaturated with other properties. Similarly, if there is no demand for the type of property you want to set up in the area then you'll struggle to get tenants interested in the first place!

Typically, HMOs in rural locations do not work as they often lack local facilities and services which are attractive to tenants, as well as nearby employment opportunities. When choosing a property to live in, tenants will want to be located close to amenities and places of employment and often don't want to have to rely on needing a car to get around. Therefore most property developers tend to look at setting up HMOs in towns and cities. Having said that, there are a greater number of more 'mature' renters now seeking to live in HMOs. Coupled with the rise in working from home and high speed internet connections, more rural or semi-rural HMOs with larger outdoor spaces, for example, could be an attractive, yet largely untapped avenue worth exploring. To aid with finding potential HMO properties, there are several useful online resources which can be used to assess the supply and demand of an area, which I'll discuss below.

HMO Property Set Up

SpareRoom

SpareRoom[34] is the biggest flatmate finding platform in the UK and receives over two million visitors to its site every month, with people typically finding somewhere to live every three minutes. To assist with your research, you can assess the number rooms available in a certain area of your choosing, as well as the number of rooms sought by potential tenants. This helps you to work out the ratio of demand for rooms against the number of tenants seeking accommodation in that area, as well as your potential competition and the average room rental rates being sought.

To work this ratio out, simply go to the website and select 'Rooms for rent' and then add in your location of interest. Start with a wide search area, for example 'Coventry' and click 'Search'. You will probably end up with loads of results. Don't worry about excluding any of the other options at this stage; you just want a high-level overview of what is around in that area.

You will be shown a list of rooms available to rent across the chosen town or city and the monthly or weekly rental rates. Make a note of these numbers, then go through the list of posts, now excluding the ones which relate to non-HMO properties. It is worth looking at the adverts as well because some of the descriptions of available rooms may relate to people letting out spare rooms in their own houses, rather than in HMOs specifically. What you should be left with is a list of HMO properties with rooms available to rent in your area of interest.

---

[34] https://www.spareroom.co.uk/.

HMO Property Set Up

Note down this figure, as well as the rental rates, taking account of the most expensive. Look at the posts and images people have put up as well. This can give you a feel for the quality of rooms available in the area and what rental amounts are being requested for the standard of quality.

When reviewing adverts, take account of the type of accommodation being let and the facilities it comes with as these properties will be your direct competition. If the rooms and communal facilities shown are generally not to a high standard and the images used in adverts show dim and uninviting rooms, with tired looking furniture or don't have any parking available, people looking for somewhere to live in the area with higher budgets will be willing to pay more for better quality accommodation. You'll want to use this to your advantage when creating your HMO. To aid with this, make sure you have professional photographs taken post-refurb for your marketing campaign to really show off your property and make it as attractive as possible to prospective tenants.

Another tip is to click on individual adverts and make a note of the unique advert reference number. Check this over a couple of weeks to see how long it takes for the advert to be taken down. This will give you an indication of how quickly rooms are being rented. If adverts are removed quickly, it is an indication there is strong demand and people are willing to move quickly to secure a room. Conversely, if the advert takes a long time to be removed, it may be an indication that demand is lower in that area, or that the room advertised is not attractive to prospective tenants.

The next step is to carry out a search for 'Rooms Wanted'. Input the same town or city and click 'Search'. You will be shown a list of people looking for rooms within that town or

HMO Property Set Up

city, as well as information about their budgets. Make a note of these figures. You should now be able to calculate the supply and demand ratio across the entire town or city, providing you with a good general overview of what local needs there are against the number of rooms available.

Next, you'll want to drill down further into this supply and demand relationship by repeating the previous steps for specific postcodes or wards throughout the town or city. For example, when looking at Coventry, there are 24 outward postcode districts, but only six which relate to the city itself (CV1 – CV6). Use Postcode Area[35] to identify the relevant postcode prefixes for the city. I'll come back to what else you can use Postcode Area for later on. Whilst this exercise may take some time, by carrying out an in-depth analysis of individual postcode prefixes, this provides you with a good indication of where there are specific opportunity areas or areas which should be avoided (no demand or oversaturated). Ideally, you want to find an area to invest in where demand is outstripping the supply. Make sure to put the results into a spreadsheet for each postcode area so you can easily keep track of potentially suitable areas.

Licenced HMO List

Local authorities are required to maintain a list of all licenced HMOs in their area[36]. This enables you to work out how many licenced HMOs are already in existence, their location, the number of bedrooms each property has and who the landlord or managing agent is. The list is typically updated on an

---

[35] https://www.postcodearea.co.uk/.
[36] See Section III.

HMO Property Set Up

annual basis to take account of any new HMOs set up since the last period.

This information should be readily available on the HMO section of their website. If not, you may have to contact the local authority and ask them to provide you with the list. This should be provided to you, although in some cases a 'Freedom of Information' (FOI) request may need to be submitted.

Once you have obtained the list, it can be helpful to plot the licenced HMO properties onto a map using Google My Maps[37], for example. This helps give you a clear visual picture of where licenced HMOs are located within your area of interest as well as the overall geographical spread of HMOs across a town or city, or where clusters of HMOs can be found specifically.

Local Statistics

As I've already mentioned, Postcode Area is useful for looking at postcode data and information on cities and regions. By using an area's postcode, you can search for local population demographics in specific postcode areas (for example, Bournemouth - BH13), helping you to identify the local population size, number of households, rate of unemployment and average household incomes to give you an overall picture of your potential investment area.

Taking the area analysis a step further, you can even select a specific full postcode, which provides an overview of the local population, including social 'grades', unemployment rate, type of occupations. You can also view crime statistics for the area, local house price data and details of nearby

---

[37] https://www.google.co.uk/maps/about/mymaps/.

HMO Property Set Up

amenities, such as banks and cash machines, shopping, post office locations and nearby businesses.

Postcode Area also provides details of nearby train stations and services and information on local attractions, pubs, churches and leisure facilities - it can even give you the local weather forecast – useful if you are planning a property viewing!

You may be thinking, "that's great - but what can I do with all that information?" Well, the simple answer is - use it to help inform your investment decisions! For example, if you find out an area has a high population of people in their 60s and 70s+, it probably isn't the right location for a 'young professional-type' of HMO, or if an area has a high number of burglaries or issues with anti-social behaviour, again, you'd probably want to avoid investing there. However, if your search reveals an area has a high number of economically active people, aged between 18 and 45, for example, that would likely be worth taking a closer look at.

You can even combine individual Postcode Area information together to provide a tailored and in-depth analysis of local demographics for a whole range of postcodes in your area of interest, helping you to target a specific location to look for property within and allowing you to make more informed decisions.

The 2021 Census Interactive Map[38], produced by the Office for National Statistics (ONS), is another powerful tool which provides data on population, education, identity, housing, health and work. Using the interactive map can help you drill

---

[38] https://www.ons.gov.uk/census/maps.

HMO Property Set Up

down further into specific local statistics, aiding with investment location selection.

11. HMO Licensing And Planning Legislation

Whilst supply, demand and local statistics are key components of choosing the right HMO investment location, there are many legislative considerations which naturally hamper or even exclude some locations.

First, let's take a quick look at HMO Licensing (although this is covered fully in Section III). HMO Licensing is concerned with the health and safety of tenants and making sure that a HMO property is of a suitable standard and size to be rented out. Licensing also seeks to ensure the owner or person responsible for managing the HMO is a 'fit and proper person'.

Considerations include minimum bedroom sizes, the ratio of shared kitchen and bathroom facilities to the number of tenants, the amount of communal space provided and the fire safety standards to be adhered to. The Government introduced national minimum standards which all HMOs should comply with, although each local authority also has the discretion to create and adopt their own local standards for HMO properties. These generally require the provision of larger rooms within a HMO above the national minimum standards.

It is therefore essential these minimum room size requirements are fully understood before you start looking at properties to purchase, as certain types of housing stock simply aren't suited for conversion into HMOs without extensive (and costly) modification.

Aside from standards, if you're setting up a HMO property where there are five or more occupants forming more than one household and sharing kitchen, bathroom and toilet facilities, the property qualifies for a Mandatory HMO Licence, which must be applied for. Local authorities also have the discretion to bring in separate licensing schemes across whole boroughs, districts or certain parts of a neighbourhood or estate, for example. These are known as 'Selective' and 'Additional' Licensing schemes which can have implications for the way in which you set up an HMO property.

Moving onto Planning Legislation (which I'll cover fully in Section IV), some types of HMOs do not need planning permission to be set up. However, LPAs can choose to restrict HMO development in certain areas or across whole boroughs or districts where they believe additional control is justified. This restriction is known as an 'Article 4 Direction' (A4D) and essentially means that any proposal for new HMO (or a larger HMO) accommodation within the designated area will need planning permission. As you can imagine, this has the potential to bring uncertainly into your property development plans as there are no guarantees planning permission would be granted. A4Ds can therefore often rule out large areas for investment, unless you are willing to 'roll the dice' on submitting a planning application and take the risk (although I would advise against this when looking to set up your first HMO).

Who Is The Local Authority For Your Area Of Interest?

To find out which local authority area a property you are interested in is part of, use the Government's 'Find your Local Council' search online[39]. All you'll need is a postcode. Once entered, you may be faced with either one or two options,

---

[39] www.gov.uk/find-local-council.

HMO Property Set Up

depending on how many tiers of local government exist in the area.

Some parts of England have a 'county council', followed by a 'district', 'borough' or 'city' council. Local services are split between the two tiers. Other parts of the country are made up of a 'unitary tier' of local government, which provides all services. These are usually unitary authorities, like the London boroughs or metropolitan boroughs. An example of a two-tier system can be found if searching for a postcode in Chichester. The search brings up the details of the county council (West Sussex County Council), responsible for services like education, transport and social care, as well as the district council (Chichester District Council), responsible for services like rubbish and recycling collection, council tax and housing.

If a two-tiered system is shown, you will generally need to go to the 'district', 'borough' or 'city' council website to access local information about HMO licensing, planning and building regulations. However, if you are still not sure, just look for whichever authority is responsible for 'housing' and navigate to their HMO licensing (also sometimes found under 'Private Sector Housing' or 'Environmental Health' pages) and Planning webpages to find relevant information on setting up a HMO within that local authority area.

Assessing The Location

Once you have found an area you think has a suitable supply of housing and tenant demand, the next step is to carry out a thorough assessment of the location. This should include:

- Whether there are opportunities for tenants to easily access public transport (usually within a 10 to 15-minute walk is preferable);

- Whether there are local opportunities for nearby employment;

- Whether there are local amenities and facilities (pubs, cafes, corner shops, GP surgeries and supermarkets) within walking distance of your chosen area; and

- Whether the area has good access to leisure facilities (gyms and leisure centres, cinemas, parks and gardens and restaurants).

Other factors to include are what the area is like. For example, is it on the edge of a housing estate, or within a cluster of housing surrounded by industrial estates, commercial and/or office buildings? Is it near to a train line or an airport or close to a school? An excellent way of answering these questions is by using everyone's favourite online search engine - Google!

Google Maps and Street View are very useful tools, allowing you to carry out a relatively detailed desktop analysis of an area - and any properties of interest - without having to go and physically look round each area. Google Maps also allows

HMO Property Set Up

you to see what other works (extensions, garage conversions, loft conversions, side extensions etc.) have been carried out in the streets surrounding a property you have identified with potential. This helps you get an idea of whether there is potential for works to be carried out without requiring planning permission (using permitted development rights (PD rights)). Additionally, Google Maps can help you look at the availability of on-street parking, plot sizes for potential extensions and to scope out where nearby facilities and amenities are, as well as opportunities for employment. You can even gauge how accessible the area is by looking at nearby transport links such as bus stops and train stations and work out walking or cycling distances to these places from an area of interest or a specific property.

This research can help determine the type of tenants you are likely to attract. For example, a key worker who may be employed by an airport or a hospital would likely want to be living near these sites, whilst a professional worker may be looking for accommodation near to offices in the town centre – or may be looking move closer to their job to reduce their existing office commute.

Remember though, whilst you won't have to live in the area, it is important that you get a good feel for it yourself. I would therefore always ask yourself if you would feel happy having a family member or a close friend living there. Would you feel comfortable, or would you advise them to look elsewhere? If you wouldn't be comfortable with that, don't expect your tenants to be either!

HMO Property Set Up

Flood Risk

Flood risk is an important factor to consider for a HMO property, particularly where you require planning permission for ground floor accommodation! There are three flood zones, labelled 1 to 3:

- Flood Zone 1 is the lowest level and means the area is at very low risk of flooding and will likely not need a flood risk assessment;

- Flood Zone 2 means the area is at some risk of flooding and proposed development may need a flood risk assessment; and

- Flood Zone 3[40] is the highest level and means there is a greater chance the area would flood during a flood event and proposed development may need a flood risk assessment.

Where possible, it is advisable to try and avoid Flood Zones 2 and 3, especially where you intend to create a larger HMO with rooms on the ground floor as residential uses are classed as 'more vulnerable' uses[41]. LPAs may refuse to grant permission where it places future occupants at greater risk of flooding, unless suitable mitigation, such as raised finished

---

[40] Split into 3a and 3b, where: 3a is distinguished as land which has a 'one percent or greater' annual probability of river flooding; and 3b which is a 'functional floodplain' that either stores water from rivers or the sea during flooding, or allows flood water to flow through it during periods of flooding.
[41] Annex 3: Flood risk vulnerability classification.

HMO Property Set Up

floor levels and protected emergency egress can be provided. To check whether a property is within a flood zone, use the Environment Agency's 'Flood Map for Planning[42]'.

Surface Water Flooding

Another useful tool is the Government's surface water flood map[43], which provides information on the long-term flood risk for an area in England and the risk of flooding from surface water. To start, all you'll need is a postcode to enter into the search box. You will then need to select the correct property address. If the property address does not appear, you can use another one nearby.

On clicking 'continue' you will be taken to a summary page of the flood risk for that property which will identify the risk from surface water flooding and river and sea flooding. The categories for surface water flooding are:

- Very low risk, meaning the area has a chance of flooding of less than 0.1 percent each year;

- Low risk, which means the area has a chance of flooding of between 0.1 percent and one percent each year;

- Medium risk, meaning the area has a chance of flooding of between one percent and 3.3 percent each year; and

- High risk, meaning that the area has a chance of flooding of greater than 3.3 percent each year.

---

[42] https://flood-map-for-planning.service.gov.uk/.
[43] https://check-long-term-flood-risk.service.gov.uk/postcode.

HMO Property Set Up

The summary page also provides details of the lead local flood authority (LLFA) for the area who are responsible for managing the flood risk from surface water and can provide more detailed information, if needed. There is also a link to a useful interactive map if you haven't been able to find the specific property address but know its location. By clicking on the map link, you can view the extent of surface water flooding for an area. Clicking on the map itself will bring up information about the flood risk from surface water flooding. This can help you to determine if there is likely to be a risk to a specific property you are interested in.

The mapping tool is also useful if you intend to extend a property as you may find part of a garden or driveway is going to be within an area at higher risk from surface water flooding. This could have wider implications for obtaining planning permission, your HMO licence, mortgage and insurance.

13. Assessing The Suitability Of Properties

When considering any potential investment property, make sure the numbers always work on paper first, otherwise there is no point wasting your time with properties that simply won't stack up. Dismiss those that don't work and move on.

Property Searching

Let's go through a quick example search together. Go to Rightmove (or any other online property search engine) and set your search criteria; for example 'Coventry' with a range of five miles. Set the number of bedrooms to 'three minimum' and 'no maximum' and then set the property type to 'houses' (you can filter later to include bungalows and /or change whether you search for detached, semi-detached and terraced houses). Don't worry about the price at this stage, unless you have a specific maximum budget in mind. If lots of results are returned, refine your search to look for the lowest price first. Click on any properties of interest, review the details and photos to get an idea of what is being offered and then review the floorplan to see the layout. The layouts of some properties can lend themselves to being converted very obviously, although some will clearly show you that conversion to a HMO may not be a straightforward option.

Reading a floorplan and working out how a conversion can take place is a skill, but it is one you can pick up through experience. Make sure to take account of where windows, doors and any shared walls are and remember, you can't create a bedroom without any windows! Where no floorplan is available, it isn't the end of the world, but means you must rely on the images a bit more. Sometimes, you can find previous listings for the property which have floorplans

HMO Property Set Up

shown, so carrying out a bit of 'property history' digging by searching for the property address on Google can be helpful here.

Next, you need to think about the refurbishment costs. Unless shown on the floorplan, you can use the property's Energy Performance Certificate (EPC) to identify the extent of the floor area[44]. This figure can be used to roughly work out the cost of refurbishment (excluding furniture, white goods and carpeting etc.). You can expect the following amounts to be reasonably accurate estimations:

Standard back-to-brick HMO Conversions	£350 - £450 per m^2
High-end back-to-brick HMO Conversions with ensuites	£450 - £550 per m^2

Table 13.1: Indicative standard and high-end back-to-brick HMO conversion costs (m^2).

Note down the Energy Performance Certificate (EPC) rating for the property as well. EPCs must currently only achieve an 'E' rating or above to be suitable for a HMO, although be aware the Government is proposing for this to be increased to a minimum 'C' rating for all tenancies from 2028[45]. It is therefore recommended to work towards providing 'C' rated accommodation post-refurb to ensure you stay ahead of any changing legislation.

---

[44] Check the property advert or go to: https://find-energy-certificate.digital.communities.gov.uk/.
[45] See Chapter 73.

HMO Property Set Up

Local House Prices And Comparables

Most valuations for HMOs will be conducted using 'brick-and-mortar' valuations, based on standard single residential dwellings. It is therefore useful to carry out a search of comparables in the local area. For example, if other dwellings in the same street have recently sold, looking at how much they sold for is very informative. Mouseprice[46] is excellent at this. It allows you to look up sold prices and valuations for an area and provides reasonably up-to-date housing data.

Create a free account and input the details of the property you are interested in. Mouseprice will then provide you with information on the current value of a property and its range of worth, the floor area, predicted rental ranges, the date the property was built, how long it was on the market for and how much it was sold for previously. Use Rightmove, Zoopla and On The Market to check for past and current property values and any recent sales too. These will give you an indication of what the property you may purchase could be valued at if re-sold, once refurbishment works have taken place.

Property Deal Analysis

To understand whether the numbers on a HMO project will stack up and make the deal viable, you should plug all the purchase, refurb and rental costs into a property deal analyser. An example property analyser is shown in Figure 13.1. You should look to add in details such as the property purchase price, stamp duty, associated legal and professional fees, refurbishment/building costs and the costs associated with getting the property 'rental ready'. You will also need to

---

[46] https://www.mouseprice.com/.

HMO Property Set Up

factor in the mortgage information, other funds and any associated interest to purchase the property and convert it to an HMO, as well as comparables, which will give you an indication of the new valuation amount.

Entering in this information, along with the expected rental income from your research, will help determine the gross profit from the property, as well as the return on investment. You want to be able to work out the property's worth after refurbishment to make sure you get as much money back out of the deal by adding value.

In the following example in Figure 13.1, sticking with Amy's search for a HMO, she decides the property she is interested in would benefit from a three-metre single storey rear extension across the back of the dwelling. The property would be extended and initially converted into a six-bedroom HMO. The extension would be carried out using PD rights and the dwelling is not located in an A4D area, so no planning permission is required for any of the works or to use the property as a 6-bedroom HMO. However, Amy plans to rent the property out as a 7-bedroom HMO in the future, so includes the seventh bedroom in the analyser, which will require planning permission to occupy.

HMO Property Set Up

Property Address	123 Example Street		
Property Type	3 bed semi-detached		
Location	Coventry		
Size (m²) (EPC)	105		
HMO Property Deal Analysis			
List Price	£245,000	**Monthly Revenue Produced**	
Purchase Price	£250,000	Lettable Rooms	7
Mortgage LTV	70%	Room 1 Rental	£650
Mortgage LTV	£175,000	Room 2 Rental	£675
Deposit (30%)	£75,000	Room 3 Rental	£700
Stamp Duty	£7,500	Room 4 Rental	£775
HMO Refurb + Furniture/House Pack	£45,000	Room 5 Rental	£785
Broker Fee	£500	Room 6 Rental	£785
Survey	£500	Room 7 Rental	£705
Legals	£1,000	Average Room Rental	£725
Planning and Architectural Fees	-	Other income (TIMS meters etc.)	£60
Total Capital invested	£129,500	Gross Revenue	£5,135
Total Costs	£304,500		
Annual Expenditure		**Key Financials**	
Total Estimated Room Bills	£9,240	Estimated Post-Refurbishment Value	£300,000
Insurance	£600	Current equity	£154,500

HMO Property Set Up

Cleaner	£2,400	Equity Growth	£25,000
Gardener	£2,400	Annual Rental Income	£61,620
Voids (10%)	£6,162	Annual Costs	£33,858
Maintenance (5%)	£3,081	Annual Gross Yield	**24.65%**
Mortgage rate (5.70%)	£9,975	Annual Net Profit	**£27,762**
Total Expenditure	£33,858	Return on Investment	**21%**

Figure 13.1: Property Deal Analyser example.

The example in Figure 13.1 identifies that to purchase the property and carry out the refurbishment work, Amy will need to invest £129,500, with a 70% LTV mortgage totalling £175,000. With 7 bedrooms, the property would generate an annual gross yield of 24.65% and an annual net profit of £27,762. Ideally, Amy would want to reduce the amount of money she has left in the deal by as much as possible to retain liquidity, although the ROI is shown to be 21%, with ten percent included for voids and five percent included for repairs per month already built in, which works out to be a respectable return.

Key figures to look out for when doing your searches are the return on investment, gross and net yields and the amount of net cash flow per month. If these meet with your minimum criteria, it's a good indication the property is suitable.

The deal analyser is important as it helps you to run various scenarios and 'stress-test' the finances for the project to the limit. Make sure to do this as it enables you to consider contingency plans. For example, this could include the cost of

HMO Property Set Up

having a high-quality refurbishment compared with a 'budget' option, the effect of having two empty rooms for three months (void periods), interest rate increases, or the impacts of refinancing. You can even look at the effect of changing the purchase costs and capital input to get an idea of whether different offers still allow the deal to work for you. Changing room rates gives you an understanding of the lowest figure you could rent the rooms for too, if necessary.

A property deal analyser is most useful in deciding whether a property is worth viewing. If the numbers add up, don't delay getting in touch with the estate agent to set up a viewing. Even in cases where you initially discount a property, it is worth keeping the details on a version of your property deal analysis, so you know what you have looked at in the area, if you decide to revisit it in the future.

Other Important Checks

Whilst you wait to view the property, there are a few other useful background checks to carry out as part of your initial due diligence. I'll start by going over using the Land Registry to review the important title documents.

Land Registry

The Land Registry[47] is useful for establishing who owns a property or a piece of land and the extent of that ownership. You can use the Title Register to check the ownership status of property or land and for any restrictions on the property's use. I'll cover this in more detail in Chapter 39.

---

[47] https://www.gov.uk/government/organisations/land-registry.

HMO Property Set Up

To get started, set yourself up with a free Land Registry business account and use the 'Map Search' function to show property/land boundaries. Title Plans and Title Registers should only cost £3 each to purchase. There are a number of companies out there that will charge higher fees to obtain the same documents, so do be sure to use the official Land Registry website. Once you have purchased and downloaded the title documents, review them carefully for any clauses, obligations, restrictions and covenants. If in doubt about anything, pass the documents onto your solicitor to advise on further as they will be best placed to flag up any details which could be of concern.

Planning History

In addition to the Land Registry, I would always advise on carrying out checks of a property's planning history as part of your due diligence. This is helpful in flushing out any pitfalls and may give you an idea of whether PD rights are available for alterations or extensions, as well as whether the property is lawfully operating as a HMO, if advertised as existing or if planning permission is needed.

Where an existing HMO is offered as a tenanted property in an area where there is a planning restriction, such as within an A4D designation, when undertaking a review of the planning history, you should either find an application for full planning permission for the change of use from a 'Use Class C3' dwelling to either a 'Use Class C4 HMO' or to a 'Sui Generis HMO[48]'. Alternatively, you may find a Certificate of Lawful Existing Use or Development (CLEUD) for the change of

---

[48] More on these Use Classes in Chapter 35.

HMO Property Set Up

use[49]. This can either be within an A4D area or outside of it. The purpose of a CLEUD is to confirm the use of the property as a HMO, or that a development is lawful in planning terms.

Outside of A4D areas, and in the absence of a CLEUD, evidence of an application for full planning permission for the change of use of either a C3 dwelling or C4 HMO to a Sui Generis HMO should be confirmed. Do be aware though that not all existing HMOs will have a CLEUD to confirm the use is lawful outside of an A4D area. This is because PD rights will have likely been used for the conversion of a C3 dwelling to a C4 HMO. Where this is the case, you will need to satisfy yourself the property is operating lawfully under PD rights.

To check the planning history of a property, simply go to the LPAs webpage and find their online planning portal search page. Some portals are more advanced than others, so searching may require you to do a bit of 'detective work' to find the correct property details!

To get started, first search for the property address. If no results are found, try searching for the street address and then postcode individually. If this doesn't reveal any planning history, most LPAs have a useful 'map search' function. Scroll to your area of interest and change the filter to 'All Time'. This should bring up any results for the property in question as far back as the online records will allow.

If you find any applications, click on them and review the details of whether they have been approved, withdrawn or refused – and the date these events happened. Dates are

---

[49] See Chapter 41 for an explanation of different planning applications.

HMO Property Set Up

important because the LPAs adopted Development Plan policies changes over time, meaning proposals can become either more or less favourable, depending on the approach taken towards housing delivery by the authority. This can allow scope for a revised application to be submitted where it aligns with more recent policy approaches. For each application found, check through the application plans and documents where available. It is useful to download a copy of the application file for your own records as it saves having to search for the planning history again. Out of all the documents, two are particularly important: the decision notice and the officer report or delegated report. Make sure to pay close attention to these. The decision notice will let you know whether any conditions were attached to a planning permission that may prevent further works, for example under PD rights, or if the application was refused, what the reasons were.

The officer report or delegated report provides a useful commentary on the development in the context of local and national policies and affords details of how the application was assessed by the assigned planning officer. These reports are also useful for giving you clues as to how you could overcome a refusal (if, for example, an extension or use was previously refused for the property). Perhaps a smaller extension or less intensive use would be more favourable?

For properties which form part of a relatively modern estate (let's say circa 1990's onwards), try to look for either the estate wide outline planning application or reserved matters application as the decision notices for these will usually say whether PD rights are removed in one of the conditions. If they are removed, this usually applies across the entire estate,

HMO Property Set Up

unless stated otherwise (i.e. PD rights may only be restricted on certain plots, for example if part of the estate has been built on contaminated land or falls within a conservation area).

It is useful to look at other planning applications within the nearby area too. Make a note of whether any neighbouring properties have applied for permission and what kind of permission. If applications have been submitted for works such as garage conversions, conservatories or small extensions, this may indicate PD rights have been removed. Similarly, if the search results identify a number of existing HMOs with planning permission in the area already, you may find it more challenging to gain consent for another.

Building Control Signoff

Building Control signoff is another important due diligence check you can undertake yourself by carrying out a search of building control applications. You can do this by going directly to the local authority's online building control webpage or by going to the planning search portal and clicking on the drop-down 'search' menu and selecting 'Building Control' instead of 'Planning', then searching for the property address.

If any records are held online, these should appear in the search results. Click on any results and these should provide you with a basic description of the works carried out and the date works were accepted on. This can give you an indication of what works have been undertaken to a property and whether your solicitor should be on the lookout for any paperwork if you decided to proceed with purchasing the property.

HMO Property Set Up

When it comes to purchasing, your solicitor will routinely carry out a detailed search as part of the conveyancing process. However, the benefits of doing your own background research initially means that it can help save you time and money and avoid any nasty surprises further down the line!

HMO Licensing

Finally, if you are looking at a property which is being marketed as an existing HMO, you'll want to know whether there is a current HMO licence for the property. As mentioned in Chapter 10, checking to see if the property has a current HMO licence is vitally important. If no licence details are available, contact the agent selling it for clarification and proceed with caution, as the property could be operating as an unlicenced HMO.

It may also therefore be worthwhile enquiring about any tenancy agreements for the property and/or rooms so you can check how the property is being operated. If tenancy agreements are incorrect and deposits have not been registered properly, for example, then inheriting this kind of mess could lead to some headaches for you as the new owner of the property and as the landlord to the existing tenants!

14. Development Costs

Having established that a property on your shortlist is suitable in principle, working out the development costs is the next step in the process. Development costs vary across the county and so the following figures are for indicative purposes only but will hopefully provide you with an idea of what to budget for when setting up a HMO.

Purchasing Costs

Let's say the cost of purchasing a standard three-bedroom semi-detached property is £250,000. With a loan-to-value ratio of 75%, your deposit would typically need to be £62,500 (25%). You can expect your legal costs to be in the region of £350 - £1,000, depending on the size of the property and whether there are any complexities which need investigating. A structural survey will usually cost in the region of £800 - £1,200, but it is worth having one carried out as it may uncover issues which could end up costing you a lot more to fix. Any issued flagged could be used to negotiate the purchase price.

If you are purchasing a property and need bridging finance, you will need to include brokers fees. These vary depending on the broker and their fee structures, but you can expect anything from £400 to £1,000. It is important to ask your broker how their fees are charged as it can make a different when working out your ROI.

If you need planning permission, you will need to budget for this. A Planning Consultant is likely to charge anywhere between £500 to £3,000 for small domestic projects, depending on the extent and complexity of what you are

HMO Property Set Up

proposing. Planning application fees will also be applicable on top of any consultant fees[50]. Linked to this, you will also need to factor in the cost of Architect's fees for drawings. These are likely to be between £1,000 to £2,500, again depending on what is being proposed. For example, a simple conversion with no external changes is likely to cost less than a conversion which includes a new rear extension.

Building regulations costs need to be factored in and will depend on whether you opt to use the Local Authority Building Control Team or a private company, who may charge more. For a HMO project, you can expect to pay around £250 to £800 for building regulations signoff, depending on whether you need a full plans application, full plans inspection or building notice[51]. Your architect will also need to prepare plans for building regulations purposes which are more detailed than those for planning permission. Again, expect to pay in the region of between £700 to £1,500 for these, excluding any additional charges for structural calculations (if necessary).

Refurbishment And Furnishing Costs

The following provides a desk-top analysis of the costs associated with the conversion of a Use Class C3 dwelling into a HMO and the associated furnishings. It is therefore only able to provide an indication of what to budget for. In this example, Amy has based her conversion costs on being between £450 to £550 per square metre for a high-end, back-to-brick HMO conversion with ensuite bathrooms. Let's assume Amy's three-bedroom property is 110 square metres.

---

[50] See section IV for further details.
[51] See Section V for further details.

HMO Property Set Up

From this, she can work out the cost of a high-quality refurb to create a six-bedroom HMO is likely to be between £49,500 and £60,500. The following costs can then be applied on top of this figure.

Item	Costs
Single Storey Extension	£1,200 to £1,400/m² including footings
Loft Conversions	£30,000 to £35,000 for a brand new room with dormer window
Basement Conversions	£15,000 to £20,000 including tanking, digging down to achieve minimum head heights, escape windows and fire proofing
Garage Conversions	£9,000 to £11,000 including removal and bricking up of garage door, installation of windows, fire proofing, insulation and stud work
Ensuite Bathroom	£1,500 to £2,000 including all bathroom fixtures and fittings, soil stacking and stud work

Table 14.1: Indicative extension and conversion costs.

Item	Cost
UPVC Trickle Vent Windows	£300 to £500 depending on window size
Fire Doors	£150 to £175 including intumescent smoke seal
Grade A Fire Alarm System	£2,000 to £2,500
Grade D Fire Alarm System	£50 to £90 per unit
Full Re-Wire, including Fire Alarm System	£5,500 to £7,500

HMO Property Set Up

Full Plumbing and Central Heating	£12,000 to £14,000, depending on existing set up and work required
Plumbing in a Bathroom	£1,500 to £1,700
Stud Walls	£350 to £400 per wall, including battens, insulation, sound proofing, stud work and plastering
Plastering	£15 to £20/m²
Painting and Decorating	£3,000 to £3,500 for a five/six-bedroom HMO

Table 14.2: Indicative other costs.

Item	Cost
Fully Fitted Kitchen	£3,000 to £3,500
Carpets	£2,500 to £3,500 for a five/six-bedroom HMO
Bedroom Furniture	£500 to £600 per room, including a double bed and mattress, large wardrobe, chest of drawers, desk and chair
Curtains	£50 to £65 per set (black out)
Lounge Furniture	£600 to £700, including two sofas, a coffee table and TV stand
Lounge TV	£200 to £250
Dressing/Soft Furnishings	£200 to £300 including cushions, pictures/prints, ornaments etc.
Boiler	£1,000 to £2,000
Vacuum Cleaner	£100 to £150

Table 14.3: Indicative fixtures and fittings costs.

HMO Property Set Up

Item	Cost
Fridge Freezers	£300 to £350
Cooker with 4-ring Hob	£250 to £300
Microwave	£70 to £90
Washing Machine	£250 to £300
Tumble Dryer	£200 to £250
Dishwasher	£250 to £300
Refuse/Recycling Bins	£50 to £60
Cooking Items	£200 to £250, including pots and pans, utensils
Cutlery and Crockery	£60 to £100

Table 14.4: Indicative kitchen item costs.

Taking the above indicative 'working costs' to extend, refurbish and furnish a property for use as a HMO, it is always worth adding at least a five to ten percent contingency 'buffer' to cover any unexpected issues or costs you may encounter (such as material expenses rising etc.). Run your ROI based on this figure to make sure the deal stacks up and achieves what you are looking for.

15. Arranging And Conducting Viewings

So, let's assume you've now found a few properties which work on paper and achieve your requirements - now it's time to go and see if they measure up in real life! Obviously, the first step here is to contact the estate agent's marketing the properties you are interested in, or respond directly to the seller, if advertised on a social media or other platform.

When contacting estate agents, it is worthwhile bearing in mind that they *hate* dealing with timewasters, so make sure that you come across as a credible buyer. When enquiring, go and see them face-to-face if possible and if you have not already done so previously, explain you are an active HMO investor/property developer in the area and are looking for suitable properties in certain areas. Provide them with details of your budget and let them know you are willing and able to move quickly, if the right property becomes available. I would advise against contacting estate agents by email, or relying on the online contact forms typically provided as you don't want to miss out on an opportunity simply because you were waiting for a reply!

When you visit the estate agents, it is worth taking along all the information they will need to review to proceed with a purchase, such as proof of funds (either a bank statement or your JV partners' statement), or a mortgage/decision in principle (MIP/DIP) from your mortgage broker, proof of ID and solicitor details. Having this information up front without being asked for it helps to demonstrate your seriousness and professionalism. You should then aim to arrange a property viewing as quickly as possible, as the chances are if you've spotted this opportunity, someone else will have too!

HMO Property Set Up

Viewings

Once you've booked a viewing, I know it sounds obvious, but make sure you are organised: know where you are going so you aren't late and have your essential viewing kit ready to go. Maybe take a drive the day before to scout out the route and get a feel for the local area. Below is a list of essential items I would recommend you take for any property viewing:

Property Viewing Kit
Laser measurer to check room sizes
Handheld/head torch to check areas which aren't well lit (basements, lofts, understairs cupboards)
Binoculars to check the roof and chimney from ground level (not to spy on neighbours!)
Telescopic/collapsible ladder to access the loft space or other hard to reach areas
Selfie stick to take external photo of the condition of first floor windows
A damp meter to determine if the property has any damp issues
Two sets of floorplans – one for reference and one for scribing notes/redrawing walls or mocking up extensions
A copy of your local HMO licensing standards
A digital camera/smartphone

Table 15.1: Property viewing kit basics.

On the day of the viewing, arrive at the property 10 to 15 minutes ahead of your arranged time so you can watch the comings and goings of people/vehicles in the area. Google Streetview can only tell you so much and first impressions count - if you are put off by the area, the chances are you can bet potential tenants may be too! Once conducting the viewing, follow these essentials tips:

HMO Property Set Up

- Make an effort to build a rapport with the estate agent on arrival. If they consider you to be an approachable person and a credible buyer, they can often help tip the balance in favour of a smooth transaction;

- Take a friend/family member/partner, JV partner, builder or even a friendly surveyor with you. Try to avoid conducting viewings on your own as you may miss something. You can also bounce ideas off your viewing partner and get a second opinion;

- If the seller is likely to be present during your viewing, tell the estate agent beforehand not to let them know you intend to turn their home into an HMO. Some sellers don't like the idea their home will be sold to a developer, even if they aren't going to be living there;

- Similarly, if the seller has spent a lot of money refurbishing the kitchen, for example, they may not like the idea of it being stripped out to meet licensing standards;

- The same goes for speaking with any neighbours who may greet you outside. If the current owner gets on well with their neighbours, you may find your offer is rejected in principle because the sellers don't want to upset the neighbours when they move;

- If the seller or any neighbours ask what your intentions for the property are, at the most just say that you intend for the property to be a buy-to-let purchase and leave it at that;

HMO Property Set Up

- Once inside the property, always start the viewing upstairs. This is where most of the bedrooms in your HMO are likely to be located. Additionally, you can see whether a loft conversion would be possible;

- Look at and knock on walls. Check to see if they are solid/load bearing walls, or if they can be removed to enable you to reconfigure the space, for example:

    - Would moving a door enable more usable space to be created?

    - Would a jack-and-jill bathroom setup be suitable to serve two bedrooms?

    - Would the removal of a wall create a suitably sized communal area for the number of tenants you are thinking of having?

- Check the drainage - where do the wastepipes run in the property? This could affect where you can move kitchens and bathrooms to, as well as where you place any ensuites;

- Where do the sewage pipes run through the plot? Do they run across the plot and into a neighbour's land or straight out to the road?[52]

- Check the location of manholes on the property; they could pose an extra headache for an extension if they are too close to the property;

---

[52] See chapter 65 for further details.

HMO Property Set Up

- Ask what is included in the sale of the property - if the oven is staying, it is suitable for the number of proposed tenants? An existing shed in the garden could provide to be handy for bicycle storage;

- Check for any issues with damp or mould - you don't want to have to inherit problems that could affect the health of your tenants;

- If the property is currently furnished, always ask to move and check behind large items - they could be strategically placed to hide something;

- Bear in mind the location of doors and windows for emergency egress - are they convenient and easily accessible?

- If the seller/estate agent is happy for you to do so, take pictures or a video - it's easier to refer to these later on when you are trying to remember all the details of a property, particularly if you have conducted a number of viewings and are now considering your options;

- Run the taps to check what the water pressure is like and whether it may need upgrading; and

- Ask what works have been carried out in the property - is there an existing conservatory, has the garage previously been converted? How long ago were these works carried out and if so, were they carried out by the current or another previous owner?

HMO Property Set Up

Estate Agent Relationships

Cultivating a good relationship with estate agents can be very beneficial. They'll often remember you for other properties which tick your investment criteria if they know you are approachable and are serious. There may even be new deals to discuss that haven't been made available to the wider public yet that they could bring to your attention.

Like with all relationships in life, once established, you need to put the effort in to keep it going. It can therefore be worthwhile popping in regularly for a chat, maybe with a coffee and a cake, to see how things are and what's new on their patch. This will help them get to know you better and help make you stand out so you aren't just 'another person' at the other end of a keyboard or phone.

16. Acquiring Property

This chapter covers the property acquisition process, firstly following the more 'traditional purchasing route' of going through an estate agent and secondly the 'auction purchase route', before explaining the steps you will need to take following the acceptance of an offer or on submission of the winning bid.

Traditional Purchasing Route

So, you've seen the house you want to buy, you've carried out your due diligence on the area and you've made sure the property stacks up financially. The next step is to put in your offer to the estate agent - exciting times lay ahead! If your offer is accepted, request that the property is taken down from the market immediately. Some sellers and/or estate agents may resist this but politely be firm with them on this. You want to be sure no one else has the opportunity 'gazump' your offer.

'Gazumping' is generally regarded as a rather distasteful business whereby another party makes a higher offer on a property after an offer has already been accepted. Obviously though, the higher the sale price is, the better it is for the seller and the estate agent, who'll then receive a larger commission. This practice is allowed as estate agents have a duty to pass on all offers made and the agreement between yourself and the seller does not become legally binding until the contracts have been exchanged. It does however result in a waste of your time and effort if someone comes along and swoops in with a higher offer as you'll then lose out on the property, unless you counteract the offer with a higher one, forcing the purchase price up. This will obviously impact on your costs so make

HMO Property Set Up

sure to re-run the property deal analyser before issuing a counter offer. If the costs mean the property is no longer viable, you may have to consider walking away from the deal.

Assuming that no gazumping takes place and to show your commitment to the purchase and that you want to move quickly, you could arrange for surveys to be undertaken immediately after the offer has been accepted. You could also consider entering into a 'lock out' agreement. This is a contract between yourself and the seller which states you have the exclusive right to buy the property by a certain date. A seller may be reluctant to commit to this however, but it does show you are serious about purchasing the property. Your solicitor should be able to advise on what is involved in this, including the costs.

If your initial offer is rejected, revisit the property deal analyser and see if you can work out another offer price which the vendor is likely to be happier to accept. If you are certain the figure still works for you from a financial perspective, resubmit your offer to the estate agent. You may have to do this several times by offering counteroffers if other parties are interested in purchasing the property. As with gazumping, be prepared to walk away if you feel you are getting drawn into a bidding war and the figures being reached are higher than you would be comfortable paying. This will only put additional pressure on your finances.

Buying A Property Subject To Planning Permission

It may be necessary sometimes to try and secure planning permission before exchanging on a property, i.e. buying 'subject to planning permission' (STPP). Provided you obtain the owner's written consent and server them the appropriate

HMO Property Set Up

notice[53], you can apply for planning permission on a property you do not yet own whilst it is going through the conveyancing process. Both the conveyancing and the planning process *should* take roughly about the same time to complete. This approach is useful where you consider the house will need planning permission for an extension or other alterations, if the property will only work as a larger HMO with seven (or more) tenants or is located within an A4D area. This approach also protects you from tying your money up in a property you cannot use as you intend to. Agreeing with the vendor to purchase the property once permission has been granted provides time to prepare and submit a planning application and wait for the outcome, prior to exchanging contracts and committing you to the purchase.

To incentive the seller to agree to this approach, try offering them a non-refundable deposit on the property to take it off the market, or reject any other offers made whilst the planning application progresses. You could negotiate a figure with the vendor, which could be a nominal figure of say around one percent of the total purchase price. If you find your planning application is likely to be refused and your proposal for the property relies on gaining that planning permission, you still have the ability to walk away from the purchase before contracts are exchanged.

Other than time, the seller won't have lost too much as the deposit you paid would likely cover any expenses incurred, plus a bit extra for themselves - and you won't end up buying a property that doesn't suit your needs. If planning permission is granted however, then you can proceed with the sale,

---

[53] See Chapter 42.

HMO Property Set Up

knowing you will be able to carry out the works or use the property as you intend to. There is obviously a risk the seller could decide to pull out of the sale once you have achieved planning permission, as having the permission can increase the value of their property, but this is usually quite low.

Auction Purchasing Route

As mentioned in Chapter 9, property auctions are a great way to source property, aside from more traditional methods. Having undertaken your due diligence regarding supply and demand, HMO licensing and planning legislation, as well as assessing the location, you may come across properties advertised for sale at upcoming auctions that fit your criteria and are within your budget.

Buying property at auction can be great for speed and efficiency, avoids the potential for gazumping as you can see other bids for yourself and there is no pressure to submit and receive confirmation that an offer is accepted first. Once the hammer goes down, the deal is effectively 'done', reducing the possibilities for lengthy delays as the exchanging of contracts process is completed quickly.

However, there are downsides too. Because of the nature of auctions, the due diligence process can often be short, meaning you might not have time to carry out as thorough a check as you would like to. Properties with structural issues and/or restrictions on their use can often be sold at auction, so be careful. This is where doing your research and checking the legal pack carefully, whilst getting your solicitor to do the same is vitally important. Arranging to visit the property with a builder, architect or surveyor, if possible, is also essential as photographs and mapping software can only tell you so much.

HMO Property Set Up

Don't rely on the guide price either as these are often set low by auctioneers to attract interest. A rising guide price may indicate there is likely to be a number of other people looking to buy the lot, so the property may end up being sold for more that you expect and are willing to pay. Where this happens, over-bidding above your budget can mean you end up paying a lot more for a property if you get into a bidding war with other parties. It is therefore important to run your analyser and set a maximum bid beforehand that you can afford and stick to it.

Buying at auction may require you to have funding in place quickly, which unless you are a cash buyer, can take some time to arrange and be costly. As the hammer falls, you will need to pay a deposit and the remainder of the amount, usually within 28 days to a month. If you fail to do so, not only will you lose your deposit but also your chance to buy the property. In addition, you may have to cover the costs of re-selling the property and possibly be charged interest for every day that passes until the property is sold. Another downside is that if on the day someone outbids you above your maximum bid, you will have lost any time and money spent on surveys and solicitors.

If the auction is online, you have carried out your due diligence and you and your solicitor are satisfied everything looks ok, the next step is to create an account with the auction house if you have not already done so and register to bid. You will usually just need to provide a few details such as your name and contact details. Auction houses also request proof of ID, such as a passport, drivers' licence and/or statements with proof of address when registering an account or signing up to bid.

HMO Property Set Up

Once you've signed up you will need to add a payment method before you can begin bidding on lots. A 'hold' is often placed on a payment card prior to bidding so that if you win the lot, the deposit can be taken immediately. Where you are unsuccessful or decide not to bid, the 'hold' will be released after the auction has ended.

For in-person auctions, the process is slightly different as you do not have to register beforehand – you can simply turn up on the day as they are open for anyone to attend. Some auction rooms do however operate a pre-registration system for all bidders and may ask you which lots you wish to bid on. It is prudent to arrive a good 30 to 45 minutes before the auction begins to give you plenty of time to review the auction catalogue and register to bid, if you wish to. You may just want to go along for the experience initially. If you do wish to bid, you must provide photographic ID and proof of residency. If seeking to buy through a company, you'll need to bring along a letter of authority signed by a director or officer of the company, confirming you have authority to bid on the company's behalf. You'll also need to provide the company registration number and registered address.

Having your finances in order is another vital step if you are not a cash buyer. Make sure to get a 'mortgage in principle' arranged before the auction so it is ready as soon as you win the lot. Auction finance is typically available to auction buyers as well to provide short term finance, bridging loans, commercial finance, buy-to-let mortgages and secured loans, to name a few products. Funds can be made available very quickly, for a fee, but can neatly fit in with the tight purchasing timescales associated with auctions. Specialist lenders are often very flexible about the types of property you are looking to purchase. Exploring your financing options in advance is key to a smooth purchasing process.

Sometimes, if you've found an ideal property and are happy with the results of your background research, you can seek to make a pre-auction offer to secure the property. However, this can be a gamble as you could either end up paying more than the lot might have sold for at auction, or your offer could be refused and you'll have shown your hand to the auctioneer. If you do manage to secure a deal, you will need to work quickly as contracts will typically need to be exchanged ahead of the auction date.

On the day of the auction, look to arrive early and try to find a spot at the back of the room. This will give you an advantage when bidding on the lots you are interested in as you can read the interest in the room and see the other bidders you are competing against. When bidding, make sure the auctioneer is able to see you clearly and make your bids obvious. Try not to get 'caught up in the moment' and remember to stick to your budget – if you are outbid, don't be too disheartened as there will always be more properties. If any lots remain unsold, the auctioneer can invite interested buyers to make a post-auction offer afterwards, particularly where the highest bid is close to the reserve fee.

After Going 'Sale Agreed' Or Submitting The 'Winning Bid'

Once you have gone 'sale agreed' or have won your lot at auction you need to take on an active 'project management' role to keep the purchase on track and drive it toward completion as quickly as possible. Many people may be involved in this process, such as brokers, solicitors, estate agents and surveyors.

HMO Property Set Up

For the traditional buying method, it is typically known for being a slow, drawn-out process, so it is important to keep on top of the process and chase people regularly to make sure everything runs smoothly. Conversely, auctions purchases are known for their quick turnarounds – so be prepared and make sure you have everything in order as far as is reasonably practical beforehand.

Solicitors

Instruct your solicitor formally in writing as soon as your offer is accepted, or you receive confirmation of a winning bid. Make sure they are provided with all the information and contacts they will need, including your broker's details, where necessary. Complete and return their terms of business form if you have not already engaged them and provide some money on account for conveyancing purposes.

For traditional purchases, ensure the basic details of the property and the estate agent's details are provided to your solicitor so they can contact the agent and find out the information they need about the seller and their solicitor.

For auction purchases, if the auction was held online, the auction house should contact you to provide the seller's solicitors details, to prepare draft contracts and collect any buyer's premium and deposits from you. For in-person auctions, where you are successful, the auction team will approach you after the hammer has gone down to congratulate you and take copies of your ID and proof of residency. You'll also need to provide other personal details such as your national insurance number and time lived at current/past addresses. These details are used for anti-money laundering purposes. You will then pay the required deposit and any

HMO Property Set Up

other fees stated in the auction catalogue. This can include a 'Buyer's Premium' and an administration fee. Following this, you'll need to complete and sign the memorandum of sale. Once completed, this will need to be passed onto your solicitor. After the auction, the auction team will confirm your purchase of the lot in writing, notify your solicitor and explain the next steps in the process.

For traditional purchases, make sure to keep in regular contact with your solicitor and the selling agent; ask them to chase the seller's solicitor regularly and if you can, ask the seller to chase their solicitor as well. The solicitors will oversee the whole buying process, so you will need to follow their guidance and instructions to avoid any delays or issues with the sale.

Broker

Once you are 'sale agreed' or win the lot, you will also need to contact your broker and ask them to prepare the mortgage application form, if you intend to fund the purchase this way. Providing them with the information from the property deal analyser can help speed up their processes, as they can use the information to find an appropriate mortgage.

Once your broker has found a suitable mortgage and prepared the application form, they will send it to you to agree, sign and return. Do this without delay. On receipt, your broker will then submit it to the lender. Your broker will then monitor the application as it progresses and will forward onto you the acceptance offer once this has been received.

HMO Property Set Up

Surveyor

As part of the buying process, having a surveyor visit the property to ensure it is safe and suitable without any major issues is essential. Knowing in advance will help you make informed decisions about whether the property remains financially viable and may provide some scope for negotiation if any repairs needed are likely to be expensive.

There are a couple of different surveys which can be instructed, including a Condition Report, Homebuyer Report and Building or full structural survey. These should be carried out by a RICS surveyor to ensure they are of a high standard and accord with industry regulations.

The Condition Report is the cheapest and most basic survey. It simply describes the property's condition, identifies any urgent issues and categorises any potential risks or legal problems using a traffic light system. Typically, it is designed for new build dwellings and properties in already in good condition. A Homebuyer Report identifies structural issues, such as subsidence or damp and looks at both the internal and external of the property, although no investigative work below the floorboards or behind the surface of walls is carried out. It is usually suited to properties which are in a reasonable condition.

A Building or Full Structural Survey is the most in-depth and comprehensive survey. This contains detailed advice on any repairs likely to be needed. It doesn't examine below floorboards or behind the surface of walls either but will include the surveyor's opinion on any potential defects in these areas. Choosing which survey to go for will largely depend on the age of the property you are purchasing and its

HMO Property Set Up

condition. Older properties or ones in obvious disrepair and poor condition would benefit from a Building or Full Structural Survey being carried out to avoid any nasty surprises. For a property which is generally in good condition though, a Homebuyers Report is likely to be adequate.

Insurance

Your solicitor will ask you to confirm you have adequate insurance in place before finalising the exchange of contracts, so you must make certain to organise this in a timely manner. This is because if anything were to happen to the property after contracts have been exchanged, it would be at your expense to cover as you'll have committed to the purchase. Additionally, not having insurance in place could delay the exchange and completion dates for the sale.

When comparing insurance, bear in mind there will likely be a period of unoccupancy during the refurbishment stage. Typically, most insurers allow up to 60 days of unoccupancy before imposing conditions, restricting the level of cover and seeking to increasing the premium. Where you are going to be undertaking significant refurbishment works, you may need to arrange a specific insurance policy with a provider. This would extend the unoccupied period of the property until works have been completed and tenants are able to move in. Be mindful of the level of protection (and cost!) to do so. You may wish to discuss your needs with a specialist insurance broker who will be able to find policies to meet your needs and ensure you are sufficiently covered[54].

---

[54] Chapter 64 contains further information on insurance.

HMO Property Set Up

Builders Quotes And HMO Licensing Officers

Alongside going sale agreed and starting the conveyancing process, arrange to visit the property again so you can look in more detail at how you will convert the property. Some sellers and estate agents may be more accommodating of this request than others but explain to them that you'll only need a few hours at most to carry out a thorough inspection and that afterwards you won't need to come back again until the property is yours.

As when you initially viewed the property, take a friend with you and arrange for a few builders to meet you at the property at different times so you can go through the property 'top-to-bottom' to discuss the alterations you intend to make and so you can receive advice from the builders. If you have an existing builder on your Power Team already, ask them to come along. Ask the builders to prepare a schedule of works list and provide you with quotations so you can budget for the works needed.

There is typically a logical order in the way refurbishment works are carried out, so having an organised list of what needs to be done and in what order is useful. This enables you to break the project down into smaller phases. These can be compartmentalised, avoiding the risks of overlapping works and additional fees. Additionally, contact your local HMO or environmental health officer (EHO) and ask for them to visit the property as well, preferably on the same day you have builders in with you, to view the property alongside you and advise on what they would need to see to ensure the property is granted a licence. Some local authorities do charge for this service now, so don't be surprised if you are asked to pay a fee for their time and advice.

HMO Property Set Up

There are benefits to asking both a builder and HMO officer to attend the property at the same time. Firstly, it demonstrates that you are approaching the project as a professional. Secondly, if this is your first HMO property, it helps to build a good relationship between yourself and the HMO officer. Thirdly, if a builder has not carried out many HMO conversion projects before, it gives them an idea of what you expect of them if instructed and the standard you want to achieve, both on this and any other future HMO properties you chose to work with them on.

Once you have visited the property with any builders and the HMO officer, put together a summary of the initial advice received and any key actions required. This serves two purposes: Firstly, the information is fresh in your mind and secondly, you can start thinking about what you will need to do going forwards as you enter the refurbishment stage.

After you have prepared your summary, send this to the HMO officer and any builders you wish to work with. This gives them a record of what was discussed and enables them the opportunity to comment upon your understanding of the works required as well. Once you receive any builder's quotes, check the works tally with what you are expecting.

Completion

Completion happens at the time of the exchange of contracts between solicitors. It can often be a stressful time as last-minute queries are ironed-out on both sides. Once completion has taken place, you are then officially the legal owner of the property and can start making the arrangements to convert it into a HMO. You'll usually then just need to arrange a date with the estate agent to go and collect those keys!

HMO Property Set Up

Council Tax And Utilities

Now that you are the legal owner of the property (congratulations by the way), you are also now responsible for the payment of council tax and utilities (I can already hear you exclaiming in joy!)

Council Tax

As the property will most likely be vacant and unfurnished on completion, you will have to pay council tax, although you may qualify for a reduction if the property is going to be undergoing major repair work or structural alterations. This includes works to extend and rebuild walls. A completion notice is usually issued by the council setting out the date you will need to start paying council tax on, following a period of refurbishment. It is at the discretion of the council to decide whether they apply a discount, but – a word of caution here; some councils now seek to charge council tax on individual bedrooms in HMOs, where it is considered a tenant has exclusive use of a room and can live 'independently' from the rest of the dwelling, i.e. they have all the facilities needed in their room to avoid having to use the communal areas of a property. This could include a bedroom with a kitchenette and ensuite, or sometimes even just a bedroom with an ensuite. Therefore, informing the council you wish to claim a reduction to convert the property into a HMO could see the dwelling being re-banded upon completion of these works[55].

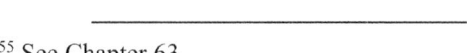

[55] See Chapter 63.

HMO Property Set Up

Utilities And Other Suppliers

If you are going to be offering 'all-bills included' accommodation, you will need to think about who you need to contact for the following services:

- Gas and electricity;
- Water and sewerage;
- Broadband;
- Netflix, Amazon, Virgin, Sky etc.; and
- TV licence.

You should be able to find out the details of all the current suppliers for the property as part of the purchasing process. You will need to inform the utility companies of the completion date for the property and provide meter readings and new direct debit details to them, if you intend to stay with the existing supplier. If you intend to switch, make sure to inform the existing suppliers and write down their details, including account numbers, so it is easier to keep track of who you have spoken with and who you need to chase.

HMOs are typically considered high energy-consumption properties because of the number of tenants and the way in which tenants typically use the facilities. Therefore, when searching for suppliers, shopping around for the best tariffs can be time consuming, so using comparison websites, such

HMO Property Set Up

as U-Switch[56], GoCompare[57] and Moneysupermarket[58] can be helpful to quickly find competitive prices. Auto-switching websites such as Switchcraft[59] and Switchd[60] can also help you find and switch to money saving deals. When speaking with suppliers, make sure to insist that all future correspondence and invoices are not sent to the property, but to your home or office address instead or are sent to you via email.

---

[56] https://www.uswitch.com/.
[57] https://www.gocompare.com/.
[58] https://www.moneysupermarket.com/.
[59] https://www.switchcraft.co.uk/.
[60] https://switchd.co.uk/.

HMO Property Set Up

Summary

In Section II, I have discussed how to get started in HMO property development and how to create your ideal search area to find a suitable investment location.

I have discussed how to go about assessing a location's supply and demand for suitability and how to check out what potential competitors in these areas are doing.

I have also provided an overview of the relevant HMO licensing and planning legislation which could influence where you wish to invest in.

Once you have found a location, I have provided you with the knowledge of how to carry out a more in-depth assessment of a town or city to assist with finding suitable properties for HMOs in these areas.

The next step I have discussed with you is how to go about assessing the suitability of any properties you find for conversion into HMOs and how to work out the typical development costs associated with this.

In the final chapters of this section, I have explained the purchase process from initial enquiries and viewings, traditional and auction purchase methods, all the way through to exchange and completion and other considerations and actions you need to take once you become the owner of a property.

Section III: HMO Licensing And Standards

In this next section, I will discuss the importance of HMO Licensing and why the standards should always be followed when looking to set up a professional HMO. I will also advise on the HMO licensing application process.

"The difference between a successful person and others is not a lack of strength, not a lack of knowledge, but rather in a lack of will."

– Vince Lombardi

17. Introduction To HMO Licensing

HMO licensing is governed by both national and local legislation and is primarily concerned with the health and safety of tenants, as well as ensuring HMOs are of a suitable standard for occupation. As mentioned in Chapter 11, there are currently three types of licensing schemes in operation in England - mandatory, additional and selective. Each local authority, whether they call themselves the 'Private Sector Housing Team', 'Environmental Health Team' or the 'HMO Licensing Team' has the power to set its own licensing and amenity standards for HMOs within their jurisdiction. These local standards are often more stringent that national standards and can lead to significant variations in the standards you are expected to meet within different local authority areas.

Local Standards And Fees

It is worth bearing in mind that as well each local authority's standards varying quite considerably between different boroughs or districts, so too do their fees for obtaining a HMO licence. It is common for fees to be paid in two separate stages as well:

1. The first payment covers the cost of administering the application and inspection of the property. The fee for this is usually based on the number of rooms being let; whilst

2. The second fee is required on the granting of the licence and covers the cost of the overall management of the HMO licence throughout the licence period.

It is always worth checking the local standards and costs for a licence before you embark on any HMO property development, either in a new area, or in an existing area you

HMO Property Set Up

may be already familiar with. This is because the local HMO standards can be updated from time to time and what may have been previously acceptable could now fall below what the local authority requires is provided. It is important to recognise that the adopted standards are typically the 'minimum' standards you should be seeking to provide in your HMO properties.

18. Mandatory Licensing

Let's start this chapter off by explaining what mandatory licensing is, as this is the most common type of licence required for a HMO in England. Part II of the Housing Act (2004[61]) requires HMOs to be licensed by local housing authorities where properties meet the definition of a HMO prescribed under Section 55 of the Act. Section 55 saw the introduction of licensing schemes for HMOs in 2006, which originally only applied to properties of three or more storeys, with five or more people living in them, making up two or more separate households.

Let's now fast-forward to October 2018, where the government changed the legislation relating to mandatory HMO licensing to apply to **any property occupied by five or more people, forming two or more separate households**, meaning that the number of stories in a property no longer makes a difference and it is about the number of occupants in a property which triggers the requirement for a HMO licence. In addition, the government's updated legislation clarified minimum room sizes required for adult[62] letting rooms as being no less than 6.51 square metres for rooms occupied by a single adult and 10.22 square metres for rooms occupied by two adults. Whilst these are the *national* minimum room size, local authorities can (and regularly do) insist on larger room sizes.

Each HMO property you own or manage must have its own HMO licence, meaning they cannot be shared between different properties. Mandatory licences are generally valid

---

[61] https://www.legislation.gov.uk/ukpga/2004/34/part/2.
[62] Defined as anyone over the age of ten.

HMO Property Set Up

for five years, although this time-period can be reduced at the discretion of the issuing authority.

Some may therefore choose to restrict licences so they are only valid for three or four years instead or require you to provide further information before they are willing to grant a licence which is valid for a longer term. Another matter to look out for is that licensing fees are usually increased on an annual every April, so don't be too surprised to learn that the fees have increased if you haven't needed to renew a HMO licence for a while!

19. Additional Licensing

I'll revert back to Part II of the Housing Act 2004 again now, as this gives local authorities the power to introduce additional licensing schemes. These are often implemented if the local authority believes there are issues with the management of HMO properties, or if a significant change in housing occupation from families to HMO properties has occurred in specific areas of a town or city. Large cities or university towns are typically subject to additional licensing requirements. The main aim of this licensing 'tool' is to seek to improve standards for HMOs in these areas and so the schemes can be introduced over whole boroughs, or restricted to certain wards, estates, streets and postcodes only.

Additional licensing is usually introduced for smaller HMOs of three or more tenants forming more than one household, but can also include any other HMO type, depending on what that local authority wishes to include. However, any decision to introduce an additional licensing scheme must be consistent with the local authority's housing strategy and must be part of their approach to dealing with homelessness, empty homes and anti-social behaviour. Where schemes are introduced, the licensing standards are usually the same as those required for mandatory licensing, although the local authority may introduce separate licensing standards for properties which fall within the additional licensing category, where it is justifiable.

Before an additional licensing scheme is introduced, there has to be a consultation period. This is so anyone affected by the designation can voice their opinion on the proposed scheme. The local authority must be satisfied there are no other courses of action which might better remedy the situation and that the introduction of a licensing scheme will actually help

HMO Property Set Up

to deal with the problems identified. Typically, once they are introduced additional licensing schemes run for up to five years before ceasing or requiring renewal by the local authority. In doing so, the local authority must then justify why they consider an additional licensing scheme needs to be continued. If the scheme has improved standards over the period of operation, there is an argument to be made that it is no longer necessary and should therefore be made redundant.

HMO Property Set Up

20. Selective Licensing

Similar to additional licensing, selective licensing schemes can be applied to cover rental properties which are let in a specific area, street, postcode or ward. This time, Part III of the Housing Act 2004[63] is relevant to consider. This gives local authorities the discretion to introduce these schemes where they believe the problems cannot be dealt with by any other means. As with additional licencing, the introduction of selective licensing must be consistent with the local authority's housing strategy and must be part of a coordinated approach to deal with homelessness, empty homes and anti-social behaviour. The main difference between the two schemes is that selective licensing applies to *all types* of privately rented residential property, including properties let to one or two people only, or flats above commercial premises, rather than just shared houses.

Selective licensing tends to be brought in where complaints have been made over the standards of accommodation available, or where there is a low demand in housing, problems with the management of private sector housing in that area, high levels of migration or sustained issues with anti-social behaviour and crime. As with additional licensing, the local authority is required to consult with local landlords and other interested parties in the area of proposed designation before introducing a new licensing scheme. They must also make the details public and must include their justification for the schemes introduction, how long it will be in place for and the area(s) which will be affected. If, for example, you have an existing HMO property which already holds a licence, such as an additional or mandatory licence

---

[63] https://www.legislation.gov.uk/ukpga/2004/34/part/3.

HMO Property Set Up

and a new selective licensing scheme is introduced, you do not need to apply again under the new scheme for a licence.

21. Management Requirements

Being the owner or operator of a HMO means you are required to undertake some specific duties, regardless of whether or not the property is licenced. These are set out in the Management of Houses in Multiple Occupation (England) Regulations 2006[64], which places a number of obligations upon the managers of all HMOs. These obligations include:

- Providing the name, address and telephone number of the manager to each household in an HMO, as well as displaying their contact details in a prominent position within the property;

- Ensuring a safe means of escape from fires which must be kept free from obstructions and kept in good order. Where provided, fire-fighting equipment and alarms must also be kept in good working order;

- Maintaining the water supply and drainage in proper working order;

- Supplying and maintaining gas and electricity, which should not be unreasonably interrupted;

- Maintaining common parts, fixtures, fittings and appliances, which must be kept clean, safe, in good decorative repair and working order and which should remain free from obstruction;

- Maintaining the living accommodation, which includes the internal structure of the property, fixtures and fittings, including windows and other means of ventilation, where

---

[64] https://www.legislation.gov.uk/uksi/2006/372/contents/made.

HMO Property Set Up

each room should be kept in good repair and in clean working order;

- Providing appropriate and suitable waste disposal facilities; and

- Providing the local authority with details of the individuals and households living in the HMO when required to do so.

There are also requirements placed on the occupier of the property, which requires them not to do anything that hinders the manager from meeting their duties, allowing the manager to enter units at a reasonable time to carry out their duties, provide information to the manager as may be necessary to assist the manager in carrying out their duties (for example, notifying you of any issues) and taking reasonable care to avoid damage to anything which the manager is under a duty to supply, maintain or repair. In addition, occupiers should store and dispose of litter in accordance with the arrangements made by the manager and comply with reasonable instructions in respect of means of escape from fire, the prevention of fire and the use of fire equipment.

22. HMO Licensing Reforms 2018

Following a period of 'extensive' consultation, on 1st October 2018, the Government's Licensing of Houses in Multiple Occupation (Prescribed Description) (England) Order 2018[65] came into effect. The purpose of this legislation was to extend the scope of Section 55(2) 9(a) of the Housing Act 2004, so that mandatory HMO licensing also applies to HMO properties which are less than three storeys high.

The purpose of the reforms to the HMO licensing criteria were to "combat rogues from being able to operate substandard accommodation for maximum profit" by altering the criteria for when a HMO licence is needed, to provide clarification over minimum size of bedrooms and for the inclusion of requirements relating to the provision of appropriate refuse disposal in licensed properties. Therefore, since the legislation was introduced, local authorities have been required to impose mandatory conditions on the minimum room size which can be occupied as sleeping accommodation in a HMO. Where rooms are smaller than the specified size, they must not be used as sleeping accommodation, unless they can be altered to meet the minimum room sizes. Other communal rooms in a HMO property cannot be used to compensate for rooms which are smaller than the prescribed minimum, as was sometimes allowed previously.

The clarification over minimum bedroom sizes was introduced to ensure a consistent approach to the size of rooms used for sleeping in HMOs, giving certainty to

---

[65] https://www.legislation.gov.uk/uksi/2018/221/made.

HMO Property Set Up

landlords, tenants and local authorities on the minimum standards acceptable. The requirement for HMOs to have proper waste disposal provisions ensures that waste produced by tenants is stored appropriately prior to collection.

Ultimately, the changes to legislation should be viewed as a positive step forward for tenants and landlords as it means standards are raised across the board, with 'shoebox rooms' to become a thing of the past and waste stored so it does not become a health hazard, providing tenants with a better standard and quality of accommodation overall.

23. National Minimum Standards

Ok, now let's dig into minimum standards for HMOs. The following minimum standards are set at national level, but as has been previously mentioned, local authorities have the power to require higher standards, although this is only provided they are able to justify why higher standards are necessary.

Bedroom Sizes

Minimum sleeping room floor area	m^2
One-person unit (aged over 10 years old)	6.51 m^2
Two-person unit (aged over 10 years old)	10.22 m^2
One child under 10 years old	4.64 m^2

Table 23.1: Minimum sleeping room floor areas (m^2).

Washing Facilities

- All baths, showers and wash hand basins must be equipped with taps providing an 'adequate' supply of cold and constant hot water;

- All bathrooms must be suitably and adequately heated and ventilated;

- All baths, toilets and wash hand basins must be fit for purpose;

- All bathrooms and toilets must be suitably located; and

- An 'adequate' number of toilets, bathrooms and wash hand basins for the number of people living in the property must be provided.

HMO Property Set Up

Shared Kitchens

Where any of the units of accommodation do not contain their own facilities for cooking:

- There must be a suitably located kitchen in relation to the living accommodation; and

- The kitchen must have a layout and be of a size and equipped with such facilities to enable those sharing the facilities to store, prepare and cook food.

Kitchens must also include the following:
Sinks with draining boards
An 'adequate' supply of cold and constant hot water to each sink installation
Electrical sockets
Worktops for the preparation of food
Cupboards for the storage of food or kitchen and cooking utensils
Refrigerators with an 'adequate' freezer compartment
Appropriate refuse disposal facilities
Appropriate extractor fans
Fire blankets

Table 23.2: Indicative minimum kitchen provisions.

24. Locally Adopted Standards

As mentioned in previous chapters, local HMO standards will vary between different local authority areas, but you will generally find that the following standards are to be expected. Other than the national standards mentioned, the standards in this chapter are for indicative purposes only.

Example Space Standards - Bedrooms

All habitable rooms, kitchens, bathrooms and toilet compartments should have a minimum floor to ceiling height of 2.13cm. Where rooms have sloping ceilings, a minimum room height of 2.13cm must be available for over half the floor area of the room to be regarded as usable space. Measurements should be taken on a plane 150cm above the floor and any floor area where the ceiling height is less than 150cm high shall be regarded as 'unusable space' and should not be included in any floor space calculations. Typically, more and more local authorities – as well as tenants – are looking for landlords to provide larger bedrooms above national standards. This is good for a number of reasons:

1. Where you can provide larger rooms this will 'future-proof' your property from any further national legislative changes to room sizes and reduces the potential to have to retrospectively refurbish a bedroom to make it larger;

2. It sets your HMO apart from other HMOs available to rent in the area, making your property more attractive to prospective tenants;

3. Tenants have more possessions and therefore require larger rooms in which to store their possessions in; and

HMO Property Set Up

4. It helps to retain your existing tenants as other landlord's HMOs in the area may not be able to offer the same sized rooms.

As identified in the previous chapter, the national standards are **6.51 square metres** for a single-person unit of accommodation. However, based on the above, I would recommend that you seek to provide a room which measures **at least 8 square metres**. Similarly, the national standards are **10.22 square metres** for a two-person unit of accommodation. Again, I would advise on seeking to provide a room which measures **at least 13 square metres**.

In some cases, local authorities are already requesting rooms are provided above the national standards. These larger rooms can, at the discretion of the licensing officer, be reduced to the national standards if you are able to justify why the space is adequate. This is often only provided the inspecting officer is satisfied the communal living rooms or kitchens with dining areas are being offered and that suitable standards of management will take place.

Example Space Standards For Communal Rooms

Kitchens	m^2
Used by up to five occupants	6 m^2
Used by six to ten occupants	11 m^2

Table 24.1: Indicative minimum kitchen sizes (m^2).

Typically, you may find that where you have more than five occupants sharing a kitchen and there is no separate dining area, then the inspecting officer will require the facilities you provide are doubled. But in doing so, you must also factor

HMO Property Set Up

into the design and layout of a kitchen adequate circulation space for tenants to move around comfortably.

Dining Rooms/Kitchens	m²
Used by up to five occupants	8.5 m²
Used by six to ten occupants	11 m²

Table 24.2: Indicative dining room and kitchen sizes (m²).

Living Rooms or Dining Rooms	m²
Used by up to five occupants	8.5 m²
Used by six to ten occupants	12.5 m²

Table 24.3: Indicative living room or dining room sizes (m²).

Example Kitchen Facilities

The standards for kitchen facilities can vary considerably depending on the number of intended occupants. In general, kitchens must be of a suitable size and layout with adequate equipment to enable occupants to store, prepare and cook food. For between one and five occupants, a kitchen must typically include:

Kitchen Facilities (up to five occupants)
A suitably sized sink and drainer in good condition approximately 500mm x 1000mm
A full-sized cooker with a minimum of four-ring burners, a standard sized oven and a grill
Four electrical sockets per five occupants sharing a kitchen to be sited above worktops, in addition to one socket for each fixed appliance
Electric cookers shall be provided with a dedicated cooker point outlet suitable for the rating of the cooker
Fixed electric space or water heating appliances sited within a kitchen shall be provided with a separate, dedicated point

HMO Property Set Up

A worktop or table of smooth impervious material of at least 500mm x 1500mm per five occupants. This should be in addition to any space taken up by any large appliances, sink unit or cooker
Each occupant should be provided with their own lockable and secure dry good storage space either within the kitchen or in an adjacent, accessible location in the dwelling
One double wall cupboard or a single base unit is required per occupant for the storage of dry goods and utensils. Space below the sink unit is not considered as useable space
Refrigerators with an adequate space for at least one shelf per occupant and equivalent freezer compartment. Where the freezer compartment is not adequate, additional separate freezers will be required
Suitable refuse and recycling containers sufficient for the number of occupants, which should be located away from habitable rooms and where they do not obstruct access
Appropriate extractor fans to provide a minimum of one air change per hour
Fire blankets

Table 24.4: Indicative kitchen facilities for up to five occupants.

In addition to the above, for between six and ten occupants, a kitchen must include:

Kitchen Facilities (six to ten occupants)
Either a double bowled sink or dishwasher in addition to a single sink
Two full sized cookers with a minimum of four-ring burners, a standard size oven and a grill or one full size cooker plus microwaves as required

Table 24.5: Indicative kitchen facilities for between six and ten occupants.

HMO Property Set Up

Example Washing Facilities And Sanitary Conveniences For Shared Occupation

Where you are not seeking to have individual ensuite facilities for the exclusive use of occupants in your HMO, the following standards for shared facilities will usually apply. In HMOs where there are four or fewer occupants sharing bathing and toilet facilities, there must be at least one bathroom with a fixed bath or shower and a toilet, which may be situated in the bathroom, or separately.

In HMOs where there a five or more occupiers sharing bathing and toilet facilities, there must be one separate toilet with a wash hand basin and splashback for every five sharing occupiers and at least one bathroom (which may contain a toilet) with a fixed bath or shower for every five occupants sharing). The provision of washing facilities should also be as follows:

Washing Facilities	Provision
Up to five people	One bathroom with wash basin and bath or shower
Six to ten people	Two bathrooms

Table 24.6: Indicative washing facilities by occupant numbers.

Example Wash Basins

Wash hand basins should be approximately 550mm x 400mm with a 300mm waterproof splashback, with cold and constant hot running water to be supplied in each shared bath/shower room, serving up to a maximum of five occupants.

Example Bath And Shower Facilities

A standard sized bath in a bathroom or a standard sized shower in a suitable room together with suitable drying and

HMO Property Set Up

changing spaces should be provided. A 300mm waterproof splashback to a bath is required, whilst the splashback for a shower, whether it is over the bath or separate should be 150mm above where the showerhead is and up to at least the edge of a fixed shower screen. Any showers should have fully tiled walls or be within a complete self-standing cubicle.

Example Toilet Facilities

Number of Occupants	Toilet Facilities
Up to five occupants	One toilet, separate from the bathroom
Six to eight occupants	Two toilets, sited in two separate bathrooms
Nine to ten occupants	Two toilets, with one separate from any bathrooms
Eleven or more occupants	Three toilets. One must be separate from any bathrooms, or a fourth toilet must be provided separate from any bathroom

Table 24.7: Indicative toilet facilities by occupant numbers.

Each separate toilet should be provided with a wash hand basin with cold and constant hot water and a 300mm tiled splashback. All bathrooms must be suitably heated and ventilated and be no more than one floor distance in relation to a bedroom. Toilets should be no more than one floor distance from living and bedrooms and where these facilities are shared, should be accessible from a common area.

Some local authorities do expect wash hand basins to be included in bedrooms; however, where these are not reasonably practical, there is generally some flexibility on this requirement. Additionally, highlighting the obvious hygiene issues with providing wash hand basins in bedrooms without a

HMO Property Set Up

toilet can often make licensing officers reconsider their requests!

Example Heating

Heating should be provided in every habitable room and bathroom. The installed heating system should be capable of maintaining a temperature of 20 degrees Celsius (°C) when the outside temperature is -1° C. The heating provisions provided must be able to be used safely at any time and be suitably protected.

Central heating is the most common option for HMOs as it is relatively cost effective and is less of a fire safety hazard than a gas or electric heater. Portable paraffin or oil-fired heaters and liquid petroleum gas heaters (LPG) are not allowed under any circumstances due to the obvious fire safety concerns they present. If tenants buy or bring their own, you will need to explain to them that they are not allowed to be used on the premises.

Example Ventilation

All habitable rooms should have opening windows of no less than $1/20^{th}$ of the floor area of the room to allow for adequate levels of ventilation to be achieved. All bathrooms should have mechanical ventilation providing a minimum of four air changes per hour. All toilet compartments must have either an opening window or mechanical ventilation providing at least one air change per hour. A kitchen should have extraction ventilation capable of providing at least one air change per hour. These should be fitted with an overrun device which allows an extractor fan to remain on for a pre-set time after being switched off to help further control humidity in the room.

HMO Property Set Up

Example Natural And Artificial Lighting

All habitable rooms should have adequate levels of natural lighting, which is to be provided through clear glazed windows and/or windows and doors. Windows should be positioned to allow light to illuminate most of a room. Windows in bathrooms and toilets should usually be obscure glazed or high level to protect privacy.

Artificial lighting should be provided in all habitable rooms, staircases landings, passages, kitchens, bathrooms and toilets. Lighting to staircases, landings and passages may be controlled by timer switches or other devices and two-way switches should be provided on stairs and passageways, as necessary.

Example Electrical And USB Sockets

Electrical sockets should be provided to both individual rooms and common areas. The minimum standards for each are set out in table 24.8.

Room	Number of Sockets
Living Room	Six double sockets
Kitchens	As set out previously
Hallways and Passages	One double socket on each level
Bedroom/Study areas	Six double sockets

Table 24.8: Indicative provision of electrical and USB sockets.

It is advisable to include sockets with USB charging ports as well as for standard electrical appliances. All socket outlets should be located in positions which allow for safe and convenient use and should avoid being located in areas where appliance cables are likely to pose safety hazards.

HMO Property Set Up

Example Personal Safety And Security

Your HMO should be able to provide a safe and secure environment for the occupiers, with appropriate locks to external doors and to tenant's own rooms to prevent unauthorised access whilst also allowing for safe egress in the event of an emergency situation. Simple locks should be provided to shared bathrooms and toilets to provide privacy. In addition, windows must be capable of being effectively secured against entry without compromising them as a means of escape in the event of a fire or other emergency.

Licensing Conditions

In cases where the correct amenities are not present within a property, the local authority has the discretion to issue a HMO licence with conditions attached to it. This will state the alterations needed to provide the required amenities/facilities and when any work must be completed by. Failure to implement the necessary changes in time could lead to the licence being withheld and costly fines for non-compliance.

Please remember that the above example standards are **not** prescriptive for every local authority, so do make sure to check the standards required for a HMO with your local authority before purchasing a property and undertaking any works.

HMO Property Set Up

25. Fire Safety And Risk Assessment

HMO properties must be provided with suitable fire safety and prevention measures to ensure the safety of the occupants. Appropriate fire precaution facilities and equipment must be provided. Some local authorities have their own adopted guidance, although most choose to follow Local Authorities Coordinators of Regulatory Services (LACORS) guidance.

LACORS guidance includes national guidance for landlords on how to properly undertake a Fire Risk Assessment (FRA) on existing residential accommodation and what measures are typically deemed suitable for different types of residential properties. The guidance is not aimed at new build housing which is built to modern regulations.

Fire Risk Assessment

The Fire Safety Act 2021[66], which builds on the Regulatory Reform (Fire Safety) Order 2005[67] came into effect in May 2022 and places a duty on the responsible person (i.e. you as the landlord/property owner or an appointed property manager) to take general fire safety precautions to ensure the safety of people on the premises and in the immediate vicinity.

The responsible person must conduct a FRA to identify general fire precautions and other measures covering common parts of the property. This should also include the property's structure, external walls and entrance doors; although for good practice, the FRA should take account of all areas in the

---

[66] https://www.legislation.gov.uk/ukpga/2021/24.
[67] https://www.legislation.gov.uk/uksi/2005/1541/contents.

property. The FRA is an organised and methodical review of the property, the activities likely to be conducted and the likelihood that a fire could start, as well as the harm it could cause to those in and around the property.

FRAs should be used as 'tools' to help identify risk hazards, reduce the risk of those hazards causing harm to as low as is reasonably practicable and help to decide on what physical fire precautions and management systems are needed to ensure the safety of people in the property, in the event of a fire occurring. FRAs should therefore be conducted in a practical and systematic way by dividing the property into rooms or areas and assessing each individually. Conducting a FRA can be broken down into five steps:

1. Identify any fire hazards, such as sources of ignition, sources of fuel and sources of oxygen;

2. Identify any people at risk and where they are likely to be found in the event of a fire;

3. Evaluate, remove or reduce the identified risks and protect against any remaining risks by looking at what the risk is, who is at risk and the action needed to remove and/or reduce the hazards that may cause a fire;

4. Record, plan and inform against the identified risks – keeping a written record of your assessment(s) and any significant findings; and

5. Review regularly – although there is no specific timescale for doing this, for good practice, the FRA exercise should be conducted at least every twelve months.

HMO Property Set Up

Once you have identified the general fire risks and necessary precautions and implemented them, you will need to put in a place a system of maintenance, for either yourself or a competent person, such as your managing agent, to implement.

Example Fire Safety Requirements For A Standard Two Storey HMO

The following requirements for a two-storey HMO converted from a standard dwelling are for indicative purposes only and should not be relied upon for the specification of your HMO but should provide you with a basic understanding of what fire safety provisions should be installed. Please discuss your specific requirements with your local HMO officer.

- A system of mains powered interlinked automatic smoke and heat detectors to form a Grade D LD2 system, in accordance with BS 5839 Part 6 or equivalent;

- In kitchens, a heat detector should be installed in place of a smoke detector;

- All detectors must be interlinked so that if one is triggered, the alarm sounds in each and every alarm location;

- Conventional light is required throughout escape routes. Emergency lighting may be required if the route is 'complex' or there is no effective borrowed light. Where necessary, lighting must be designed and installed in accordance with BS 5266 Part 1 or equivalent;

HMO Property Set Up

- The escape route should allow occupants from all parts of the building to reach a place of safety outside, without passing through a higher fire risk area;

- The route should always be kept free of obstructions and combustible materials;

- Walls and ceiling should be free from flammable materials;

- At least 30-minutes of fire resistance should be provided by the route.

- Electricity and gas meters located in the fire escape route should be either relocated or contained within a fire resisting construction, to provide at least 30-minutes of fire resistance;

- A fire door of at least 30-minute fore resistance must be installed in each doorway leading onto the fire escape, except for bathrooms and WCs;

- Security devices on bedrooms and final exit doors must be capable of being opened from the inside without the use of keys (such as Yale type or thumb turn keys);

- A fire blanket should be provided in each area where there are cooking facilities and be wall mounted 1.5m high adjacent to an exit door and away from cooking appliances; and

- Fire extinguishers, where provided, should be multipurpose extinguishers and located for ease of access.

26. Housing Health And Safety Rating System

The Housing Health and Safety Rating System (HHSRS) was introduced under the Housing Act 2004 and applies to residential properties in England and Wales. It is a risk-based evaluation tool used to help identify and protect against potential risks and hazards to health and safety from any deficiencies identified in dwellings. The HHSRS is applied to any form of dwelling, whether it is a self-contained property or a large building. As part of the HMO licensing inspection process, the local authority officer has a duty to examine all the parts of the property to ensure they are acceptable and fit for purpose. Where rooms and areas are shared, officers will look at any possible increase in the likelihood and/or outcomes which could be hazardous as a result of sharing.

There is a guidance document for landlords[68] which does not set out minimum standards but instead seeks to avoid, or at the very least, minimise potential hazards and sets out a landlord's responsibilities as being required to look after:

- The exterior of the dwelling and structural elements of the dwelling; and

- The inside facilities which are part of the dwelling.

---

[68] https://www.gov.uk/government/publications/housing-health-and-safety-rating-system-guidance-for-landlords-and-property-related-professionals.

HMO Property Set Up

This includes:

- Water, gas and electricity; including all equipment necessary to supply these utilities, which must be fully installed in a correct and safe manner;

- Personal hygiene facilities, such as wash hand basins and/or baths;

- Sanitation and drainage; including lavatories, WC basins, drains, waste pipes, rainwater goods, inlet gullies and inspection chambers;

- Food safety; covering sinks, drainage boards, work tops, cooking facilities, cupboards and/or shelves for storing cooking and eating utensils and equipment and food storage facilities;

- Ventilation; covering elements such as airbricks, trickle vents, opening lights to windows and ventilation equipment; and

- Space and water heating installations; including any kind of fitted space heating appliances or central heating system.

When a property is being assessed for conditions which could cause hazards, the local authority officer will take account of the likelihood for a particular hazard for the type and age of the property, any deficiencies which may increase the likelihood of occurrence and how serious the outcome of such an occurrence will be to the occupants. Assessments will

HMO Property Set Up

inform decisions on the most appropriate action that an officer can recommend to the landlord to take and/or remove or minimise any identified hazards. A rating system is used to categorise hazards into bands. These bands range from A (most dangerous) to J (least dangerous).

If the rating system identifies there is likely to be a hazardous occurrence within the next twelve months which could have serious consequences for occupants, the local authority is required to take 'appropriate action' to remedy the situation. This could mean requiring the landlord to undertake works to remove or minimise the identified risk immediately.

The Assessment Process

In Appendix II of the guidance there is a suggested assessment process to help minimise the chances of any unacceptable hazards:

1. Inspect the property:

    a. Room-by-room, checking elements, fixtures and fittings;

    b. Thoroughly check common parts;

    c. Check outside the building, external elements, yards/gardens and paths; and

    d. Record any deficiencies or disrepair.

2. Deficiencies:

    a. Check if any deficiencies and faults contribute to any of the identified common hazards; and

HMO Property Set Up

    b. Make a judgement on whether the deficiencies increase the likelihood of a harmful occurrence or increase the severity of the harm.

3. Remedial work:

   a. Decided what needs to be done to remedy deficiencies and reduce risks;

   b. Identify the urgency of works; and

   c. Work out a timetable for having works conducted.

4. Keep records:

   a. Record the programme of works; and

   b. Record the dates works were completed on.

5. Review:

   a. Check the hazards have been removed/minimised; and

   b. Re-inspect the property on a regular basis.

Following this process should ensure your HMO properties are safe places which tenants are happy to live in and will ensure that you can sleep easy at night knowing you have done all you can as a responsible landlord to minimise the risks of any hazards.

HMO Property Set Up

For reference, appendix III of the guidance details the profiles of potential health and safety hazards in dwellings, including issues such as damp and mould growth, excessive heat or cold, crowding and space, lighting, noise, domestic and personal hygiene, food safety and water supply and protection against accidents such as falls and electrical hazards. Additionally, appendix IV provides useful examples of how to assess hazards such as falling on the stairs, fire, electrical hazards and hot surfaces. The examples included should serve as a guide for how to assess potential hazards in your HMO properties.

27. The Licence Application Process

The process of applying for a HMO licence is relatively straightforward, provided you have all the information you need up front and know you will be already meeting (or exceeding) the correct standards for your area, which should have been informed by the pre-refurbishment discussions held with the HMO officer. However, if you have 'cut corners', it is likely an inspecting officer will spot where this has happened, which could result in delaying receipt of your licence, or additional works being needed to rectify any issue(s) found.

Applications for a HMO licence are made directly to the local authority. Remember, the person who will be managing or having control of the HMO must apply for the licence and this could be yourself or an agent. To apply, you will need to complete and sign either a paper or online application form. This can usually be found on the local authority's website, either in their private sector housing section, environmental health or HMO licensing section. You will need a number of supporting documents to accompany the application and you will need to pay the appropriate fee. There can sometimes be a 'stage one' fee which must accompany the application form and is paid to cover the 'administrative costs' of processing the application and determining whether to grant the licence. A 'stage two' fee may then be required where a draft licence is issued, which covers the costs of inspections over the lifetime of the licence, plus a contribution towards the costs of 'identifying and enforcing HMOs'. The supporting documents required may vary depending on the local authority, but will typically include the following:

HMO Property Set Up

HMO Licensing Documents
Application Form
Passport picture of the Applicant
Gas Safety Certificate
Portable Electrical Appliance Test (PAT) Certificate
Electrical Installation Safety Certificate
Automatic Fire Detection Certificate
Fire Risk Assessment (FRA)
Emergency Lighting Inspection Certificate
Statement of Safety of Furniture and Fittings
Tenancy Management Agreement
A full copy of the Title Deeds (Title Absolute)
Energy Performance Certificate (EPC)
Property Floorplans (to a standard scale, i.e. 1:50 or 1:100 on A4/A3 paper)
Disclosure and Barring Service (DBS) Certificate
Details of any planning consent for building works or conversions
Details of any building regulations approval for works or conversions
Details of any building regulation completion certificates for works or conversions

Table 27.1: Indicative documents and certificates required when applying for a HMO licence.

It may be that when you come to apply for your HMO licence you are unable to provide all the supporting documentation in one go. Usually, the licensing authority will allow you time to gather and provide this information, up to three months after the application has been made, to give you sufficient time if you are awaiting signoff or other confirmation certificates to be issued. If the details are not provided in good time, the authority may close the application and refund any fees paid.

HMO Property Set Up

Once an application is deemed to be 'valid', a licencing inspection will be arranged. The inspection will include a thorough check of the property to look for significant hazards under the HHSRS and will check for any HMO Management Regulation breaches. An assessment of the property's overall suitability for occupation against the Licensing and Management of HMOs Regulations[69] (2006) and whether the property meets the local authority's adopted HMO standards. A check will also be undertaken on the prospective licence holder and/or manager to determine whether they are considered a 'fit and proper' person. This is aptly named the 'fit and proper person test'. But what does this *actually* mean?

A person is deemed to be a 'fit and proper' if:

- They do not have any unspent convictions that may be relevant to their role as either licence holder or manager;

- They have not been found by a court or tribunal to have practiced unlawful discrimination on grounds of sex, colour, race, ethnic or national origin or disability;

- They do not have any unspent conviction in relation to any housing, public health, environmental health or land and tenant law;

- They have not been in control of a property which has been subject to a control order under Section 379 of the Housing Act 1985 in the last five years;

---

[69] https://www.legislation.gov.uk/uksi/2006/373/contents.

HMO Property Set Up

- They have not had a licence refused, been convicted of breaching the conditions of a licence or have acted otherwise than in accordance with the Code of Practice approved under Section 233 of the Act that concerns a property in their ownership;

- They do not own or have not previously owned property that has been the subject of an interim or final management order or a special interim management order under the Housing Act 2004; and

- They are not subject to a banning order under the Housing and Planning Act 2016 (Banning Order Offences) Regulations 2017.

Following inspection, provided nothing is identified during or after the consultation process, the authority will issue a notice of intent to grant a licence (the draft licence). This will generally be issued by email. At this point, you may be asked to pay any remaining ('stage two') fee. Make sure to check all the details are correct, such as the licence holder's name and the property address are correct. Make sure to carefully check through any conditions attached to the licence as well. You don't want to be caught out if there are any works listed that need to be completed by a certain time! Also, be sure to check and make a note of when the licence is due for renewal.

Typically, the draft HMO licence is issued with mandatory licence conditions, such as presenting a gas safety certificate annually to the local authority if gas is supplied, maintaining electrical appliances and furniture supplied by the landlord in a safe condition and providing confirmation to the local

HMO Property Set Up

authority, if requested, that the electrical items and furniture in the property are safe, the provision of smoke and/or carbon monoxide alarms to be kept in good working order and their positions in the property, maintenance records and the provision of a written statement to each occupant the terms of their occupancy (sample tenancy agreement).

The issuing authority also has the option to include a number of discretionary licence conditions, which may be property specific conditions to help regulate the management, use, occupation, condition or contents of a particular HMO. On receipt of the draft licence, you have the option to make representations to the issuing authority if you do not agree with the conditions. If no representations are received within 14 to 21 days, the full HMO licence will then be issued. Where you do make representations, the issuing authority can either accept or reject them and will inform you accordingly. If any changes are accepted, a revised draft licence is issued (a modification notice), which gives you a further window of opportunity to make representations or to accept the revised draft licence.

Once the representation period has expired, the issuing authority will issue the actual HMO licence (also known as the decision notice). This is valid from the date it is issued, meaning that the licence conditions are fully enforceable from that date. Remember, once issued, the licence is valid for a maximum of five years and is property and person specific. So if you wish to change the agent or manager, you will need to apply for a new licence as they are not transferrable.

Where licences are refused, the authority will issue you with a notice explaining why the licence cannot be granted. If you do not agree with this decision, there is an appeal process which

HMO Property Set Up

can be made to the First-tier Tribunal (Property Chamber). Appeals can be made up to 28 days after receiving the decision notice.

Should you fail to apply for a licence altogether, you could face a fine of up to £20,000 and be banned from operating as a landlord. Non-compliance with conditions can also result in significant fines and cause issues if you wish to evict tenants as the AST agreement will not be considered 'valid'.

28. Accreditation Schemes For Landlords

At a national level, the National Residential Landlord Association[70] (NRLA) is one of the largest membership organisations for private residential landlords in the UK. The NRLA have their own accreditation scheme which provides training, advice and guidance to landlords and helps its members to navigate the challenges of the private residential sector by offering comprehensive learning resources and sector intelligence, with the aim of enabling its members to help provide safe, legal and secure homes. Landlords can become accredited by applying to the NRLA for membership and will need to comply with the NRLA Code of Practice as well as complete and retain records of Continuing Professional Development (CPD) training. At more local and regional levels, some local authorities have their own accredited landlord registers, which allow you to become registered with them as an accredited landlord. Some local authorities recognise different bodies, so do make sure to check this beforehand.

As a landlord, being accredited can help you gain various discounts, access to training, support and advice and enable you to gain entry to local CPD and networking events. It also provides you with a chance to meet up with and get to know other landlords operating in your area. Accredited landlords may also attract and retain tenants over a longer period, which can help to reduce void periods. This is because tenants will recognise that as a professional landlord, you will work to resolve any issues raised quickly and that the standard of accommodation is likely to be better than other landlords may

---

[70] https://www.nrla.org.uk/.

HMO Property Set Up

be providing. Being accredited may also have the benefit of 'adding value' to a landlord's property and being able to command higher rental rates.

For tenants, being with an accredited landlord can help demonstrate that they have a professional landlord who meets professional standards, giving them confidence the property they are renting is of a good standard, is properly managed and regulated. This can obviously be very attractive, particularly if tenants have previously had bad experiences of landlords and/or HMOs.

For local authorities, landlord accreditation schemes are a good thing as in addition to HMO licensing standards, schemes can also help with raising housing standards in the area and with singling out poor accommodation providers who cannot (or choose not to) improve their properties. Schemes can also help improve relationships between local authorities and the landlord community by seeking to improve standards through mutually beneficial partnerships.

Once registered with an accreditation scheme, depending on the local authority, you may receive a certificate and can become eligible for discounted HMO licence fees, grants for insultation and other works to improve your property and receive invitations to discounted accredited CPD training. A useful list of landlord accreditation schemes nationally and by region is available from the Accreditation Network UK[71].

---

[71] https://www.anuk.org.uk/schemes-near-you.

HMO Property Set Up

29. HMO Officer Relationships

Where possible, I would encourage you to try and build a good relationship with your local HMO officer from the start as they can certainly help to make a big difference when applying for a HMO licence, or even in allowing some flexibility regarding amenities and facilities in a new HMO you may be looking to set up. This can be particularly beneficial if you have existing high-quality HMOs elsewhere in the area, as they'll know the standards you work to.

Building a good relationship can also lend help in cases where you submit a planning application for a larger HMO, for example, as the HMO officer may be able to provide a supporting statement or respond as a 'statutory consultee[72]' on the application. If you have previously been able to demonstrate to them that you are able to provide good standards of living for your tenants, they can attest to this, which could help tip the outcome of a planning application in your favour. Therefore, when starting out in your HMO journey, try to introduce yourself at an early stage and explain what it is you are trying to achieve (i.e. high-quality, affordable homes for professionals and key workers) and that you want to work with the local authority and build a relationship so you can help to provide good places for people to live in in the area.

---

[72] An organisation or body defined by statute which local planning authorities are legally required to consult with on relevant planning applications.

HMO Property Set Up

Advisory Visits

A number of local authorities now conduct a HMO 'advisory visit' service or offer HMO 'pre-licensing advice', usually for a fee, for landlords who are thinking of converting existing dwellings into HMOs. The visits are generally carried out by an EHO or private sector housing officer (PSHO), specialising in HMOs. The officer will typically visit the property, along with the landlord, or their representative and conduct a full inspection, including calculating the room sizes. Following the officer's visit, a schedule of works, alongside their advice is issued, highlighting all the necessary works required to bring the property up to the licensable standards of the local authority.

Costs for this service will vary, but you can expect to pay around £200-£300 for this. Whilst it may seem expensive and potentially unnecessary when you have the local authority's HMO standards to work from, it is worth doing as it can really help to build a good working relationship with officers and it allows you the security of carrying out refurbishment works with an officer's up-to-date advice (I've known of plenty of HMO officers whose advice has deviated from the local authority's HMO standards). Additionally, for any future licence applications on this or other HMO properties you set up, the officer's will recognise your name and know you will be seeking to provide a high-quality HMO. As already mentioned, this may allow for some 'wiggle room' on the size of communal rooms and/or other facilities required (although don't expect any wiggle room on the minimum room sizes for sleeping accommodation).

Some authorities will enable you to request a visit when the property is vacant, so you could seek to book the visit during

HMO Property Set Up

the purchasing stage. Once the advice is received and you have completed on the purchase, you can get started straight away. If the property is currently occupied, you will obviously need to seek to owners' permission before booking a visit.

30. Enforcement

I cannot stress this enough - if your HMO qualifies as being licensable, you **MUST** apply for a licence! This applies to both mandatory and additional licensing schemes. Claiming ignorance over the issue will not be looked upon favourably either. Failure to apply for a licence where one is required or failing to comply with licence conditions is a punishable offence and if convicted, you could find yourself receiving an unlimited fine – per offence. Alternatively, you could be issued with a Civil Penalty Notice of up to £30,000.

Tenants who currently live at, or previously lived at the property, whilst it was unlicenced or where licence conditions were not properly complied with may also be eligible to apply for a Rent Repayment Order (RRO) to reclaim up to 12 months' rent from you. In addition, the duration of the remaining licence could be shorted by the local authority where there is 'reasonable evidence' to show the property should have had a licence, although the full licensing fee would still be payable.

Furthermore, the 'fit and proper person' status of a landlord and/or their managing agent may be reviewed if the person or persons responsible are prosecuted or sanctioned for an offence. In circumstances where there is evidence of continuous poor management, breach of licensing conditions and other relevant factors, an individual's 'fit and proper person' status can be revoked altogether. Should this happen, the landlord and/or their agent will be prevented from being involved in the management of a licenced property – essentially it would result in an effective ban on being a HMO landlord/manager.

HMO Property Set Up

Not having a licenced HMO has other implications for landlords, including not being able to serve notice on tenants under the Section 21[73] procedure where you wish to regain possession of the property.

---

[73] See Chapter 73.

HMO Property Set Up

Summary

In Section III, I have discussed the three different types of HMO licences which exist within England (two of which are most applicable to HMOs) and have outlined some of the standards which HMOs are expected to meet, along with providing you with an indication of the facilities they should be provided with.

I have also gone over the basics of the fire safety and risk assessment processes and provided an example of the fire safety requirements for a HMO. Further, I have discussed the Housing Health and Safety Rating System (HHSRS) to help identify and protect against risks and hazards to health within a HMO.

I have also examined the HMO licensing application process, landlord accreditation schemes and the importance of building a good working relationship with HMO officers.

Finally, I have outlined how HMO licensing legislation can be enforced by the local authority and emphasised the importance of having a HMO licence in place where one is required.

Section IV: The Planning System And HMOs

This section is all about the Planning System in England and how it applies to HMO development and will cover how the planning system operates, applicable Permitted Development rights and their restrictions, what use classes are and why they are relevant, as well as outlining a number of other planning strategies for HMO development.

"Good buildings come from good people, and all problems are solved by good design."

– Stephen Gardiner

31. Introduction To The Planning System

The planning system in England in its current form has existed for over 70 years, although as a result of various methods of 'government tinkering' it has been added to, amended and had parts removed altogether many times over since its introduction.

Further 'comprehensive reforms' of the planning system could potentially be on the horizon (at the time of writing) as the Levelling Up and Regeneration Bill[74] (LURB) proposes a raft of addition changes, building on the 'Planning for the Future' white paper (2020). The main elements of the LURB relevant to HMO development include:

- The introduction of 'National Development Management Policies', which would carry the same weight in the decision making process as Local Development Plan policies;

- Changes to simply the local plan process to make it faster, with more community involvement;

- Limiting the scope of local plans to 'locally specific' matters;

- 'Neighbourhood priorities statements' to be used to aid the preparation of local plans;

---

[74] https://bills.parliament.uk/bills/3155

HMO Property Set Up

- Mandatory infrastructure levy ('IL') to capture some of the financial gain created by development, where local authorities can set differential rates;

- A new power for minor variations to existing planning permissions for 'non-substantial changes' such as the description of a development and conditions attached to a permission;

- 'Design Codes' for each local planning authority;

- The strengthening of neighbourhood planning and the introduction of *'street votes'*, allowing residents to propose development on their street and hold votes over whether permission should be granted; and

- Planning application fee rises, which are currently still subject to consultation, but if brought in, this could see fees rise by as much as 35% for 'major' applications and 25% for all other application types [75].

A consultation on revisions to the National Planning Policy Framework (NPPF), the Government's planning policies for England and how these are expected to be applied began in December 2022 and closed in March 2023. The Department for Levelling Up, Housing and Communities sought views on how to update and develop policy to support levelling up, which has impacted upon approaches to housing need and achieving a suitable housing mix for local communities. The

---

[75]: https://www.gov.uk/government/consultations/increasing-planning-fees-and-performance-technical-consultation.

HMO Property Set Up

consultation feedback is currently being analysed by the Government (as at May 2023[76]).

Changes to the planning system are frequently proposed and as a result, it is an ever-evolving entity. However, before I get too carried away with delving into the complexities of planning itself, let's take a step back and start from the beginning by discussing the planning system itself and planning legislation.

The Planning System And Planning Legislation

The planning system is often considered to be complex and confusing and as a result of this, it can be misunderstood, causing people who are unfamiliar with the many foibles of the planning system and planning legislation to be apprehensive about engaging with it. Where they do, they can often be left feeling a bit puzzled! Within the United Kingdom, the planning system is devolved, but operates similarly in England, Scotland, Wales and Northern Ireland. For each of the devolved nations there are separate laws, rules and policies setting out how planning legislation should be undertaken. For the purposes of this book, I will only be discussing the English planning system[77].

The planning system was introduced so that land and property development and uses could be controlled in the interests of the public and to ensure that appropriate development and uses are allowed to take place in suitable locations, when and where it is needed, for the benefit of communities, the

---

[76] https://www.gov.uk/government/consultations/levelling-up-and-regeneration-bill-reforms-to-national-planning-policy.
[77] Whereby references to the 'planning system' mean the English planning system.

economy and the environment. It is primarily concerned with development, the use of land and what it looks like. In planning terms, 'development' is defined under the Town and County Planning Act 1990[78] as:

"The carrying out of building, engineering mining or other operation in, on, over or under land, or the making of any material change in the use of any building or other land."

I think you'd agree that's a rather broad and all-encompassing definition, right?

Planning Permission and Material Considerations

Planning permission is sought through a wide variety of different applications and legislation, depending on the development or use proposed. Planning decisions are based on compliance with local and nationally adopted planning policies contained within documents such as the National Planning Policy Framework ('NPPF') and the Local Development Plan, which sets out a LPAs approach to planning and development in its area of authority.

Planning decisions are also based on matters called 'material considerations'. The scope of what can constitute a material consideration is not well defined, allowing for a wide variety of issues to be considered by the decision taker (the LPA). The Government recognises that a material planning consideration is one which is relevant to making the planning decision in question and the scope of what can constitute a material consideration is very wide. In general, courts have taken the view that planning is concerned with land use in the

---

[78] Section 55 of The Town and Country Planning Act 1990 (as amended).

HMO Property Set Up

public interest, so that considerations should not include those which related purely to private interests only[79]. This could include private interests such as the potential for the value of a house decreasing due to being next to a neighbouring development or someone simply objecting because they do not like the idea of living next to a proposed development – an objection must instead be linked to a planning matter.

In relation to HMO developments in particular, material considerations can include issues such as overlooking and loss of privacy, overshadowing, traffic, highway safety and parking concerns, noise, design and appearance, layout and density of a building, intensification of use, type of materials proposed, effect on listed buildings or conservation areas, as well as many others. As a material consideration is judged on its planning merits, this can lead to a degree of discretion and flexibility in the approach of the LPA towards proposals, allowing each application to be considered individually.

A Flexible Approach

Local planning policies allow you to tailor your proposal to suit the attitude of the LPA. For example, you may find if you look at two different authority areas to invest in that they have a completely different approach to HMO developments. One may have no specific policies relating to HMO development and you may instead have to rely on more general housing policies, focused on providing sufficient levels of housing for its population. Another LPA may have more restrictive policies towards HMO development and include specific policies which allow the LPA to retain a greater measure of

---

[79] National Planning Practice Guidance Paragraph 008 Reference ID: 21b-008-20140306 Revision date: 06 03 2014.

HMO Property Set Up

control over the number of HMOs in their area, typically in a student city or town.

It is worth noting in planning that a 'one size fits all' approach towards proposals does not work, as each application is assessed individually – and by different planning officers. This means that when preparing an application, you need to carefully tailor your planning application to suit the circumstances of the area and the planning policy context, including any relevant material considerations.

32. National Planning Policy

Planning is a 'policy-led' activity. The Government is therefore responsible for setting out the approach towards development, which has been translated into a document called the National Planning Policy Framework (the 'NPPF'). First introduced in 2012, the most recent version of the NPPF was published in July 2021[80]. It sets out that first and foremost, the purpose of the planning system is to contribute to the achievement of sustainable development. This is defined in paragraph 7 of the NPPF as *"meeting the needs of the present without compromising the ability of future generations to meet their own needs."*

To achieve this, the NPPF identifies three overarching objectives relating to economic, social and environmental objectives, which paragraph 9 notes should be delivered through the preparation and implementation of plans and the application of the policies in the NPPF. Crucially, the policies of the NPPF are noted as not being criteria which every decision can or should be judged against. Instead, they should play an active role in guiding development towards sustainable solutions, taking local circumstances into account to reflect the character, needs and opportunities of each area. The NPPF includes a broad range of policies, including the approach LPAs should take toward plan-making and decision-taking, the provision of housing, business and economic development, transport, flooding and the natural and historic environment. The NPPF sets out how these policies should be applied and provides guidance for LPAs, who are required to

---

[80] Although as Chapter 31 notes, consultation on an updated version of the NPPF took place in December 2022.

HMO Property Set Up

preparing local plans to guide development in their areas. The policies within the NPPF are also regarded as 'material considerations' in the determination of applications and appeals.

In relation to HMOs, the NPPF seeks to support the Government's objective of significantly boosting the supply of homes and to help the needs of groups with specific housing requirements, with the overall aim being to meet as much housing need as possible with an appropriate mix of housing types in local communities. Further, the size, type and tenure of housing need for different groups should be reflected in planning policies, including for students and people who rent their homes. Planning decisions are also encouraged to promote and achieve healthy, inclusive and safe places for people to live and work in, underpinned by good design.

The NPPF is supported by the National Planning Practice Guidance (PPG), an online resource that is regularly updated. The PPG adds further context to the NPPF, which it is intended to be read alongside. It is also a material consideration in the determination of planning applications, particularly where a relevant local policy is regarded as being 'out of date' and can therefore add weight to an argument for approval. The PPG is arranged into over 50 different categories to provide guidance on the interpretation of the NPPF and how its policies are to be applied. Its aims are to ensure the planning system allows land to be used for new homes and jobs, whilst protecting natural and historic environments. Whilst the PPG does not mention HMOs specifically, it includes paragraphs on the housing needs of

HMO Property Set Up

different groups and design considerations to be take account of as part of proposals.

33. Local Planning Policy

Each LPA has the authority to design and adopt its own local plans to assist with guiding development in their areas, in accordance with the aims of the NPPF. These form part of the overall Development Plan for the authority area. The local plan sets out the LPA's approach to development decisions over the designated plan period (which must cover a minimum of 15 years but are typically prepared to span a 20-year period). Local plans contain policies on all matter of issues, from where housing will be allocated, to the design and use of buildings, what forms of development will be acceptable and how proposals should demonstrate they comply with relevant local and national policies in relation to housing provision, the local economy transport, ecology and biodiversity, natural and heritage assets and the urban and rural landscape, for example.

Neighbourhood plans (NPs), introduced under the Localism Act 2011[81], form an important addition to local plans and the Development Plan as a whole. These are plans which are often written and prepared by local community groups and/or parish councils rather than the LPA and typically cover a designated neighbourhood area (often the parish area). NPs were brought in to help guide the local development of these designated areas, enabling communities to "get the right types of development, in the right place.[82]"

The planning policies included within NPs should typically be in conformity with those contained in the local plan. NPs normally last for five years before they need to be reviewed

---

[81] https://www.legislation.gov.uk/ukpga/2011/20/contents.
[82] https://locality.org.uk/neighbourhood-planning.

HMO Property Set Up

and updated. Once adopted, NPs form part of the Development plan, meaning their polices become material considerations in the decision-making process.

The adopted Development Plan policies of the LPA are the main tools used to test applications for planning permission and can either result in a grant of permission or a refusal, where proposals are judged not to comply with relevant policies. Local plans and neighbourhood plans therefore play an important role in development and the way in which planning applications should be determined in line with the relevant policies of the Development Plan, unless there are other material considerations to be taken account of.

The Development Plan is often supported by Supplementary Planning Documents (SPDs) or Supplementary Planning Guidance (SPGs). These build upon and provide more detailed explanations over how polices contained within the local plan should be applied. Once adopted, they typically become material considerations in the determining of applications. SPDs and SPGs can relate to a number of specific topics, including:

- Housing;
- Transport and Parking Standards;
- Design;
- Landscaping;
- Refuse Management; and
- Extensions, alterations and improvements.

HMO Property Set Up

The Local Development Scheme

The process of preparing and adopting a local plan or any other plans to help guide local development is set out in a document called the 'Local Development Scheme' ('LDS'). All LPAs are required to prepare and maintain an up-to-date LDS.

If you are not sure what the current development plan documents are for an area you are interested in, or you know the LPA is in the process of preparing a new local plan, but don't know how far it has been progressed, refer to the LDS. This document will contain information on the status of the current development plan documents and will provide a timetable for the preparation and predicted adoption date of either a new or revised local plan. It will also provide details of any other supporting development plan documents which are in the process of being progressed by the LPA or a neighbourhood plan group.

HMO Property Set Up

34. Introduction To Permitted Development Rights

After that quick introduction to national and local planning policy, you may now be wondering what you can actually do without needing planning permission? Well, the next few chapters will provide you with an overview of what types of development can be carried out without planning permission being required, subject to proposals complying with certain restrictions and limitations. This type of development is known as Permitted Development (PD). PD rights were introduced by the Government[83] to allow for a whole raft of small-scale development projects to take place without planning permission being required, removing the need for LPAs to determine 'small' applications in an effort to help speed up the planning process. These rights supersede local plan policies and allow you to carry out some works without even notifying the LPA.

As part of your due diligence, I would always encourage you to check for local restrictions on PD rights, through the use of tools such as Article 4 Directions[84] (A4Ds), conservation areas and restrictive covenants[85], but I'll come onto these in more detail later in this section.

---

[83] Under the Town and Country Planning (General Permitted Development) (GPDO) (England) Order 2015 (as amended).
[84] Under Article 4 of the Town and Country Planning (General Permitted Development) (GPDO) (England) Order 2015 (as amended).
[85] These are not related to planning permission but can supersede PD rights. See Chapter 59 for further details.

HMO Property Set Up

The General Permitted Development Order (GDPO) is a statutory instrument which grants planning permission for certain types of development. It has a broad scope which delves into may topics such as development within the curtilage of a dwellinghouse, changes of use, temporary buildings, agricultural and forestry, non-domestic alterations, transport related development, heritage and demolition, renewable energy, communications and the construction of new dwellinghouses to name a few.

For the purposes of this book, I am only going to discuss two parts of the GPDO which are of most relevant to you as an HMO property developer. These are development within the curtilage of a dwellinghouse (Householder PD rights), under Schedule 2, Part 1 of the GPDO and Change of Use Classes, under schedule 2, Part 3, Class L (small HMOs to dwellinghouses and vice versa). In the next chapter, I'll start with Use Classes as these PD rights can dramatically affect how you intend to use a property.

HMO Property Set Up

35. Use Classes

Firstly, let's go over a bit of background on Use Classes. Most buildings are classified into a specific 'Use Class' under the Town and County Planning (Use Classes) Order 1987 (as amended). This puts buildings into various categories and uses, depending on what their intended use is and, in some cases, the maximum size of buildings for that particular use. Until 1st September 2020, the Use Classes Order consisted of four main Use Class groups (A to D), each containing several subgroups:

Class	Building Type
A	Shops, restaurants, cafes, pubs and takeaways
B	Business, industrial and commercial premises
C	Residential uses
D	Doctor's surgeries, assembly and leisure uses etc.

Table 35.1: Former Use Classes by building type.

However, on 21st July 2020, the Government published an update to the Use Classes Order, which came into effect on 1st September 2020. The purpose of these changes was to allow for a greater degree of flexibility in the way buildings are used. In England, these changes saw the removal of Classes A and D, as well as B1(a), whilst introducing new Use Classes E and F. Use Class E (Commercial, business and service) amalgamates the following uses into one Use Class:

HMO Property Set Up

Use Class E
A1 shops
A2 financial/professional services
A3 cafes/restaurants
D1 medical health facilities, creches and nurseries
D2 indoor sports/fitness centres
B1 office/business/light industrial uses

Table 35.2: Updated uses now falling within Use Class E.

Use Class F1 relates to learning and non-residential institutions, whilst Use Class F2 relates to local community uses.

<u>Use Class C3</u>

Now, you may well be thinking "what does this have to do with HMOs?" Well, crucially, the updates to PD rights still enable certain changes of use to occur without planning permission being required. This is important because most HMO developers will seek to purchase a 'C3' Use Class dwellinghouse (C3 dwellinghouse) for conversion into a HMO. There are three distinct types of C3 dwellinghouse, defined as:

HMO Property Set Up

Definitions of a dwellinghouse	
C3(a)	Occupied by a single person or by people in a single household, such as a family or a couple (whether married or not)
C3(b)	Occupied by up to six people living together as a single household and receiving care, such as a supported housing scheme for people with learning disabilities
C3(c)	Occupied by a group of up to six people living together as a single household, where no care is provided, such as a small religious community or a homeowner with a lodger(s)

Table 35.3 Definitions of a C3 dwellinghouse.

Under the provisions of Class L (small HMOs to dwellinghouses and vice versa) of the GPDO, C3 dwellinghouses benefit from PD rights to convert them into 'C4' Use Class HMOs (C4 HMOs). These are defined as small, shared houses occupied by between **three and six** unrelated individuals, as their only or main residence, who share basic amenities such as a kitchen or bathroom. This means you can purchase a C3 dwellinghouse and convert it, without needing planning permission in most cases, into a C4 HMO for occupation by a maximum of six people unrelated people. You may even move a property back and forth (unless stated otherwise) between C3 and C4 uses as they share PD rights to do so. This gives you a large degree of flexibility over how the property is occupied – pretty amazing right? There are, however, several ways in which PD rights for these changes of use can be removed which I'll discuss in Chapter 39. In the meantime, let's go back to Use Classes (yay, I can hear you shout!)

HMO Property Set Up

There is one more Use Class relevant to HMOs, called 'Sui Generis'. Sui Generis is Latin for 'of its own kind' and in planning terms, this basically applies to all other buildings or uses which do not easily fit within any particular use class. Examples of other Sui Generis buildings or uses includes petrol stations, amusement arcades, takeaways, cinemas and casinos and scrap yards. In relation to HMOs specifically, Sui Generis HMOs are defined as large HMOs occupied by **seven or more** unrelated individuals.

It is important to note here that **planning permission is always required to convert either a C3 dwellinghouse or C4 HMO into a Sui Generis HMO**. Similarly, if you wanted to convert a Sui Generis HMO back into a C3 or C4 use, you would need to apply for planning permission as the change of use would be considered 'material' by the LPA. Therefore, if you are intending to carry out physical works to a C3 dwellinghouse, such as PD extensions or other alterations to later convert it into a HMO, you may wish to think carefully about how you go about staging the order of development. I'll pick this up again in Chapter 38.

Introduction To Changes Of Use Using Prior Approval

As I mentioned before, the changes to the Use Classes Order still enable changes of use to be undertaken without needing planning permission. Other changes of use may only need a 'light touch' planning submission to be made in the form of a 'Prior Approval' application (or sometimes referred to as 'Prior Notification').

I won't go into too much detail here as many HMO developers will likely be happy sticking with converting C3 dwellinghouses. Certainty, if you don't have much experience

HMO Property Set Up

with development projects in the first place, it is advisable to get comfortable with more 'basic' or 'vanilla' conversion projects before embarking on any complex office or retail shops to residential conversion schemes using the prior approval method. These specific PD rights provide another level of development to get your teeth into, perhaps further down the line when you are more experienced.

For reference though, these types of application are where the principle of development is established through PD rights, but proposals must demonstrate they comply with certain other limitations and restrictions, as set out in legislation. Prior approval/notification is a formal submission to your LPA to seek confirmation that specified parts of a development are acceptable, prior to any works being allowed to commence. Usually, applications take up to 56 days for a decision to be issued, depending upon the request being made.

There are different types of prior approval requiring varying levels of detail. Generally, prior approval allows the LPA to assess the impacts and risks of a particular scheme on the current/existing and proposed use of the land or building and its location. LPAs are also often required to take account of the impacts of noise, design and external appearance, amenity, transport and highways considerations and the risk of any flooding or contamination issues.

Any HMO conversion project relying on prior approval would need to be approached in stages as it is potentially risky. Stage 1 would be to establish the conversion to residential use is acceptable. Stage 2 would then require you to establish the approved residential use. Stage 3 would be to apply for permission to convert the building to a HMO. This is explained further in the next part of this chapter.

HMO Property Set Up

Alternatively, there are options to go straight in with a planning application for the change of use of the existing building into a HMO, but this can be a risky strategy in itself. In many ways though, it is often better to establish a C3 residential use as a 'fallback' position first, provided the financials add up and then go back in with an alternative proposal to convert the building into a HMO.

Use Class E To Residential

Following the updates to the Use Classes Order in September 2020 which introduced Use Class E (commercial, business and service uses), from 1st August 2021, Class MA was also brought into effect, allowing for the conversion of the following Class E uses to Class C3 residential uses, subject to prior approval:

Class E Uses to Class C3 Residential Uses	
E(a)	Display of retail sale of goods, other than hot food
E(b)	Sale of food and drink for consumption (mostly) on the premises
E(c)	Provision of financial services, professional services or other services in a commercial, business or service locality
E(d)	Indoor sport and recreation
E(e)	Medical services
E(f)	Non-residential creche, day centres or nurseries

Table 35.4: Use Class E uses to Use Class C3 uses.

This prior approval process only allows you to convert a property into a C3 dwellinghouse, subject to other considerations. If your prior approval application is successful, you would need to carry out works to convert the property to a C3 dwellinghouse and then have it occupied as a single dwellinghouse to establish its residential use.

HMO Property Set Up

Following this period of use solely as a C3 dwellinghouse, you could apply to the LPA for planning permission to change the property into a HMO, subject to local planning policies and other material considerations. If the proposed use as a HMO is refused, or any conditions relating to the prior approval application prevents using the property as anything but a C3 dwellinghouse, this could be problematic for you. Further, if securing the use of the property as a HMO is the only way to make the project financially viable, do think carefully about your investment strategy.

Before embarking on this type of project, I would strongly advise speaking with a suitably experienced Planning Consultant for their opinion. Alternatively, you could apply to the LPA for pre-application advice to 'test' the acceptability of a proposal in principle. This approach would depend on whether you own the site already, or if the seller is willing to wait for a response to be received from the LPA, as they may be in receipt of other offers not subject to planning enquiries. Chapter 41 provides guidance on pre-application advice submissions.

36. Householder PD rights

Ok, after that trip down the 'change of uses' rabbit hole, let's move onto another part of the GPDO and take a closer look at the PD rights available for development within the curtilage of a dwellinghouse. As mentioned before, these PD rights are set out in Schedule 2, Part 1 of the Order. Classes A – H (known as 'development within the curtilage of a dwellinghouse') are relevant here and as you may have guessed, these apply specifically to Use Class C3 dwellinghouses and their residential curtilages.

Do bear in mind that flats, maisonettes, converted house or houses created through PD rights via change of use and other non-household buildings (such as former offices or agricultural buildings) do not benefit from these PD rights under Classes A – H. In addition, there are other restrictions to PD rights which prevent these householder developments from being carried out. These are discussed further in Chapter 39.

Firstly, let's start off by clarifying what I mean by 'curtilage'. Curtilage is the area of land immediately surrounding or associated with a house, forming one enclosure with it. This can include land comprised of a garden, yard or any outbuildings and structures. Curtilage is explained further by Figure 36.1. The light grey indicates the extent of the 'curtilage' around the dark grey 'dwellinghouse' within the plot:

HMO Property Set Up

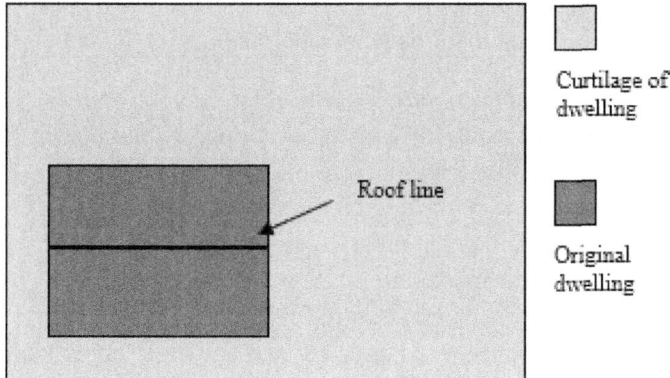

Figure 36.1: Birds eye view of a detached dwelling and its curtilage.

In many cases, most residential houses you will be looking to purchase for conversion will require some sort of addition or extension to add value to them, make them more comfortable for tenants, future-proofed - and ultimately more profitable, as you may seek to create as many lettable bedrooms as is reasonably possible.

When I say 'future-proofed', I mean in terms of only needing to carry out significant building works once (i.e. building an extension or converting the loft space into habitable accommodation). When you have the property tenanted as a six-bedroom HMO, for example, you really don't want to have to carry out extra works to create an additional bedroom, should you later decide you wish to operate a seven-bedroom HMO. In another scenario, you don't want to find you have to get the builders back in to create larger communal areas if HMO Licensing standards are updated. It would certainly be very expensive to provide tenants with alternative accommodation whilst any works are carried out and would result in the loss of income for a month or so at least, not to mention noise and disturbance for neighbours!

Having a good understanding of the changes you can make to a dwellinghouse using PD rights is therefore essential. These will allow you to increase the size of a dwelling quite significantly, without the need to apply for planning permission beforehand in most cases. Of course, you will need to take into consideration HMO Licensing standards when looking at extending or altering a property to create additional bedrooms, or a larger kitchen and other communal areas, but referring to the guidance in Section III should help to ensure you stay on the right side of the licensing requirements. The next part of this chapter discusses some of the many PD options available to you and the various limitations of those rights. I'll start at the top of a dwellinghouse and go through loft conversions and dormer extensions first.

Loft Conversions And Dormer Extensions

Using PD rights under Schedule 2, Class B allows you to create up to an additional 40 m^3 of roof space on a terraced house, whilst on detached and semi-detached houses this limit increases to 50 m^3. These PD rights enable you to create additional habitable accommodation though extension and conversion of the loft space, such as a spacious bedroom (or bedrooms) where the original loft space may not have been suitable due to its size or roof pitch, for example. This is, of course, subject to certain limitations and conditions, including:

- Any existing loft conversions or dormer extensions must be included as part of the volume allowance (i.e. if a

HMO Property Set Up

previous owner has carried out a loft extension before, this will 'eat' into the volume allowance);

- The loft extension must not protrude over the edge of the existing roof slope of the 'principal elevation' where it fronts the highway;

- The extension must not be built higher than the highest part of the existing roof;

- Similar colours and materials must be used which match with the existing dwelling;

- Any proposed windows facing a side elevation must be 'obscure glazed' to protect privacy. Any openings must be at least 1.7 metres above the floor level;

- Any extension created cannot overhang the outer face of a wall on the original dwellinghouse; and

- The roof extension must be set back from the roof edge as far as reasonably practical, at least 200 millimetres from the original eaves (excluding hip-to-gable extensions).

HMO Property Set Up

Figure 36.2.1: Side-on view of dormer extension to rear elevation of roof space.

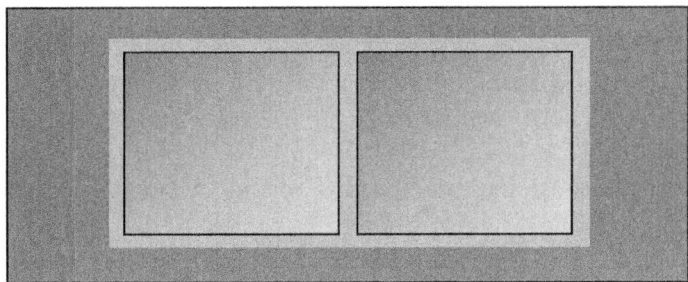

Figure 36.2.2: Front-on view of dormer extension to rear elevation of roof space.

Roof Alterations And Roof Lights/Skylights

In general, you won't need to apply for planning permission to either re-roof a dwellinghouse, provided that you use similar materials, colours and textures, or to insert roof lights/skylights (such as Velux windows), which can certainly help brighten up a loft space to a sufficient degree so it can be used as a bedroom. These PD rights, available under Schedule 2, Class C, are handy if you are simply looking to utilise the existing roof space of a property without wishing to extend

HMO Property Set Up

any further outwards. These are again subject to some limitations, which include:

- Ensuring no alteration projects more than 150 millimetres above the existing slope of the roof;

- Ensuring no alterations are built higher than the highest part of the existing roof; and

- Ensuring any proposed windows facing a side elevation are 'obscure glazed' to protect privacy, whilst any openings must be at least 1.7 metres above the floor level.

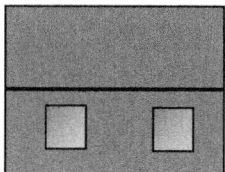

Figure 36.3.1: Birds eye view of roof lights/skylights installed on front elevation of roof space.

HMO Property Set Up

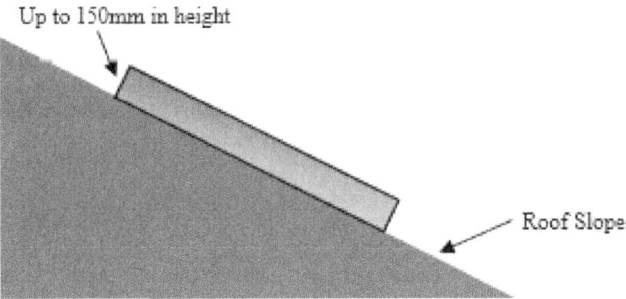

Figure 36.3.2: Side on view of roof lights/skylights installed on front elevation of roof space.

This is going to be a long one as I'll discuss the PD rights available for single storey and double storey extensions on various parts of a dwellinghouse, as well as the prior approval process for larger rear extensions. Firstly, I'll go through some basic points to think about when considering PD extension, before getting stuck into the details of the extensions themselves, so go grab yourself a cuppa and make yourself comfortable...

There are all manner of PD extensions available to you for consideration, depending on the layout of the existing dwellinghouse, what you want to achieve and whether there are any existing extensions which have been carried out by previous owners. For all PD extensions, it is important to remember that only half the area of land around the 'original dwellinghouse' can be covered by extensions or other buildings.

In planning terms, the original dwellinghouse is understood to be either the house as it was first built; or the house as it stood

HMO Property Set Up

on 1st July 1948, if it was built before this date. Additionally, when using PD rights to extend, no part of an extension can be built higher than the highest part of the existing roof, or higher than the eaves of the existing roof. Where an extension comes within two metres of 'boundary', the height at eaves level must not exceed three metres.

A boundary is understood to be the edge of the area of enclosed space surrounding the house and can be known as the 'boundary of the curtilage'. It is worth mentioning here that some LPAs may have a different opinion of what constitutes a 'boundary', but it is generally accepted this applies to a wall or fence between houses or gardens, or the wall of an adjoining building. Further, no extensions are allowed where they are built forward of the 'principal elevation' or on a side elevation where this fronts a highway. The principal elevation is often considered to be the 'front' of a house, as most houses are built to face a road. This is the elevation which is often most prominently seen by members of the public. The principal elevation can include more than one wall facing in the same direction. An example of this is where bay windows have been built on the front elevation, or if the house has been built in an 'L' or 'U' shape. In these cases, all walls facing in the same 'front' direction are deemed to form the principal elevation, as demonstrated in figure 36.4.

HMO Property Set Up

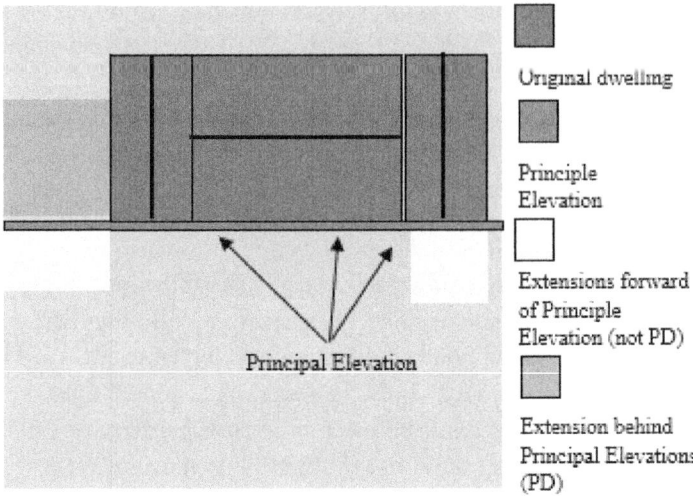

Figure 36.4: Birds eye view of Principal Elevation and extensions.

In some cases, you can end up in a situation where you may not be able to easily identify the principal elevation of a dwellinghouse, particularly where houses are built on corner plots. This can have significant impacts on your options for PD extensions. This is because where you may consider a side extension to be achievable, your LPA may think of it as an extension forward of the principal elevation - which would not be PD! I'll come back to this point in Chapter 40.

Finally, for all extensions, any materials used on the exterior of a dwelling must be either the same where practical, or of a similar appearance to those which are visible on the exterior of the existing dwelling.

HMO Property Set Up

Rear Extensions

With that brief overview, let's now turn our attention to looking at rear extensions, as these are commonly used to provide additional rooms within a HMO due to the availability of space often found at the back of a house. Rear extensions are popular as cost effective ways to create extra space and allow for the ground floor of a dwellinghouse to be easily reconfigured, whilst still providing access to the rear garden space.

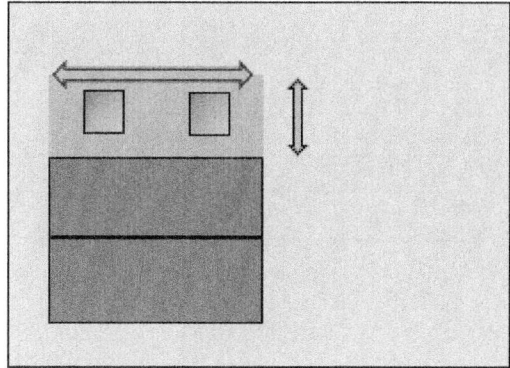

Figure 36.5: Birds eye view of a single storey rear extension across the full width of a detached dwelling, with skylights.

Single Storey Rear Extensions

Single storey extensions can be built beyond the rear wall of the original dwellinghouse up to four metres deep on detached houses, whilst for semi-detached and terraced houses, this is reduced to three metres deep. Regardless of the house type, for all extensions, the maximum roof height cannot be more

HMO Property Set Up

than four metres. This applies whether the roof is a flat roof or a pitched roof.

The width of the extension on the back of the dwellinghouse can be built across its full width, provided the original rear wall is 'flat' across the entire width of the house (i.e. there is no 'step' either in or out from the rear wall). Alternatively, the extension can be built part way across the width of the house to allow for access to the rear garden if a passageway runs along a side elevation of the property.

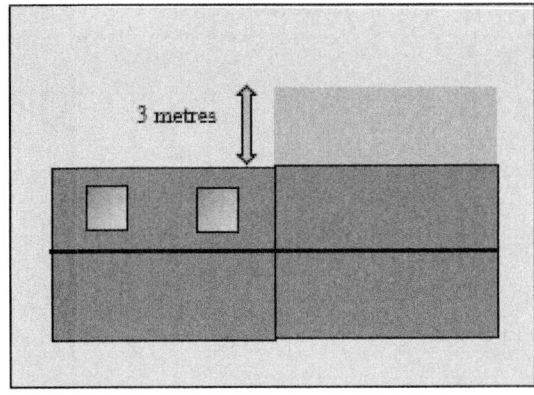

Figure 36.6.1: Birds eye view of single storey 3m deep rear extension across the full width of a semi-detached dwelling.

HMO Property Set Up

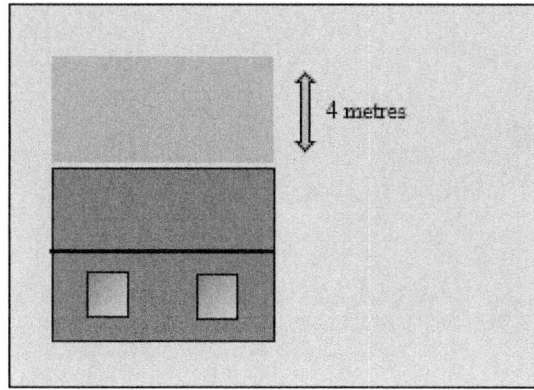

Figure 36.6.2: Birds eye view of single storey 4m deep rear extension across the full width of a detached dwelling, with skylights.

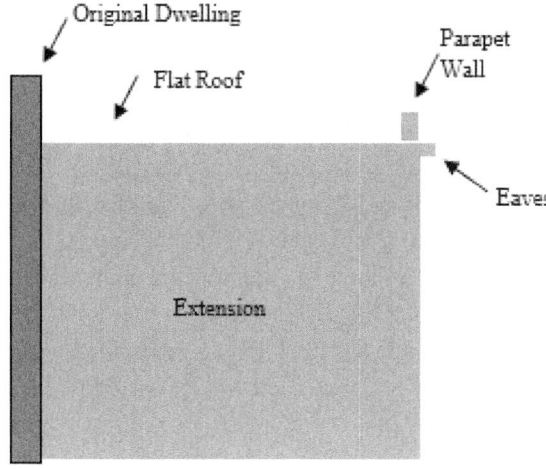

Figure 36.6.3: Side on view of an extension with a flat roof.

HMO Property Set Up

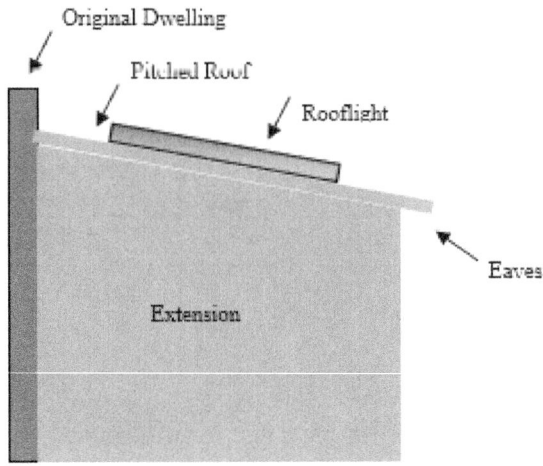

Figure 36.6.4: Side on view of an extension with a mono-pitched roof.

Prior Approval Rear Extensions

The respective four metre deep and three metre deep limits for single storey rear extensions can be doubled if an application for prior approval is submitted to your LPA. The prior approval application (known as a 'prior approval larger home extension application') currently carries a fee of £96 since being made permanent in 2019. This means on detached houses, a rear extension can be built up to eight metres deep, whilst on semi-detached and terraced houses, an extension can be built up to six metres deep, again across the whole width of the house, unless it is 'stepped', or if an access passageway is intended. The height of the extension is restricted to a maximum of four metres as well. These options for rear extensions create huge amounts of additional space either for use as bedrooms, or as large communal kitchen/diner areas,

HMO Property Set Up

for example, freeing up other rooms in a property for conversion to bedrooms.

Prior approval applications require the submission of an application form and scaled floorplans/elevations to the relevant LPA. The submission must include a written description of the proposed development including how far the enlarged part of the dwellinghouse extends beyond the rear wall of the original dwellinghouse, the maximum height of the enlarged part of the dwellinghouse and the height of the eaves of the enlarged part of the dwellinghouse. The submission should also include the addresses of any adjoining premises.

On validation, the LPA will notify you and consult with any adjoining neighbours they deem may be affected by the extension. This typically includes neighbours either side of a property, as well as to the rear, in some cases. Should any adjoining neighbours raise concerns or submit objections, the LPA is required to determine whether the impact on the amenities of adjoining properties is acceptable or not. Amenity impacts are material considerations and as such, can be tricky to distinguish. Usually they will include considerations such as loss of privacy, overshadowing, noise and loss of natural light. Importantly though, if a neighbour responds to say they are against the proposal, simply because they do not like the idea of it, this is not a planning concern and will likely be ignored by the LPA.

Provided your proposal is well-designed, doesn't have a significant impact on neighbour amenity and accords with relevant planning policy, there should be little justification for the LPA to reject your proposal. A decision should be issued within 42 days of validation being confirmed. If a decision is

HMO Property Set Up

not issued within the 42 day window and you have not agreed to an extension of time, this is typically deemed to signal an 'approval' by the LPA as they are obliged to notify the applicant as to whether prior approval is given or refused. Where prior approval is not required, the proposal can proceed in accordance with the submitted details.

In cases where it is considered the prior approval of the LPA is required, you may have to submit an application for householder planning permission, or provide additional information as part of a new application for prior approval.

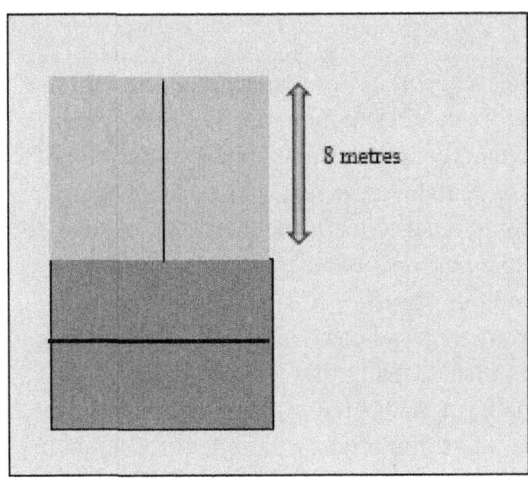

Figure 36.7.1: Birds eye view of a single storey 8m deep Prior Approval rear extension with pitched roof to a detached dwelling.

HMO Property Set Up

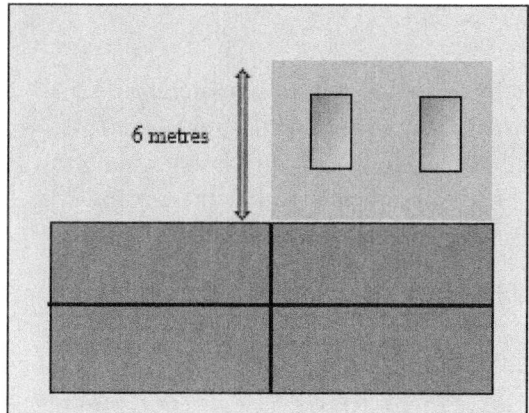

Figure 36.7.2: Birds eye view of a single storey 6m deep Prior Approval rear extension to a semi-detached dwelling, with skylights.

Rear Extensions Greater Than One Storey In Height

PD extensions where more than one storey is proposed are only able to be extended beyond the rear wall of the original dwellinghouse by a maximum of three metres deep, regardless of house type. These types of rear extensions can usually only be carried out where the extension would not result in there being less than seven metres between the rear wall of the extension and that of any rear boundary. Like single storey rear extensions, the width of the extension across the back of the dwellinghouse can be built full width, provided the original rear wall is flat across the entire width of the house (i.e. there is no 'step' either in or out from the rear wall) and the extension doesn't result in a wall of the extension being built within two metres of a side boundary (i.e. there must be a minimum two metre gap maintained). Due to the restrictions in relation to boundaries, it is likely that only detached houses

HMO Property Set Up

set amongst wide plots will be capable of benefitting from this type of PD.

The roof pitch on the extension must also match that of the existing house as far as is practical, whilst any upper floor windows proposed in a side elevation of the extension must be obscure-glazed and non-opening, unless the window opening is more than 1.7 metres above the floor level.

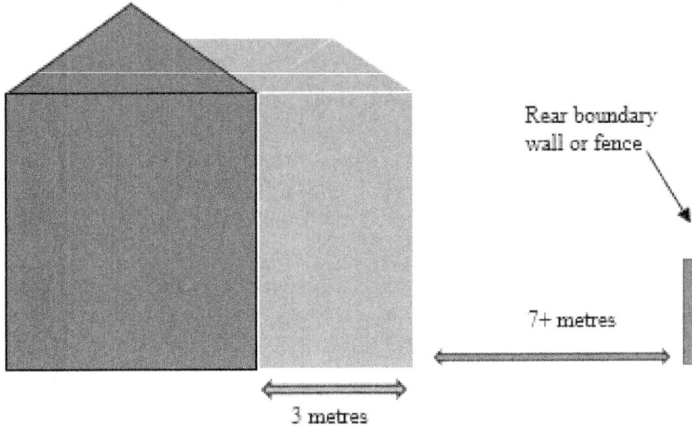

Figure 36.8: Side on view of a rear extension greater than one storey in height.

Single Storey Side Extensions

This type of extension can provide a generous ground floor addition to a property which may have been underutilised, either as a driveway or as part of a garden/garage previously. Side extensions can be built up to a maximum of half the width of the original house. Therefore, if the house is six metres wide, the extension can be up to three metres wide. Obviously, this width limit depends on the size of the plot and having space to extend to that width. When thinking about

HMO Property Set Up

side extensions, you may wish to consider how the rear of the property will be accessed. If you intend to build a side extension right up to the boundary, the rear garden and back of the house may only then be accessed through the house. This is potentially something which could be an issue during maintenance or repair works or if you intend to have bicycle storage or refuse storage in the rear garden space. It could also be a fire or emergency hazard, in the event that tenants need to leave the property. Many HMO developers therefore choose to leave enough space for a gateway and a side passage wide enough for bikes and refuse bins to fit through, as well as for emergency egress.

Single storey side extensions can only be built up to a maximum of four metres in height. If you wish to create a side extension of more than one storey, it will require planning permission as discussed previously. Roofs can be either flat or pitched and their design may depend on whether you want to mirror the existing roof form of the original house.

HMO Property Set Up

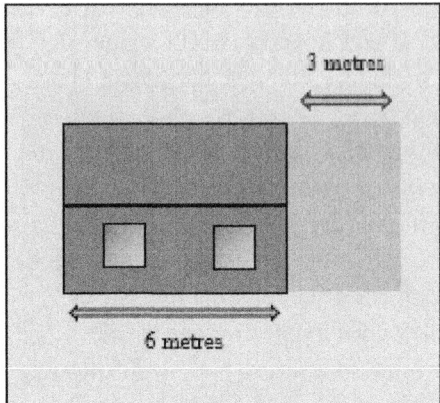

Figure 36.9: Birds eye view of single storey flat roof side extension.

Single Storey Side And Rear Extension Combinations

Using a combination of the above PD rights and their various limitations, you can create conjoined single storey side and rear extension, which help to maximise the floorspace and flexibility of the ground floor space for bedrooms or communal rooms. A number of the achievable combinations are available, including those shown in the following figures.

HMO Property Set Up

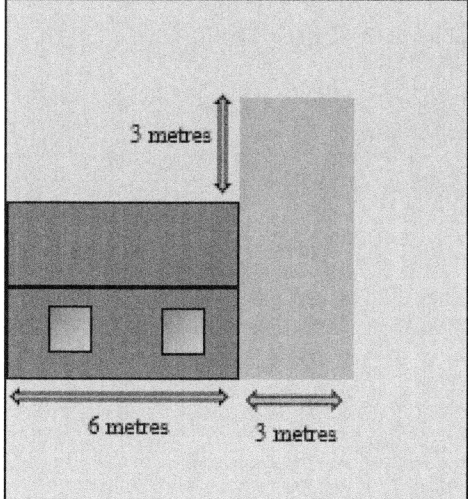

Figure 36.10.1: Birds eye view of a single storey side and rear extension combination to a semi-detached dwelling.

HMO Property Set Up

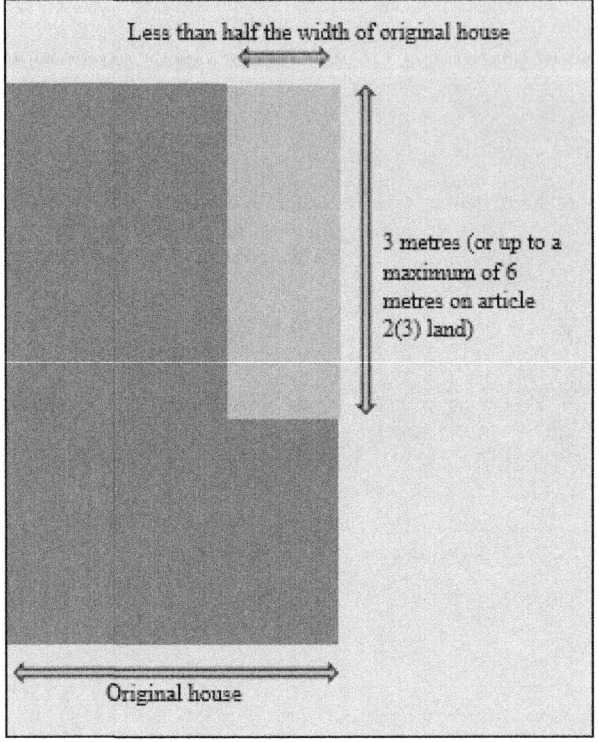

Figure 36.10.2: Birds eye view of a single storey side and rear extension combination to a semi-detached dwelling.

HMO Property Set Up

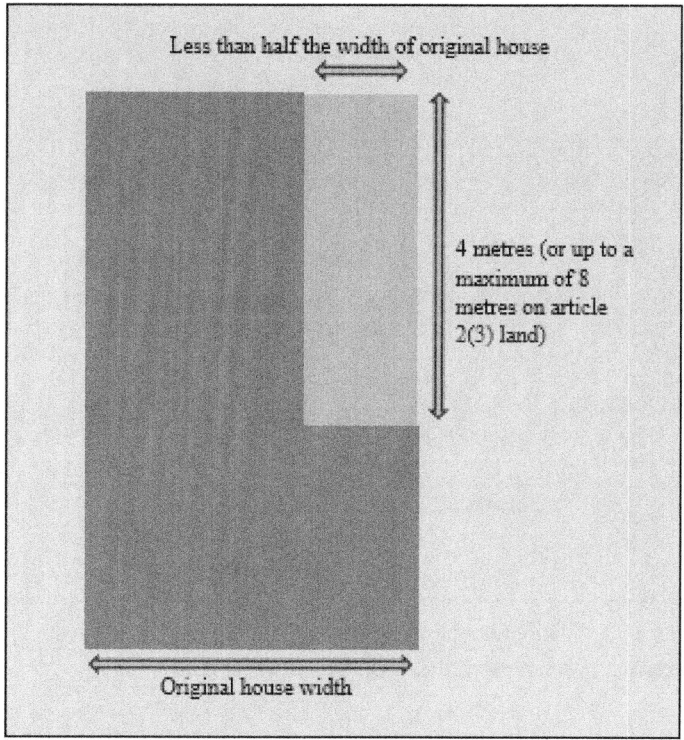

Figure 36.10.3: Birds eye view of a single storey side and rear extension combination to a detached dwelling.

HMO Property Set Up

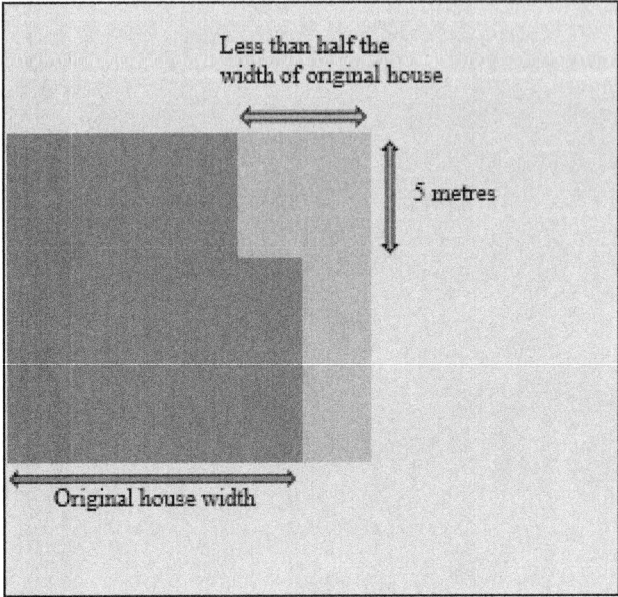

Figure 36.10.4: Birds eye view of a single storey side and rear extension combination to a semi-detached dwelling.

HMO Property Set Up

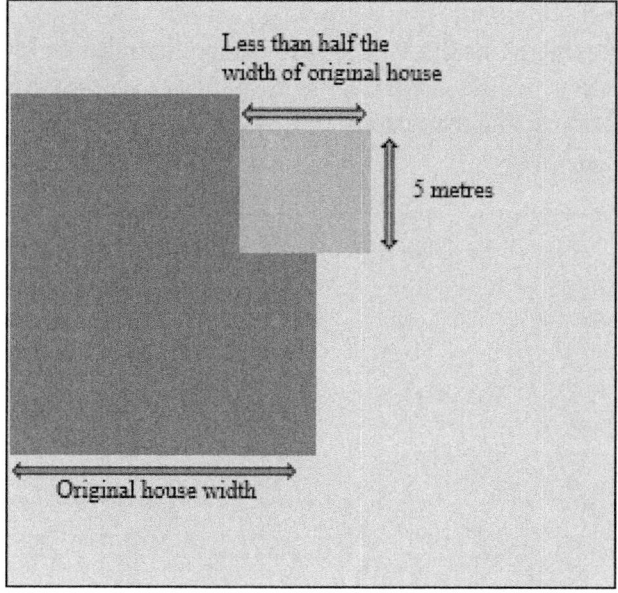

Figure 36.10.5: Birds eye view of a single storey side and rear extension combination to a semi-detached dwelling.

HMO Property Set Up

Separate Single Storey Side And Rear Extensions

Again, sticking to the limitations and requirements set out by the GPDO, there are options here to create both a single storey side extension and a rear extension which remain separate from one another:

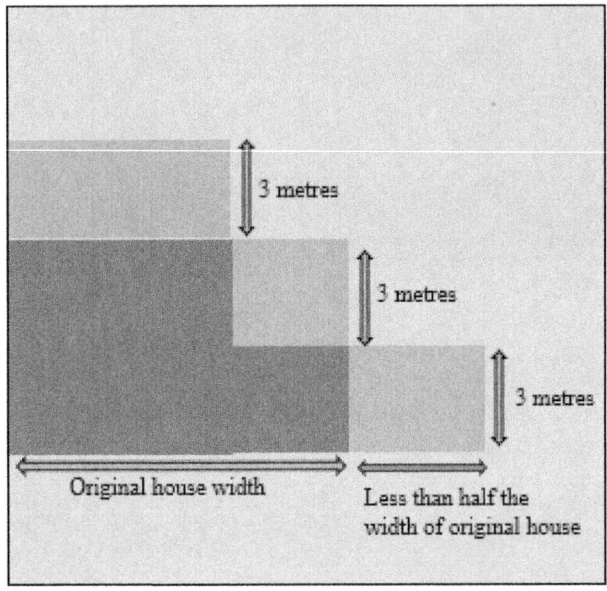

Figure 36.11.1: Birds eye view of separate single storey side and rear extension combinations to a semi-detached dwelling.

HMO Property Set Up

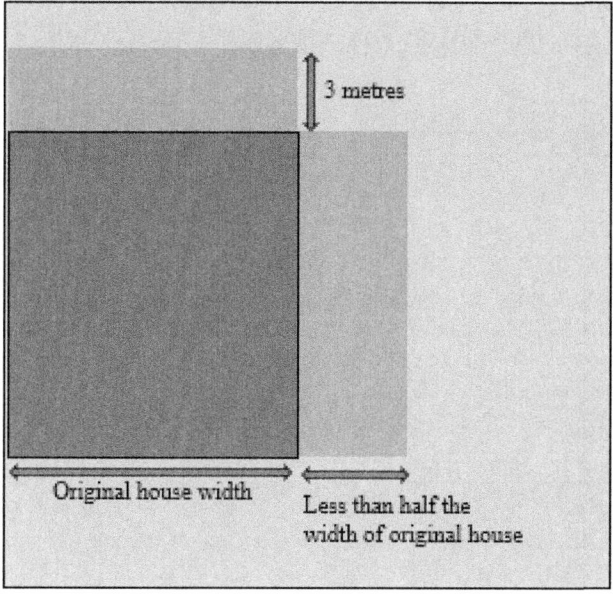

Figure 36.11.2: Birds eye view of separate single storey side and rear extension combinations to a semi-detached dwelling.

Conservatories

I have included conservatories as a separate option, but they are essentially subjected to the same limitations as single storey side and rear extensions. Some HMO developers choose to build conservatories as communal rooms, rather than extensions as it is typically cheaper to erect a conservatory than to create a brick-built extension. Conservatories can free up reception rooms to be used as bedrooms on the ground floor, but in general, the usefulness of these spaces for tenants may be limited, as conservatories are often known to either be too cold in the winter or too hot in the summer. Be sure to ask your HMO officer whether they would allow for a conservatory to be used as a dining room or lounge area – some might allow it where the room is well insulated.

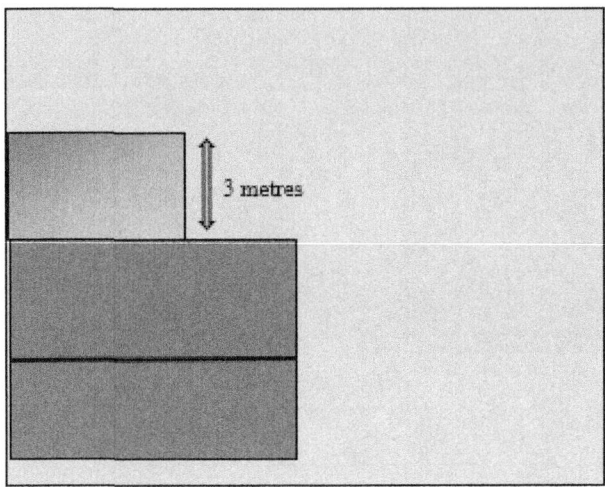

Figure 36.12: Birds eye view of conservatory to rear of semi-detached dwelling.

Other Householder PD Rights

These next few options now look at more general changes or works you can undertake to a property using householder PD rights.

Doors and Windows

Doors and windows can usually be repaired, replaced and/or installed using PD rights, provided the materials and styles used are in-keeping with those installed elsewhere around the

HMO Property Set Up

dwellinghouse. If a house is in a designated area[86], there may be additional restrictions placed on what you can and cannot do. Where any new windows are to be installed on the side elevation of an upper floor, these are required to be either non-opening, or more than 1.7 metres above the floor level. They must also be obscure glazed to protect privacy and prevent overlooking.

It is worth noting that the creation of new bay windows on a front elevation would require planning permission as these are classed as extensions forward of the principal elevation. However, bay windows on any other elevations (side or rear elevation) would be subject to the relevant PD rights for that

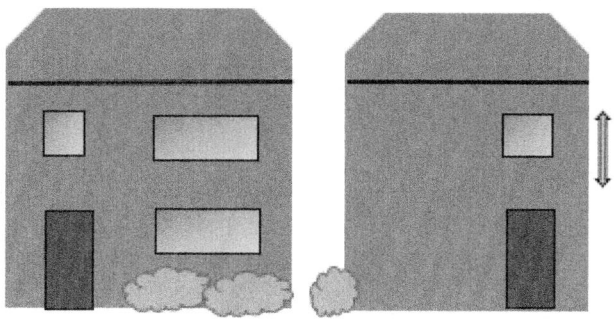

Doors and windows to be of a similar appearance to those already installed

Window to be obscure glazed and non-opening or more than 1.7 metres above floor level

Figure 36.13: Front and side view of doors and windows.

---

[86] See Chapter 39.

HMO Property Set Up

Garage Conversions – Integral Garages

Converting an existing garage attached to the main house (an integral garage) into a habitable room is an easy way to add additional space to a property without having to extend it further. Garage conversions largely involve internal works, which can usually be carried out using PD rights, alongside the removal of the garage door and the insertion of a new window and surrounding brickwork.

This is provided the brickwork and window do not extend forward of the principal elevation (i.e. the window elevation is flush with the side elevation brickwork and does not create a bay window) and the works do not involve enlarging the garage in any way, such as increasing the roof height, or digging down through the floor to achieve minimum ceiling heights, as these works would fall outside the scope of PD rights.

HMO Property Set Up

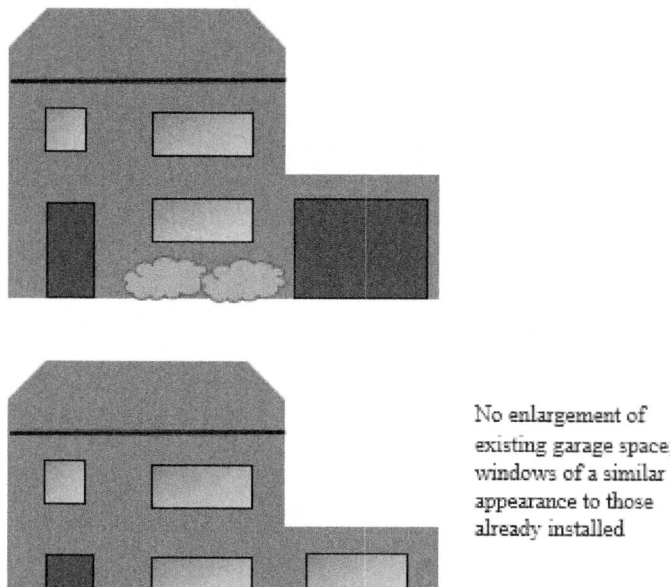

No enlargement of existing garage space; windows of a similar appearance to those already installed

Figure 36.14: Front view of integral garage conversion.

Garage Conversions – Detached Garages

If you come across a property where the garage is close to, but separate (detached) from the main house, you could either choose to do one of two things; 1) demolish the existing garage and erect a new extension adjoining the house in its place; or 2) seek to 'bridge the gap' between the house and the garage with a PD side or rear extension. Any extension to bridge this gap must be within the limits of PD rights (i.e. no more than half the width of the original house if to the side of the dwellinghouse or no more than three or four metres deep

HMO Property Set Up

if to the rear of the dwellinghouse), otherwise planning permission would be required. Once 'joined' to the main house, the garage could then be converted to provide additional sleeping accommodation or communal space. However, it would be advisable to check with your LPA that they agree with this strategy prior to undertaking any 'joining' works.

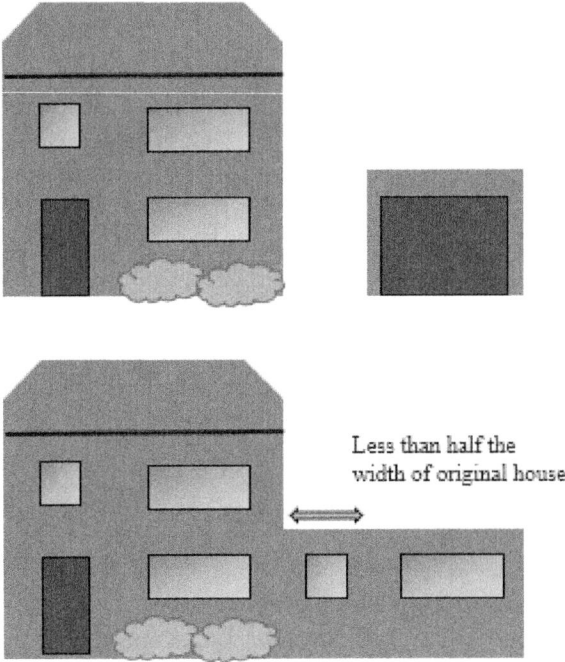

Figure 36.15: Front view of side extension and detached garage conversion.

HMO Property Set Up

Maximise Your PD Rights

Whilst conversions can usually be carried out with minimal disruption to the rest of the house, if you are already carrying out refurbishment works to the main dwelling, it makes sense to convert the garage at the same time. This maximises your PD rights whilst the property is still in C3 use and avoids having to call your builders back at a later stage to undertake further works. For example, you may wish to run a seven-bedroom Sui Generis HMO in the future, but you may initially only let the property as a six-bedroom C4 HMO to establish its use. Once converted, the garage can remain unoccupied until such time as you wish to apply for planning permission for the change of use. The disadvantage of this is that you may not be granted planning permission for use of the additional room. However, the room created could still be used in other ways, such as a home office for a tenant or a flexible communal workspace, storage room for either yours or your tenant's possessions, or as an additional communal space (gaming room/TV lounge).

Conversions To Separate Accommodation

Should you choose to convert a garage, whether integral or detached, into a separate dwelling from the main house, this cannot be carried out within the scope of PD rights. Instead you would require full planning permission as the garage would essentially become a separate planning unit. There would also be other considerations to think about such as access and parking, private amenity space, refuse provisions, utilities and amenity impacts.

HMO Property Set Up

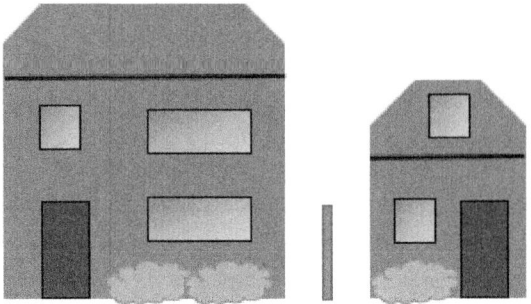

Figure 36.16: Conversions to separate accommodation.

Basement Conversion

In general, converting an existing basement into usable space can be achieved through PD rights, provide the conversion does not require any alterations to be made to the external appearance of the dwelling, for example, the installation of a new light well, and that the space will not be used to create a separate dwelling.

The creation of any new basement or works to deepen an existing basement would however require planning permission as it the works would involve significant excavation works beyond the scope of PD rights. Basement conversions only work if you are able to provide adequate space, lighting and headroom for the intended purpose. In most cases it is not likely you will be able to use a basement as a bedroom for tenants as it would not provide an acceptable amount of natural light or headroom. However, there is the option of using them for communal purposes or as utility areas, provided the ceiling height is sufficient. As with garage conversions, a converted basement could be used as a home office for a tenant or as a flexible workspace, storage room for

HMO Property Set Up

either yours or your tenant's possessions, or as an additional communal space (gaming room/TV lounge).

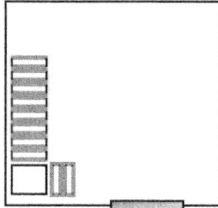 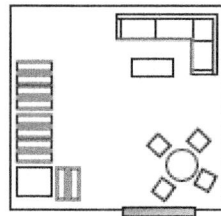

Figure 36.17: Birds eye view of basement conversion.

Paving A Front Garden

As is often the case, tenants will have cars they wish to park securely when living at your property. Expanding a driveway to include additional car parking spaces on a front garden can therefore be a great way of attracting tenants whilst avoiding on-street parking issues with neighbours! PD rights allow you to install or replace a driveway of any size on a front garden where permeable or porous surfacing is used. Permeable or porous surfacing can include gravel, shingle, loose stones, reinforced grass or resin-bound aggregates. However, should you wish to use impermeable materials for a driveway which don't allow water to drain to a permeable area, the area which can be covered is then limited to five square metres (about the size of two standard car parking spaces). Any larger than this and planning permission would be required.

HMO Property Set Up

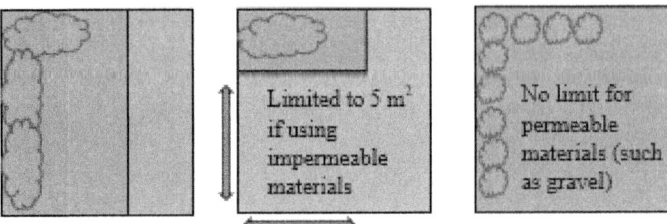

Figure 36.18: Birds eye view of paving a front garden.

Patio And Driveway

Excluding the front garden, should you wish to cover the rest of the land around a house, there are no size restrictions applicable in relation to what can be covered with hard surfacing at ground level. Whilst covering a garden in paving slabs or a patio may result in low maintenance, it is not likely to be very attractive to tenants, particularly in light of the Covid-19 pandemic where the benefits of quality outdoor amenity space became very important factors for tenants when deciding on where they wish to live. Where access allows and where you may not have space at the front of the property, you could cover a rear or side garden area in either a hard or permeable surfacing to provide off-road parking provisions. A permeable surface is preferrable as it will allow water to drain and avoid surface water flooding and runoff issues. If you are going to be using the rear garden for parking purposes, make sure there is suitable room for vehicles to access the rear parking area and to then turn and exit the property in a forward gear.

HMO Property Set Up

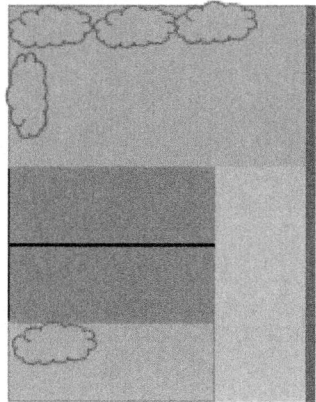 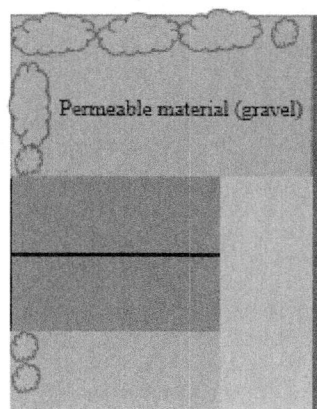

Figure 36.19: Patio and driveway alterations (to a detached dwelling with side access to rear garden).

Fences, Gates And Garden Walls

PD rights enable you to erect a new fence, gate or garden wall, provided that where it is located next to a highway used by vehicles, or a footpath of such a highway (pavement etc.), it would not be greater than one metre in height. Where it is to be erected away from a highway or footpath of such a highway, it should be no greater than two metres in height. Where any existing fences, walls or gates have been erected higher that the limits set out above, their height cannot be further increased and if you wished to replace, alter, maintain or improve any existing fences, walls or gates above the PD rights limitations, you would need to apply for planning permission.

PD rights for fences, walls and gates are removed where any part of the site forms part of a listed building or where it is within the curtilage of a listed building. Additionally, no fence, wall or gate or any other boundary involved can form a boundary with a neighbouring listed building or its curtilage.

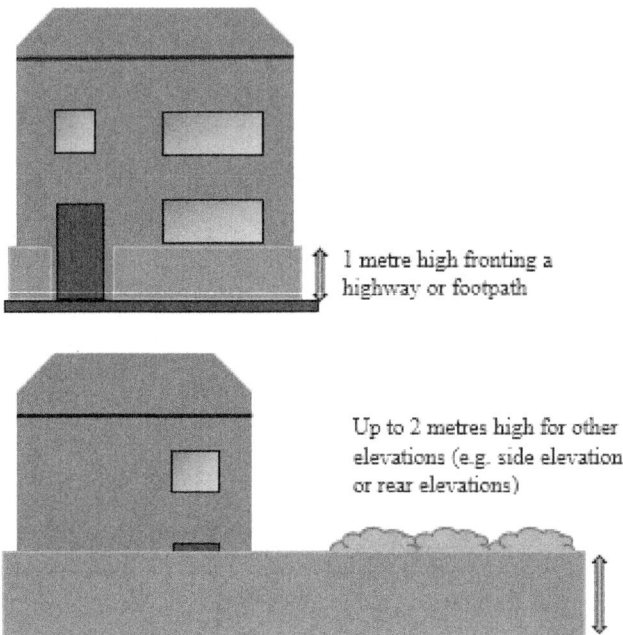

Figure 36.20: Fences, gates and garden wall alterations.

Trees And Hedging

When viewing a property which has trees within its curtilage, it is always worth checking whether any of these trees are protected by Tree Preservation Orders (TPOs). Most councils keep an interactive map of protected trees so you can check whether any trees are included by simply typing in 'TPO' or 'Tree Protection Map' into the search bar of the council's website and inputting the property address. As part of your checks, it is also worthwhile checking whether the property is within a conservation area as trees are automatically protected within these designations without a TPO, whilst the properties themselves may be subject to reduced PD rights (more on this in Chapter 39).

Where a property you are interested in is located within a Conservation Area and has trees within its curtilage, works to prune or fell these protected trees requires consent from the LPA. It is an offence to fell or prune a protected tree without prior consent and you could risk a hefty fine for unauthorised works. Planning permission, however, is not required when planting hedging and whilst there are no laws controlling how high hedges are allowed to be grown, as the property owner, you have a responsibility to ensure that any hedge planted is maintained and does not become a nuisance to either tenants or neighbours. In most domestic cases, where you wish to remove a hedge, no planning permission is required either, although some special circumstances may apply. These special circumstances can include if the hedge is part of a condition of planning permission, or if it is on or runs alongside a local nature reserve. Remember – if in doubt about the status of a tree or hedge, contact your LPA for further advice before pulling out the chainsaw and branch cutters!

Trees Within Conservation Areas

As briefly explained, TPOs are not normally designated to trees within a conservation area. However, as you may know, local councils have a duty to preserve or enhance the character and appearance of conservation areas. Trees can play a significant role in achieving this objective; hence they are protected by the conservation area.

HMO Property Set Up

If you wished to carry out works to a tree within a conservation area that is not subject to a TPO, you are still required to give at least six weeks' notice to the LPA, unless the tree is dead, dying or dangerous (i.e. it could fall and injure someone). Upon receipt of a notification of intention to prune or remove a tree, the LPA must decide if the tree is considered to 'preserve and enhance' the conservation area. Where it is decided the tree does not fulfil these purposes, the LPA should provide consent for its removal or pruning, or they may allow the notice to lapse without response. Where notifications are refused, a TPO is likely to then be imposed to protect the tree, although you can challenge this.

Electric Vehicle Charging Points

As you will no doubt be aware, electric vehicles are becoming increasingly popular - and with them is a growing demand for convenient charging points. By installing at least one charging point, this can help future-proof the property against any changes in legislation or local policy and it may even help with attracting tenants who are seeking to, or who already use, more sustainable modes of transport.

There are two options when providing a charging point - a wall mounted outlet and an outlet mounted on an upstand. For wall mounted electrical outlets to recharge electric vehicles, PD rights exist provided that the area where the outlet is located is used for off-street parking. The outlet and its casing must be smaller than 0.2 cubic metres and must not face onto or be within two metres of a highway. Additionally, the outlet must not be within the curtilage of a listed building or within a site designated as a Scheduled Monument.

HMO Property Set Up

For outlets mounted on an upstand, PD rights also allow these to be installed, again provided the area where the outlet is located is used for off-street parking. The upstand and the outlet must be smaller than 1.6 metres in height from ground level, where the vehicle will be parked within the curtilage of a dwellinghouse. The upstand must not be within two metres of a highway either. As with outlets, the upstand must not be within the curtilage of a listed building or within a site designated as a Scheduled Monument. PD rights also only allow for one upstand to be provided for each parking space.

Additional Storeys And Upwards Extensions

You may be aware that the Government introduced new PD rights on 31st August 2020, allowing for upwards extensions on a number of existing properties, including dwellinghouses. This PD right does not extend to allowing for C3 dwellinghouses to be converted into C4 HMOs, however, this does not mean you couldn't apply for full planning permission to convert the extended dwellinghouse into a Sui Generis HMO. I would point out here though that this would be considered a high-risk strategy, particularly when you think about the reason why this PD right was brough in:

"It will mean that families can add up to two storeys to their home, providing much-needed additional space for children or elderly relatives as their household grows[87]."

Therefore, unless your fallback position would be to operate the extended property as a standard buy-to-let, you would be better off applying for planning permission from the get-go

---

[87] Housing Secretary Rt Hon Robert Jenrick MP, 21st July 2020.

HMO Property Set Up

for an upward extension, or just sticking with normal PD rights if there is sufficient space to do so.

Outbuildings

Outbuildings are considered as separate structures from the main dwellinghouse, used for a purpose 'incidental to the enjoyment of a dwellinghouse[88]' and can be constructed using PD rights. The definition of an outbuilding is broad and so it can be applied to any number of structures, including sheds, greenhouses, home offices and even swimming pools and gyms to name a few. From a HMO perspective, outbuildings cannot be used as sleeping accommodation. Firstly, you would need planning permission as it would be akin to a separate dwelling. Secondly, you would not be granted an HMO license where one bedroom was separate from the rest of the house (this could potentially be seen as having a 'beds in sheds' setup, which is definitely frowned upon by the local authority).

So, what benefits can an outbuilding provide for your HMO? Well, you could use one to provide a safe and secure place for tenants to store their bicycles, as a refuse and recycling storage area or as an area for tenants to some of their possessions. It could even be used as a place for you to keep spare furniture or replacement fixtures and fixings on site but separate from the main dwelling. Additionally, as outbuildings are such versatile spaces, they can also be used as part of a separate communal space for your tenants to

---

[88] This is a broad concept, subject to matter and fact of degree in each case but Planning Inspectors have concluded this can include uses connected with the running of a dwellinghouse or with domestic and leisure activities of the persons living in it.

HMO Property Set Up

enjoy, for example, as a garden room in the summer. This can be particularly useful if you need to negotiate with an HMO licensing officer over the amount of communal space available. Of course, as with all PD rights, there are a number of conditions which need to be met in order for an outbuilding to be erected under PD. These include:

- No more than half the area of land around the original house can be covered by additions or outbuildings;

- Outbuildings are not allowed on land which is in front of a wall forming a principal elevation (i.e. you can't put a shed in the front garden without planning permission);

- Outbuildings, including garages, can only be single storey structures with a maximum eaves height of 2.5 metres and a maximum overall height of three metres if a mono-pitch or a flat roof is constructed;

- For outbuildings with a duo-pitched roof, the maximum eaves height remains at 2.5 metres, but the overall maximum height allowed is four metres;

- Where an outbuilding is located within two metres of a boundary of the curtilage of the dwelling house, the maximum height is reduced down to 2.5 metres; and

- Balconies, verandas and raised platforms above 0.3 metres in height are prohibited.

HMO Property Set Up

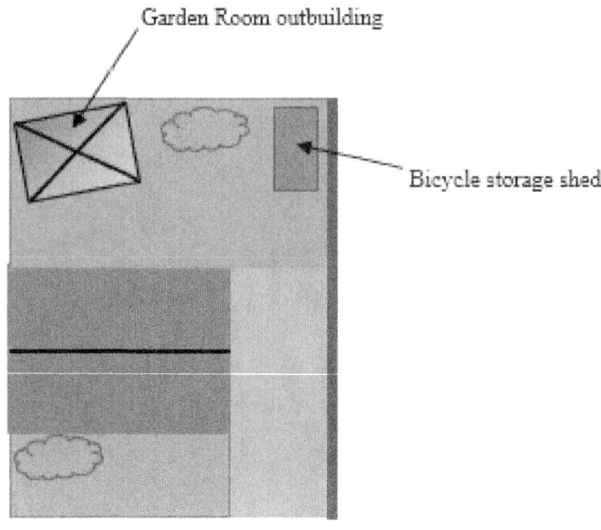

Figure 36.21: Birds eye view of outbuilding examples.

37. Adding Value And Fallback Positions

Adding Value

Property is a competitive market, so knowing how to add value to a dwelling is essential for capitalising on your investment. Now that you have a good understanding of what can be done to a property using householder PD rights and through change of use, this can feed into how you approach the refurbishment of a dwelling, although it remains important to ensure that what you are intending to do will actually result in value being added to the property.

Extensions, such as single storey or double storey and conversions, including garage, basement and loft conversions can increase the value of a property by up to 20%, although as extensions and conversions come in all shapes and sizes, this figure will obviously vary depending on exactly what is proposed. The key thing to take away here is that by extending a property to make use of the space around it, you can really improve its potential as a HMO when it is revalued, although works to extend will obviously depend more heavily on capital investment. Research by Checkatrade[89] identifies that a loft conversion or a garage conversion which creates a bedroom with an ensuite can increase the value of a property by 20%, whilst a single storey extension will add on average five to eight percent. A double storey extension can add up to 12%. Internally, a new kitchen can add up to ten percent to the value of a property, whilst a bathroom can add five percent.

---

[89] https://www.checkatrade.com/blog/how-to/add-value-to-your-home/.

HMO Property Set Up

This, combined with good interior design, is also a great way of increasing your return on a HMO.

If you are on a budget, works to the interior can be effective at increasing the value of your HMO property and are often simpler to undertake, being relatively cost-effective. However, these works can provide a significant 'wow' factor – both for a valuer and for prospective tenants and can increase interest in your property as well as bump up your returns, as many HMO properties available can appear rundown and tired looking. By taking the opportunity to improve the interior of your property through the installation of new doors, new flooring and carpets, painting walls, adding feature walls and eye-catching art or pictures, these small changes can improve the rental rates for each room. Interesting and creative designs alongside spacious bedrooms are particularly desirable and in demand for tenants. Chapters 69 to 71 go into more detail around refurbishment and design.

External spaces are just as important to tenants nowadays as internal spaces. A well-designed garden space can therefore increase the value of your property by up to ten percent in some cases, and make it more appealing to tenants, so it is well worth spending some of your budget on the landscaping of private garden spaces which your tenants can make use of and enjoy. Even where you propose to use some of the rear garden space for parking, a well-designed and attractive courtyard space or patio area, for example, can dramatically improve the attractiveness of a property and add value.

Fallback Positions

Smaller HMOs will naturally have less wear and tear as fewer people live in them, but they are less profitable because of

HMO Property Set Up

this, whilst larger HMOs are typically more profitable, but often are more expensive to set up and maintain. There is usually a balance to be had between the two types of HMO, where the set up and ongoing costs provide suitable income, without great expense. When looking for properties, it is important to try and find where value can be added without overspending on refurbishments and works to extend. Therefore, should you decide you do need to apply for planning permission for a larger extension or alteration than PD rights allow to make the property 'work', always have in the back of your mind a PD rights 'fallback position'. This is so that if permission is refused, the property you buy, or are in the process of buying, will still work for you from a financial and operational perspective. For example, if a larger rear extension is refused planning permission, will a smaller standard PD extension still offer the space you need without compromising the layout of the property?

Another example would be if you bought a property with the intention of using it as a seven-bedroom Sui Generis HMO. You could carry out the necessary building and refurbishment works to create seven bedrooms and the communal space required. However, you may then find your application is refused planning permission for occupancy by seven people. Whilst you can appeal the decision, it is essential you make sure the property still works financially as a six-bedroom C4 HMO. If the figures only stack up as a six-bedroom HMO, don't then over-extend your finances by carrying out the extra building works to make that seventh bedroom. Where you over stretch your budget, you may well only find yourself struggling to make up the difference, particularly if you have any void periods, or there is a change to legislation which

HMO Property Set Up

requires you to spend extra money to improve your property (such as meeting changes to EPC legislation, for example[90]).

Unless you resubmit an amended planning application to address the reason(s) for refusal, or appeal against the decision (see Chapter 45), that seventh room, if built, must remain unoccupied. However, as discussed previously and as a fallback position, that seventh room could be used as a separate storeroom for a tenant's possessions, or even as a 'work from home' office or additional communal area or TV/gaming room for your tenants. Use of the room in this way may allow you to increase the collective rental rate, as your tenants will be able to benefit from the use of the extra space. It may not add up to the amount you'd receive if the room was let to another tenant, but it can certainly help plug the gap!

---

[90] See Chapter 73.

38. When To Carry Out Works Using PD Rights

It is important to remember that if you obtain planning permission for a Sui Generis HMO, only once that permission is enacted (i.e. the seventh tenant moves into the property), you lose the right to carry out any householder PD works discussed in the previous chapters. This is because the use of the property is no longer deemed to be in the 'C3' use class and so householder PD rights do not apply. Therefore, if you wish to make the most of these PD rights, it is advisable to carry out all PD works whilst the property is in the C3 use class, including the creation of additional bedrooms through extensions, garage conversions or loft conversions.

Assuming the property is not within an A4D area, once all the works under PD have been completed and you have obtained a HMO licence, you can then let the property out as a C4 HMO for occupation by up to six tenants. Any additional bedrooms above six can remain empty, or can be used as part of the communal space, or for storage, until such time as you are ready to apply for planning permission to rent the remaining rooms out.

When going through the licensing process, if you intend for the property to be occupied by seven or more tenants in individual bedrooms, make sure to apply for a licence for the intended maximum number of occupants. That way you won't have to amend the licence once planning permission is granted. Some HMO officers do request that planning permission is in place for the maximum number of tenants/bedrooms prior to the licence being issued, but there is usually some discretion in this. Obviously, there is a risk of

HMO Property Set Up

having planning permission refused, meaning any additional rooms created remain empty, but as discussed in the previous chapter, you should ensure the property is capable of covering its costs and works for you from a financial perspective as a C4 HMO as a minimum.

39. Removal/Reduction Of PD Rights And Other Common HMO Planning Obstacles

As I mentioned in previous chapters, there are several ways in which PD rights can be withdrawn. In these circumstances, you would need to apply for planning permission. In some cases, you may even need to obtain consent from a benefactor or seek insurance against enforcement (more on this in Chapter 59). There are also several common 'planning obstacles' that may affect the way you approach a HMO development project, which I have sought to cover for you below. Let's start by discussing previous works carried out by others using PD rights.

Previous Works Under PD Rights By Others

Imagine that you come across a good-sized semi-detached house which has already been extended by a previous owner. A three metre deep, full width extension has been built across the back of the house and a dormer extension utilising 30 cubic metres of additional space in the loft using PD rights. In this situation, the rear extension could not be extended any further using ordinary PD rights because you are unable to extend an extension and the extension which has been built utilises the full three metre depth allowance for a semi-detached dwelling.

If, however, the existing rear extension was built to be only two metres deep, you would be able to extend back a further meter, utilising the remaining one metre allowance under PD rights. However, you would not be able to extend back any further as this would be outside of the PD allowance. Therefore, should you wish to extend any further, you could either apply for prior approval to extend up to an additional

HMO Property Set Up

three metres deep (utilising the full six metre allowance), including demolition of the existing extension where necessary or apply for householder planning permission to either demolish the existing extension completely and rebuild a new extension in its place, or extend what has already been built, which would be subject to planning policies and the LPAs design guidance.

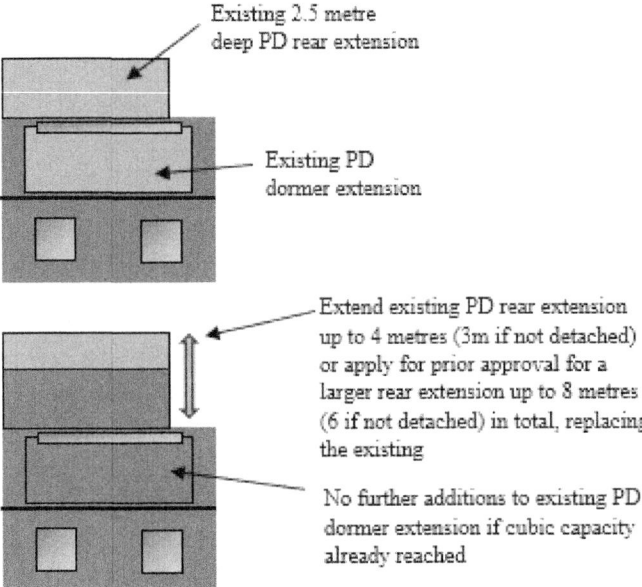

Figure 39.1: Birds eye view of previous PD work by others to a detached dwelling and options for remaining PD rights for a rear extension.

HMO Property Set Up

Let's now take a look at a dormer extension in this example.

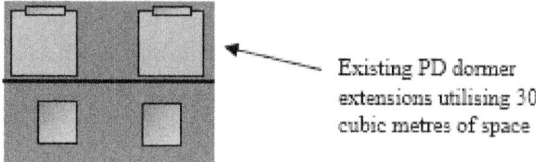

Existing PD dormer extensions utilising 30 cubic metres of space

Figure 39.2: birds eye view of previous works under PD to create a dormer extension.

Let's assume the previous owners of a detached dwelling decided they didn't need to utilise the full 50 cubic metre allowance and only built a dormer extension which gave them 30 cubic metres of additional space in the loft. Therefore, if you intended to create further additional loft space, this would be limited to the remaining 20 cubic metres of space only, again unless you applied for something larger via planning permission, which would be subject to planning policies and the LPAs design guidance.

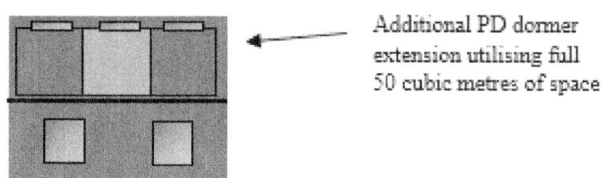

Additional PD dormer extension utilising full 50 cubic metres of space

Figure 39.3: Birds eye view of PD rights for a dormer extension/loft conversion on a detached dwelling, where full allowance is utilised.

Instead of extending the existing loft or rear extension further, you may consider there is suitable space for a side extension

293

HMO Property Set Up

to be erected which would provide a good layout for your HMO. However, this is where you may need to take account of the size of the plot and the extent of existing extensions, as only half the area of land around the original house is able to be covered by extensions or other buildings (outbuildings).

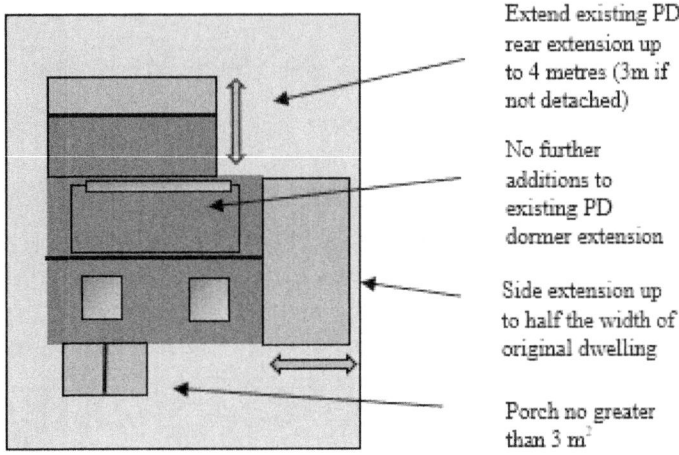

Figure 39.4: Birds eye view of maximising your remaining PD rights on a detached dwelling.

Whilst there may therefore be adequate space for a side extension to be built, if it would exceed the above 50% limit, you would need to apply for planning permission. Most houses have reasonable sized plots allowing you to build side and rear extensions without exceeding this limit, but it is always worth bearing in mind the extent of works carried out by previous owners and how this may remove or reduce your options when it comes to PD rights.

HMO Property Set Up

Previous Planning History

In this scenario, imagine the same house as before, but the previous owners have chosen to carry out a two-storey rear extension which was larger than PD rights allow and so required householder planning permission. If you can, be sure to check the decision notice for that permission very carefully to see if there are any restrictions on further works to the property. An example of this would be the removal of PD rights by way of a condition. Where this kind of condition exists, you would need to apply for planning permission to carry out any further physical works to alter the external of the property or seek to try and get the condition removed or varied.

It is worthwhile also checking for any refusal notices relating to the property too, as this provides a good indication of what the LPA may find acceptable in the context of that location. Bear in mind the age of any decisions as if they are over ten years old, the local development plan will likely have been updated and the LPAs approach to residential extensions and design may have changed as well.

Article 4 Directions

An Article 4 Direction (A4D) is a piece of legislation under Article 4 of the GPDO, which allows either the Secretary of State, or the LPA to remove certain PD rights related to either an operational development or the change of use of a property or group of buildings across a defined geographic area. Essentially, an A4D allows the LPA to maintain a greater degree of control over a specified type of development or use. The removal of PD rights can be temporary or made permanent, depending on whether its introduction is deemed to be 'successful' in doing what it was brought in to increase control over.

Where PD rights are removed by an A4D, that development is deemed to require planning permission. It is important to note that the introduction of an A4D does not mean that the type of development is no longer allowed. It simply enables the LPA the opportunity to have greater control over the development by considering any proposals received in more detail. The LPA is then able to decide whether permission should be granted or refused.

A4Ds can be introduced as immediate or non-immediate directions. Due to the level of consultation required, non-immediate directions usually take a year to be brought into force. This time period generally allows for works or changes to be completed prior to the introduction of the direction. For example, if you are midway through a HMO refurbishment when an announcement is made, you should have plenty of time to finish the works and tenant your property before the Direction is introduced.

Provided the house is occupied by at least three unrelated individuals prior to the introduction date, the property is lawfully considered to be a HMO. If timelines for completion are looking tight but your property is largely finished to an acceptable licensing standard, you may even be able to let it to your builders whilst they complete the works to establish the use as a HMO. Another important matter to note is that A4Ds cannot prevent development which has already been commenced or which has already been carried out (i.e. Directions are not applied retrospectively).

HMO Property Set Up

Article 4 Directions and Houses In Multiple Occupation

A4Ds relating to HMOs are usually known as Article 4(1) Directions (directions affecting other buildings). These are generally introduced by the LPA when increasingly large numbers of HMO properties already exist in either one particular area or street, or across a whole borough which might have the effect of changing the character of the area. The introduction of this A4D relates specifically to the PD right for the change of use of C3 dwellinghouses to C4 HMOs so other PD rights for householder works are not affected unless other restrictions apply.

As mentioned, the introduction of an A4D allows the LPA to regain an element of control over how many new HMOs are able to be created and can therefore be used as 'tools' in some cases to prevent 'sandwiching', to avoid standard residential dwellings from being 'flanked' on either side by HMOs, which could affect their amenities and quality of living. Always check whether a property you are interested in is covered by an A4D. The simplest way to check this is to go onto your local authority's website and search for 'Article 4 Direction'. Alternatively, navigate to the planning section and look for advice on PD rights or planning policy.

If A4Ds have been brought in, or are being brought in, look for the map of the area covered or the list of streets covered by the A4D. Make sure to check the boundaries thoroughly as in some cases, the boundary can mean C3 dwellinghouses on one side of a road have their PD rights removed for change of use to HMOs, whilst other dwellinghouses on the other side do not. Getting this wrong can obviously have a great impact upon your ability to convert a property into a C4 HMO without planning permission!

HMO Property Set Up

It is worth noting that some LPAs opt for implementing an A4D over specific areas, wards or streets, as is found in Bristol and Poole for example, whilst other LPAs opt for a blanket covering, meaning properties across entire cities, such as Manchester, Southampton and Portsmouth, have no PD rights for change of use to a HMO. Usually, where a new A4D is introduced, a Supplementary Planning Document (SPD) or Guidance (SPG) is prepared alongside it by the LPA to provide advice on when new C4 HMOs or Sui Generis HMOs may be acceptable. For example, the LPA may introduce a policy which permits only a certain percentage of properties to be converted to HMOs in any given street, or within a 50-metre radius of an application site.

If you are seeking to buy a C3 dwellinghouse in an A4D area, it is advisable to buy the property subject to planning permission, as there is no guaranteed planning permission would be granted. However, if you are seeking to buy an existing HMO in an A4D area, these can often fetch quite a premium as their perceived value is greater because there are either no more or reduced numbers of new HMOs being permitted in that area. There are other considerations to think about when buying existing HMOs, particularly in A4D areas, but I'll come onto those in Chapter 41.

Other Common HMO Planning Obstacles

This next part of the chapter covers a number of other considerations for HMO property developers to take account of when setting up a HMO, which can affect the location of a HMO and the use of householder PD rights.

HMO Property Set Up

Article 2(3) and Article 2(4) Designated Land

Under Schedule 1, Parts 1 and 2 of the GPDO 2015 (as amended), PD rights are restricted or can be removed altogether on Article 2(3) and 2(4) designated land. This relates to land within:

Article 2(3) Designated Land
Conservation Areas
An Area of Outstanding Natural Beauty (AONB)
An area specified by the Secretary of State for the purposes of Section 41(3) of the Wildlife and Countryside Act 1981 (enhancement and protection of the natural beauty and amenity of the countryside)
The Broads
A National Park
A World Heritage Site
Article 2(4) Designated Land
The Broads
A National Park
Land outside the boundaries of a National Park within specific parishes of the districts of Allerdale, Eden and South Lakeland and the borough of High Peak

Table 39.1: Article 2(3) and Article 2(4) Designated Land.

In most of the above cases, with the exception of conservation areas, it is unlikely you would want to set up an HMO property in any of these designed land areas anyway as most are likely to be rural locations which do not benefit from suitable population densities or would present inaccessible locations for the majority of tenants. However, it is worth noting you may need to apply for planning permission for some works which would ordinarily be allowed using PD

HMO Property Set Up

rights, so checking with your LPA and the guidance on their website before undertaking any works is worthwhile.

Conservation Areas

Conservation areas are designated under the Planning (Listed Building and Conservation Areas) Act 1990[91]. The purpose of a conservation area is to protect the look and character of buildings or structures within these designated areas. Conservation areas represent one of the most common ways in which PD rights are reduced or removed, typically removing PD rights for minor works, such as erecting fences or walls, installing satellite dishes or external repainting, for example.

Restrictions can also include extensions or additions to existing properties, outbuildings, flues, chimneys and soil pipes or vents, the type of external cladding allowed and the insertion of dormer windows in some cases, as well as proposals to demolish or partially demolish buildings.

A4Ds can be introduced in conservation areas, where the LPA deems works under PD rights could harm the special character and significance of the area due to the existence of buildings of special historical or architectural importance. These are known as Article 4(2) Directions (directions affecting dwellinghouses in Conservation Areas) and can be introduced to control works which have the potential to threaten the character of an area of acknowledge importance. Like Article 4(1) directions, Article 4(2) directions allow LPAs a much greater degree of control over what works can or cannot be

---

[91] https://www.legislation.gov.uk/ukpga/1990/9/contents.

carried out to a property, as the LPA has a duty to preserve and where possible enhance these areas.

Any works restricted through the A4D would therefore need planning permission and you may need to produce a heritage assessment or statement to support a planning application and specify the use of specific conservation area-friendly materials and items such as windows, doors, brick types and tiles in keeping with the character and local context of the area. It is important as part of your due diligence to check whether a property you are interested in is within a conservation area as this may affect your options to extend or alter the property and the materials, colours and textures you are able to use.

To find out whether a property is within a conservation area, head to the LPAs website as most will either have online maps which show the conservation area boundaries, whilst others may only have a list of areas or parishes which are affected by these areas. Typing in 'Conservation Area' into the LPA search box should bring up the information you need. Alternatively, navigate to the planning pages and then look for the links to either heritage or conservation. Some conservation areas are also accompanied by their own appraisals or management plans, which detail the history of the area, the range of restrictions applicable and what types of development are considered 'in-keeping'. Some LPAs may even have their own design guidance for specific conservation areas, so it is worth considering this with an experienced architect before embarking on a project which would result in external changes to a property in a conservation area.

It is worth remembering that in a conservation area, PD rights do still exist for the change of use of a C3 dwellinghouse into

HMO Property Set Up

a C4 HMO and vice versa, unless removed by a separate A4D. However, do be sure to clarify this with your LPA prior to commencing any works, just to make sure they are of the same understanding. Whilst this may not be specifically applicable to most HMO development projects, it is worth noting that the demolition of an unlisted building of more than 115 cubic metres in a conservation area or the demolition of a gate, fence or other type of enclosure higher than one metre if abutting a highway, or two metres elsewhere, without the consent of the LPA is not allowed and would be a seen as 'unlawful' demolition which is a criminal offence, for which the maximum penalty can be up to two years' imprisonment or an unlimited fine.

Listed Buildings

Listed Buildings are buildings, objects or structures which have been judged to be of national importance due to their architectural or historic interest and are protected buildings or structures under the Planning (Listed Buildings and Conservation Areas) Act 1990. This could be due to their age, rarity, aesthetic merits, selectivity and state of repair. Listed buildings can be either within a designated conservation area or simply stand as individual buildings, objects or structures. There are three grades of listing, where the higher the grade, the more importance is attached to the preservation of the building:

HMO Property Set Up

Grade Listings
Grade I – buildings of exceptional national importance
Grade II* - important buildings of more than special interest with some national significance
Grade II – buildings of special interest but of more local importance

Table 39.2: Graded Listings.

A searchable register and interactive map of listed buildings, their descriptions and why they are considered important is kept by Historic England[92]. Where a property is registered as a listed building, most PD rights will no longer apply and planning permission would be required for pretty much all external alterations and extensions.

Your LPA is also likely to retain a register of listed buildings, as well as a register of 'locally listed buildings' which are not on the official register but are nonetheless considered locally important 'landmark' buildings, objects or structures. The full range of PD rights is available for locally listed buildings, provided they are not located within a conservation area. Where a property is a locally listed building within a conservation area, PD rights will be reduced and subject to the same restrictions as other unlisted buildings within the conservation area. Where proposals are perceived to result in harm to a building or group of buildings, the LPA can seek to introduce an A4D for a specific building or buildings within that area to protect them from works under PD rights.

Buildings, objects, sites, places and structures can also be deemed as 'non-designated' heritage assets (NDHAs), which is slightly different from local listings. Identified NDHAs can

---

[92] https://historicengland.org.uk/.

have a degree of significance earning consideration in planning decisions because of their heritage interest, but do not meet the criteria for a designated heritage asset (DHA). Locally listed buildings are NDHAs, but not all NDHAs are locally listed. LPAs can identify a NDHA at any point, with many only being identified following the submission of a planning application. However, the LPA must provide sound justification for doing so as just because a building is old does not mean it should automatically be considered as an NDHA.

Listed Building Consent

As with conservation areas, it is an offence to carry out works that would require listed building consent, without first obtaining consent from the LPA where demolition or works which would alter or extend a building noted as having special architectural or historic interest would affect its character. Again, the maximum penalty would be two years' imprisonment or an unlimited fine.

This means you will typically be required to apply for listed building consent for any proposed works to alter, extend or demolish where it may affect the character of a building which is of special interest. Designated buildings are protected both internally and externally, so works which require consent include the replacement of windows or any internal alterations, such as moving doorways or staircases or the removal of a chimney breast, for example.

To apply for listed building consent, this is a separate process from planning permission. Applications are submitted to the LPA, whether planning permission is required or not. If planning permission is required, for external works, for example, the two applications can be submitted and are often

HMO Property Set Up

determined in conjunction with one another. Applications for listed building consent are free of charge, but a fee would still be required for the planning application.

Once submitted, the LPA will review the application, in liaison with a conservation or heritage officer, who will consider the impact of the proposal on the significance of the building, its curtilage and the character of the area. In some circumstances where notable internal and/or external alterations are proposed or there are a number of other listed buildings in close proximity to the property, it may be worth engaging the services of a specialist heritage or archaeology consultant who can advise on the significance of the changes proposed and whether the LPA is likely to find them acceptable. A report is typically prepared, discussing the impacts of any proposed development and any enhancements, which can be submitted in support of your application.

Special Protection Areas

Special Protection Areas (SPAs) are sites which have been designated under the EU Birds Directive[93]. SPAs are introduced to protect rare, vulnerable and migratory bird species and form part of Natura 2000, a European-wide network of Sites of Importance for Nature Conservation (SINC). Since leaving the EU, the UK is no longer part of the EU's Natura 2000 ecological network. Instead, SPAs are subject to the draft Conservation of Habitats and Species (Amended) (EU Exit) Regulations 2019[94], which have created

---

[93] Directive 2009/147/EC of the European Parliament and of the Council of 30th November 2009 on the conservation of wild birds.
[94] https://www.legislation.gov.uk/ukdsi/2019/9780111176573.

HMO Property Set Up

a national site network on land and at sea which includes existing and proposed SPAs.

SPAs can affect new development, as the regulations seek to ensure any proposed development scheme or plan does not adversely affect the integrity of an SPA. This is particularly the case for development within the Thames Basin Heaths SPA 'zone of influence', an area of heathland which spans across large parts of Surrey, Hampshire and Berkshire.

Some LPAs have been advised by Natural England that new housing, including an increase in the number of occupants in a dwelling, within five kilometres of the SPA may harm rare breed bird populations and that particular harm can occur from additional new development within 400 metres of an SPA. Typically, additional new housing development, including change of use, is not permitted within 400 metres of an SPA.

Harm is considered to be caused by disturbing birds through additional number of walkers using the area, as well as cats and dogs who may then frequent the SPA as a result of increased housing in the area. LPAs have put in place mitigation measures to avoid causing harm to SPA areas, caused by new housing development, including change of use. HMOs are cumulatively considered to significantly affect SPAs due to the intensity of use within one dwelling.

SPA Mitigation Fees

Whilst PD rights do exist for the conversion of C3 dwellings to C4 HMOs, Article 3(1) of the GPDO requires compliance with Regulations 75 to 78 of the Conservation of Habitats and Species Regulations 2017 (now superseded by the 2019 Regulations), meaning conversions to HMOs must comply

HMO Property Set Up

with these regulations and are therefore required to contribute towards avoidance or mitigation measures. These measures can affect the favourability of an area for a HMO property developer, as mitigation fees are typically quite steep.

Mitigation is typically in the form of fees to contribute towards Suitable Alternative Natural Greenspaces (SANG) and Strategic Access Management and Monitoring (SAMM) schemes. Some LPAs choose to charge fees by the number of rooms created in a HMO, whilst others calculate the contribution amount based on the net additional person capacity, or the amount of residential floorspace created through conversion of a dwelling to a HMO. However you look at it, these one-off contributions can become quite expensive for HMO developments, often costing a few thousand pounds. Therefore, if you do wish to consider purchasing a property for use as a HMO within a SPA zone of influence, make sure to check whether mitigation is needed and if so, how much it will cost you up front. You may take a strategic long term view and decided that the upfront mitigation fee is outweighed by the rental returns and increase in property value over the length of your ownership.

Nutrient Pollution and Nitrate Neutrality

Nutrient pollution is an increasingly problematic environmental issue, particularly in freshwater habitats and estuaries which are important wildlife and/or protected sites covered by the 'Habitat Regulations[95]', where increased levels of nutrients (nitrogen and phosphorous) are resulting in the

---

[95] Conservation of Habitats and Species Regulations 2017 (as amended) https://www.gov.uk/guidance/habitats-regulations-assessments-protecting-a-european-site.

HMO Property Set Up

growth of algae blooms ('eutrophication') that starve the water of oxygen and causes fish to die, removing an essential food source for birds and other local wildlife. Sources of nutrients include sewage treatment works, septic tanks, livestock and arable farming and industrial processes. Where freshwater sites are already in 'unfavourable' conditions, increased residential accommodation can add to the problem. Since 2018, there are a significant number of LPAs across England which are affected by nutrient pollution in their areas of authority.

To combat these adverse impacts on protected sites, Natural England first released guidance to LPAs in 2019 advising that developments within *designated catchment areas* only[96] which result in additional overnight accommodation, should demonstrate they are 'nitrate neutral', meaning they should not result in any additional water pollution.

This can include HMO development.

To demonstrate a development is nitrate neutral, for small scale proposals which require planning permission (such as a new HMO within a A4D area, or an existing C3 dwelling and/or a C4 HMO changing to a Sui Generis HMO), many LPAs have introduced a Nitrogen/Nutrient Budget Calculator. Where the dwelling size (number of bedrooms) and/or occupancy rates are specified in the planning application, applicants will need to complete an occupancy calculator and

---

[96] See 'Nutrient Neutrality Catchments' map: https://www.local.gov.uk/pas/topics/environment/nutrient-neutrality-and-planning-system.

HMO Property Set Up

input the results into Natural England's latest Nutrient Budget Calculator.

If the outcome of the nitrogen budget calculation results in a net increase in nutrients, where planning permission is required, applicants must provide details of how it is intended to mitigate the impact of the additional nutrients generated. If suitable space is available, an on-site mitigation scheme can be achieved through a non-mains drainage package, such as a small-scale Package Treatment Plant (PTP). Alternatively, if space is not available, off-site mitigation can be achieved using an official mitigation scheme. Often, nitrogen 'credits' can be purchased via a nutrient trading scheme to offset the impacts of additional overnight accommodation, or contributions can be put towards wetlands which strip nutrients, upgrading sewage treatment works or taking land out of use and converting it to open space. Mitigation contributions can be secured by way of a 'Section 106 agreement[97]' (S106) planning obligation attached to a grant of planning permission.

Unfortunately, where proposed HMOs which require planning permission are within catchment areas for nitrate neutrality (NN), this can delay the outcome of a planning application quite significantly, particularly if off-site mitigation is necessary to secure beforehand. Therefore, if you are intending to set up a HMO quickly in an area affected by nitrates, it would be advisable to look at small C4 HMOs with up to six people initially, outside of A4D areas.

---

[97] https://www.gov.uk/guidance/planning-obligations.

HMO Property Set Up

Restrictive Covenants

Restrictive covenants are effectively legal 'rules' imposed on land or property being sold, setting out what can or cannot be done to that specific parcel of land or building. They are usually introduced to prevent purchasers from using sites in a particular way that may be deemed 'inappropriate'. I would always recommend purchasing the Title Register for a property as part of your due diligence as it can save you thousands in the long run - and potentially a lot of unnecessary headaches!

Restrictive covenants are usually found on the Title Register for a property or piece of land in the Charges Register section. Title Registers can be purchased and viewed from the Land Registry and will let you know whether there are any covenants attached to a property or land which could prevent you from using it in a certain way or carrying out certain works. Occasionally, the Charges Register may only state the Register 'contains restrictive covenants', in which case, it would be wise to ask your solicitor to carry out a deeper background check to find out what those covenants relate to and how they may impact on your use of the property.

An important point to remember is that restrictive covenants supersede PD rights and planning permission. Therefore, should you find a covenant which restricts the use of a property to a 'single private family dwellinghouse', for example, converting the property into either a C4 or Sui Generis HMO would be considered a breach of that covenant, which could be enforceable, even if you were to obtain planning permission! This is because under the definition of an HMO, the tenants would not form a family. But, if you came across a covenant which simply stated the property

HMO Property Set Up

could only be used as a 'single private dwellinghouse' for example, using the property as a HMO is likely to be acceptable because there would usually only be one front door, one set of utility meters and the house would remain as a single private residence, unlike a block of flats.

Similarly, if a property you were interested in had a covenant stating the garage had to remain as a garage for 'vehicle parking only', or restricted any alterations or extensions being carried out, you would not be able to undertake these works to convert the garage or extend using either PD rights or through applying for planning permission because works or a use which involved using the garage for something other than vehicle parking would be a breach of the covenant. If in doubt about the wording of any covenants, always seek the advice of your solicitor or another legally qualified person.

Should you decided to apply for planning permission and assuming permission was granted, because the charges register for a property is not reviewed as part of the planning process this could mean any works undertaken could still be considered as breaching the covenant, which could be legally enforceable. Where you happen to find a restrictive covenant on a property you are interested in and if everything else checks out ok as part of your due diligence process, there are some options available to you to overcome these obstacles - such as removing or varying the covenant - but I'll go through these options fully in Chapter 59.

Corner Plots

As briefly mentioned in previous chapters, corner plot houses can impact upon your PD rights for an extension or alterations. This can occur when a property has two elevations

HMO Property Set Up

and both could be reasonably considered as the 'principal elevation'. Where houses are set on corner plots and the side elevation fronts a highway, PD rights are restricted on that side of the house. But, deciding whether the elevations fronting a highway is a side elevation or not is depended on a number of factors, such as:

- The address and postcode of the property – what road serves the property?

- The location of the front door, entrance porches and/or bay windows – are these at the 'front' or 'side' of the property?

- Access to the property's driveway from the road – is the main highway serving the house from the 'front' or 'side'?

- The distance between the 'side' elevation of the property and the highway. If there is a reasonable gap and it is separated by a grass verge and/or pavements, it is unlikely the property could be seen to be 'fronting the highway'.

- The angle between the elevation of the house and the highway. If this is greater than 45°, the elevation is not usually considered as fronting the highway.

The above is not exhaustive but gives you an indication of the kind of questions you need to be asking if you come across a suitable property for conversion to a HMO on a corner plot.

HMO Property Set Up

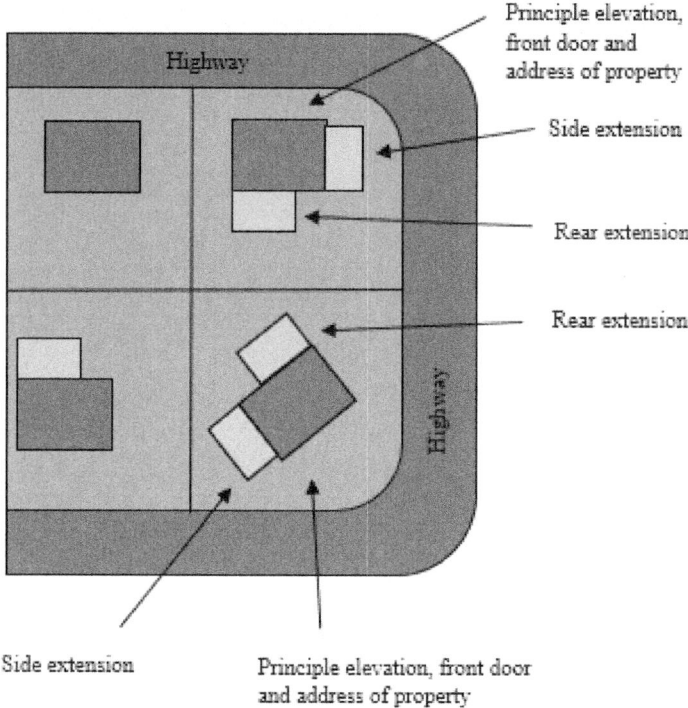

Figure 39.5: Birds eye view of dwellings on corner plots and applicable PD rights.

A useful tip is to take note of other corner plot properties within the area and see whether planning permission has been sought for any extensions. If you find applications for works which are normally considered to be PD, this helps you to assess how the LPA perceive which is the principal elevation. If in doubt though, discuss your proposal with the LPA. Bear in mind that where 'side' extensions on a corner plot property are considered to require planning permission, the LPA typically seek a minimum of two metres from the public

HMO Property Set Up

highway to the side wall of the proposed extension, unless the prevailing pattern of development in that area is made up of frontages which are already built closer to the highway.

40. Checking For PD Rights And Pre-application Advice

Knowing whether PD rights are available for a property is an important part of property development and should form part of your due diligence process. A lot of the time, it simply comes down to experience and understanding what to look for and where, which you will instinctively build up as you progress on your HMO property development journey. As mentioned in Chapter 13, checking the planning history of a property is one of the easiest and quickest ways to undertake an informal assessment of whether PD rights have been removed, but there are also a few ways in which you can check whether PD rights exists for a dwelling in a more formal capacity. Additionally, if you are proposing something outside of the limitations of PD rights, you may want to consider pre-application advice instead, particularly if you are proposing something which you think is likely to attract objections from neighbours.

Duty Planner Service

Most LPAs do have a 'Duty Planner' service offering informal advice relating to householder and PD queries, but not all duty planners will provide advice for free. Try calling your LPA and asking for the Duty Planner firstly (noting that some LPAs are more helpful than others!) and if the Duty Planner is happy to answer basic enquiries, that may be all the advice you need (albeit in an informal capacity).

In some cases, much of what the Duty Planner may be able to tell you could be contained within the LPAs design guidance, which should be part of their planning policy documents or on the Planning Portal. Sometimes if you give them a specific

HMO Property Set Up

property address, they can even check the planning history of a property for you and advise on any restrictions. However, the Duty Planner may also say that they are only able to provide paid for advice and direct you towards submitting a permitted development enquiry or pre-application advice submission.

If you do have any property-specific conversations with the Duty Planner which are beneficial to your proposal, it can help to send a brief email to either the officer you spoke with after a call, or to the LPAs generic planning email, noting the officer's name in the subject line to summarise the conversation and your understanding of what was discussed. The LPA may not reply, but it just helps to keep a record of what was discussed, which could be useful to you at a later stage.

Permitted Development Enquiry

Some but not all LPAs offer a 'PD rights enquiry service', also known as a 'Householder Enquiry' form, for which a small fee is often required[98]. This informal service allows you to submit details of your proposal and the LPA will notify you of whether they believe the works would require planning permission or can be carried out using PD rights. Often, details such as the property address and a description of the existing property, along with a description of the proposed works and any supporting drawings/documents are provided. If your intention is to convert the property to a HMO as well as carry out other works under PD rights, I would advise on not mention the proposed use of the property as a HMO on these forms as this can result in unnecessarily complicating

---

[98] Expect to pay anywhere from £50-£100.

HMO Property Set Up

matters. For example, if you wish to know whether PD rights exist for a 3-metre rear extension to a dwellinghouse or conversion of a garage to a habitable room, just simply ask for advice on that. The LPA does not need to know at this stage about the future use of the property as an HMO, that is unless the property is within a A4D area, or you are aware the property has had PD rights removed as part of a previous planning condition or covenant, otherwise conversion to a C4 HMO should be allowed under PD rights.

Lawful Development Certificates

I'll cover these types of planning application in more detail in Chapter 41, but if you are in doubt about whether you have PD rights on a C3 residential dwelling, you can apply for confirmation from your LPA via a formal application for a Lawful Development Certificate (LDC), sometime also referred to as either a Certificate of Lawfulness for a Proposed Use or Development (CLOPUD) or Certificate of Lawfulness of Existing Use or Development (CLEUD). A LDC application can provide you with written confirmation from the LPA over whether a proposed or existing use, operation or development is lawful in terms of planning for certain PD householder projects, works or uses. This obviously depends on whether the use or development is proposed or existing. For example, if you weren't certain whether PD rights existed for a garage conversion, or a side extension within the limits of PD rights, applying for determination by the LPA would ensure you received confirmation the works would be considered PD. The same applies for whether the conversion of a C3 dwelling to a C4 HMO would be considered 'lawful'. Where a certificate is refused, it will explain why the LPA

HMO Property Set Up

have reached that decision and could potentially unearth some unknown issue.

LDCs are also useful when in discussions with a mortgage broker or lender, as it can give the lender peace of mind that any works or uses proposed would be lawful and are therefore not at risk of planning enforcement action being taken. Some lenders can be very strict on having formal written confirmation on a proposal from the LPA, so even if you are positive PD rights exist for whatever you are proposing, you may find yourself being forced into applying, unless you can convince the lender otherwise by providing them with a relevant extract of the GPDO legislation for review, which identifies the specific PD rights you intend to carry out the works under. For example, if a query arises concerning the change of use of a C3 dwellinghouse to a C4 HMO, providing an exact except of 'Schedule 2, Part 3, Class L – small HMOs to dwellinghouses and vice versa' could be enough to convince the lender that planning permission is not needed, where the property is not in an A4D area.

Pre-application Advice

Pre-application advice is not compulsory, but it can be useful to assist with your planning strategy where you are unsure of what the LPAs attitude is going to be toward your proposal. Fees for this service vary between LPAs but expect to pay anywhere between £50 and £250. Pre-application advice may cost more upfront than simply submitting a planning application, but it can help avoid any issues and potentially offer a smoother pathway toward achieving planning permission.

HMO Property Set Up

Where you expect to receive objections from neighbours, you may want to receive some prior informal reassurance from the LPA that the principle of your proposal is acceptable. Pre-application advice can therefore be a useful tool in helping to resolve 'in principle' issues upfront, prior to the submission of a formal planning application and can save you time and money. For example, you can establish whether the principle of an extension or use of the property as a HMO is acceptable to the LPA before going to the expense of having detailed plans drawn up for a large extension, carry out works to convert a dwelling into a Sui Generis HMO, or a C4 HMO in an A4D area.

To apply, the process is quite straightforward and only a simple form with a clear description of your proposal is required, along with a site location plan, some basic scaled sketches, plans and/or photographs. Depending on what you are proposing, some technical surveys and reports may be useful to include as well. For example, if you are proposing a large householder extension, a daylight/sunlight assessment might be useful. For a Sui Generis HMO, an on-street parking survey might be worthwhile commissioning. Tailor your pre-application submission to suit your proposal. It is useful to include a cover letter, to provide details of the existing property, your proposal and explaining how it complies with local and national planning policies. Once you have all the information, the package can usually be submitted directly to the LPA for registration either by email directly to the LPA or by using an online portal on the LPAs website.

On registration, a planning officer will be assigned who will identify the relevant policies which your proposal will be assessed against and the key constraints affecting the

HMO Property Set Up

property. A summary of any planning history is often provided, which may identify the removal of PD rights or specific conditions relating to the use of the property. An assessment of the proposal is then put together by the planning officer, setting out the principle of the development. Depending on the proposal and level of pre-application advice sought, this may include comments on design considerations, highway matters, environmental health input, impact on residential amenity and any issues, such as the existing number of HMOs already in the street, potential parking and refuse storage issues etc.

Advice is also provided on what supporting information would be required to accompany a formal submission to the LPA (for example, a heritage statement if the proposal site is a listed building) and the planning officer's opinion on the likely outcome of the proposed development (i.e. where the LPA would support an application), plus how any issues contrary to planning policy could be overcome, or if the proposal is completely unacceptable. Usually on receipt of the advice, the planning officer is happy to enter into an informal dialogue and discuss any next steps you would need to take, for example, further meetings or a different approach to the scheme proposed.

If you have concerns you may face local opposition to your proposal, applying for pre-application advice gives you an opportunity to refine your plans, build a relationship with the LPA and then go on to publicly submit the best version of your proposal, provided the advice received is favourable. Should the advice received be unfavourable, this gives you the chance to rethink and revise your strategy and potentially implement a PD rights fallback position instead – plus you

HMO Property Set Up

have the added bonus of knowing you haven't unnecessarily antagonised any neighbours through the submission of a formal planning application! One thing to bear in mind however it that whilst requests for pre-application advice and the LPAs responses are not placed on the LPAs website (enabling them to be confidential), under the Freedom of Information Regulations (FOI), members of the public can request the details of your submission. Additionally, the details may be made available if/when a formal planning application is submitted to the LPA for the development.

41. Planning Permission: Different Types Of Permission And Application Documents

When applying for planning permission, there are many different types of planning applications for various projects and proposals, depending on what type of development is being applied for. In most cases, particularly for HMO developments, it is likely you will only need to know about a select few application types, detailed below:

Application Type
Full Planning Permission
Householder Planning Permission
Lawful Development Certificates
Approval of Details Reserved by a Condition
Removal/Variation of a Condition
Non-Material Amendments (NMAs)
Prior Approval: Larger Home Extensions

Table 41.1: Different types of planning applications relevant to HMOs.

To support your proposal, you will typically need to provide a number of forms, statements or reports and scaled drawings and plans. Before I discuss the different application types themselves, let's go through a few of the application requirements themselves.

Application Form, Completed Ownership Certificates and Community Infrastructure Levy Forms

All of the above applications require the appropriate application form to be completed, available from the Planning Portal, or from some LPA websites directly. The details and amount of information required for each application type vary

HMO Property Set Up

depending on what you are proposing to do. As you'd expect, an application for full planning permission will require more information than a householder application, whilst an application for a non-material amendment (allowing for minor changes to an approved application) will only require basic information about a proposal because the 'principle of development' has already been established as acceptable. All application types will however need the name and address of the applicant and/or their agent (if using an agent), the address of the site and a description of the proposal. From there, you will need to tailor the remainder of the application form to suit your proposal.

Application forms also require information about the ownership of the property or site. If you are the owner and have been for 21 days or more, you can complete the form and do not have to serve notice on anyone, but if you are not currently the owner and have not been for a period of at least 21 days than you will need to serve notice on the current owner(s) so they are aware you are submitting the application. For most HMO property development projects, you will likely know who the owner of the property is, but on some occasions if you are unable to identify a land or property owner, you may have to have a notice placed in a local newspaper to raise awareness, allowing the owner(s) the opportunity to come forward. The Planning Portal has different notice letters which can be downloaded and completed to suit either of the above circumstances. It is unlikely a property you are seeking to convert to a HMO will form part of an agricultural holding, so you shouldn't need to serve that type of notice.

HMO Property Set Up

Another type of form which most applications require to be filled in and submitted with a planning application is a Community Infrastructure Levy (CIL) form, also known as 'CIL Form 1: CIL Additional Information'. This needs to be completed accurately and should include the details of any existing and proposed changes to the gross internal area (GIA) of a building. even if no changes to the GIA are proposed, you still need to complete and submit CIL Form 1. In cases where you are proposing an extension larger than 100 square metres you may be liable to pay a CIL contribution per square metre. Each LPA has the authority to adopt its own charging schedule, meaning that fees for CIL contributions vary by area.

Covering Letter

Your covering letter should provide the site address, as well as briefly explain the proposal. For example:

"Application for full planning permission for the change of use of a six-bedroom HMO (Use Class C4) to an eight-bedroom HMO (Use Class Sui Generis), including two additional parking spaces and a bicycle storage shed and associated works at 123 Example Street, Coventry."

For good practice, the covering letter should also list the information being submitted with the application (i.e. a list of drawings, plans and supporting reports/statements, including reference numbers), the application fee amount and details of who will be paying it (i.e. you as the applicant/a business partner/your agent).

HMO Property Set Up

Planning Statement/Design And Access Statement

Whilst they may seem similar, these two documents are quite different. A Planning Statement is a key part of successful planning application, providing a balanced justification for a proposal, whilst a Design and Access Statement (DAS) typically provides more details on the design and access of the proposal in relation to the site and its setting. A DAS is usually more suited to larger development projects where more detail is required and a new access may be proposed. Both statements however are two of the most important documents to submit alongside a planning application. They offer an opportunity to demonstrate to the planning officer, the public and statutory consultees why your proposal complies with planning policy and enables you to provide a justified argument for why your application should be approved.

The length of the Planning Statement/Design and Access Statement should be tailored to suit the scale of your proposal, but should generally include the following information:

- Introduction to the proposal;

- Outline of the site context and surroundings;

- An explanation of any relevant planning history;

- A detailed description of the proposal;

- An overview of the key planning policies and other material considerations;

HMO Property Set Up

- An assessment of the planning argument which should demonstrate how the proposal complies with planning policies and other material considerations; and

- A summary and conclusions highlighting the reasons for approval.

Where proposals are fairly straightforward, you shouldn't need to go into too much detail. A top tip is to try to keep your arguments relevant to the proposal and focused on the policies of greatest importance to what you are applying for specifically. Your planning officer won't appreciate having to wade through a rambling, disjointed and poorly structured statement.

Site Location Plans

Site Location Plans (SLP) are typically required for most applications. These identify the site area, which should be outlined with a red line around it, along with the surrounding context. Access to the site should be included within the red line boundary. A blue line must also be added where an applicant owns any other property or land which does not form part of the application site but may adjoin it.

Plans should include a 'north' point or arrow and included two named roads or buildings to assist with the identification of the site. SLPs should typically be scaled at either 1:1250 or 1:2500 on a standard paper size (A1, A3, A4 are usually used) and are available to purchase from a number of online websites for as little as £12, or your architect can obtain these as part of the package of plans they prepare to support your application.

HMO Property Set Up

Site Plan/Block Plans

Site Plans, also known as 'Block Plans' show the development site in more detail than a SLP. Again, a red line should be included around the site boundary, including the site access and any other land owned by the applicant should be outlined in blue. These plans should typically be scaled at 1:500 or 1:200 on a standard paper size.

Some site plans can be prepared to show the existing and proposed development, which allows the LPA to easily compare the two. However, for most HMO or householder development projects, a simple 'proposed site plan' will likely be sufficient. If you are proposing something more complex, your architect or draughtsperson can provide an 'existing site plan' so the LPA can quickly compare the changes.

Other Plans

Depending on the size, scale and complexity of your proposal, you may need to submit a number of other scaled plans to support your proposal. These can typically include:

- Existing and proposed floorplans;

- Existing and proposed elevations;

- Existing and proposed roof plans;

- Section drawings;

- Proposed landscaping plans; and

- Car parking/bicycle storage/refuse storage plans.

HMO Property Set Up

All of these plans should typically be scaled at either 1:100 or 1:50 and be provided on a standard paper size.

Other Supporting Reports And Statements

Again, depending on what your proposal is for, it may be necessary to submit other reports and statements to address technical issues or certain designations. These are likely to be listed on the LPAs local validation list and can include the following:

Report/Statement	Justification
Heritage Statement	Useful if the property is a listed building/near to a listed building or within a Conservation Area
Ecological statement	Useful if a proposal is likely to have an impact on biodiversity sites within or nearby to the site
Contamination Statement	Useful if the site has the potential to be contaminated, for example, if a property to be converted is part of a former petrol station
Arboricultural Statement and Tree Protection Plan	Useful if the proposal is likely to affect any trees or hedges within or nearby to the site
Flood Risk Assessment	Useful if the property is within either flood zone 2 or 3
Parking and Accessibility Statement	Useful if your proposal for a HMO is reliant on on-street parking
Accessibility Statement	Useful if you want to demonstrate good public transport/sustainable modes of transport are available

HMO Property Set Up

	and the accessibility of nearby services, facilities and amenities

Table 41.2: Supporting technical reports or statements for planning applications.

These reports and statements will typically need to be prepared by a suitably qualified consultant, who will charge a fee for their services, so do bear this in mind when preparing an application for planning permission. The list in Table 4.2 is not exhaustive and there may be other reports and statements required as part of your planning application. To find a specialist consultant to assist with a specific matter, you can either review other similar planning applications and see who prepared the supporting reports and contact the consultants directly or carry out a Google search for relevant consultants in your area, for example, typing in 'transport consultant Coventry' should bring up details of any transport consultants operating in the area.

Where you are not sure what other information may be necessary to accompany your submission, I would always recommend looking at your LPAs 'Local Validation List' and familiarising yourself with the LPAs local requirements when seeking to submit an application. The lists will provide details of what supporting information will be needed for each application type, although some of the items listed will not be relevant to small scale HMO developments. You will therefore need to decide what is likely to be appropriate for the scale of your proposal and its location. The validation list can usually be found by simply typing in 'validation list' or 'validation checklist' on the LPAs website or searching through the planning pages.

HMO Property Set Up

Let's now take a closer look at each of the relevant application types for HMO developments and what they can be used for.

Full Planning Permission Application

A full planning application is often used for detailed development proposals which are not covered by PD rights or householder planning applications and at this scale include proposals for change of use, creation of new dwellings or extensive external works. For example, a C3 dwellinghouse changing into a Sui Generis HMO or a C4 HMO into a Sui Generis HMO and vice versa and for combining applications for a change of use with an application to extend and/or carry out other works which alter the external appearance of the property. This could include the change of use of a C3 dwelling house into a Sui Generis HMO, with two-storey side extension.

The following documents will be required for a full planning application:

Full Planning Permission Application
Completed Application Form
Ownership Certificates (as necessary)
Community Infrastructure Levy (CIL) Form
Covering Letter
Planning Statement/Design and Access Statement
Site Location Plan (usually 1:1250 or 1:2500)
Site Plan/Block Plan (usually 1:200 or 1:500)
Other Plans (as necessary) (usually 1:100 or 1:50)
Specialist/Technical Reports or Statements (as deemed necessary)

Table 42.3: Typical application requirements for Full Planning Permission.

HMO Property Set Up

Currently, the fee for this application is £462 + Planning Portal admin fee. Applications should be determined within eight weeks from the date of validation by the LPA.

Householder Planning Permission Application

This application is used to apply for works which will alter the external appearance of a domestic (C3) dwellinghouse (excluding flats and apartments), including works within the boundary or garden and can only be used when the property is still in use as a C3 dwelling (pre-conversion). Householder applications can therefore be used for projects where PD rights have been removed, or where proposals are larger than PD rights allow. Examples of common projects include, extensions, the erection of outbuildings, walls and fences, loft conversions, porches and garage conversions.

The documents required as part of a householder application will vary depending on what is proposed, but will typically include the following:

Householder Planning Permission Application
Completed Application Form
Ownership Certificates (as necessary)
Community Infrastructure Levy (CIL) Form
Covering Letter
Planning Statement
Site Location Plan (usually 1:1250 or 1:2500)
Site Plan/Block Plan (usually 1:200 or 1:500)
Other Plans (as necessary) (usually 1:100 or 1:50)
Specialist/Technical Reports or Statements (as deemed necessary)

Table 41.4: Typical application requirements for Householder Planning Permission.

HMO Property Set Up

Currently, the fee for this application is £206 + Planning Portal admin fee. Applications should again be determined within eight weeks from the date of validation by the LPA.

Lawful Development Certificates (Existing And Proposed Uses)

This application type is slightly different from full and householder applications and is particularly useful to confirm that a use or development doesn't need any further planning consent and is lawful in planning terms.

Lawful Development Certificates (also referred to as LDCs, CLOPUDs or CLEUDs) are evidence-based applications, so clear and unambiguous evidence is required to be submitted with the application to confirm that a use or development is lawful. It is solely up to the applicant to demonstrate and justify why a certificate should be granted. As such, there is a 'burden of proof' upon the applicant.

Proposed Use Or Development

As discussed in Chapter 40, LDCs are useful to confirm that proposed works or uses are considered by the LPA to be permitted development, or that you have PD rights intact for your proposed development. For example, if you wished to carry out a garage or loft conversion, or wanted to extend a property using PD. For applications of this type, you can usually rely on providing the LPA with the relevant section of the GDPO, along with a summary of the property history to demonstrate that PD rights have not been removed and any previous works under PD have not 'used up' your PD rights allowance. Where the LPA is satisfied with this proof, this should be sufficient for them to issue a certificate.

HMO Property Set Up

Existing Developments

I've split this next part into two parts for existing developments and existing uses as the approach taken for each is slightly different. Let's say that you are buying a standard C3 dwellinghouse which has an existing physical *development*. For arguments sake, let's say it is a side and rear extension built over ten years ago which is larger than PD rights would usually allow for and neither you nor other current owner have been able to find any evidence of planning permission being granted. For your own peace of mind, you may wish to apply for confirmation from the LPA that the existing extension is considered 'lawful' in terms of planning and would therefore not be at risk of enforcement action being taken. To do this, you will currently need to provide at least four-years-worth of evidence of the extension being in place. This is because the property is still in C3 use, so only four years' worth of evidence is required in this situation.

HMO Property Set Up

The type of evidence used to confirm that **existing physical development** is lawful can include:

Evidence for Existing Physical Developments
Historic aerial images (using Google Earth's 'Timehop' function showing the structure in place
Dated photographs of interior/exterior
Builders/contractors invoices
Building Regulations completion certificates
Statutory Declarations or sworn affidavits, signed and witnessed by an appropriate person (i.e., a solicitor or Commissioner for Oaths) attesting to the development being there for the requisite time period.
Council tax/valuation tax letters
Architectural plans and elevations (as these are usually dated)

Table 41.5: Typical application requirements for CLEUD applications for physical works.

Existing Use

For an existing use, a LDC could be applied for if you are purchasing (or selling) an existing C4 or Sui Generis HMO and wish to confirm that the property is lawfully in use for that purpose. Applications for existing *uses* not related to C3 dwellinghouses require the applicant to provide at least ten-years' worth of evidence, unless planning permission has been granted for the change of use to a HMO. For HMOs specifically, ten years' worth of evidence is required because the property is no longer considered to fall within a 'C3 residential' use.

Where A4Ds are proposed to be introduced, some LPAs may encourage landlords and HMO property owners to apply for LDCs which will confirm their existing HMOs are in lawful

334

HMO Property Set Up

use (assuming there is sufficient evidence to demonstrate this) prior to the implementation of the A4D[99]. It is worth pointing out here again that existing HMOs are not affected by the introduction of a new A4D; the A4D only applies to new HMOs being proposed after the A4D is introduced.

If you decided to apply for a LDC to confirm the lawfulness of an existing HMO, this is where proof of at least ten years continuous use as a HMO is necessary. Evidence, such as HMO licences, previous and current tenancy agreements, sworn statements from previous and current tenants and neighbours (if you have a good relationship with them), photographs, building regulation certificates, work invoices and utility bills can be used to prove your HMO property is lawful. In cases where evidence of use is not readily available or is incomplete and 'patchy', this could mean an established HMO without planning permission is refused an LDC as the LPA won't, on the 'balance of probability', be able to establish that the use has been in operation for the requisite time-period. In which case, unless the landlord or owner and/or purchaser can produce more 'robust' evidence, they may be forced into seeking planning permission retrospectively. This again highlights the importance of good record keeping.

---

[99] This can help speed up HMO licensing application or renewals but may make your HMO more 'visible' to the Council, which has the potential to result in re-banding for council tax purposes.

HMO Property Set Up

Evidence for **existing uses** can include:

Evidence for Existing Uses
Council tax/valuation tax letter identifying the unit
Tenancy agreements
Dated photographs of interior/exterior
Building Regulations completion certificates
Builders/contractors invoices, including for regular servicing
HMO Licence (current and previous)
Utility bills
Statutory Declarations or sworn affidavits, signed and witnessed by an appropriate person
Rental/account documents
Marketing information/brochures
Email correspondence from tenants/letting agents

Table 41.6: Typical application requirements for CLEUD applications for existing uses.

HMO Property Set Up

Lawful Development Certificates – Other Requirements

To fully support an application for a LDC, whether it is for an existing or proposed use or development, there are a number of items required. These will vary depending on the purpose of the application, but will typically include the following:

Lawful Development Certificate Application
Completed Application Form
Ownership Certificates (as necessary)
Community Infrastructure Levy (CIL) Form (as necessary)
Covering Letter
Planning Statement
Site Location Plan (usually 1:1250 or 1:2500)
Site Plan/Block Plan (usually 1:200 or 1:500)
Other Plans (as necessary) (usually 1:100 or 1:50)
Specialist/Technical Reports or Statements (as deemed necessary)
Evidence to verify the application

Table 41.7: Typical application requirements for Lawful Development Certificates – other submission requirements.

Naturally, there are different fees applicable to the different types of LDC applications. Currently these are £103 + Planning Portal admin fee for proposed uses or developments, whilst for existing uses or developments, the fee is currently £231 + Planning Portal admin fee. Once validated by the LPA, applications for both existing and proposed uses or development should be determined within eight weeks, although as these type of applications delve into legal matters, the local authority's legal department is often involved. This can result in delays to the determination date.

HMO Property Set Up

Approval Of Details Reserved By Conditions

Applications for planning permission are often approved subject to a number of conditions. These conditions are attached to control and limit the way in which the planning consent is implemented by making sure that developments are enacted appropriately and to mitigate any adverse impacts. There are a few different types of conditions, some of which are compliance conditions for informative purposes only, but others require 'discharging' (i.e. the submission of further information to the LPA for approval) prior to either the commencement or occupation and/or use of an approved development.

The above type of application is used to discharge pre-commencement or pre-occupation conditions. As part of the application you must demonstrate to the LPA and any relevant statutory consultees how you intend to meet the wording of the condition. This can be done by providing additional or supplementary information on top of what was submitted at the planning application stage. For HMOs, conditions which might need discharging could relate to the installation of frosted glazing on windows to protect amenities, or the provision of refuse and recycling facilities and bicycle storage facilities within the curtilage of the property, if not already adequately provided. Conditions requiring discharge can also relate to matters such as the provision of suitable off-street parking or the materials, colours and textures to be used in an extension, or for the submission of additional technical information. An example of this could be if the development requires excavation works or the removal of trees and hedges. In which case, you may then need to have specialist reports prepared, such as an archaeological watching brief for works

HMO Property Set Up

which may uncover historical artefacts or arboricultural method statement to cover tree works for submission to the LPA to address the conditions.

However, through discussions with your planning officer prior to the determination of the application, you may be able to provide the information up front, negating the need to discharge any conditions. The knock-on effect of this is that it may take longer for your application to be decided as comments will be sought from any relevant statutory consultees on the information or plans provided; but it could save you time later down the line knowing you don't have to submit any further applications to the LPA for determination – and pay a fee for doing so.

The documents required as part of an application for the approval of details reserved by condition will vary depending on the conditions you are seeking to discharge, but will typically include:

Approval of Details Reserved By Conditions Application
Completed Application Form
Covering Letter/a brief Planning Statement
Site Plan/Block Plan (usually 1:200 or 1:500) (as necessary)
Other Plans (as necessary) (usually 1:100 or 1:50) can included, but are not limited to: • Proposed Landscaping Plan • Car Parking/Bicycle Storge Plan • Refuse/Recycling Storage Product Specification

HMO Property Set Up

• Materials Schedule and Sample Images
Specialist/Technical Reports or Statements (as deemed necessary – these are condition specific)

Table 41.8: Typical application requirements for Approval of Details Reserved by Conditions applications.

If the application relates to a householder application (i.e. the property is currently a C3 dwellinghouse), the current fee is set at £34. However, where the application relates to any other permission (e.g. full planning permission), the current fee increases to £116 + Planning Portal admin fee. You can discharge more than one pre-commencement or pre-occupation condition at a time, so you don't have to keep paying separately for each condition. Your covering letter and application form should clearly refer to the original planning application reference and set out which of the conditions discharge is being sought for, as well as the information being provided for each condition.

Applications should be determined within eight weeks from the date of validation by the LPA. Once all conditions are discharged and you have received decision letters confirming this from the LPA, the development can proceed and/or the property can be occupied.

Removal/Variation Of A Condition

This type of application is also referred to as a 'Section 73' application[100] and as the name suggests, can be used to either remove or vary a condition placed on a development or use, following a grant of planning permission. The use of these types of application and another one known as a non-material

---

[100] Under Section 73 of the Town and Country Planning Act 1990.

amended (which I'll cover later) allows for flexible options to be taken towards proposals which have already been granted planning permission.

As previously mentioned, conditions are typically applied to a grant of planning permission to limit and control the approved development or use. Conditions may sometimes be added which can end up being restrictive, or after having received permission, you may change your mind about a certain detail and want to amend the approved plans without having to go through the whole process of applying for permission all over again. This is where these types of application are useful tools as they allow you to vary the way in which the condition is worded so you can carry out the development in a way which is more beneficial to you. Alternatively, you could seek to have the condition removed altogether, if you are able to demonstrate it is sufficiently redundant and would not serve a useful purpose.

The type of changes proposed under Section 73 ('s73') applications are often considered to 'materially' alter the original consent. An example of this may be if you find a condition has been imposed requiring you to construct a loft conversion with dormer extension (in this example, larger than PD rights allow for) in accordance with the approved plans. On reviewing your plans for the property, you may decide that instead of creating the dormer with one large window, you want to increase the size of the dormer and insert two windows with a gap in between, as well as two rooflights, so two bedrooms can be accommodated in the loft space instead of one.

You have already established the principle of the development is acceptable through the original consent, but as the changes

HMO Property Set Up

you'd now like to make would be considered 'materially' different from what was approved, you would therefore be seeking to vary the condition which deals with the approved plans by substituting one set of plans for another. The plans submitted would need to show the revised floorplans, elevations and roof plan.

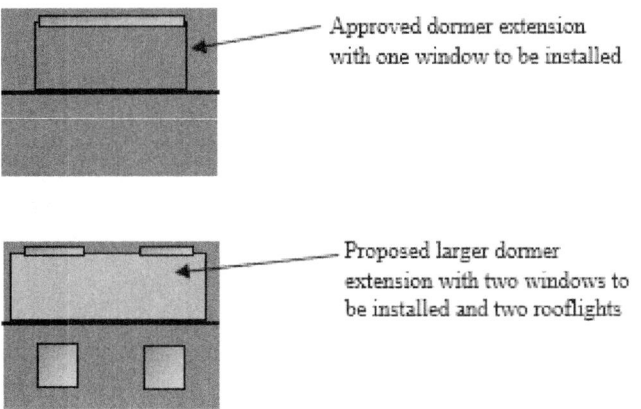

Figure 41.1: Birds eye view of approved and proposed alterations to dormer extension for Variation of Condition application to change approved plans.

An example of where you may seek to remove a condition rather than vary it could be where a planning application is granted for a two-storey side extension with a condition that requires you to provide an additional parking space in place of one lost to the side of the property to make way for the extension. You may consider this unnecessary if you already have suitable parking provisions on the driveway for your HMO. In which case, you could argue that the condition is unreasonable and should be removed.

HMO Property Set Up

Crucially, whatever the outcome of the s73 application is, the original permission will still stand and can be implemented, typically within three years. However, where approved, the s73 application has the effect of creating a 'new' permission which sits side-by-side with the original but allows the LPA the opportunity to add other conditions to this new permission, which may then need additional information to be submitted for considered by the LPA, prior to the commencement of works or occupation (pre-commencement or pre-occupation conditions). Implementing the s73 application means the original application will subsequently expire after three years. The documents required as part of an application will differ depending on what is proposed, but typically include:

Removal or Variation of a Condition Application
Completed Application Form
Covering Letter/a brief Planning Statement
Site Location Plan (usually 1:1250 or 1:2500)
Site Plan/Block Plan (usually 1:200 or 1:500)
Other Plans (as necessary) (usually 1:100 or 1:50) depending on your proposal/what details you wish to vary

Table 41.9: Typical application requirements for Removal or Variation of a Condition applications.

The current fee for this type of application is currently £234 + Planning Portal admin fee. Applications should be determined within eight weeks from the date of validation by the LPA.

Non-Material Amendments (NMAs)

This application is quite similar to an application for the removal or variation of a condition in that it allows you to amend the details of a consented scheme without submitting an entirely new planning application. However, this type of

HMO Property Set Up

application is limited to only small changes being carried out to the proposal which are considered to be either 'non-material' or 'minor material' changes. If a non-material amendment application is successful, no 'new' planning permission will be created as the original permission will still stand, but it will have been amended by the NMA.

It is difficult to define what is considered as a 'non-material' and 'material' amendment. Indeed, the Government sets out in the NPPG that it is dependent on the context of the overall scheme, where an amendment that is non-material in one context may be material in another[101]. You'll therefore find LPAs have their own views on what they would consider this to be, so discussing with the planning officer who worked on the original permission ahead of a submission could be beneficial. In general, NMAs are considered non-material where:

---

[101] NPPG Paragraph: 002 Reference ID: 17a-002-20140306.

HMO Property Set Up

Non-Material Amendment Examples
The application site and description of development does not differ from the original application
The proposed amendment does not increase the size of any part of the development
The proposed amendment does not locate any part of the development closer to neighbours
The proposed amendment does not change windows in any elevation facing a neighbour which increased overlooking in any way
The proposed amendment does not result in the development moving more than one metre in any direction
The proposed amendment does not result in a greater visual intrusion to interested parties
The proposed amendment does not result in changes to the external details of the proposal which would materially alter the appearance of the building

Table 41.10: Non-Material Amendment examples.

Where changes are deemed non-material, it is unlikely public consultation will be needed, although anyone who may be affected by the proposal must be informed.

An example of where a NMA could be sought is if planning approval is granted for an extension to an existing dwelling. On reviewing the layout and internal configuration of the extension, you may wish to amend the position and sizing of the windows in a rear elevation to provide additional natural light and an improved outlook for your tenants.

HMO Property Set Up

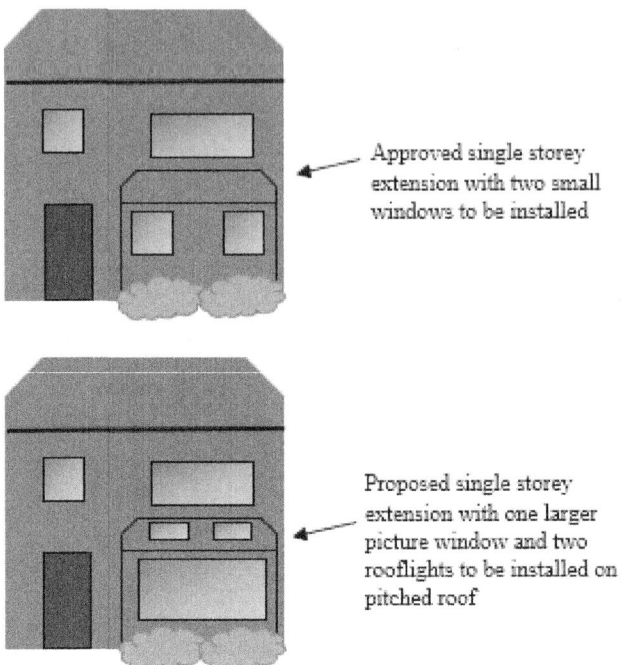

Figure 41.2: Rear elevation views of approved and proposed alterations to single storey rear extension for a NMA application.

Where you can demonstrate the changes would not 'materially' affect the original consent and that no amenities or privacy would be adversely impacted, then the LPA should not unreasonably withhold permission for such a minor amendment. NMA applications can also be used for amending the wording of a condition, if the amendment proposed would not alter the overall permission in any material way. For example, a condition added which requires a stringent level of professional monitoring for works around a TPO could be amended to one that is less stringent where you are able to

HMO Property Set Up

demonstrate to the satisfaction of the LPA that the works would not harm a tree or its roots following the erection of tree protection fencing. Supporting documents include:

Non-Material Amendment Application
Completed Application Form
Covering Letter/a brief Planning Statement
Site Location Plan (usually 1:1250 or 1:2500)
Site Plan/Block Plan (usually 1:200 or 1:500)
Other Plans (as necessary) (usually 1:100 or 1:50) depending on your proposal/what details you wish to amend

Table 41.11: Typical application requirements for a Non-Material Amendment application.

If the application relates to a householder application, the fee is currently set at £34. However, where applications relate to any other permissions (e.g. full planning permission) the current fee increases to £234 + Planning Portal admin fee). Once validated, a decision should be issued by the LPA within 28 days.

Prior Approval: Larger Home Extension

Under the GPDO[102], householders are able to construct larger singe-storey rear extensions than PD rights would usually allow for[103]. Flats and maisonettes do not benefit from this type of application, nor do 'converted' buildings to residential dwellings. The size limits for these types of rear extension to qualifying houses are increased from four metres up to eight metres for a detached house and three metres up to six metres

---

[102] Schedule 2, Part 1, Class A(g).
[103] Subject to the site not being on Article 2(3) land or within a Site of Special Scientific Interest (SSSI).

HMO Property Set Up

for any other type of house (i.e. terraced and semi-detached houses).

Prior to any development commencing, the LPA must be notified of the proposal. This notification should include details of how far the enlarged part of the dwellinghouse will extend beyond the rear wall of the original house, the maximum height of the extension and the eaves height of the extension. They will subsequently determine if their prior approval is needed and will usually consult with immediate neighbours only. This can be either side of the application property – and sometimes to the rear, if deemed appropriate.

Supporting documents for this type of application include:

Prior Approval – Larger Single Storey Rear Extensions
Completed Application Form
Covering Letter/a brief Planning Statement
Site Location Plan (usually 1:1250 or 1:2500)
Site Plan/Block Plan (usually 1:200 or 1:500)
Other Plans (as necessary) (usually 1:100 or 1:50): • Existing and proposed floorplans • Existing and proposed elevations • Existing and proposed roof plans • Section drawings.

Table 41.12: Typical application requirements for Prior Approval for a larger single storey rear extension application.

Currently, the application fee for this type of application is set at £96 + Planning Portal admin fee. Applications should

HMO Property Set Up

generally be determined within 42-days from the date the application is received. If no decision is issued after this period has expired, consent is generally deemed to have been granted, unless otherwise agreed (although I would advise checking this with the LPA before commencing any development).

Good Design Principles

Regardless of whether your proposal requires planning permission or can be carried out using PD rights, good design principles should be applied. These form an important aspect of the development process and can help make a HMO property more desirable to live in and more visually appealing, which can boost its rental potential and capital value. It can also help make neighbours more content with the idea of having a HMO in their neighbourhood. However, design is more than just the appearance of the property. It is also about improving functionality and the useable space provided within a property. This can have a beneficial impact on the health and wellbeing of any tenants where the design and layout of a HMO has been carefully planned to provide bright, spacious and inviting spaces.

When considering alterations or extensions, think carefully about how each room of your HMO will be used and where tenants will be spending most of their time when they are living there. Good design creates buildings which are sufficiently resilient and able to carry out their functions without deteriorating too quickly. All buildings, extensions and spaces must therefore be designed to perform well for the purposes they were designed for and over a long period of time, so they remain as both practical and inviting spaces for tenants to occupy.

HMO Property Set Up

Good design should also positively respond to the local character, history and identity of the street. Whilst PD rights allow you almost 'free reign' in terms of design, any proposed extension or alteration to an existing dwelling, whether it needs planning permission or not, should try to blend in well with the surrounding properties and be 'in harmony' with what already exists in the street scene and surrounding local area. To this end, most LPAs will have a Residential Design Guide as a Supplementary planning Document (SPD) available in the planning policy section of their website. Take a look at this and see what advice is provided by the LPA in terms of design, layout, scale, character, local materials, vernacular and setting as this will give you and your architect a good indication of what the LPA would expect to see for a planning application, as well as providing a useful guide for what would be acceptable in the local area. Where no local design guidance is published by the LPA, the Government have produced the National Design Guide[104] (January 2021) which provides a high-level framework for design and a useful reference point to applying good design principles to all forms and scales of development by demonstrating what good design means in practice.

The 45° 'Rule'

Part of including good design principles in your HMO projects should also include taking note of the '45° rule'. This is not a 'legislative requirement' and does not apply to PD legislation but is simply a common 'guideline' used by LPAs to determine the impact of proposed extensions on the amount

---

[104] https://www.gov.uk/government/publications/national-design-guide.

HMO Property Set Up

of direct sunlight and daylight received by neighbouring properties (usually where these are terraced or semi-detached) and is an assessment of the depth, width and height a proposed extension.

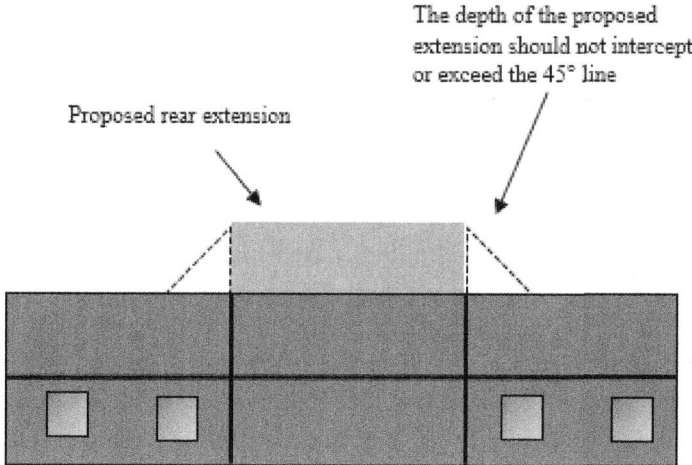

Figure 41.3: Birds eye view of the '45° rule', demonstrated on a terraced dwelling.

Where extensions are poorly designed, it can dramatically affect the amount of light received into the main 'living spaces' of neighbouring dwellings. Rooms used as bathrooms, halls, utilities, landings and stairs are not typically considered as 'living spaces' and whilst overshadowing of a neighbour's garden may be annoying for them, it rarely results in adequate grounds to justify refusing planning permission for a scheme, unless it completely dominates their outdoor amenity space. Whilst not a legislative requirement, the 45° rule and the impacts of a proposed extension or other works on the

HMO Property Set Up

amenity of others should be a consideration for you as any neighbours must live with whatever you build. Keeping on good terms with neighbours can help you later down the line if you do need planning permission for your HMO. I'll talk more about neighbours in Chapter 67.

For extensions or alterations requiring planning permission, it is the responsibility of the LPA when considering an application to protect the amenities of neighbouring properties, but it is important you take account of how your proposal will influence any neighbours. A good tip to remember is that there's little merit in putting forward an application which will immediately get knocked back due to amenity issues. All that will do is waste your time and money and annoy your neighbours, making them very aware (and possibly hyper-critical) of anything else you seek to do next! In all cases, extensions and new buildings should therefore be well designed from the start to minimise any overshadowing and loss of light for neighbouring properties. As part of the design process, you should consider the following:

The 45° Rule and Design Considerations
What the sun's maximum height at noon will be
Where the sun's path will fall during winter months, where there are fewer hours of daylight
The height of your proposed development
The optimum location for your proposed development
The size of your plot and any neighbouring plots
The orientation of your property and any neighbouring properties
The distance between any shared boundaries
The topography of your plot and any neighbouring plots

Table 41.13: The 45° 'rule' and design considerations.

HMO Property Set Up

When designing an extension to take account of the 45° rule, either working on your own or with your architect, start by sketching the existing property along with any neighbouring properties. You can use a block plan to do this. Add in the maximum depth and width of your proposed extension. Next, you need to mark the nearest window of a main living space in the neighbouring houses and draw a line at a 45° angle on to your sketch plan. Where possible, ensure that your planned extension does not fall inside this line. The centre point should be the centre of your neighbour's window. If the line you've drawn crosses over further than this, you may need to alter the scale of your extension.

Another way of calculating the impact is to work out the maximum height and width of your proposed extension. Draw out a sketch plan of the front or back of your house (depending on where the proposed extension will be) and include your neighbours' house on the drawing too. Next, draw the centre point of your 45° angle on the top of the window of the nearest 'key' room of your neighbour's property to see whether your plan will affect your neighbour's property.

HMO Property Set Up

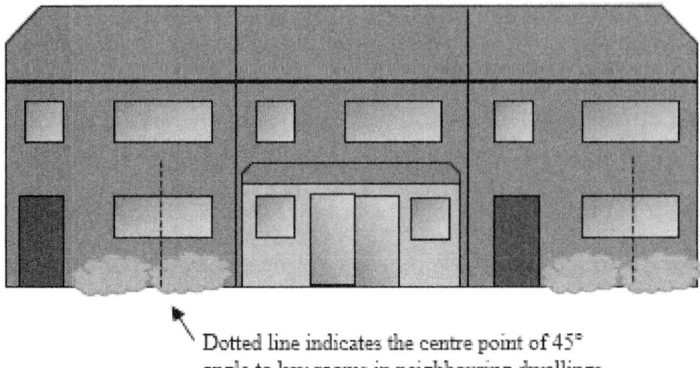

Figure 41.4: Rear elevation view of single storey rear extension to a terraced dwelling, taking account of the 45° rule.

Taking the above into account, most properties can accommodate a single storey extension without impacting too much on the amount of direct light received by neighbouring properties. From experience however, most mid-terrace properties are not suitable for two-storey extensions, although end-of-terraced, detached and semi-detached properties are more capable of accommodating this type of development, subject to complying with other planning policies.

HMO Property Set Up

42. Applying For Planning Permission, The Planning Process And Timescales

To help you understand the planning process better, I have prepared a simple flowchart, starting with the submission of an application and ending with the issuing of a decision:

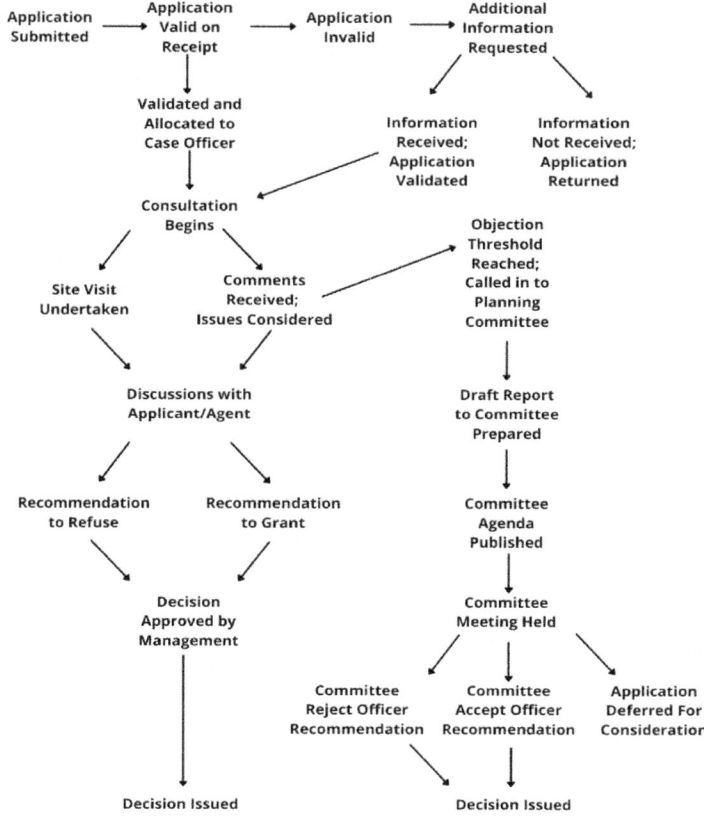

Figure 42.1: Planning Process Flowchart.

HMO Property Set Up

Most applications are now able to be submitted online via the Planning Portal[105]. If you haven't come across the Planning Portal before, it is an online system allowing for planning applications (and building regulations applications) to be prepared, submitted and processed electronically. It also contains useful advice and guidance on a range of development topics and easy to follow explanations on planning legislation.

To prepare an application, you will need to create a free account, unless you are using an agent (such as a planning consultant or architect), who can prepare the application on your behalf. If doing it yourself, once your account has been set up, you will need to create a new application. You can do this by inputting the address of the property and then selecting the type of application you wish to apply for planning permission for. If you are not sure, the Planning Portal offers guidance on what applications are most likely to be suited to your proposal. Once the application has been created you will then be required to complete the application form and ownership certificates (where necessary) with details about the proposal. Where questions are not directly applicable to your proposal, it is acceptable to simply type 'not applicable' (for example, on a full planning application you will be asked about matters such as 'employment', 'hours of opening', 'non-residential floorspace' and 'hazardous substances').

Once you have completed your application on the Planning Portal, uploaded any mandatory and supporting documents and calculate the relevant fee. As previously mentioned, all LPAs have a list of local requirements (validation list) that

---

[105] https://www.planningportal.co.uk/.

HMO Property Set Up

detail the specific documentation required to be submitted with an application which allow it to be made valid. The requirements do vary depending on the LPA and application type, so it is always important to check whether you have all the necessary documents needed before you submit your application. Remember – these are specific to your proposal, so some listed requirements for full planning permission submissions may not be applicable.

On completion of the application and following the uploading of all supporting documents, the application can be submitted. You can either pay for the application then and there or nominate someone else to pay for it. On confirmation of payment, the application is then transferred to the LPA and the process of registration and validation begins. Where you need to serve notice on existing owners or other interested parties, you should do so now too.

The next stage is over to the LPAs validation or registration team, who will review the submitted information to check the application meets all the criteria to enable it to be made valid. If information is missing the validation team can refuse to validate your application until the information is provided. Usually you are given up to 21 days to provide any requested information before your application is returned to you. This can obviously cause unnecessary delays, so it is important to double check that all the information required for validation is provided prior to submission.

Validation can sometimes take up to two weeks (or longer if there is a backlog of applications). Once your application has been made valid, you will receive an acknowledgement letter from the LPA. This provides the application reference number and a description of the proposal. Pay close attention to the

HMO Property Set Up

description of development as it may have been changed to something less accurate. If you do not agree with the new description of your proposal, you can ask the validation team to amend this or revert back to your original description. The acknowledgement letter will also include details of the assigned planning officer, including their contact details and when a decision is expected to be issued by (known as the 'target determination date'). The application will also be made public on the LPAs online planning register.

Following the acknowledgement letter, the LPA will begin the consultation period by publicising the proposal so that members of the public and statutory consultees (such as the Environmental Health/HMO Licensing Team, the Highways Authority and the Refuse/Waste Management Team, for example) can provide their comments on the scheme. Site notices, letters to nearby neighbours and the notification of the parish council are the usual methods used by the LPA to advertise the proposal, but this depends on the type of application submitted. You may be asked to display the site notice yourself, or your planning officer may come out and do this on your behalf. The formal consultation period typically lasts 21 days. Any comments received during that time are posted on the LPAs online planning register. It is important you check this regularly and see what comments are received and by whom. Comments relating to 'non-planning' issues, such as the impact on house values in the area due to a proposed HMO or other private matters, for example, will be published but will not be taken into account by your planning officer. However, concerns such as the impact of the proposal on neighbour amenities (increased noise, loss of privacy and a lack of on-street parking etc.) will be reflected on as they are 'material considerations'.

HMO Property Set Up

You can prepare and provide your planning officer with a response to any public or statutory consultee comments made, however it is advisable to wait until the consultation period has ended so you are able to address all the comments in one succinct letter, without having to submit further responses or address requests for additional information more than once.

You will typically have the option to discuss any issues or concerns your planning officer has prior to a formal determination of your application, allowing you the opportunity, at the planning officer's discretion, to make some minor changes to the scheme in an effort to make it more acceptable or to address a specific concern which your planning officer flags up to you. In cases where your planning officer informally advises they will be recommending your application for approval, you should ask to see a list of any proposed conditions which may require the submission of additional information at the discharging of conditions stage and to make sure that any proposed conditions are not unreasonable or overly restrictive.

Following this and on the assumption that your planning officer is satisfied with all the details, they will review all the comments and prepare their report, (known as an officer report or delegated report), summarising the application and setting out their formal recommendations. This report is reviewed and signed off by your planning officer's manager. Once signed off, a decision notice will be issued, either granting permission for your proposal, or refusing it. The decision notice will include a list of conditions the application must comply with where it is approved. If refused, the decision notice will identify the reasons the LPA has for refusing it, along with the specific policies or material considerations the proposal fails to accord with.

Sometimes, a planning application may be 'called in' for determination at a planning committee meeting, usually where it is 'controversial' or where the number of objections received exceeds a certain 'threshold'. I'll cover this in Chapter 43. It is worth noting that you can withdraw your application at any point in time to avoid an unfavourable determination (i.e. a refusal) being added to the property's history, if the officer advises that they would be looking to refuse your application and are not willing to accept any amendments to make it more acceptable. However, if you do decide to formally withdraw your application, you then forfeit the right to appeal against any refusal.

How Long Does The Application Process Take?

From the point of validation, your assigned planning officer usually has up to eight weeks to issue a decision on most minor[106] applications. Formal extensions of time to allow for determination can be requested if further information is submitted and/or additional comments from consultees are required. Negotiations with your planning officer over certain details of your proposal can also lead to delaying the determination date. Do not be surprised if the determination date passes without a decision being issued! Unfortunately, this is quite normal due to officer's having high numbers of caseloads to work on. Planning officers do try to keep to determination dates as it is important for their internal targets, but it is imperative you (or your agent) keep in regular contact

---

[106] A minor application is less than 10 dwellinghouses or a site area of less than 0.5 hectares.

HMO Property Set Up

with your planning officer (at least once a week) and don't be afraid to chase them for updates.

Where you can, it is advisable to agree to a reasonable extension of time request for the determination of an application, particularly if it is likely to go over the target determination date. Firstly this is because it helps your officer to maintain the focus on your application so it doesn't just 'drift' or get put to the bottom of the pile. Secondly, it provides you with the opportunity to address any concerns or provide further relevant information ahead of determination. Thirdly, if you wished to submit an appeal against the LPA for failing to decide within the agreed time period (non-determination), you only have six months from the last date agreed in which to prepare and submit your appeal. However, where you agree to an extension of time request – or suggest one yourself, this supersedes the original determination date (or any previously agreed extension) and effectively buys you more time if you wished to prepare an appeal under non-determination, should it come to that.

A word of caution though – in some cases, if you fail to agree to an extension of time request, your planning officer can refuse your application due to not having 'sufficient time' or 'information' to consider your proposal fully. Alternatively, they can simply put your application to the back of their worklist and instead focus on other applications where they have a chance of meeting their internal targets for applications which are still within the target determination date period. I would therefore advise that you always try to work with your planning officer rather than against them on determination dates and reasonable requests for extensions of time.

43. Planning Committee

Usually, most minor and 'uncontroversial' applications can be determined under 'delegated powers[107]' by the assigned planning officer. However, more controversial applications (sometimes including HMOs), or larger (major[108]) applications can often be 'called in' for a decision to be made at a Planning Committee meeting instead, often by local councillors and/or if a number of relevant 'planning' objections are received from members of the public. Depending on the LPA, the threshold for applications being called in typically ranges from between three and five objections.

Committee meetings are made up of local councillors, who meet on a fortnightly or monthly basis to discuss certain planning applications and determine whether they should be approved, deferred for further consideration or refused. Your planning officer will inform you if your application is likely to go to committee for a decision. On confirmation, they will work on preparing a report to the committee (a Committee Report) setting out an appraisal of your application, their recommendations and a list of suggested conditions. This will be circulated to the committee members prior to the meeting so they have a chance to review the details of the proposal fully.

You, or your agent, may have the opportunity to speak at a committee meeting to explain why your application should be

---

[107] These powers enable planning officers to determine applications themselves without decisions being issued by a planning committee.
[108] Developments over 10 dwellinghouses are proposed or the site area of the development is over 0.5 hectares.

HMO Property Set Up

approved. To do this you will need to register beforehand with the LA's delegated services officer so you can be included in the meeting agenda. When you or your agent speak, you are usually allowed between three and five minutes to present your case. Again, this depends on the LPAs policy, as some permit shorter speeches and may even only allow a supporter of an application to address the committee if an objector has registered to speak as well.

Once representations have been provided to the committee, the members' role is to debate the planning issues, objections received and the merits of an application, including the recommendations of the planning officer, then consider the key points and decide on the application by putting it to a vote for either deferral, refusal or approval. It is worth bearing in mind that committee members are not obliged to follow the planning officer's recommendations and can go against their advice when determining an application.

Once the committee's vote has been cast, the decision is noted and recorded in the meeting minutes. If deferred, the application will go undetermined until it can be added to the agenda for the next committee meeting. Requests for further information or clarification over certain aspects of the proposal may be made. Depending on the information requested and/or whether there is a backlog of other applications waiting to be heard at committee, it may take a month on two before your application is relisted on an upcoming committee meeting agenda. Once a decision has been made at committee, you will be issued with a decision notice by the LPA over the following few days.

HMO Property Set Up

44. The Planning Decision

<u>Approval And Next Steps</u>

Whether your application is approved under delegated powers or at a committee meeting, you will receive a decision notice from the LPA. As discussed previously, these often contain a number of conditions which should be read, checked and understood as you may be required to submit further information before commencing development or occupation of a property. As a HMO developer, you will no doubt want to implement the permission as soon as possible to get the property set up and tenanted, but failure to discharge any conditions properly, for whatever reason, could lead to enforcement action being taken or the need to apply for retrospective planning permission. Therefore, if you have any queries about the conditions, do contact your planning officer who will be able to explain any additional requirements or submissions you may need to make to lawfully implement the permission.

You'll likely find a condition requiring the permission to be implemented within three years too. It is worth noting that failure to implement the permission before the expiry date can result in it lapsing, meaning you'd need to re-apply for permission again!

In addition to the decision notice, an officer report will be provided, which goes into more detail about how the officer has assessed the proposal and how they came to a decision. This is useful to read through and can help to provide you with 'pointers' for any other HMO properties or other permissions you may wish to apply for in the area as you'll be able to see the relevant policies of the development plan and how the planning officer has applied them to your proposal.

Refusal And Resubmission

If your application is refused under delegated powers or at a committee meeting, the LPA will subsequently issue a refusal notice. This will outline the reasons why permission has not been granted and the policies the proposal fails to comply with. Bear in mind that if a planning committee goes against an officer recommendation for approval and decides to refuse permission, there will need to be a justifiable planning reason, which will be added to the refusal notice. This will note which policies the proposal fails against. Again, an officer report will be provided. It is important that both documents are read and understood as it may affect how you wish to proceed next; i.e. do you:

- Submit a revised application to address the specific reasons for refusal; or

- Submit an appeal against the decision to the Planning Inspectorate; or

- Submit a revised application and prepare an appeal at the same time; or

- Look to do something else with the property which doesn't require planning permission (your PD rights 'fallback' position).

HMO Property Set Up

Officer Report

For any planning decision, it is important to read the accompanying officer report, also sometimes referred to as a delegated report. This covers all the issues the planning officer considered, the consultee and public responses (in favour, neutral or objecting to the proposal) and will highlight what the proposal complies with in terms of local and national policy. There will often be a discussion on the principle of the development and the planning balance before going into more detail on the specific impacts and benefits of the proposed development, for example, the impact of a HMO on neighbour amenities could be weighed against the provision of affordable, high-quality accommodation.

Where you find your application has been refused, the report will provide you with a 'guide' on what may be considered acceptable if you revise your proposal, or the likelihood of success at appeal if you don't agree with the officer's justification(s) for refusal. For example, if your application is refused for a relatively minor reason (such as the position of a proposed window in an extension which compromises the privacy of neighbours), but everything else within the proposal is acceptable, you could simply revise the appropriate drawings, move the window and resubmit the application. Another common reason for the refusal of permission could be the ability to demonstrate suitable off-road parking. This could be remedied by applying to have a kerb dropped and creating additional parking in the front garden (or back garden, if access allows).

Where minor issues are identified, it can be worth discussing these with your planning officer informally or via the pre-application route as they can advise on what needs to be done

HMO Property Set Up

to make the proposal acceptable. Where development or a use is considered 'unacceptable' in principle, this can be more difficult (but not impossible) to overcome and may require significant changes to be undertaken to the proposal to allow it to be considered acceptable. Pre-application advice could be particularly beneficial here to help 'iron out' officer concerns ahead of a resubmission.

Revised Applications And A 'Free Go'

Under planning legislation, you are entitled to what's is essentially a 'free go', following the determination or withdrawal of your application. This allows you to submit a revised application where a previous application has either been approved, refused or withdrawn, without needing to pay the application fee again. This is of course provided the resubmission is:

- The first revision to the application; and

- The development is of the same character or description as previously submitted; and

- Is submitted by the same applicant; and

- Is submitted within 12 months of the previous application being withdrawn; or

- Is submitted within 12 months of the previous application being granted or refused.

The process of preparing a 'free go' application is exactly the same, except when it comes to calculating the application fee

HMO Property Set Up

on the Planning Portal. Instead, you'll simply need to select the most appropriate reason for either a fee reduction or exemption from the list provided. Where no fee is applicable, the application will be issued directly to the LPAs validation team on submission.

45. The Appeal Process

There are a number of reasons why you may wish to submit a planning appeal. Appeals are typically submitted where an application has been refused planning permission. However, you can also submit an appeal for:

- The refusal of permission to vary or remove a condition(s);

- The refusal of prior approval for PD rights;

- Permission granted, subject to conditions which you object to; or

- The failure of the LPA to determine an application within the appropriate time period (usually eight weeks, unless otherwise agreed in writing), also known as 'non-determination'.

Planning appeals can be submitted in relation to householder applications, full planning applications, listed building applications, lawful development certificates and enforcement notices.

Who Are Appeals Submitted To?

Planning appeals are submitted to the Planning Inspectorate, who are an independent body. Their purpose is to make decisions and provide recommendations and advice on a range of land use and planning-related issues across England and Wales. They are also the body who deal with planning appeals, national infrastructure planning applications, the

HMO Property Set Up

examination of local plans and other planning-related and specialist casework.

You can prepare and submit an appeal directly to the Planning Inspectorate[109] free of charge, although there is a cost involved in the preparation and management of an appeal if you choose to engage with a planning agent. It is worth remembering that only the 'original applicant' can submit an appeal, so if for example, you applied for permission using a company name as the applicant, you'd need to use that same name on the appeal form rather than your given name.

Before you go down the appeal route however, it is worth carefully considering the merits of whether it is right to appeal a planning decision. This is because appeals can be time consuming for all parties involved and are not quick processes, often taking many months for a decision to be reached. Even then, there is no guarantee an inspector will allow an appeal as they may draw the same conclusions as the LPA and decide to dismiss the appeal. There can be a danger too that if the Planning Inspectorate does dismiss your appeal, this can effectively 'close the door' on the proposal, leaving you no further room to negotiate with the LPA on a revised scheme. Instead therefore, it can sometimes be more beneficial to try and negotiate with the LPA, depending on the scheme. You may wish to consider informal discussions with your planning officer to make the proposal more acceptable. Alternatively, you could apply for pre-application advice for a more formal response on the prospects of a revised proposal, as outlined in Chapter 41. Provided a general agreement can

---

[109] https://www.gov.uk/government/organisations/planning-inspectorate.

HMO Property Set Up

be reached, you can go back in with a revised proposal which the LPA is more likely to support and you can even make use of the free go.

In some cases where you cannot afford to wait for an appeal decision, it may not be a feasible or appropriate option for you to pursue. This can typically be where you are seeking to set up your HMO property quickly. It is therefore worth making a note of the appeal timescales before seeking to prepare an appeal, particularly if you are on bridging finance! Anyway, I digress… back to appeals!

Submitting An Appeal

Following on from the determination of your planning application, you have the right to appeal to the Planning Inspectorate within six months of the date on the LPAs decision notice, or if the LPA failed to issue a decision (non-determination), you can appeal up to six months after the decision was due, or the last date from any agreed extension of time. In cases where an enforcement notice has been received, you must submit your appeal within the time frame set out in the notice, which is usually 28 days. Failure to do so could lead to enforcement action being taken.

To prepare your appeal, unless you are using a planning agent, you will need to create a free account on the Planning Inspectorate's website and then complete the appropriate appeal form. This is also where you would submit your appeal from once complete. There are three different procedures that an appeal can follow. These are:

HMO Property Set Up

Appeal Procedures	
Written Representations	The most straightforward and quickest method of appeal, where an Inspector decides the appeal on the basis of written representations and a site visit
Hearings	This allows the parties involved to informally present their case before an Inspector, who leads a discussion on the appeal issues
Inquiries	This is typically used for larger, more complex cases and can take several weeks. The Inspector hears evidence from witnesses, who may be cross-examined by legal representatives

Table 45.1: Types of planning appeal procedure.

Generally, the Written Representations appeal procedure is most applicable for HMO-related development applications and other smaller-scale development, including householder extensions/alterations and appeals against planning conditions. Alongside the application form, to fully support your appeal, you will need to prepare a Statement of Case (SoC). This is similar to a planning statement, but should typically include the following information:

HMO Property Set Up

Statement of Case
An introduction briefly setting out why the appeal is being made, the reasons it was refused or not determined
A description of the appeal site and its surroundings to provide context on the proposal
A summary of the relevant planning history, including the most recent application and a summary of any other relevant appeal cases for similar proposals
An overview of the appeal proposal
The relevant planning policies and material considerations most applicable to the appeal proposal
A statement of case, addressing any reasons for refusal and why permission should be granted for the scheme
Final conclusions

Table 45.2: Typical appeal Statement of Case format.

As part of the appeal submission, you will also need to provide copies of the following documents:

Appeal Documents
A copy of the original planning application form
A copy of the LPAs Decision Notice (if issued)
The Site Location Plan
Copies of all the plans, drawings and documents sent to the LPA as part of the application
Copies of any additional plans, drawings and document sent to the LPA but which did not form part of the original application
Any additional plans, drawings or documents relating to the application but not previously seen by the LPA, including any specialist or technical reports commissioned to support your appeal
Any relevant correspondence between yourself and the LPA, statutory consultees and other parties

Table 45.3: Typical appeal documents for submission.

HMO Property Set Up

The Appeal Process

On submission of a completed appeal, you will receive an acknowledgement letter from the Planning Inspectorate with the appeal reference. You will also receive the 'appeal form'. This form must be sent to the LPAs appeal team or co-ordinator, along with any other supporting documents that were not submitted to them as part of the original application so that the appeal can be registered. The form is accompanied by a cover letter which outlines how to find out who at the LPA the appeal form and any other relevant documents/plans should be issued to. Failure to submit the appeal form to the LPA can result in delays, or the Planning Inspectorate refusing to accept your appeal as valid.

Once an appeal has been submitted, the Planning Inspectorate will then check and review the information and confirm whether the appeal is valid, or if anything is missing, ask for further information or documents. On validation, an appropriately experienced Inspector will be assigned to the appeal and you will subsequently be issued with a 'start letter'. This letter provides details of the assigned Inspector's name and contact details, along with a timetable for the progress of the appeal. It also outlines when any supporting documents and final comments should be sent and received by yourself and the LPA as well as any other interested third parties as part of the process.

Planning appeals do not have a set timescale for decisions to be issued within, although average timescales are updated regularly by the Planning Inspectorate and published

HMO Property Set Up

online[110]. The timescale also depends on the type of appeal submitted and the complexity of the appeal proposal. Whilst there is no financial cost to you for the appeal itself, there is obviously a cost in terms of lost time attached to any appeal being submitted and in waiting for its determination, which could result in delays starting refurbishment works and subsequent loss of rental income for HMO proposals.

You could seek to try and recoup some costs by applying for an 'award of costs[111]' as part of your appeal. You can claim costs directly associated with your appeal (but not for costs relating to your original application). This requires an additional form to be completed and issued to the Planning Inspectorate. However, claims can only be made where you believe a party behaves unreasonably which ends up costing you money. This includes if a party fails to co-operate with you, misses deadlines, fails to turn up to a site visit or gives information which is wrong or declared after a deadline. You can also claim costs for the time spent preparing for an appeal, the use of consultants to provide any technical advice and any paid witnesses needed (as necessary). If you are successful in being granted an award by the inspector, you'll then need to reach an agreement with the other party over how much will be paid.

For the appeal itself, the assigned inspector will review both yours and the LPAs SoCs and will go through a round of final comments received from the appellant, the LPA and other

---

[110] https://www.gov.uk/guidance/appeals-average-timescales-for-arranging-inquiries-and-hearings.
[111] https://www.gov.uk/claim-planning-appeal-costs.

interested parties. They will also conduct a site visit (usually unaccompanied), prepare their report and issue their decision.

The inspector can either allow the appeal, or dismiss it and their report will detail how they have come to reach their decision. It is not guaranteed that the inspector will overturn an LPAs decision, so do not rely on this route if you are refused permission initially. However, where an appeal is allowed, this has the effect of granting planning permission. As with LPA decision notices, a list of conditions is usually attached to an inspector's decision. These may need discharging to allow for the development or use to commence and/or be occupied.

If an appeal is dismissed, the inspector's decision is often final. You can seek to challenge an inspector's decision in the High Court, but only if you believe the inspector has made a 'legal error'. Costs for pursuing this can quickly escalate, so unless you have deep pockets and are confident that a legal error has occurred, the inspector's decision will stand.

The report issued as part of the inspector's decision will often reveal the aspects of the proposal the inspector did not agree with. Depending on the wording and the reasons for dismissal, you can use this information to prepare an amended proposal, which can be submitted to the LPA, possibly under the 'free go' route.

46. Planning Enforcement

Hopefully you won't ever have to deal with the LPAs planning enforcement officers, but just in case you do, I have explained the main processes and actions in this next chapter. As part of their planning department, LPAs will have a team of enforcement officers dedicated to dealing with alleged breaches of planning permission. Breaches include where alterations have been made or something has been built without planning permission being granted. For example, a garage converted into habitable accommodation where PD rights have been withdrawn and no planning consent was sought, or a two-storey extension which has not been built in accordance with approved plans (perhaps the roof height has been increased slightly or additional windows installed).

Breaches also include when the use of land or a building has been altered without planning permission. For example, the change of use of a C4 HMO into a Sui Generis HMO, or where conditions attached to a planning approval have not been complied with. An example of this may be if a HMO developer fails to provide details of a cycle storage shed to the LPA for written approval prior to the occupation of their property as a HMO.

If brought to their attention, enforcement officers will typically investigate any unauthorised building works and changes of use, unauthorised works carried out on listed buildings, unauthorised works to protected trees, breaches of conditions attached to planning consents. They may also investigate any potential failures to properly maintain land (if it affects the amenity of an area) and works carried out using

HMO Property Set Up

PD rights, where these appear to be outside the limits of PD rights.

How Do Enforcement Officers Find Out About A Potential Breach?

Most breaches are identified by members of the public, bringing an 'issue' to the LPAs attention. Enforcement officers are obliged to investigate any potential breach of planning permission, so even where you are certain you have done nothing 'wrong', you could find yourself speaking to an enforcement officer if a complaint is lodged. Sometimes complaints can be made because of neighbour disputes, but it is the LPAs duty to listen to both sides of the case before deciding whether any action needs to be taken.

If you wished to make a complaint about a potential breach of planning permission, most LPAs have an online portal or specific email address and phone number where complaints can be submitted. All complaints are treated confidentially. You will have to provide the exact address and details of the harm being caused by the alleged breach. You will also need to leave your name and contact details so the enforcement team can reach you to check information and keep you informed of any proceedings.

Where harm to amenity is demonstrated or when breaches of permission are identified, the enforcement officer will usually contact the person causing the breach to talk about the problem. This can result in the submission of a retrospective planning application to regularise an identified breach, if it is considered this route would be acceptable by the officer. However, where a breach is considered unacceptable, discussions will be held about removing the offending works

HMO Property Set Up

or remedying them or halting or changing a use so it is acceptable. Where a person causing the breach refuses to discuss the situation with the enforcement officer or fails to resolve the issue in an acceptable way, the enforcement officer can take enforcement action to settle the issue on a discretionary basis. This means an enforcement officer's decision over whether enforcement action is taken or not is based on whether it is in the 'public interest' to do so. There needs to be identifiable harm being caused which is sufficient to warrant action being taken.

What Is The Enforcement Process?

If you are contacted by an enforcement officer about an alleged breach of planning control, you are entitled to know what the allegation is and explain your side of the case. Initially, a member of the enforcement team may want to visit the site to establish what works have taken place, or what the land/building is being used for. If an allegation refers to land or buildings where you have an interest, the enforcement officer will provide details of the breach and how it can be rectified. You may also be served with a 'Planning Contravention Notice'. This often requires information concerning the alleged development to be provided and is used to establish the facts of what has occurred and the details of those with an interest in the land, so the enforcement officer can determine whether a breach has taken place and who is responsible. Where a breach is established to have occurred, as the developer/owner, the enforcement officer will expect your co-operation in resolving the situation, either through the removal or modification of the unauthorised development or ceasing/modifying the unauthorised use or activity.

HMO Property Set Up

Depending on the nature of the breach, a reasonable time period will be provided in order to do this – for example, where seven tenants are living in a licenced HMO which may be operating without planning permission, the seventh tenant cannot just be 'kicked out' onto the street so the property can return to C4 use.

This is an important point to note: you cannot be made to stop the use of a property as a larger HMO if you already have a planning application submitted (for example, for change of use to a Sui Generis HMO). That application must be determined before any action is taken. If refused, you then have the right to an appeal, so you could choose to continue operating the property as a larger HMO until an appeal is decided. As the appeals process is quite lengthy you may find by the time an appeal decision is issued that one or two of your tenant's AST agreements have come to an end. In which case, you can simply leave the room(s) empty and drop back down to a C4 HMO use. If the appeal is then dismissed, you are no longer in breach of planning permission as the property will have returned to C4 use. However, if the appeal is allowed, you can look to tenant the room(s) again, of course, only where you have a HMO licence suitable for the intended number of tenants in the property. Anyway, back to enforcement...

In some circumstances you may be invited to submit a retrospective planning application or other appropriate application, where the enforcement officer considers that consent may be granted. Submitting a retrospective application is the same as submitting a standard application via the Planning Portal, except that the word 'retrospective' is inserted into the description of the proposal. Alternatively, an

HMO Property Set Up

application for a CLEUD may be suitable, where evidence can demonstrate the breach would be immune from enforcement action and would therefore be lawful. This is where relevant evidence of either four or ten-years' worth of use/existence can significantly help with the determination of your application.

Formal action can be taken if compliance is not secured through negotiations or the submission of a retrospective application, or where a Certificate of Lawfulness is refused.

Formal Powers

Enforcement officers have a range of powers they can call upon to use to rectify identified breaches of planning control. These currently include the following:

Formal Planning Enforcement Powers	
Planning Contravention Notice	Requires the provision of information relating to the development and/or activities taking place. Often served first as a 'fact-finding' step before determining whether is it in the public interest to serve other formal notices
Breach of Conditions Notice	Served to ensure compliance with any conditions of the planning permission. It is often used to help resolve problems quickly
Enforcement Notice	The most frequently used notice, providing a set of 'steps' to rectify an identified breach
Stop Notice/Temporary Stop Notice	Require any unauthorised activities to be ceased either immediately or after a three-day notice period

Section 215 Notice[112]	Provides the LPA with power to secure the proper maintenance of land and buildings where there is an adverse effect on the amenity of the area
Injunctions	Obtained from the High Court or County Court and often served in anticipation of a breach, taking effect with very little notice. Harm must be considerable to warrant the serving of an injunction
Prosecution	Usually only enacted if any of the above notices are not complied with by a specific date. A formal reminder is sent prompting a person or persons responsibilities to comply with a Notice. Failure to act will normally lead to prosecution, where significant fines can be issued
Direct Action	Used only in extreme circumstances, this enables the LPA to enter land, carry out works and place a 'charge' over the land for the repayment of the costs incurred. If the amount due remains unpaid, this can be converted to a 'Charing Order' or an 'Order for Sale'

Table 46.1: Summary of planning enforcement powers.

The Levelling Up and Regeneration Bill (LURB) (2022) is seeking to make changes to LPAs enforcement powers, by extending the time period in which LPAs can take

---

[112] Section 215 of the Town and Country Planning Act 1990, Chapter 2, Part 8.

enforcement action against unauthorised developments such as building and engineering works and the change of use of any building to use as a single dwellinghouse in England from four years to ten years. For HMO-related developments and uses, this means it will be more important than ever to keep and maintain accurate records for the use of a property as a HMO and any other building works carried out, just in case you need to provide evidence of lawful use or development.

HMO Property Set Up

Summary

In Section IV, I have provided an overview of the English planning system and how it has developed over time from inception. I have explained how national and local planning policies and material considerations can influence HMOs and other associated development proposals.

I have also provided an introduction to householder PD rights and use classes and have explained how you can utilise these rights to extend or alter existing residential properties. I have outlined the importance of adding value to a property and when PD rights should be utilised to gain maximum return on investment as well as utilising PD rights as 'fallback' positions. Additionally, I have explained how PD rights can be removed and other relevant planning and legislative considerations which may affect how a property is used.

I have explained the process of checking whether PD rights exist for a property and the various planning applications which you may need to submit as part of the HMO set up process, as well as key information on what to include in an application.

I have discussed the application process and the timescales involved from submission to a decision, including decisions at planning committee and the appeal process. Finally, I have explained the planning enforcement process and how to navigate this, should any issues arise.

Section V: Building Regulations

This section explains what Building Regulations are and how to ensure that your development complies with them.

It also explains what Approved Documents are and why they are important, along with providing an overview of the types of building regulations applications, the building control process, enforcement and regularisation.

"The road to success is always under construction… there are lots of potholes but no traffic jams."

– Dan Pena

47. Introduction To Building Regulations

There can often be a degree of confusion between planning and building regulations legislation, but I can assure you they are very different matters from one another! As I have explained in the previous section, planning is concerned with the use or development of land or property. Building regulations on the other hand are concerned with the structural safety and integrity of buildings. Both aim to ensure only good quality development takes place.

Building regulations are a set of national minimum standards for England which lay out the 'rules' for the design and construction of most types of buildings. These regulations also apply to conversions, renovations and extensions and ensure that buildings and other structures are fit for purpose for people to either occupy or use. Building regulations are informed by a series of detailed guidance documents, known as 'Approved Documents', which cover anything from structure and fire safety to accessibility, energy performance and electronic communications.

48. Why Are Building Regulations Important For HMOs?

Building regulations are important for HMOs because, primarily, they certify that any works undertaken on a property are built to the correct standards by whoever is carrying out the works. There are a whole range of checks which must be carried out prior to and throughout the construction period, before completion and final signoff is achieved, allowing the property to be occupied. Without achieving signoff on these works you may not be able to tenant the property and will likely not be granted a HMO licence if the proper paperwork cannot be provided.

Compliance with building regulations is important for when it comes to selling your HMO too, or if you seek to refinance the property. Completion or final certificates are often used by solicitors and agents to provide peace of mind for any potential buyers. Because of this, HMOs without a completion certificate are typically valued at less than they might actually be worth, which could deter buyers or only attract 'low-ball' offers, if there is uncertainty over the safety of any works and whether they meet building regulations, forcing down the value of your property further. Mortgage lenders will wish to see the correct certificates prior to releasing funds too. Lenders may even seek some form of protection from the risks, which could be another cost for you.

Furthermore, buildings insurance may be deemed invalid where no completion certificate is available. Companies may even refuse to insure your HMO, or pay out in the event of an incident, meaning you could have to cover any costs yourself.

The above briefly demonstrates why building control and compliance with building regulations is such an important

HMO Property Set Up

aspect of any property development project, let alone HMOs. Engaging properly with the relevant legislation, which I'll go into further over the next few chapters, is clearly of upmost importance.

49. Approved Documents

Building works are informed by Approved Documents, given legal status under the Building Act 1984 (as amended)[113]. These documents provide detailed guidance on how building regulations can be satisfied when carrying out building works to create, for example, a HMO, by laying out the minimum standards expected to be complied with for such a domestic project. There are a whole range of Approved Documents listed A – S which are regularly updated. For the majority of HMO developments, the following Approved Documents are likely to be of particular relevance[114]:

Approved Documents typically relevant to HMO Projects	
Part Name	**What is covered**
Part A: Structural	The loading of buildings, the construction of structural elements (foundations, walls, floors, roofs and chimneys)
Part B: Fire Safety	Fire safety in residential homes, new and existing dwellings and residential accommodation (Volume 1: Dwellings)
Part E: Resistance to Sound (soundproofing)	Sound insulation requirements in dwellings, flats and rooms for residential use
Part F: Ventilation	Ventilation requirements for dwellings (Volume 1: Dwellings))
Part G: Sanitation, hot water safety	Standards required for cold water supply, water efficiency, hot water

---

[113] https://www.legislation.gov.uk/ukpga/1984/55.
[114] Depending upon the extent of works proposed, other approved documents not listed may also be relevant.

HMO Property Set Up

and water efficiency	supply and systems, sanitary conveniences and washing facilities, bathrooms, kitchens and food preparation areas
Part H: Drainage and waste efficiency	Foul water drainage above and below ground level, pipe sizes, protection of pipes, manholes and inspection chambers
Part J: Combustion appliances and fuel storage system	Air supply, discharge of combustion products and protection of buildings for solid fuel, gas and oil appliances and the provision of information for hearths fireplaces, flues and chimneys
Part L: Conservation of fuel and power	Energy efficiency requirements for dwellings (Volume 1: Dwellings)
Part M: Access to and use of buildings	Access to and use of buildings in dwellings; baseline for accessibility in the built environment (Volume 1: Dwellings)
Part P: Electrical Safety	Explanation of when notification of work is required; guidance on the design, installation, inspection, testing and provisions of information
Part Q: Security in dwellings	Standards for doors and windows to resist physical attack or unauthorised access to any dwelling
Part R: High speed electronic communications networks	In-building physical infrastructure to enable connections to broadband networks for new buildings and existing buildings undergoing major renovation works.
Part S: Infrastructure for	Technical guidance on the installation and charge point

HMO Property Set Up

| charging electric vehicles | requirement for new residential buildings and buildings undergoing major renovation |

Table 49.1: Approved Documents typically relevant to HMO projects.

50. Who Has The Responsibility For Building Regulations Compliance?

As you are likely going to be the owner or agent for the HMO you are setting up, you ultimately hold legal responsibly for any works being carried out to the correct standards. However, that is not to say your builder, contractor or installer has no responsibility. As the contracted professional, they must be competent enough to carry out any works to the expected standards and then be capable of rectifying any issues raised by a building control body as part of the signoff process.

Building control bodies have a duty to inspect works as they progress and site visits ensure works are being carried out properly and in the correct order - minimising the potential for any costly mistakes which you'll need to put right. Where substandard works are identified, modifications may be needed. Costly penalties often exist for those who do not follow the standards accurately and Local Authority Building Control (LABC) teams have the power to enforce these penalties under the Building Act 1984, should non-compliant works be identified, where fines and even legal action can be pursued in serious cases.

Therefore, it is important to appoint a competent, professional builder, contractor or installer to carry out any works or installations. Whilst it might be tempting to try and save some money on your budget, the cheapest option isn't always the best. Appointing a builder or contractor just because they seem inexpensive could end up costing you much more in the long run, in terms of time and expense to fix issues as a result of poor-quality workmanship and non-compliance with standards.

HMO Property Set Up

When searching for a competent person to carry out works, where possible, it can often be worthwhile using your local network of landlords, agents and other property professionals to seek out people or companies recommended by others and asking to see examples of their work. If they are already familiar with high-quality HMO projects, they will understand the standards you will be seeking to emanate. A useful guide on how to avoid 'Cowboy Builders' is available from the LABCs website[115].

---

[115] https://www.labc.co.uk/homeowners/how-to-avoid-cowboy-builders-and-how-labc-can-help.

51. The Building Control Process

For most HMO property developers, the building control process will involve building control inspectors approving aspects of any relevant works which have been carried out to reconfigure an existing dwelling into a HMO. Unless works are proposed under PD rights, you will need to wait until planning permission has been granted before making a submission for building control sign off on a project.

Before any works are able to be started, you will need to decide whether to make a 'Full Plans' or 'Building Notice' application. It is worth noting however that a Building Notice enables you to carry out works without the prior approval of a building control body, whilst a Full Plans application requires you to submit plans and documents to a building control body to be approved. For most HMO construction projects involving conversion and/or extensions to an existing dwellinghouse, a Full Plans application will likely be needed. I'll go into more detail over the types of building control applications in Chapter 53. For now, I have produced a helpful flowchart of the building control process, showing you how applications are typically progressed.

HMO Property Set Up

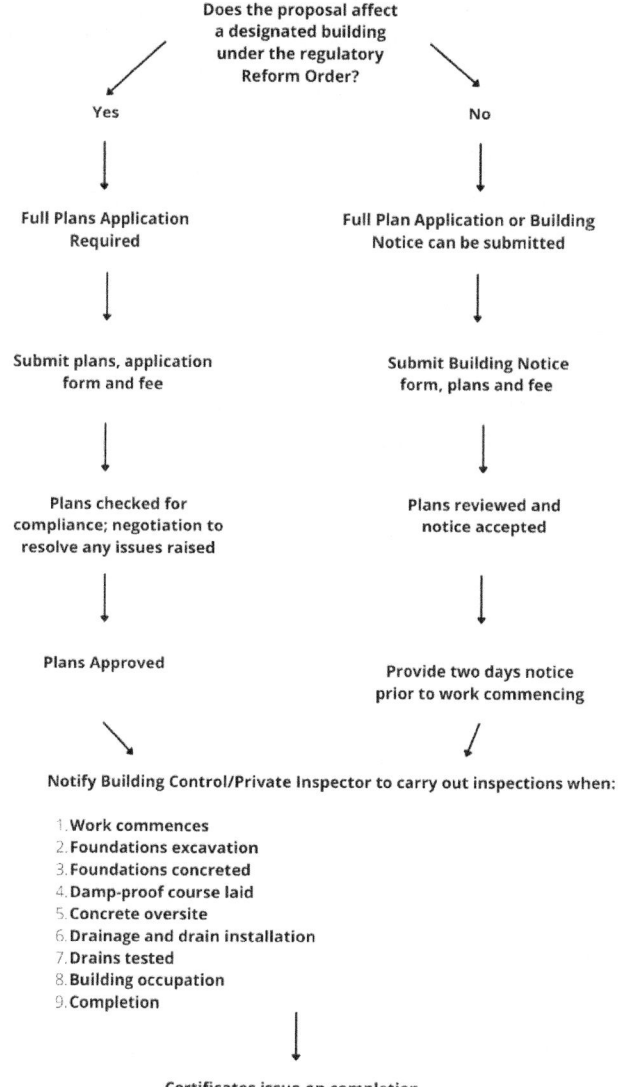

Figure 51.1: Basic Building Control Process Flowchart.

HMO Property Set Up

There are three main choices in the building control process where works may be checked by one of the following building control bodies:

- A local authority building control inspector, run through the Local Authority Building Control (LABC); or

- An approved inspector from a government-approved private building inspection company; or

- A 'competent person' who is usually a qualified fitter or installer working under an approved government scheme, such as NICEIC[116], APHC[117], HETAS[118] FENSA[119] and who is able to sign off work and report it to the Local Authority.

---

[116] National Inspection Council for Electrical Installation Contracting.
[117] Association of Plumbing and Heating Contractors.
[118] Heating Equipment Testing and Approval Scheme.
[119] Fenestration Self-Assessment Scheme.

52. What Works Require Signoff?

In general, where 'light touch' renovation works, such as general painting and decorating or changing kitchen cupboards are proposed, signing off these works is not needed and so no notification is required. However, building regulations will apply where more substantial or structural works are proposed to a building. For example, the erection of a new building, carrying out an extension on an existing building, the change the use of an existing building, the insertion of insulation into a cavity wall or works to underpin the foundations of an existing building. Works which alter an existing buildings' services, such as the thermal elements and electrical status of the building (energy performance), washing and sanitary facilities, hot water cylinders, foul water and rainwater drainage, the installation of replacement windows and fuel burning appliances of any type also require signoff.

As an example, for an extension, most will need to meet the minimum set of technical standards. You will therefore need to consider the extension's energy performance to ensure it is well insulated and has good airtightness, it is structurally sound and has the correct foundations, there is adequate protection against falls and unsafe walls, electric and gas installations have been fitted safely and securely and fire protection measures must be in place, including ensuring there is a safe passage for emergency egress to a safe external area.

There will be many other building works and processes involved in converting a property into a HMO which also require sign-off. Therefore, if you are in any doubt, make sure to always discuss any queries with a building control body beforehand as they will be able to advise you accordingly on

HMO Property Set Up

what is necessary and ensure you do not miss out anything of importance.

53. The Signoff Process And Obtaining Building Regulations Approval

Carrying out building works controlled by building regulations means you will need to gain approval from a relevant building control body prior to starting works, regardless of whether planning permission has been granted or works are proposed under PD rights. This is known as 'giving notice', although this does not apply to works carried out under a competent person scheme, as discussed in Chapter 54.

Approved Private Inspector or LABC Team?

Whether you choose to appoint a local authority inspector through your LABC team or an approved private inspector to carry out the signoff process is completely up to you. As with most things, there are pros and cons for both options, although both are required to adhere to the same building regulations standards. Both must sign off technical plans and drawings and both must also attend site visits when certain work stages are reached on your project to enable them to review the work completed and to ensure your build team are progressing the works in line with the correct regulations and plans.

Although there is no difference in the outcome achieved, there are some variations between application processes if you opt to appoint a private inspector or a LABC inspector. Where you appoint a LABC inspector, you will need to prepare and submit your application via the Planning Portal, or make contact with the LABC team directly, who will then be able to advise you on the process, including how to submit an application. Their contact details are usually found on your local authority's website. However, where you wish to appoint a private inspector, they will apply for approval on your behalf. In general, when appointing a private inspector to oversee the building control process, you are more likely to have a single dedicated person with specialist experience assigned to your project, whilst if appointing a LABC inspector, you may be appointed to different inspectors at different stages who may have more general knowledge and experience.

One thing to note is that only LABC inspectors have the power of enforcement. Therefore, if problems with a build are identified, the LABC can work to resolve these directly, however a private inspector would have to hand the project over to the LABC team to deal any enforcement issues at that stage if the issues cannot be resolved informally. It is also worth noting that if works have started, or have been completed, and you have failed to properly notify a building control body beforehand, only the LABC team can approve those works which have been carried out or completed. However, because the correct approval procedure has not been followed, the LABC team are not obliged to approve any works already carried out without the proper notification taking place. This could result in you being asked to rectify or remove any unauthorised works they have not signed off themselves.

The Inspection Process

Although not all works need formal approval before being commenced (works requiring a Building Notice only), it is important to remember that no works can proceed beyond certain inspection stages without the approval of an inspector. For a HMO project where an extension is being added, these inspection stages would typically be at the following stages:

- Excavations for an extension's foundations;

HMO Property Set Up

- Pouring concrete for the foundations;
- Constructing the oversite;
- Construction of the damp-proof course;
- Drainage installation;
- Pre-occupation completion ('second fix' stage); and
- Completion.

Private inspectors may often be able to attend site visits on a more regular basis and often have the time to provide more detailed advice, particularly if they have specialist experience of HMO projects, whereas a LABC inspector may only be able to provide more general advice on HMO projects. LABC inspectors may also conduct fewer site visits due to existing workload commitments. The knock-on effect of this is the level of feedback provided on building works may be reduced, although in both cases, works will still need to meet minimum standards to enable signoff.

<u>Fees</u>

Fees for appointing the LABC team for their services are based on the costs of the LABC team's work. What you'll pay depends on the type of works involved, the number of rooms in the building and the total floor area. A comprehensive schedule of fees is usually published on the local authority's website. Fees for private inspectors are likely to be slightly more expensive as they are quoted for on an individual project basis, but they can offer more flexibility over payment arrangements and fees can often be negotiated.

HMO Property Set Up

The additional fee expense can often be balanced by savings elsewhere, as some LABC inspectors consider HMOs require additional building works to be undertaken, which may not strictly be necessary. This can include costly works for extra sound proofing between walls, floors and ceilings (under Approved Document E). Whether Approved Document E applies to HMOs depends on the interpretation of the regulations by an inspector and whether a HMO is defined as creating 'rooms for residential purposes'. These are described as rooms, or a suite of rooms, which are not part of a dwelling house, but which are used by one of more persons to live and sleep in and include rooms in a hostel, a hotel, a boarding house, a hall of residence or a residential home. Where HMO rooms are interpreted as creating rooms for residential purposes, there is a requirement for these rooms to be designed and constructed to provide 'reasonable' resistance to sound.

Typically, these standards can be applied to larger HMO properties (seven or more tenants). However, some LABC teams can apply these standards to HMOs with six or fewer tenants. In most cases, these 'sound proofing' standards can be excessive and add significantly to refurbishment budgets, which could be better spent elsewhere.

Types Of Application

As mentioned previously, there are two main types of application you can apply for under the building regulations process. These are a Full Plans application and a Building Notice. A third type is for regularisation, which I'll come on to later in chapter 56. The extent of works to be undertaken on your project will dictate the most appropriate option. Typically though, HMO conversions will require extensive

HMO Property Set Up

works, so the Full Plans application route will be most appropriate.

It is worth noting here that plans for planning permission are different from plans prepared for building control purposes. The level of detail required for building control plans and drawings is much more rigorous and are often accompanied by detailed annotations and scaled section drawings.

For building regulations drawings, you can expect to pay from around £700 to £900 for a single storey extension to around £1,500 to £1,800 for a two storey extension and/or internal structural reconfigurations. This may exclude additional charges involved for structural calculations. Therefore, make sure when instructing works to prepare any drawings for planning purposes that the architect or draughtsperson you appoint can produce plans suitable for building control as well. This could save you time and money in not having to go to someone else to prepare a package of plans for building control purposes. If the works proposed are PD, you will still need suitable drawings for building control signoff.

Full Plans Application

Under the Full Plans procedure, the application should comprise of a full description of the proposed works, a set of technical drawings, structural calculations (where necessary) and a site location plan or block plan identifying the site. The package, including detailed drawings and other technical information, such as construction details and sections of the proposed works are submitted to building control for review in advance of any works starting on site. These plans and details are then checked to ensure the proposals meet the relevant building regulations. If queries are raised about the

HMO Property Set Up

level of detail, a request may be made for modifications or further information.

Once it has been determined the plans demonstrate compliance, they are generally approved or approved conditionally, specifying any modifications which must be made to the plans. Following this, you will receive a notice stating that the plans have been approved and building works can begin. If your plans are rejected, the reasons for rejection will be explained in a notice letter. On issuing, a Full Plans approval notice is valid for three years from the date the plans were deposited.

Building works do not need to conform exactly to the plans (as things do inevitably change on site for one reason or another!) but importantly, works must comply with the requirements of the relevant building regulations. However, significant deviations from the plans could result in needing to submit amended plans for approval[120]. In some cases where deviations are considered too great, these works may even need to be taken down or altered. A completion certificate should be received within five to eight weeks of building works being completed and the final completion inspection being undertaken.

Building Notices

A Building Notice is required where works proposed are simpler and so plans are generally not necessary initially, although you may need to provide drawings and/or structural calculations later. Typically, this route is best suited to smaller works (internal alterations to remove one or two walls, the

---

[120] And may require an amended planning application to be submitted and approved.

HMO Property Set Up

installation of boilers, insertion of windows and the installation of bathrooms and small extensions). It does, however, exclude works which are built close to or on top of rain water and foul drains, where a new building will front onto a private street and where the fire authority will need to be consulted. As you are essentially promising to adhere to building regulations 'in advance', this route allows works to be commenced quickly, although does mean you are reliant on your builder being familiar with the relevant regulations and following them appropriately.

Prior to the commencement of any works, two full days' notice must be given to the LABC team, along with a completed form providing details of the building work proposed and a site location plan or block plan, showing the boundaries of the site and any drainage details. On receipt of a building notice, the LABC team can request further information is provided, either before works begin or while the works are progressing. Once the details are accepted, works may then commence. A building notice is then valid for three years from the date notice is given to the local authority. If building works are not commenced within this time, the notice will lapse.

As with the Full Plans route, works are reliant on inspections being carried out on site when certain stages are reached to confirm compliance. As such, all works taking place should be programmed to allow for inspections at the required stages. Failure to notify an inspector at the relevant work stages may result in the works needing to be 'opened up' for inspection. This can obviously eat into your budget, increasing costs and extending the timeframe for your project's completion.

Following the completion of works, where the LABC team or private inspector are satisfied the works comply with the

HMO Property Set Up

relevant building regulations, a completion certificate should be issued. This provides evidence of compliance with building regulations and should be kept safe.

54. Competent Person Schemes

Competent person schemes (CPS) are schemes set up by the government which allow fitters and installers who are registered with a CPS (such as APHC, HETAS, NICEIC and FENSA) to prove their ability to carry out works to a certain standard and then self-certify that those works comply with the relevant building regulations. Examples of the types of work which can be certified under the CPS are the installation of mechanical ventilation systems, electrical works, plumbing and heating systems and home window replacement.

Where works qualify, this is as an alternative to submitting a Building Notice, although it is worth mentioning here that you can appoint a self-certified installer to work on the relevant part of a project (i.e. install a new heating system), as well as an approved private inspector or a LABC inspector. On completion of works, the fitter or installer will update the local authority on your behalf about the works they've carried out. Once the local authority has been notified, you will receive a certificate from the installer within 30-days of completion of the works, confirming the work complies with building regulations. This will subsequently show up on any solicitor searches if/when you come to sell the property.

It is worth noting that even where works are carried out under CPS schemes, where any works are later found to contravene building regulations, the LABC team have the power to carry out enforcement action to ensure the offending works are rectified, removed or replaced, where this course of action is considered appropriate.

55. Contravention Of Building Regulations And Enforcement Action

A local authority has a general duty to enforce building regulations across its area of authority. Contravention of building regulations can occur through a failure to follow the correct procedures or a failure to meet the expected minimum technical requirements. Sometimes, an owner or a builder may not be conscious that certain works require sign off.

As mentioned previously, approved private inspectors do not have the power to enforce building regulations. However, where a private inspector considers works do not comply with the correct building regulations, they can issue a written notice to deal with the issue informally. Should any offending works not then be rectified, typically within a three month period, the approved private inspector can cancel the initial notice and will provide the person carrying out the works and the LABC team with a cancellation notice. If no other approved private inspector takes on the works, the building control function would be picked up by the LABC team, who are then able to use their enforcement powers, where necessary, to rectify any areas of non-compliance which they have been made aware of.

Aside from informal enforcement to achieve building regulations compliance, the local authority has two formal enforcement powers it can call upon where needed. Firstly, where a person carrying out building work contravenes building regulations, the local authority may seek to prosecute them in the Magistrates' Court and an unlimited fine may be imposed under Sections 35 and 35A of the Building Act

HMO Property Set Up

1984[121]. Prosecution is also possible up to two years after the completion of any offending works, where action will usually be taken against the person carrying out the work (i.e. the main contractor, builder or installer).

Secondly, the local authority may serve an enforcement notice on the building owner during building works, or up to one year after their completion under Section 36 of the Building Act 1984[122], if the LABC team considers any works carried out contravene building regulations. The notice will typically require those specific works to be taken down or altered within 28 days. Where this occurs, an independent report can be obtained if you disagree with the LABC team's decision. Based on the findings of any such report, the LABC team can either withdraw their notice, if the report demonstrates the works have been completed to the correct standards, or if the independent report fails to adequately demonstrate compliance you could seek to appeal to the Magistrates' Court under Section 102 of the Building Act 1984 to resolve the matter. However, as you can probably guess, this option does come at a considerable cost.

You should be aware that the local authority also has the ability to undertake any works to rectify or remove offending works itself and charge you as the building owner for doing so. Such actions are rare, particularly for relatively small projects such as HMO, but if you do find yourself in this situation, it could become extremely costly very quickly for

---

[121] This section can be used to fine people who fail to comply with building regulations. It can be used to ensure that applications are made, and that the builder removes defective work.

[122] This allows the authority to remove defective work by way of a notice signed by an authorised officer. It can only be served on the owner of the property, not the builder.

HMO Property Set Up

you! Importantly though, a Section 36 enforcement notice cannot be served on you after the expiry of a 12 month period from the date of work being completed. This means if any works were not identified as non-compliant within this time period, no further enforcement action can be taken, but you would likely be encouraged to regularise the issue, discussed in the next chapter. In addition, the local authority cannot take enforcement action under Section 36 if you have undertaken works in accordance with a Full Plans application that the authority either approved or failed to reject.

To avoid contravening building regulations it is therefore always good practice to use reputable and experienced builders and installers on your projects to make sure the correct standards are achieved first time round as this will save you time and money, both of which are obviously important factors when setting up a HMO property.

56. Regularisation

As mentioned in Chapter 53, there is a third type of building control application, which is for regularisation. It can be particularly helpful where you are purchasing a property with the intention of converting it into a HMO and your due diligence uncovers unauthorised building works have previously taken place where no completion of final certificate has been issued. Depending on the extent of issues uncovered, you could even seek to negotiate with the seller over the cost of getting the works 'regularised' as part of the selling price. The chances are they will be willing to enter into some form of agreement, as if you have discovered the issues, there is a high probability anyone else interested in the property will too, which could delay or halt the sale of their property. Because you will likely be carrying out works to extend the property and internally reconfigure it so that it is suitable as a HMO, this offers an opportunity for the works to be regularised, whereas if the property were to be purchased by a family for example, it is unlikely they'd be willing to undertake the works necessary so early into their ownership.

The regularisation process is used where unauthorised building works carried out on or after 11th November 1985 can be made 'compliant' through the issuing of a regularisation certificate from the LABC team only. This certificate will act in the same way as a completion certificate. An approved private inspector is not able to issue these certificates as they do not have the authority to do so. If a regularisation certificate is issued, following an inspection of the works by a local authority inspector, this will demonstrate the works complied with the building regulations in place when the unauthorised works were carried out and provides you with peace of mind that you are not inheriting substandard works you may then need to fix at your own expense. An application for a regularisation certificate should comprise the following information:

- A description, with scaled drawing and sections (if possible), of the unauthorised works; and

- Scaled plans, diagrams and sections showing any additional works needed to ensure compliance with the relevant building regulations in effect when the work was originally carried out.

The LABC team may require the building owner to open the works for inspection or for testing to ensure it will comply with building regulations. Where any works have been completed properly, a certificate can be issued to the building owner, although it is worth bearing in mind the LABC team has no obligation to issue a regularisation certificate. In cases where the LABC finds the works completed are not up to the expected standards, works to rectify the issues may be needed - again, the cost for these works could be negotiated with the seller.

Obtaining regularisation for any previously unauthorised works could also help you with refinancing the property and with selling the property on again in the future. Although they should show up in any property searches undertaken, you may be required to physically produce the certificates, so having them easily to hand can help speed up the process.

HMO Property Set Up

Summary

In Section V, I have discussed building regulations and those which are likely to be relevant to HMOs. I have discussed why compliance with the regulations is important and explained how compliance with approved documents is achieved so that any buildings works carried out are safe and fit for purpose.

I have provided an outline of the building control process and explained what works are likely to require signoff, as well as discussing the routes to achieving approval for various works carried out on a HMO project.

Additionally, I have explained the contravention, enforcement and regularisation processes for building regulations and expressed the importance of keeping any certificates issued safe for future reference.

Section VI: Additional Legislation And Considerations

In this penultimate section, I will discuss a range of other legislation and considerations which may crop up as your progress along your property development journeys.

"It takes a deep commitment to change and an even deeper commitment to grow."

– Ralph Ellison

HMO Property Set Up

57. Introduction

Aside from the three primary legislative matters of HMO Licencing, Planning and Building Regulations, there are a number of other secondary pieces of legislation and frequent considerations which come into play when you are setting up a HMO. No one property development project is the same, but you will often find common themes and threads will arise for each one.

This next section therefore sets out to give you additional knowledge and understanding which will help you avoid some common pitfalls and issues that may arise on development projects and enable you to progress your HMO projects without being hindered by these obstacles.

This section also contains general advice on best practice to ensure your HMO projects stay on track and are compliant with the relevant health and safety legislation. Once you know what additional matters to look out for on your property development journeys and the more experience you gain as you undertake additional projects, the entire HMO development process will become much easier.

58. Party Walls

Let's kick this section off by discussing Party Walls. For most projects where you intend to carry out works to an existing property with shared walls and where those works involve working on or near to a wall which is shared by two or more adjoining properties, you are likely to have to engage with the Party Wall Act 1996 to some degree[123]. This can include for both internal and external works. The Act applies to properties in England and Wales only and was devised to prevent building work that could compromise the structural integrity of any shared wall or adjoining properties. Essentially, it provides a framework to firstly help prevent and secondly resolve disputes between adjoining owners in relation to party walls, boundary walls and excavations, should these types of disputes arise.

What Are Party Walls?

I'm sure you will most likely have come across at least one type of party wall before, but if not, there are three main types. Firstly, a party wall can be a shared wall that stands on the lands of two (or more) 'adjoining owners' and forms part of a building. It can be part of a single building (see Figure 59.1).

---

[123] Further guidance on the Party Wall Act is available from the Government's Explanatory Booklet:
https://www.gov.uk/government/publications/preventing-and-resolving-disputes-in-relation-to-party-walls/the-party-wall-etc-act-1996-explanatory-booklet.

HMO Property Set Up

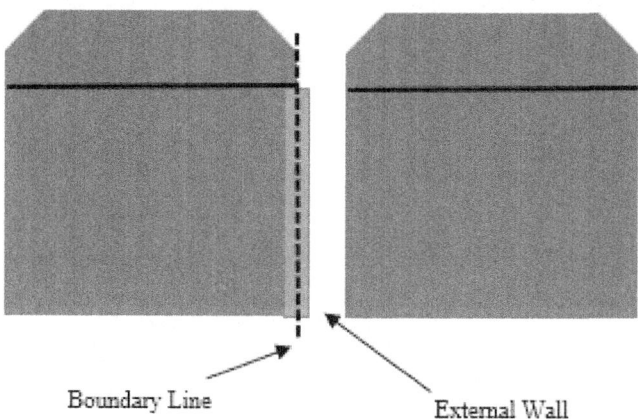

Figure 58.1: A typical Party Wall forming part of one building.

Secondly, it can separate two or more buildings belonging to different or 'adjoining' owners.

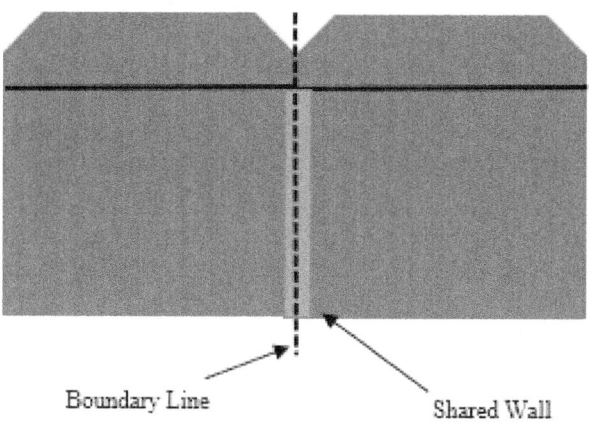

Figure 58.2: A typical Party Wall between to (or more) buildings.

HMO Property Set Up

A third type of party wall is known as a 'Party Fence Wall'. This is not part of a building, but typically stands astride the boundary lines of land in different ownership. Party fence walls are typically brick walls and do not include wooden fencing or hedges.

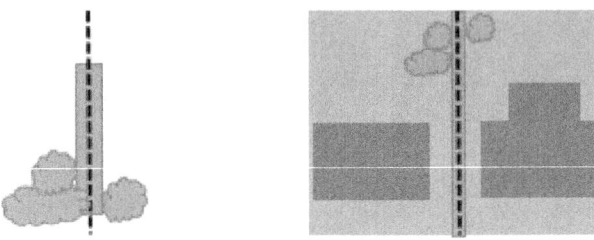

Figure 58.3: Front view and birds eye view of a typical Party Fence Wall astride of two boundaries.

A wall is also considered a party wall where it stands wholly on one owner's land and is used by two (or more) owners to separate their buildings. This could occur where an owner has built a wall and an adjoining owner has built up to the original wall, without construction their own wall. The part of the wall which separates the two buildings is considered to be the party wall, whilst the parts on either side or above are not party walls.

HMO Property Set Up

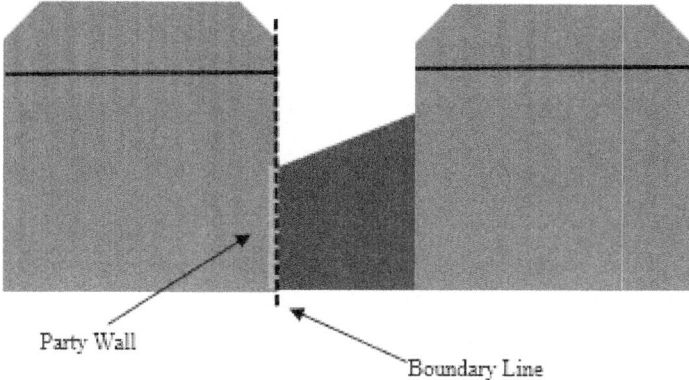

Figure 58.4: typical Party Wall between adjoining owners, separating two buildings, where construction has taken place up to an original wall.

An additional type of Party Wall is known as a 'party structure'. This can be a wall or a floor partition, or another type of structure which separates buildings or parts of buildings which are in different ownerships and which are accessed by separate staircases or entrances, for example, in a block of apartments.

HMO Property Set Up

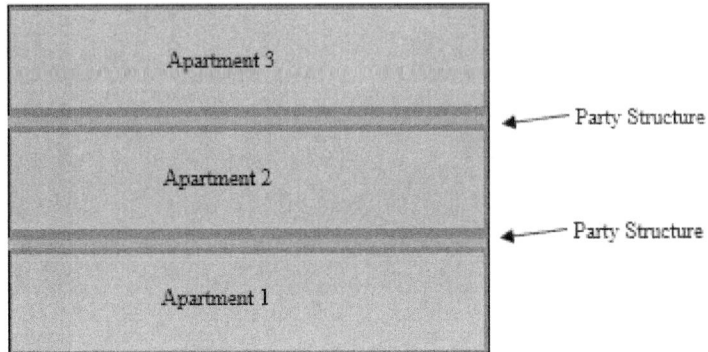

Figure 58.5: Typical Party Structures between adjoining owners.

Walls which are not considered to be party walls include boundary walls, such as a fenced wall or a garden wall constructed wholly on an owner's land and the external walls of a building built up to, but not astride, the boundary line.

What Are Your Obligations Under The Act?

Under the provisions of the Act, you are required to inform 'adjoining owners' and provide them with a Party Wall Notice where any of the following common works are proposed:

HMO Property Set Up

Common Works Requiring a Party Wall Notice
Works to shared walls between semi-detached and terraced dwellings
Works involving shared 'party structures', i.e. floors between flats/apartments
Works to garden boundary walls
Excavation works for extensions or underpinning within three to six metres of a party wall (depending on what is being proposed)
Loft conversions which impact on a party wall i.e. inserting a beam
Works to make a party wall thicker or higher
Constructing a second-storey extension above a shared wall
Works to extend a party wall downwards i.e. to create a basement
Constructing a new wall up to or off a party wall
Removal of a shared chimney breast/chimney
The insertion of a damp-proof course into a party wall
Works to repair an existing party wall

Table 58.1: Common works where a Party Wall Notice is required.

Table 58.1 is not however an exhaustive list and other works may require notification. It is worth noting here though that minor works, such as drilling into a party wall for shelving, hanging pictures or kitchen/bathroom units, or carrying out plastering, adding or changing electrical wiring or sockets and painting do not require notice to be given to neighbours as none of these types of works are likely to impact the structural integrity of a shared wall. Where you are planning works which have the potential to affect the structural strength and supporting function of a party wall, or which might cause damage to an adjoining owner's side of the party wall it is likely you will need to serve a Party Wall Notice on any 'adjoining owners'.

HMO Property Set Up

What Is An Adjoining Owner?

An adjoining owner can be either a person or a company who is the freehold or leasehold owner of any adjoining property. Where properties are not physically touching one another (i.e. detached properties), if they are within three metres (or six metres) of your property, depending on type and extent of the works you wish to carry out, they are considered to be 'adjoining' and will therefore need to be informed of any proposed works to a party wall, prior to those works commencing. Aside from providing any adjoining owners with the correct type of notice, you will also need to ensure the correct notice period is observed.

What Is A Party Wall Notice?

A Party Wall Notice is a written letter (or an email) which must be provided to any affected or potentially affected adjoining owners ahead of works being carried out to a party wall. Generally, at least two months' notice should be provided before any work is due to commence, although one month for new party walls or structures and any excavations is considered to be acceptable. Prior to serving a party wall notice, it is advisable to speak to any adjoining owners in person, where possible, before serving them written notice for the works. This can often help to reassure them and gives them the opportunity to ask any questions about what you intend to do. However, in cases where you may be seeking to carry out an extension, for example, I would recommend withholding the details about the future use of the property as a HMO. This is because whilst they may not have a problem with an extension being built, as soon as it is linked to a HMO use, in an adjoining owners mind, it may cause unnecessary

HMO Property Set Up

concerns to arise and detract from the works you are actually notifying adjoining owner(s) of.

The process of formally serving notice will involve drafting the party wall notice in letter or email format. Your letter or email should include your contact details, the details of the works proposed affecting the party wall, the date you (or your builder) intent to start the works on. You should also include details of any access requirements (including for materials and equipment) that may be necessary over any adjoining owner's property or land and can include details of the work hours and days (i.e. works will take place Monday to Friday 9:00 to 17:30 and on Saturdays 9:00 to 13:30). Additionally, it is useful to provide the date works should be completed by as well so adjoining owners have an indication of how long any disruption may go on for.

Where an adjoining property is rented out or is a leasehold property, you will need to serve notice on both the owner(s) of the building as well as the tenant. You can use the Land Registry to find out who owns the property if it is not clear, or a tenant does not know. Where owners are not local, or you are unable to drop off the notice letter in person, I would recommend sending the letters via recorded delivery or request read receipts if sending via email.

To make the process easier for adjoining owners to agree to the works, it is worthwhile enclosing a drafted reply letter which can be filled out by adjoining owners and where necessary, a stamped addressed envelope for neighbours/owners to sign and then return to you. The Government has produced a useful guidance document which contains a number of Party Wall Notice example letters. These cover a range of party wall issues and templated letters that can be printed, filled out and served on adjoining neighbours and/or owners. To access these, simply go to Google and type in 'Party Wall Act Explanatory Booklet', then go to the gov.uk website.

Once an appropriate notice has been prepared, served and hopefully accepted by your neighbour(s), it is valid for a year. If you are on a tight schedule, this can be useful in avoiding delays, particularly where you need to apply for planning permission as the notice can be provided to adjoining owners at the same time as a planning application is submitted. Where works do not require planning permission however, such as works under PD rights, once the proper notice period has been observed, you can commence works straight away, provided the adjoining owner is satisfied with the details set out in the notice letter and has provided their formal written agreement to you.

What Happens Once I Have Served Notice?

Once you have handed, emailed, or had delivered the notice letter to any adjoining owners, they have three options before them:

1. Provide their consent for the works. Where they may verbally tell you they are happy to consent, ask them to return the reply letter confirming this or draft their own response; or

2. Refuse to give their consent. This begins the 'dispute resolution' process; or

3. Issue a 'counter notice'. This can include additional works they would like carried out at the same time, costs for which should be split between both parties where there is a mutual benefit.

HMO Property Set Up

From the date notice is served, adjoining owners must respond to your notice letter within 14 days. As above, verbal consent is not valid as it cannot be proven. However, where written consent is given, this concludes the process, allowing you to make a start on the works once the notice period expires. Be aware that unless the adjoining owner has agreed in writing to the work starting earlier than is stated in the notice, you will need to wait until the notice period has expired before starting the works. In cases where no written response is received within the 14-day period, you automatically enter the 'dispute resolution' process, even if the adjoining owner has verbally agreed to the works. If you do speak with any adjoining owner, it is worth mentioning this as it can encourage them to provide their written response, saving you time and money on appointing Party Wall Surveyors when they are not necessary.

Consent Refused And Dispute Resolution

If any adjoining owners refuse to provide their consent for the works, or where they fail to respond in time, under the Party Wall Act legislation, you are considered to be 'in dispute' with one another. Firstly, the easiest thing to do in this situation is to try and speak to the adjoining owner(s), find out what their concerns are and seek to come to an agreement with them. Where they produce a counter notice, you could seek to come to an agreement over these terms where they are reasonable. Counter notice terms can typically include changes to the works, additional works or changing the working hours which you have specified. Where minor additional works are sought, such a replacing an old fence panel, you may wish to pay for and undertake these works as a 'goodwill gesture', particularly if you feel an adjoining owner is likely to raise concerns over the future use of your property as a HMO. Any agreements reached, including who pays for what works, must be put in writing and signed by yourself and the adjoining owner.

In circumstances where agreements are still not possible, you will need to appoint a suitably qualified Party Wall Surveyor. You can appoint one to work for both yourself and any adjoining owner(s), although an adjoining owner also has the option to appoint their own independent surveyor and you would typically be liable for both surveyor's fees as the works being proposed would be for your benefit. The surveyor(s) would then work to help try and resolve the dispute so that the works can take place.

Party Wall Awards

Once appointed, a surveyor will assess the proposed works and put together a document called a 'Party Wall Award'. This is a legal document setting out what, how and when works can be carried out, including access details, any necessary protections taken to minimise the risk of damage to an adjoining owner's property – and also who is responsible for paying for the works and any damage caused. A 'Schedule of Condition Report' is often prepared by surveyor(s) for an adjoining owner's property, prior to any works being carried out. This includes a site inspection of both internal and external elements, where appropriate. The report will document any pre-existing damage, cracks and the condition of an adjoining owner's property to ensure that any 'new' damage as a result of works to the party wall are accurately recorded.

Under the Act, whilst anyone can be appointed as a party wall surveyor, provided they are not a beneficiary of the works (i.e. the building owner or adjoining owner) and they are not

HMO Property Set Up

already involved in the building work (i.e. your builder), they should have a good knowledge of construction and the Act itself. It is therefore recommended you contact a suitably qualified building professional for both yours and an adjoining owner's peace of mind. Many surveyors are often RICS accredited, giving you the reassurance they are fully capable of acting responsibly for both parties. It is worth mentioning here that if you end up in a disagreement with an appointed surveyor, perhaps acting on behalf of an adjoining owner, you cannot revoke their appointment, but you can approach a third surveyor to resolve the issue. This option, however, is only available where you and the adjoining owner have chosen to appoint separate surveyors.

Where a surveyor issues an Award, this is final and allows the building owner the legal right to commence party wall works to their property which affect an adjoining owner's party wall. Awards also allow for the checking of works to ensure they have been carried out in accordance with best practice. In cases where either you or the adjoining owner consider the Award is unfair, it can be appealed at county court within 14 days from the date it was served, although as with everything 'court' related, the costs for this can escalate quickly for both parties. Should you wish to challenge an Award, it is worthwhile seeking appropriate legal advice. In most cases, however, adjoining owners do not seek to challenge an Award when it has been prepared by a professional, so if you are then in agreement over the Award and extent of works, consent is deemed to have been given for the works to be carried out.

HMO Property Set Up

What Happens If I Fail To Serve Notice?

In cases where you fail to serve notice on an adjoining owner, it is not a legal offence, but it does leave you exposed to the threat of civil action from an adjoining owner. Courts typically take a dim view of owners who fail to serve a party wall notice. As a result, you could find yourself being forced to pay for the cost of repairing any damage caused to a party wall, regardless of whether any damage stemmed from the works you carry out or not, as there would be no record of an adjoining owner's party wall condition prior to any works being carried out. Additionally, where works have commenced without notice being provided, an adjoining owner can seek to obtain a court injunction, halting the works and causing unnecessary delays to you, throwing your HMO refurbishment schedule out the window. A surveyor will then need to prepare an Award before any further works are able to continue and you'd be liable to cover the costs associated with this.

I would therefore always recommend serving notice on an adjoining owner as soon as possible where works are proposed to a party wall or structure. If you are not sure whether notice should be served, a precautionary approach can often be the best way forwards. This reduces the risk of delays and additional costs, although seeking the advice of a professional beforehand can be invaluable, particularly as many party wall surveyors can offer initial free advice on party wall matters.

59. Restrictive Covenants

I briefly touched on restrictive covenants in Chapter 39, but I'll go through them in more detail here. Restrictive covenants are legal terms which are imposed on land or property and set out how you can use that piece of land or property. They are imposed to prevent the buyer from using the land or property in a way that the seller, or benefactor, deems to be inappropriate. This is usually in the interests of neighbours and/or the surrounding area. A benefactor is any person or company named in the title register who 'benefits' from the restriction imposed.

Details of any restrictive covenants can usually be found in the title register for a piece of land or property, in the 'Charges Register' section. Any restrictions should be uncovered as part of your due diligence before purchasing, usually by your solicitor, however you can quickly check whether any covenants may prevent you from carrying out physical works to a property, or using it in a certain way, by purchasing the title register from the Land Registry yourself and taking a look at the details.

Restrictive covenants are very much separate from the planning system, but because they are legal restrictions, they are able to supersede PD rights. This means if there are covenants contained in the title register which restrict the use of a property to anything but a *single private family dwellinghouse*, it is commonly accepted that it cannot be used as an HMO, because the unrelated tenants will not form a 'family' unit. However, properties with covenants restricting their use to a *single private dwellinghouse* are generally considered suitable for being converted into HMOs. This is because the house remains as a single private dwellinghouse with one front (main) door, one set of utility meters and one

HMO Property Set Up

council tax payment. Do check whether your solicitor agrees with this prior to moving forward on a potential purchase as they may offer an alternative view.

Similarly, if you came across a covenant which places restrictions on extending the property, you wouldn't be able to build an extension, regardless of whether the works would normally fall within PD rights or requires planning permission, without the express permission of the benefactor of the covenant. It is important to note however that a LPA will not consider any covenants when assessing a planning application or PD enquiries – it is your responsibility to check for these types of restrictions on land or a property you are interested in. Another thing to note is that restrictive covenants are increasingly being placed on new build properties by builders or property developers which prevent purchasers from altering the properties, unless a fee is agreed with the builder or developer to remove it and allow for works to be undertaken. This is different from a planning condition which may remove PD rights as part of a grant of planning permission as these covenants relate to legal matters. These covenants are typically placed by builders/developers to maintain an element of control over the look and character of estates and the use of new houses. As a result, this can rule out many suitable properties which may otherwise have good potential for being used as HMOs.

Older properties may also have some restrictions placed on their use, sometimes to protect the design and use of the building, whilst others may be more general, such as not keeping livestock, burning materials or running a business or trade, for example. Where you come across a covenant relating to business or a trade, unless it specifically mentions HMOs, these should not be classed as a business or trade as they remain primarily as residential properties in residential

HMO Property Set Up

use. These types of covenants should therefore not be an issue for most HMO projects, although again, do be certain to ask your solicitor to check the wording of any covenants uncovered carefully and advise accordingly – they are the legal professional after all!

What Happens If I Ignore A Restrictive Covenant?

If you were to breach a covenant, the benefactor of the covenant could seek to enforce it against you - potentially meaning you may have to remove any extensions built and return the property to its original condition, or cease using it as an HMO. However, this can only happen if the benefactor is either still trading (if it is a company) or is still alive (if it is a person) and the beneficiary of the covenant has not been transferred to another company or person. Additionally - and importantly - only the benefactor can seek to enforce a covenant. It is worth noting as well that in certain circumstances, if there has been a continuous breach of a covenant for a 'significant' period of time, then the breach can be considered 'unenforceable' as the benefactor has allowed for the breach to continue without taking action to enforce it.

What Can You Do If Land Or A Property Has a Covenant Restricting Its Use Or Development?

In cases where you find a covenant on a property you are interested in which affects its use as an HMO, or prevents physical works to a property, you could seek to take out a special type of insurance called 'indemnity insurance'. Alternatively, you could try to have the covenant either varied or removed altogether[124]. Where you choose to opt for

---

[124] This is not the same as a planning application to vary or remove a condition (S73 application).

HMO Property Set Up

indemnity insurance, this can be tailored to cover any works or use of a property, in the event that a benefactor seeks to enforce a covenant.

Where planning permission is sought for works that may breach a restrictive covenant, this can make obtaining indemnity insurance more difficult as the planning process is invariably public. This can result in benefactors reviewing their titles to see if anything can be used to prevent a proposed use or development – or even to obtain a 'ransom' value from the new owner of the land or property. In cases where you intend to take out indemnity insurance, you will need to speak to your solicitor to ensure the type of cover you are seeking is suitable for your needs. Additionally, your solicitor will need to liaise with a suitable insurer and organise the insurance on your behalf, as you are often not able to obtain specialised restrictive covenant indemnity insurance directly from an insurance provider as an individual.

The insurer will assess the risks of enforcement and draw up a bespoke policy that will cover any 'reasonable' legal and professional fees and expenses you may incur if you are required to make a settlement in a legal action. Typically, the insurer will seek a one-off payment to cover the cost implications of a benefactor making a claim against the way in which the property is used or has been altered in the future. This includes the cost of an out-of-court settlement, any damages, compensation, cost and/or expenses you may have to make resulting from legal action, the cost of altering, demolishing and/or reinstating all or part of the property or anything built on it as a result of legal action, the reduction in the value of the property and any money you may have spent on the property lost as a result of legal action. If the matter is considered 'low risk', a lower payment can be expected; naturally, if the insurer considers the matter to be of 'higher

HMO Property Set Up

risk' from being enforced, you can expect to pay a larger amount.

Once obtained, the duration of the policy is in perpetuity and continues to protect the buyer even when they no longer own the property, whilst extending to any future owners and mortgage lenders, providing long-term peace of mind for yourself and any future purchasers of your HMO property should you wish to sell it on.

Variation Or Removal Of A Restrictive Covenant

As mentioned earlier, aside from indemnity insurance, there is a second option available to deal with restrictive covenants. However, this option is potentially more 'high risk' than obtaining insurance as it involves approaching the benefactor directly and seeking to negotiate the variation or release of a covenant. This can sometimes be achieved for a fee. An example of this is a HMO developer in Hemel Hempstead who was looking to purchase a property which contained a covenant, placed by the local authority, which restricted the use of the property to a family residence only. The developer decided to approach the council to remove the covenant. After some negotiation (and a very patient vendor), the council agreed to lift the covenant for a fee. This fee was based on the future potential revenue generated by using the property as a HMO. The developer decided to proceed with the purchase as the fee wasn't considered significant over time, in comparison to the income the property would produce as a HMO. The developer subsequently factored in the cost of lifting the covenant into the purchase price of the property. Even with the agreed fee to be paid to the Council, the property analyser was able to show that the property could provide a healthy return as a seven bedroom HMO.

HMO Property Set Up

However, in other circumstances, a fee can often prove to be prohibitively costly and negotiations with a benefactor may take too long to come through, particularly in a competitive market or just simply break down. Ultimately, negotiations may then result in a failure to lift or vary the covenant. If your request to the benefactor is unsuccessful, you can take your case to the Upper Tribunal (Lands Chamber). The Lands Chamber is a specialist tribunal which seeks to settle legal disputes. As per most decisions involving courts or tribunals, the costs can become quite steep very quickly and legal advice should be sought before embarking on this route. Once a case has been taken to the tribunal, it will be assessed. A decision will then be issued over whether the covenant is still deemed to function and is fit for purpose. In cases where it is deemed redundant, a decision is made over whether it can be lifted to allow for the development or use proposed. Again, this can end up being a costly and drawn-out process, so is unlikely to be a viable option if you are seeking to purchase and set up a HMO property quickly.

One thing to note is that once a benefactor has been approached with the intention of varying or lifting a covenant, you are then not able to take out indemnity insurance. This is because most policies will contain a common clause stating that the insurance is invalid where you reveal the issue or reason for the policy to a third party, including the benefactor. Essentially therefore, once you choose the route of approaching the benefactor, this limits your options significantly.

I would therefore advise discussing the impact of a restrictive covenant with a solicitor as soon as possible once one has been uncovered during the due diligence process. In some cases, it can be more beneficial, both in time and cost, to discount a prospective property for HMO development rather

HMO Property Set Up

than seek to obtain indemnity insurance or lift the covenant, although ultimately it depends on your appetite for risk.

60. Vehicle Parking Standards, Bicycle Storage And Dropping A Kerb

You may be surprised to know that for HMOs created using PD rights (i.e. those outside of A4D areas), there is no obligation for you to provide any bicycle or vehicle parking spaces for your tenants at all as no planning permission is required. I would, however, advise on seeking to provide at least some off-road parking for your HMO properties where possible, in line with the adopted standards for a C3 dwellinghouse[125] as it can make your property more attractive to tenants, particularly those who commute by car or motorcycle.

It can also help to keep neighbours living in the street on your side as your tenants won't be competing with them for on-street parking, which can be very frustrating for all users; particularly on busy streets where parking is already likely to be limited. Where parking restrictions are in force, some councils do allow tenants of HMOs to apply for one or two parking permits per property in these areas. This can be attractive to prospective tenants, although tenants would then need to register their vehicles to the property, which they may not wish to do if they don't intend to stay at your property for long. When advertising rooms for rent, it is always worthwhile providing information about the availability of vehicle and cycle parking.

---

[125] Some LPAs do have adopted parking standards for C4 and Sui Generis HMOs, so compliance with these is necessary if your HMO is in an A4D area, or you need planning permission for a larger HMO.

HMO Property Set Up

Vehicle Parking Standards

For HMOs requiring planning permissions (Sui Generis or those in A4Ds areas), not complying with local parking standards can mean that planning permission is refused for your proposal. Information about adopted parking standards can typically be found in either SPDs or SPGs which accompany a local development plan, although in some cases, there may be a specific parking related policy contained with the main Development Plan Document. Levels of parking provisions required do vary from council to council and often by area within the local authority district or borough, depending on whether the area is classed as 'rural', 'suburban' or 'urban'. Occasionally, parking standards are set by the county council, rather than the district, city or borough council, so do check both if you can't immediately find what you are looking for. Looking at the officer reports or delegated reports of recently decided applications for HMOs on the LPAs website may offer clues as to what parking standards are expected and where to find the information if it is not readily available.

It is not uncommon for LPAs to set maximum vehicle parking standards for HMOs as well as minimum bicycle parking spaces, to be provided in a secure store. These maximum parking standards are put in place to avoid front gardens and driveways effectively becoming 'parking lots', to aid with reducing flooding risks from surface water runoff as a result of using impermeable hard surfacing on driveways and to help encourage the use of more sustainable forms of personal transportation. Often, as part of a grant of planning permission, you will have a condition setting out the required number of vehicle parking spaces and bicycle storage

HMO Property Set Up

necessary for your HMO development. An example of this could be the requirement to provide four car parking spaces for a seven-bedroom Sui Generis HMO, with eight bicycle parking spaces (one for each tenant, plus an extra space for any visitors).

Vehicle parking spaces are typically accepted as being 2.4 metres wide by 4.8 metres long, although as cars have become larger, LPAs are increasingly requesting car parking spaces are at least 2.5 metres wide by five metres long and that driveways must provide sufficient space for manoeuvring. LPAs are also keen for independently accessible 'side-by-side' spaces to be provided over 'tandem' parking spaces so tenants are less likely to block each other in. It is therefore important you check you have sufficient room for the number of spaces you may be asked to provide and that vehicles can turn and both enter and exit a driveway in a forward gear as reversing onto a road is not considered favourable.

Electric Vehicle Charging Points

With the Government's drive toward expanding the number of electric vehicles on the roads, electric vehicle charging points (EVCPs) are increasingly being requested for all residential developments, including HMOs. Where existing properties are undergoing major renovations, charge points are commonly being installed and if planning permission is required, a condition setting out that at least one EVCP must be provided are becoming increasingly common.

Whilst you may find that many tenants do not currently have electric vehicles, assuming the Government's drive to halt the sale of new diesel and petrol vehicles by 2030 stays on track, it is likely that more and more tenants may have electric

HMO Property Set Up

vehicles. Therefore, being able to provide at least one charging point could help to attract and keep tenants at your property, as well as helping to 'future-proof' your property.

Bicycle Storage

Secure bicycle storage can either be in the form of a discreet purpose-built lockable cycle storage unit at the front or side of the property, or a standard shed in the rear garden of a property. This is of course provided there is suitable access for this without going through the main house (i.e. a side passageway can be used). It can also be in the form of a 'Sheffield' style 'D- ring' or bicycle rack.

Most planning applications for HMOs are granted with a condition requiring the submission of additional details relating to cycle storage. Provided the type of bicycle storage you are offering is secure, this should be acceptable in most cases, although a request for covered storage may be made by the LPA.

Dropping A Kerb

Dropping a kerb, also known as a 'vehicle crossover point', is where an area of pavement and kerb is lowered to allow access from a road, across the pavement and onto a driveway or parking area. These can be particularly useful if you are seeking to create additional off-street parking for your tenants as it avoids them having to 'bump' their cars up over the pavement, which could damage them and the pavement and stops other people (in theory) from parking in front of a kerb and blocking access to your property's driveway.

Most people are not commonly aware of this, but it is not legal to drive over a pavement unless there is a vehicle

HMO Property Set Up

crossover as by doing so, this could damage the pavement and any pipes/cables below it. However, this is generally difficult to enforce and so there is often a bit of a 'grey area' over accessing off-street parking by 'bumping up' a kerb.

If you set up a C4 HMO to later change to a Sui Generis HMO, it may be necessary to apply for permission to drop a kerb for access to any off-street parking you may create. Best practice guidance advises that you should have a dropped kerb in place before constructing any off-street parking. This is because the LPA or Local Highway Authority (LHA) will often expect you to demonstrate that off-road parking is firstly accessible. When applying for planning permission, some LPAs will require you to drop a kerb where the road is designated as a 'classified road[126]', or the property is located within a conservation area, is a listed building or if PD rights have been otherwise removed. Your local authority will usually have a list of classified roads on their website so you can check this, although you will find that most dwellings in urban or suburban areas are on classified roads. Other LPAs may simply refer you to the LHA to obtain their permission for a vehicle crossover.

Permission is typically required to ensure the access is safe and provides adequate visibility onto the highway, does not adversely impact on existing levels of on-street parking or street furniture (signs, street lights, bus stops/shelters, exchange boxes etc.) and to check whether the pavement needs strengthening to protect any services buried underground (water pipes etc.). You can also apply to have an

---

[126] A classified road is a highway or proposed highway which is a classified road in accordance with section 12 of the Highways Act 1980 (section 329, Highways Act 1980).

HMO Property Set Up

existing dropped kerb made wider, which is helpful if you have a particularly wide driveway but only a comparatively small vehicle crossover point.

To apply for a dropped kerb, you will either need to be the owner of the property, or have the owner's permission. You will also need to complete a basic application form and provide information to support your application. This information may include site plans, photographs, proof of planning permission being granted and/or a letter or email from a utility company confirming they are happy the proposal won't affect any services. On receipt of an application and the appropriate fee, a LHA engineer will typically visit the site and carry out an inspection to determine its suitability. After this assessment has taken place, the LHA will notify you of the outcome, either:

- Approving the works, subject to them being completed within a certain timeframe; or

- Rejecting the application and providing the reason(s) why.

Assuming your application is approved, you will be able to appoint a contractor, or in some cases, appoint the local authority's highways team to carry out the vehicle crossover works. If rejected, depending on the reasons, you may be able to amend your application and resubmit it for further consideration. Should you choose to appoint your own contractor to carry out the vehicle crossover works, they must be suitably qualified to undertake them by demonstrating they have the proper licences in place to open the road and have an appropriate level of public liability insurance.

HMO Property Set Up

Once the works have been carried out, they will need to be inspected to ensure they are completed to a sufficient standard. The LHA will then issue a Certificate of Completion. This concludes the process and confirms that a legal right of access has been created from the highway to your property.

61. Construction Design Management (CDM)

Every construction project, regardless of its size or scale, is required to comply with the Construction (Design and Management) Regulations 2015[127]. This legislation was brought in to protect construction workers working on a site or project and seeks to ensure works are sensibly planned for so the risks involved are managed correctly from a project's start to its finish. By following the CDM regulations, this ensures risks are minimised and that workers and site visitors are protected from harm.

Essentially, CDM seeks to ensure you are suitably covered against site accidents or any unexpected incidents, such as someone breaking in and injuring themselves or a contractor injuring themselves. It also ensures that workers have the correct knowledge and skills to be working on site in the first place. For projects involving landlords who own domestic properties, the CDM regulations identify these as 'commercial' clients, comprised of organisations or individuals for whom a construction project is carried out in connection with a business. As the building owner, you are the CDM 'Duty Holder' and are ultimately responsible for the health and safety of all those entering and working on the site or project right through to the construction work being completed and until the client disposes of their interest in the building. Commercial clients have contractual control and can appoint designers and contractors. They are also accountable for the impact of their decisions and the approach taken on health, safety and welfare on the project.

Whilst most commercial clients will typically not commission construction works very often and will not be experts or have

---

[127] https://www.legislation.gov.uk/uksi/2015/51/contents.

HMO Property Set Up

detailed skills, knowledge or experience of the construction process, particularly if you are embarking on your first HMO project, the overall duty of a commercial client is to make and maintain suitable arrangements for managing a construction project so that health, safety and welfare for all involved is achieved. These responsibilities can include appointing professionals with the necessary skills, knowledge and experience to undertake the delivery of the project. Responsibility can therefore often be transferred to a contractor employed for single contractor projects or the principal designer or contractor for projects with more than one contractor, who will take the lead during the pre-construction and construction phases of a project. The differences between the two roles are that:

- A principal designer is a professional appointed by the client (you) who has a duty to plan, manage and coordinate the planning, design work and health and safety of the project during the *pre-construction* phase of any project involving more than one contractor; whilst a

- Principal contractor is a professional appointed by the client (you) who has a duty to control the construction phase of any project involving more than one contractor and must plan, manage and coordinate the construction work and health and safety of the project during the *construction* phase.

The principal designer and contractor can be separate individuals or the same person/organisation – they just need to have the correct skills, experience and knowledge for the job! It is useful to appoint a principal designer/contractor as early as possible in the project and have plans already drawn up at this point to aid with discussions. If you have already engaged

HMO Property Set Up

with building regulations, you should already have appropriately detailed plans drawn up for your project.

As principal designers/contractors are required for every project where more than one contractor will be working on the site, many HMO projects where extensions and significant internal works are to be carried out will involve more than one contractor, so appointing professionals with the necessary skills and knowledge to help manage the pre-construction and construction phases on your behalf will be appropriate. The principal designer's/contractor's roles will be to help you, as the commercial client and project manager, set up the project correctly and make you aware of your responsibilities under CDM. For all projects, commercial clients must:

- Make suitable arrangements for the management of their project, enabling those qualified to carry out the management of health and safety risks in a proportionate way;

- Allow sufficient time and resources for each stage of the project;

- Make sure that any principal designer/contractor appointed carries out their duties fully throughout the project;

- Make sure there are suitable welfare facilities provided for the duration of construction work;

- Maintain and review the management arrangements for the duration of the project;

- Provide pre-construction information to every designer and contractor bidding on or appointed to the project;

HMO Property Set Up

- Ensure the principal contractor prepares a construction phases plan before that phase of work begins;

- Ensure the principal designer prepares a health and safety file for the project which is updated and revised as necessary and which is made available to anyone who needs it for subsequent work on the project.

Due to the typical scale of HMO projects, it is unlikely that each of the above criteria will be necessary to fulfil, but for larger projects (such as the conversion of an office building or hotel into a HMO) involving construction works that are expected to last longer than 30 working days and involving more than 20 workers at any one time, commercial clients must also notify the Health and Safety Executive (HSE) in writing with details of the project and ensure a copy of the notification is displayed in the construction site office.

In cases where you choose not to appoint a principal designer or contractor, you will be responsible for fulfilling their duties yourself. However, a word of caution here – whilst it may save you some money, fulfilling the duties and responsibilities may be difficult if you have not undertaken this role before and/or do not have the correct experience. This could leave you open to prosecution should something go wrong on site.

Your appointed contractors should be able to help and advise you on the preparation of a 'working brief' for the project. This brief will include relevant information on the construction works proposed and who may be appointed on the project to carry out the works. This ensures all parties involved understand their role in the project, the project and the site itself, any existing structures and any identifiable hazards or risks. This information should be provided to designers and contractors in good time to enable them to carry

HMO Property Set Up

out their duties safely and correctly. As mentioned, you also have a responsibly to ensure contractors have made suitable arrangements for welfare facilities whilst contractors are on site. This includes suitable toilet (whether that is a portal toilet or within the existing dwelling) and washing facilities and areas for contractors to rest, change and store clothing and other items.

Your professional team will also be able to advise you on how much time should be allocated to the project and the resources that will be needed as part of a construction phase plan. This will be proportionate to the size and nature of the construction works proposed. Based on this information, you should set aside sufficient time and resources for the project to ensure it can be completed safely within an agreed upon time frame. Other duties include eliminating foreseeable risks to health and safety that could arise during the project. Control measures should be put in place to reduce any remaining risks that cannot be eliminated, such as accidents.

Once the pre-construction information has been put together, the principal designer/contractor will review and check the adequacy of the information, identify any missing information and advise you on how to obtain any missing information. Once your team is satisfied with the information, they will share this with other contractors, individuals and organisations involved in the project and communicate the pre-construction information and health and safety needs, which should be upheld until the project has been completed.

Additionally, the principal designer/contractor will put together and take charge of the health and safety file. This will contain information relating to health and safety and risk management. As the project progresses, the principal designer/contractor have a responsibility to review, update

HMO Property Set Up

and revise this file accordingly, sharing the details with anyone involved in subsequent phases of the project. On completion of the project, you will receive the health and safety file from your professional team, which should be kept for your records and be provided to anyone else involved with future alterations or building maintenance.

Where works are commenced without CDM regulations being complied with, HSE or local authority has the power to carry out investigative works and stop the construction process until they are satisfied the regulations are being complied with. This could result in significant unnecessary delays which will only add to the cost of the project. In serious situations, breaches of the regulations could even see you prosecuted, demonstrating that the regulations are not something which you can afford to ignore! Further information on the CDM Regulations and the various roles and responsibilities is available from the HSE website[128].

---

[128] https://www.hse.gov.uk/construction/cdm/2015/index.htm.

62. Joint Contracts Tribunal (JCT) Contracts

As part of appointing contractors and professionals to undertake your project, you may wish to think about engaging with Joint Contracts Tribunal (JCT) contracts[129] to ensure the smooth running of your project. The Joint Contracts Tribunal is a body founded in 1931 which represents a wide range of interests in the building and construction industry.

JCT contracts are widely used throughout the UK construction industry to help deliver a development or building project using standard forms for contracts, alongside detailed guidance notes. They are typically associated with all scales of private and commercial development. Put simply, where a development or building project requires building contractors to be employed, the JCT contract sets out the responsibilities of all parties involved with the development and their obligations to each other. This makes it very clear what works needs to be carried out, who will be doing the work, when it will be completed by and the costs or fees to be paid for doing so. This approach helps to clearly define these roles and apportions the risks in a way which is appropriate to the scale of the project.

Whilst not compulsory, if you choose not to use a JCT contract for your project, there are a number of associated risks, such as contractors not upholding the terms of any agreement, spiralling costs which you may not have budgeted for and no clear deadline for the completion of works. This can obviously cause issues, particularly where bridging finance is being used and you want to set up your HMO

---

[129] https://www.jctltd.co.uk/.

HMO Property Set Up

quickly. Further, without any documentation to cover who is responsible for what aspects of the project's design and delivery, it can be difficult to hold any parties involved accountable, if you needed to. You could even find yourself in a situation where a contractor is able to unreasonably exploit the situation by demanding payment for a half-finished property, whilst your funds run short and the property is not bringing in any income.

To help avoid situations such as these, there are a number of 'contract families' which can be used for a range of projects. However, for most HMOs and the scale of works proposed, it is likely you will only need to use one or two contracts. As the property owner, you would be classed as the 'employer' for any development works. The first contract likely to be relevant to a HMO project is the 'Minor Works Building Contract', which is designed for smaller, basic construction projects, undertaken by traditional, conventional methods.

Under the most basic contract, you would be responsible for providing detailed drawings (usually by others), a specification or work schedules to define the quantity and quality of the work and an agreement over the price and payment structure, which is usually based on a lump sum, with monthly payments. Some of this information is likely to form part of your CDM file.

The second contract likely to be relevant is the 'Home Owner Contracts', which is designed specifically for small domestic building works, such as extensions or alterations and will most likely be applicable to your HMO projects too. It offers the benefits and protection of a contract when appointing consultants or contractors to carry out the building works and is for property owners who do not wish to appoint a

HMO Property Set Up

consultant to administer the contract. As such, you would be the one who deals directly with the contractor, unless you have a principal designer/contractor in place to do this on your behalf.

As an example, for part of your HMO conversion project, you may wish to build a single storey extension, alongside the internal refurbishment and reorganisation of the rest of the house. You would be employing a builder to carry out these works, which need to be completed to a high standard. The contract would ensure your builder works to the standard you expect them to.

There are a number of further benefits to be gained from a JCT contract. These include saving time and minimising transaction costs, protection over common issues and pitfalls that can arise during projects, ensuring that contractual terms are not more favourable to one party than the other, assisting in dispute resolution (should the need arise) and protection for 'employers' against poor contractors. The contracts have been developed by a multitude of people working in and involved with the building industry and the contract process reflects benchmark provisions and accepted forms of good practice. The standard contract form you will need to prepare is set out in two parts. The first deals with the arrangements for the works required and is broken down into sections or stages, which could include the following:

HMO Property Set Up

Standard JCT Contract Part One
The works to be carried out
Details of any planning permission, building regulations and party wall considerations
The use of facilities on or at the property/development site
The working period and working hours
Any relevant product guarantees
Insurance
Relevant property security
The disputes procedure

Table 62.1: Standard Joint Contracts Tribunal (JCT) Contract Part One.

Each stage is assigned a fee which is recorded in detail in the JCT contract. The second part of the contact also sets out the conditions or obligations of the parties involved. This will usually include:

Standard JCT Contract Part Two
The Contractor's responsibilities (including signing off the works, correcting any defects picked up on a snagging list)
The Customer/Employer's responsibilities
Site Health and Safety
Any amendments to the work details
Extending the working period
Payment terms and conditions
The Contractor's ongoing responsibilities
Winding up of the contract
The right to cancel
Insolvency procedures

Table 62.2: Standard Joint Contracts Tribunal (JCT) Contract Part Two.

Where JCT contracts are to be prepared, or have been prepared, it is worthwhile discussing them with your solicitor

HMO Property Set Up

to ensure that any clauses containing legal 'jargon' are fully explained and that the contract is fair for both parties entering into it. Additionally, a solicitor will also be able to tell you whether the contract is properly written and legally binding. If all parties are happy with the contract and you receive written confirmation of this, you will be able to commence the project works with the peace of mind which comes from knowing that should any issues with your builder or any other contractors employed arise, there is a legal contract in place which you can rely on to resolve any problems, minimising your exposure to risk and helping to control and keep your budget on track.

63. Council Tax: Re-banding And Valuations

Council Tax Re-banding

As you will likely already be aware, council tax is a tax levied on domestic property, collected by local authorities in instalments throughout the year. Each local authority oversees the setting of its rates. The amount charged is based on a number of factors, such as a property's size, layout, character, location, use – and in England, unless it is a new build property, its value as at 1st April 1991. Properties can be re-banded for council tax purposes where certain changes have occurred, for example a band 'C' property may be changed to a band 'D' when it is next purchased, if the property has had a large extension carried out. A property may also be re-banded without it being sold, if it is changed from a standard house into a HMO, either with or without rooms that have ensuites and/or kitchenettes (deemed to be 'self-contained').

Re-banding is the formal process for which a property is revalued by the Valuation Office Agency (VOA) and placed into a different band, or into a combination of bands. The VOA is a government body which undertakes surveying and valuation services on properties for the purposes of council tax and non-domestic rates. It also provides advice to support taxation and benefits to the government and local authorities. In circumstances where HMOs are re-banded, it is increasingly common for each room to have its own council tax band (known as 'Individual Council Tax Banding' (ICTB)) as the VOA consider each room to be a separate dwelling within the main property, similar to flatted accommodation. It can therefore work out to be significantly more expensive if you offer 'all-inclusive room rates'. This is because you may find your previous band 'E' property, which could have been operating as a seven-bedroom HMO is then

HMO Property Set Up

re-banded as seven individual band 'A' dwellings which you'd have to cover the costs for as part of the all-inclusive rates being offer.

Naturally, the re-banding of a property can make a sizeable dent in your profit margin. You may therefore want to think carefully about adding a clause to any Assured Shorthold Tenancy (AST) agreement to clarify who would be responsible for council tax payments, should re-banding occur. Alternatively, you could also look into providing Licence Agreements for the occupation of rooms as part of a shared house instead of an AST agreement. A Licence Agreement permits a Licensee to occupy the room and use the furniture and furnishings, as well as pay for all council tax and other utilities consumed or supplied in the room or property.

HMOs And Council Tax

According to the National Residential Landlords Association (NRLA), the definition of a HMO for council tax purposes is either:

- A property originally constructed, or subsequently adapted, for occupation by more than one household; or

- Each person who lives in the property is either a tenant or licensee, only able to occupy part of the property or not liable to pay rent for the whole property.

Often where a HMO property has not been re-banded and is let to individual sharers (who typically do not know each other beforehand) on a room-by-room basis (i.e. a typical HMO), tenancies are set up so that the tenant does not have a 'material interest' in the whole building, but shares access to the communal parts of the property with other tenants. As the

HMO Property Set Up

tenants are therefore not in control of the whole property, they should only reasonably be required to pay rent for the portion they occupy. The landlord should then be liable for paying the council tax on the whole property. For HMOs which are exclusively occupied by students, no council tax is owed at all, although this exemption only lasts as long as all the tenants qualify as students[130].

Cases of ICTB for each room are on the rise across the country, but to the frustration of many a landlord, there appears to be no set criteria from one location to another and the VOAs decisions appear to be quite random, even where HMO rooms do not have all the facilities required to be self-contained. This means a great deal of inconstancy remains in the approach and interpretation of HMOs taken by VOA officers toward re-banding.

Having said that, HMOs which have their own kitchenette and separate shower/bathroom and WC facilities are more likely to be given their own individual band, even though the occupant may still share some of the communal facilities, such as a main kitchen and living area. This is because the room is considered to have all the amenities required to sustain an occupant and is effectively a 'self-contained' room. In which case, this often increases the chances of the room being given its own band. Whilst ICTB remains by-and-large a small issue, it is increasingly having significant cost implications for both landlords and tenants in re-banded houses and currently remains a difficult situation to advise on.

---

[130] Households where everyone is a full time student on a course that last at least one year and involves at least 21 hours of study per week.

HMO Property Set Up

Government Consultation 2023

As part of the Levelling-up and Regeneration Bill, an amendment clause, known as 'New Clause 7' is being consulted upon, with the intention of preventing the imposition of council tax individually on tenants of a room in a house with shared facilities, or in a licenced HMO. In response, the Government published a consultation on 17th February 2023[131] to seek views on the council tax valuation of HMOs, covering the scope of the issue, current landscape for the valuation of HMOs and the Government's proposal to *"provide greater certainty and consistency in the way that accommodation in the HMO sector is banded for council tax, and to ensure that HMOs are banded as one property and have one council tax band, other than in exceptional circumstances."*

Importantly, the Government seeks to ensure that the liability for council tax remains with the HMO landlord and that their tenants do not become subject to individual council tax bills. At the time of writing, the results of the Consultation have not been published (May 2023).

Council Tax And Refurbishment

Until the outcome of the Consultation is known, the following advice may be a useful way for you to proceed when commencing HMO conversion projects.

---

[131] https://www.gov.uk/government/consultations/council-tax-valuation-of-houses-in-multiple-occupation-hmos/council-tax-valuation-of-houses-in-multiple-occupation-hmos-consultation.

HMO Property Set Up

As you may be aware, whilst a property is vacant and undergoing refurbishments works, you may be entitled to a short period of exemption from council tax payments. To apply for this 'break' you can contact your local authority to advise them the property is not currently occupied. However, I would advise on being cautious in this approach as re-banding often occurs once refurbishments have been completed and by notifying the local authority that the property will no longer be vacant following the completion of works could trigger an inspection. You should therefore think carefully about whether the amount saved in council tax payments during the refurbishment period is worth the potential of the property being re-banded, as your local authority may pass information about the property onto the VOA for them to come out and assess.

The Government sets out that when looking at a property, the VOA must consider what a 'dwelling' actually is for council tax purposes, as set out under Section 3 of the Local Government Finance Act 1992[132]. If the test set out under Section 114(1) of the General Rate Act 1967[133] are satisfied, each unit will be considered a 'dwelling', capable of having its own council tax band. In other works, qualifying units can be banded individually, even if they are not self-contained and where some facilities are shared with others.

Where the VOA becomes notified of changes to a property and discussions are held with you, the VOA may not be able to obtain enough information to band a property from written or verbal conversations with yourself. In which case – and with your permission, they will arrange a visit to inspect the interior of your property and take photographs. Following

---

[132] https://www.legislation.gov.uk/ukpga/1992/14/contents.
[133] https://www.legislation.gov.uk/ukpga/1967/9/contents/enacted.

HMO Property Set Up

inspection, should the VOA determine your property contains more than one area of separate living accommodation, each unit could be re-banded individually. The VOA is required by law to apply a separate council tax band for every building, or part of a building, which has been constructed or adapted for use as separate living accommodation. A room with an ensuite and a small kitchenette with a sink, worktop and microwave could and has been deemed to fall within this definition.

However, decisions over whether to re-band a property into individual units currently depends largely on the degree to which the dwelling has been adapted and the discretion of the inspecting VOA officer. For example, if you choose to have ensuites installed in ground floor bedrooms where they would not typically be found in standard domestic properties; or decided to provide kitchenettes in each room so tenants would not necessarily need to use the shared facilities in the HMO, this could tip the scales in favour of re-banding. Additionally, if you sought to provide an independent access from the main front door of the property for any lettable rooms, this too could result in re-banding occurring. A further consideration for an inspecting VOA officer would be how easily the HMO could be converted back into a standard dwelling, should its HMO use cease. If only relatively minor works would be necessary, you may avoid re-banding; conversely, if major modifications were needed, the chances of re-banding occurring are greater. There may however be circumstances and exceptions where the VOA can seek to combine the bands into one. These exceptions include:

HMO Property Set Up

Exceptions for Combined Bands
HMOs with little or no adaptation from standard domestic properties. These minor adaptations can include where door locks are added and the occupants of the separately let rooms in the property share the kitchen and bathroom facilities of the original house
HMOs with adaptions to each floor, where a single band can be assigned to each floor of a house let in parts which has standard facilities and can be treated as a self-contained unit, typically where occupiers of the floor share a kitchen and a bathroom

Table 63.1: Council Tax re-banding exceptions for combined bands.

Ensuites and Kitchenettes

Ensuites and kitchenettes can be more popular with tenants in some areas and there is a tendency for tenants to stay longer in a HMO because of this. Often, demand from tenants ensures they are willing to pay extra for the benefits of having an ensuite and they may be more willing to accept paying council tax on an individual room if the property is re-banded. This is particularly in light of the Covid-19 pandemic, where some tenants may now prefer having their own kitchenette and/or bathroom facilities. As part of your due diligence on an area, you should be able to determine whether this type of accommodation is in demand and whether the benefits of providing this type of accommodation outweighs the potential for a property being re-banded because of these changes.

In a six- or seven-bedroom HMO, it is advisable to have a good mix of two to three ensuites, with between two and four large double bedrooms sharing bathroom facilities. Having a mix of different room types in your HMO properties also means they are capable of attracting a more diverse range of tenants with different budget limits and may save each room

HMO Property Set Up

from being subject to ICTB in the event that re-banding occurs. Further, a mix of room types to suit different budgets enables tenants who maybe can't afford to pay extra for facilities, but still want to live in a high-quality HMO, with a functional and spacious room, and are happy using the shared facilities are not priced out. Don't forget that room size is key for a lot of tenants who may have more possessions. Squeezing in an ensuite or a kitchenette may actually be off-putting in some smaller rooms, in addition to having to comply with licencing and fire safety requirements. Further, when you consider the cost of installing an ensuite may be around £2,000+, along with ongoing maintenance work, upkeep costs and running costs for individuals who may take long, hot showers, or forget to turn taps off in their ensuite before leaving for the day, not to mention increasing the potential for re-banding, this can become the deciding factor over whether to install additional facilities for individuals in rooms.

How Can HMOs Be Identified For Council Tax Purposes?

In addition to carrying out refurbishment works, new or existing HMOs can be identified and their details passed to the VOA for assessment via a number of methods, including the following:

HMO Property Set Up

Other methods of HMO identification
The LPAs online planning register (where you may have applied for planning permission for a HMO development, or to confirm the lawful of use of the property as a HMO)
Information gathered from the electoral register, usually if three or more seemingly unrelated people are registered as living at the same address
Council tax records (these may identify whether a property is exempt from council tax if it is occupied by full time students)
HMO Licence Register, which are regularly updated to identify all known licenced HMOs within an area
Complaints made by neighbours or members of the public to the council who then pass the details onto the VOA

Table 63.2: HMO identification methods for Council Tax re-banding.

Unfortunately, where HMOs are identified and their details passed onto the VOA for assessment, as I've already mentioned, there is currently no standard approach the VOA will take when assessing a property for re-banding. Therefore, each valuation is judged on an individual basis where the layout and use of a property is considered on a 'case-by-case' basis. This can obviously pose a significant financial gamble for landlords wanting to offer tenants something a bit more than 'just a bed in a room' and is something the Government has picked up on as part of its consultation, identifying that concerns over re-banding may be deterring some landlords from making improvements to existing HMOs which would ultimately improve tenant's living conditions. Re-banding could also make rooms for tenants unaffordable if they are then made liable for council tax payments, putting extra pressure on personal finances and adding to the ongoing housing affordability crisis.

HMO Property Set Up

Can I Challenge The Re-banding Of A Property?

In cases where you are informed your property is to be re-banded, there is an appeal process to the Valuation Tribunal for England. As the property owner, you have three months in which to challenge the decision to re-band. You may also want to challenge the council tax bill with the VOA by issuing a proposal to the listing officer, setting out that the rooms form part of a shared house and should not be listed as separate dwellings on their own. Where individual rooms are listed for ICTB, you should challenge each one; otherwise contest the whole property. You should receive confirmation for each room to be challenged. As part of your challenge, you will be required to provide evidence to support your opinion. However, this may be difficult to produce, particularly if you are aware of other similar HMO properties being re-banded in your area of operation. In all challenges, there is a danger that listing officer may also simply choose to agree with the VOA officer's original assessment of the property.

Aside from challenging the council tax bill, on submission of an appeal to the VOA, you can also contact your local authority to inform them a challenge has been made and request they treat the rooms as part of a single property, with the landlord paying a single council tax bill, under the Council Tax (Liability of Owners) Regulations 1992 Statutory Instrument 551[134] and request an inspection is undertaken. You should request that all correspondence between the local authority and VOA be provided to you under a 'Subject Access Request'. Additionally, you can ask to make a formal complaint to the local authority's monitoring officer. Should your appeal to the VOA be declined, a decision notice will be

---

[134] https://www.legislation.gov.uk/uksi/1992/551/contents/made.

issued to you. On receipt, the next stage of the process would be to directly raise an appeal for each individual room with the Valuation Tribunal Service (VTS). This enables you to challenge each room separately, ensuring your case does not get 'rebuffed' in one hearing. Following the raising of a challenge and appeal, the local authority may continue to send bills to you as landlord as well as to tenants. You can ask them to halt issuing bills whilst the appeal process is undertaken, although do not be surprised is a summons is issued if bills were to go unpaid. If a summons is received you can contact the Clerk of the Court to request either an adjournment or withdrawal of the summons, providing the VOA and VTS appeal references. Always ask for email confirmation of their decision.

In cases where you seek to challenge a decision for ICTB on rooms in your HMO properties, it is worthwhile discussing the options available to you with a suitably qualified professional beforehand as the above strategy may not be a suitable approach for you and your circumstances.

Acceptance Of Re-banding

Where you choose to accept the re-banding of your HMO property, your tenants may subsequently be liable to pay the council tax, which would obviously reduce your cost as a landlord if you passed the costs onto them. However, this could have the knock-on effect of reducing the amount of interest in the room/property where competitors, who may not have had their properties re-banded, can still offer 'all-inclusive' room rates. Existing tenants may also choose or be forced to leave your property due to affordability concerns and you could find yourself having to deal with increased void periods.

HMO Property Set Up

On the flip side of this, if you choose to continue offering all-inclusive room rates and pay the council tax for all the individual rooms yourself, this will obviously have a significant impact on the amount of income the property produces and should be factored into an updated property analyser. If you find your property is re-banded, a 25% reduction is usually applied for single occupancy of rooms, although there will be an increase in cost for you as the landlord if you still wish to offer all bills included accommodation. Well-performing HMOs can still make healthy profits after ICTB, especially if some of the costs are offset in rent increases. Whilst not always the case, most HMO landlords with quality HMOs should still be capable of making profit.

Ultimately, when considering whether to undertake adaptions to a property which could result in re-banding, you will need to carefully balance the attractiveness, affordability and desirability of the property to tenants against seeking to provide better amenities through individual ensuites and kitchenettes and being liable to paying the additional council tax, if offering all-inclusive rates. Naturally, there are arguments for and against both approaches. Following the Government's consultation on council tax re-banding for HMOs, there may be changes to the law governing council tax emerging soon, which could provide further clarity and certainty for landlords and tenants alike,. This clarification could present an opportunity for landlords and HMO developers to provide better accommodation without the worry of whether HMO rooms will be re-banded as individual 'dwellings'.

64. HMO Insurance

Insurance can often be seen as a bit of a 'dry' and boring subject to discuss, but should you need to rely on it to make a claim, having a good policy in place can certainly make a big difference and offer you peace of mind when you need it most. It is therefore always worth spending some extra time making sure you do your research and ensure you have the right policies in place to protect both yourself as a landlord and your HMO properties. For all types of insurance you wish to take out, always read the policy documents carefully so you know the policy will provide you with the appropriate level of cover. A cheaper policy usually means something important is likely to have been left out, or that it comes with a whole host of complicated conditions and exclusions that essentially make it ineffective when you need to call on it. In addition, when applying for insurance, make sure you are honest and provide accurate information about all aspects of your property and how it is used – the last thing you want to be faced with if you need to make a claim is the insurance company deciding it won't pay out because you didn't provide the correct information!

As Chapter 16 briefly outlined, you must ensure the property is correctly insured not only prior to the exchange of contracts, but also during the refurbishment stage when the property will be unoccupied. Once refurbishment has been completed and tenants are able to move in, you then need to have other insurance policies in place so that your asset is fully protected in the event of any accidents, theft or damages. I'll go through a list of common insurances you may want to think about now, although there may be others not listed you want to take out, depending on the circumstances and your appetite for risk.

HMO Property Set Up

Buildings Insurance

This type of insurance covers you against the cost of damages to the structure of your property. Basically, this means anything which is either fixed or cannot be easily taken out and moved somewhere else is insured. It can also be extended to include structures such as garages, sheds and fencing. As you may already know, buildings insurance is compulsory when buying a property with a mortgage and it will usually be a condition of the mortgage that adequate insurance is in place to cover the property for mortgage purposes. In cases where you may be buying a property without a mortgage, it is still advisable to purchase buildings insurance to cover you and your assets in the event of any loss or damages. Without it, you could end up losing both your asset and the ability to reclaim your financial investment.

The buildings insurance policy should cover the full cost of repairing any damages or rebuilding your property, including demolition, site clearance and any associated professional fees involved. There are naturally different levels of cover available. These typically cover loss or damage as a result of fire, explosions, storms, floods, theft and vandalism, frozen and burst pipes, fallen trees and damage caused by street furniture, subsidence and vehicle collisions. Obviously, some of the policy criteria may not be applicable to your property, depending on its location and surroundings (such as flooding and the potential for falling trees, for example) and could therefore be safely discounted from the policy. When reviewing insurance policies, it is worthwhile looking out for how the property is treated when it is 'empty', what is considered an 'empty' property and how long a property can be left empty for before the cover ends (for example, during long refurbishment stages or briefly between tenancies) as

HMO Property Set Up

well as whether there is any need to regularly visit an empty property to check it is secure.

Premiums are calculated by working out the rebuild value. This is different from the market value of the property as rebuild costs are generally lower than current market value. You will therefore need to ensure you don't over-or-under insure your property so you should seek to account for any costs associated with rebuilding, refurbishment or replacement items as accurately as possible. Remember to factor in any improvements you have made, or intend to make, such as building an extension, or adding a loft conversion, which may add value to your property. Where a property has been recently valued, most likely when you bought the property or for mortgage purposes, the valuation will have included the rebuild value. However, if you don't have a recent valuation figure, there is a free building cost calculator provided by the Association of British Insurers[135]. To work out the rebuild value, all you'll need is the size of the property, which can be found on the EPC or may be on any architectural plans you've had prepared for the property. However, do bear in mind this valuation is an estimate and will not be as accurate as a professional surveyor's report.

Finally, when putting together your requirements for the policy, it is a good idea to request that cover is issued on an *'all-risks'* basis and includes both accidental damage and subsidence cover, as well as malicious damage by tenants, therefore covering as many bases as possible. For a higher premium, you can add extra cover to protect your asset against other risks. For example, if the property is in a high flood risk zone, becomes infested or a tenant causes damage,

---

[135] https://www.abi.org.uk/

HMO Property Set Up

as well as for the provision of alternative accommodation in the event of an incident occurring.

HMO Landlord Insurance

HMO landlord insurance is specifically designed for the protection of property owners renting property to tenants. By earning money through renting out a property, you are, for insurance purposes, classified as a 'business'. As a result, the terms for HMO insurance are slightly more complex than those for regular landlord insurance policies, typically because HMOs are placed in a higher risk category for insurance purposes due to the number of occupants and the (perceived) increased risks.

As a landlord, having the correct insurance in place for your HMO is vital to ensure you are sufficiently covered. Should a worst-case scenario occur, it will protect you against the risk of loss (including financial), damage by tenants/weather and theft. Whilst you are not under any legal obligation to obtain landlord insurance, your mortgage lender may insist upon it as part of their lending terms. Equally, your tenancy agreements may require you to adhere to certain responsibilities that are best served by having appropriate insurance in place.

To obtain a HMO landlord insurance policy, you will need to register your property as an HMO and discuss your requirements with a suitably qualified insurance broker who will be able to go through the options with you and tailor a policy that best suits your needs. Premiums are often based on the size of your property, number or rooms and number of tenants. Because of the bespoke nature of these insurance policies, the costs of HMO landlord insurance can vary significantly between insurers, so don't be afraid to shop around to find the best deal.

HMO Property Set Up

Landlord Contents Insurance

As HMOs are usually provided as fully furnished properties, with appliances and soft furnishings included, you will need to make sure these items are also suitably insured. Any policy you wish to take out should include all free-standing item such as cookers, washing machines, tumble dryers, fridges, tables, beds and sofas. Contents insurance should also cover damage to floor coverings such as carpets, lino and laminate floors. This ensures there is adequate coverage in the event of damage, whether accidental or malicious, or in the event of a fire or flood, as these items would need to be replaced. This demonstrates the importance of having an accurate and up-to-date inventory, providing a clear record of what contents are within your property and their condition. As with most insurance policies, the cost of landlord contents insurance differs according to a number of factors, including size and type of property you have, number of tenants, the location of the property and the level of cover you're looking for, including specific items. Again, there is no harm in shopping around to find the best deal.

It is worth bearing in mind that landlord contents insurance does not cover any tenant's possessions, so if they ask whether their possessions are insured, be sure to advise them to take out their own individual insurance policy to protect their personal belongings, including bicycles, laptops, clothing, jewellery and other items which have been brought to the property.

Other Insurances

Aside from the insurance polies already mentioned, there are several other policies you may wish to investigate and take out to offer you greater protection. Obviously, the more policies you have, the greater the expense will be for your business, but having additional insurances in place could provide you with extra peace of mind should a worst case scenario occur.

Should You Have Public Liability Insurance And Property Owners Liability Insurance?

Whilst not mandatory, both public liability insurance and property owners' liability insurance can be worth looking into. They both cover injuries, illnesses or property damage to third parties. The main differences between the two are essentially who the policyholder is.

Public liability insurance is generally bought by businesses as they face some exposure to third party liability risk. Public liability insurance can protect a business financially from the litigation costs and compensation payments that can follow as a result of accidents. In comparison, property owners' liability insurance is typically purchased by private property owners and is a type of public liability insurance. You may find you are required to have property owners' liability insurance if you have a mortgage, as it may be a condition of your contract. Do be sure to check this point when arranging a mortgage.

Property owners' liability insurance will protect your legal liabilities as a property owner against the risk of any third-party losses, property damage or bodily injury in the event that a legal claim is made by a third party who is on your property. Examples of claims could be from a tenant who trips and falls down the stairs and is then unable to work for a period of time, to contractors who may injure themselves whilst carrying out maintenance or fixing something in your existing HMO property. You could even receive a claim from a delivery driver who might trip on the driveway and injure themselves! Personal injury claims or property damage claims are on the rise and can prove to be quite expensive, so do make sure to make sure you are adequately covered in the event that something untoward does occur!

Rent Guarantee Insurance

This type of insurance can cover the payments of your rental income, usually for a period of between six and 12 months, should a tenant either be unable to pay their rent or decide to withhold it. Often the legal fees involved with the recovery of rent arrears, repossession and evicting a tenant can be included too, for a slightly higher premium. Again, costs for this type of policy will vary significantly depending on the type of property you are renting out, its size and location and the number of tenants in a property, as these considerations all factor into the amount of rent you are likely to receive.

Policies are typically issued with a number of stipulations and exclusions, such as deferral periods, for example, where you may find you aren't covered for the first month of rent arrears or are unable to make a claim for a set period of time (say three months) after the policy is taken out. Other common exclusions relate to the type of tenants you have in your property. For example, people who are unemployed, on benefits or are students may be excluded as they are seen as being at a higher risk of defaulting on their payment obligations. In these circumstances, insurance providers may therefore wish to see any references obtained, sometimes requesting these are provided through a recognised referencing service. Where tenants have a poor credit or payment history, rent guarantee is not likely to cover them. This is quite understanding from an insurance providers point of view as they only wish to cover tenants who are very likely

HMO Property Set Up

to pay their rent on time – so you may ask, why bother with it at all? Well, it is worth noting that it can typically take between six and ten months (under normal circumstances) to evict a tenant where they have stopped paying rent. This obviously adds up to a significant amount of lost rental income! During this time, you'll still be liable for any mortgage payments, utilities and other payments to make on the property as you'll need to keep meeting your financial commitments. Whilst you may have to cover some of the costs for a few months before the insurance policy kicks in, you won't need dip into your contingency fund for quite as long.

Having rent guarantee insurance in place also has the added advantage of ensuring you are 'disciplined' in who you rent your property/rooms to. If a prospective tenant fails referencing and you know they won't be covered by your insurance policy, you are less likely to take a chance on them and risk your potential income.

Another aspect of protection, which is separate from rent guarantee insurance, comes in the form of rental income protection. This can cover the amount of rent you would have received during a period of unoccupancy, for example if the property is damaged by fire or flooding and cannot be rented out again until the issue has been satisfactorily resolved. Again, it is likely there will be certain exclusions and stipulations attached, so make sure you review the wording of any policies carefully before agreeing to anything.

Summary Of Insurances

As discussed, there are a number of different insurance policies which can be taken out to protect you as a landlord, your property and its contents. Some insurers will offer

HMO Property Set Up

combined or 'bundled' policies, incorporating several of these policies such as buildings, landlords and contents insurance together, which will be much easier for you to administer and keep track of. These bundles may even result in a discount being applied.

As previously mentioned, when discussing your requirements with an insurance provider and setting up any policies, it is worthwhile being as honest as possible and disclosing all the information about the property you wish to insure and the way it is to be used. This helps minimise the possibility of any 'loopholes' being exploited by an insurer to get out of making a payment in the event you need to make a claim.

Where multiple policies are sought, it is worthwhile asking to review a quotation schedule to ensure that any policies taken out will cover all the necessary aspects you need them to. Make sure to read the policy documentation carefully to check it matches with the level of cover you require. If there are clauses you don't understand or need explained, don't be afraid to query them with the provider.

Having the right insurance in place for you and your property is crucial and will provide you with assurance that you have mitigated all the risks of owning and renting out a property as far as is reasonably practical. Whilst you are obligated in certain circumstances to take out insurance policies, some of the other optional polices can seem like a further unnecessary expense. However, whilst you may not (and hopefully won't) have to make a claim, knowing you have these policies in place can provide you with much needed 'security blanket' in the event you do face any issues. Remember, you can't put a price on peace of mind!

65. Drainage, Water Supply And Build Over Agreements

A matter which is commonly overlooked but can be crucially important when considering the layout and facilities of a proposed HMO is drainage and the location of your water supply. Where you are seeking to add bathrooms or ensuites to a property, make sure to note where you can access the drainage from and where it flows out to the grounds of the property. Whilst on paper a design and layout might look good, it is no use proposing to put an ensuite in a bedroom or installing a new bathroom where the installation of the necessary pipework has to come from over the other side of the property and you end up having pipework snaking around the house to make it work!

When viewing a property, have in mind a couple of key questions, such as: do the drains run to the front or back garden and from there, where do they run to? Are the drains on private or shared land? Will a drain or sewer be in the way of any foundations for extensions or other additions you are proposing? Knowing the answers to these questions can help you with re-configuring the property for HMO use and enable you to save time and money on refurbishment works.

In relation to the water supply, your supply pipe is owned by you and at the point of entry into your property, you own this and have a responsibility to maintain and fix it. Understanding where this comes into your property is therefore important, not only for refurbishment works, but in the event of an emergency where the water supply needs to be shut off. As for pipework and drainage assets outside of your property boundary, water companies own and are responsible for all public sewers and public lateral drains in their region. This is the length of pipe carrying wastewater away from a property to a sewer. It is their responsibility to maintain and fix these public assets.

Build Over Agreements

Where you are seeking to carry out works within your boundary, you don't usually need permission from the water company. However, some pipes on private land may serve as distribution mains to more than one property. In these circumstances, water companies will typically advise you to divert pipework around any proposed buildings or extensions. Where you are unable to do this, ducting any pipes and fitting them under the building so they can be accessed for repairs is recommended, although this method does come at a personal cost to you.

In some circumstances, water companies will require a build over agreement to be applied for to ensure works proposed in close proximity of public sewers and drains do not interfere with them and provide sufficient access for maintenance or repairs. These agreements also ensure that the extra weight of any new construction works undertaken won't damage the pipework. Works typically needing build over agreements include where you are seeking to extend a property, add a conservatory or any other works where new foundations, underpinning, piling or basements are proposed within three metres of an existing pipe and which serves more than one property, or is within one metre of the point where a pipe serving only your property crosses your boundary, where it becomes a public lateral drain. Under these and other circumstances, build over agreements are required before any building works commence and provide the water company's 'stamp of approval' for any works planned over or near a sewer they own.

HMO Property Set Up

Where build over agreements have not been approved, you may find that works are unable to be signed off by the relevant building control authority, which could cause issues when it comes to re-mortgaging or selling your property. Water companies do have legal powers to seek injunctions for the removal of any construction work that inhibits their ability to maintain, repair, replace or renew public sewers and are not liable for any damage caused to your property as a result of doing so, meaning it is important that agreements are in place where they are needed and are not simply ignored.

How Do You Know If You Need A Build Over Agreement?

If you are unsure whether you need approval, most water companies are happy for you to send across an initial consultation enquiry, usually accompanied by a scaled ground floor plan of your property, with any building works shown. If you've had drawings prepared for building regulations purposes, these plans should be sufficient. The water company may also request a sewer/drainage layout plan, which you may be able to obtain from them by contacting their asset enquiries team. Some water companies have an online library of maps which you can access once you have registered for an account. Usually there is a small charge for ordering any maps. Additionally, the location of any pipework may be shown on Title Plan for the property. Alternatively, you can get in touch with a property search provider. The water company will then check the plans and confirm their approval isn't required in writing, sometimes for a small fee.

If you think you may need a build over agreement for your proposed works, there are two types which can be applied for, depending on the type of work proposed and the position of any pipework nearby to where construction works will take place. These two different types are called 'self-certified build over agreements' and 'approved build over agreements'.

Self-certified Build Over Agreement

A self-certified build over agreement is required if you are going to be building over or near a domestic (Class 1) sewer which has a diameter of 160mm or less. The water company should be able to tell you what assets they have within your boundary if you are not sure. Applications can be made online on the relevant water company's website and are usually free. They involve answering several fairly basic questions about the proposed development and any known assets within the plot. Although water companies may have different criteria, you can typically apply for self-certification where:

Common criteria for Self-certified Build Over Agreements
The works proposed are to add a structure to an existing building (an extension or conservatory)
There are no obvious issues with the sewer (blockages, strong odours, flooding)
The sewer being built over or close to has a diameter of less than 160mm
Access points (manholes, inspection chambers or rodding points) are outside of or at least half a metre from the building
It is not proposed for the sewer to change direction, gradient or diameter
The sewer is comprised of plastic or clay
Your proposal allows for minimum clearances (which will be specified) to be achieved
No loadings are placed on the pipe (lintels are commonly used to support the weight of new structures)
Traditional strip or trench fill foundations are proposed

HMO Property Set Up

No easements or covenants apply to the sewer
Where any buildings works will extend across the width of a plot, the sewer must still be accessible from a neighbour's property

Table 65.1: Self-certified Build Over Agreement criteria.

It is worthwhile discussing the self-certification process and any questions you may have with your architect, builder or local building control team before submitting the application as they should be able to advise you of the details. Where you can answer the self-certification questions and can suitably demonstrate your proposal poses little risk to the pipework and any other assets in the immediate vicinity, a self-certified build over agreement should be granted.

Where a self-certified build over agreement is issued by the water company, you can start works straight away, providing they are undertaken exactly as described. However, if sufficient responses or details cannot be provided, you may be directed to applying for an approved build over agreement instead.

Approved Build Over Agreement

Approved build over agreements are required where either you are unable to confirm some aspects of proposal under the self-certification questions (or fail to qualify), even where the sewer is a Class 1 pipe, or if you intend to build on or over a Class 2 (160mm to 375mm) or Class 3 (over 375mm) pipe.

Because of the technical assessment required, there is a fee involved, payable to the relevant water company. The fee is calculated depending on the size of the sewer and whether your property is in domestic or commercial use. The fee covers the processing of the application, technical plan reviews, discussions over any design changes required for your proposal, liaison with building control and registering any agreement on the water company's records. You can include some minor sewer diversions in your application, where pipes are 160mm or less (Class 1), subject to pre- and post-construction surveys. Where surveys are needed, the water company will undertake a pre- and post-construction survey using either CCTV or by entering the sewer, depending on the diameter of the pipe. Surveys may be charged at an additional fee depending on the water company. Any proposed works to divert Class 2 or Class 3-type sewers for a small domestic project are usually considered 'unviable' by water companies due to the significant financial costs involved as diversions are usually only recommended on larger projects, such as housing estates.

As part of the application process, you will need to provide scaled drawings of the proposed works. These must show the existing building and drainage layout. You may also be asked to provide a cross-section drawing where you are building over a sewer, or within 1.5 metres of a sewer, as you will need to provide details, including sections drawings of how the foundations will be constructed. Your architect should be able to prepare these details. There are again several criteria an application will need to be assessed against to ensure it is suitable. Typically, a water company would require confirmation of the following:

HMO Property Set Up

Common Criteria for Approved Build Over Agreements
All works must comply with the latest 'Sewerage Sector Guidance' approved documents
Like-for-like materials must be used in the construction of any works
No additional loads will be transmitted to the sewer and that the foundations will be below the level of the pipe's base
The public sewer pipe's base level will be checked and verified before any works are commenced
Driven piles are not proposed where the proposal is within 15 metres of a public sewer
Sewers up to 1.1 metres deep will be at least 1.5 metres away from any foundations
Sewers over 1.1 metres deep will be at least half a metre away from any foundations
Sewers over 2 metres deep will be at least 1 metre away from any foundations

Table 65.2: Approved Build Over Agreement criteria.

As with self-build agreement applications, it is advisable to discuss any approved build over agreement application you consider making with your architect, builder or local building control team before making an application to the water company.

Where Can't You Build Over A Sewer?

There are a number of instances where a water company will not allow you to build over a sewer. These are:

HMO Property Set Up

Common circumstances where build over agreements are prohibited
Where rising mains (pressurised sewers) pumping foul sewage or rainwater are present, typically due to the prohibitive cost of moving them
Over manholes, due to the increased risk of internal flooding and odour issues. Any manhole would need to be moved to outside of the extension and be reconnected to the original pipe
Where strategic sewers are located. These are typically most significant in networks and can be very costly to relocate

Table 65.3: Circumstances where Build Over Agreements are prohibited.

Approval Process And Commencement of Works

Once your application has been received, the water company will aim to carry out their technical assessment within 21 days and provide you with their response. Where more information is required, you will be notified and asked to provide this. Where you have applied for a build over agreement for a domestic sewer of no more than 160mm in diameter, you can go ahead with the approved works once confirmation is received from the water company.

Most build over agreements do not require a CCTV survey, so approval can be issued swiftly, unless the sewer is non-domestic or over 160mm in diameter. Under these circumstances, an approval will only be issued after a pre-construction survey has been undertaken. Once this has been carried out, you may then carry out the approved works, assuming all other details are approved. In cases where sewers of more than 160mm in diameter are involved, you will need to notify the water company when building works are

HMO Property Set Up

completed. This is so a post-construction CCTV survey can be arranged to check the condition of the sewer. The CCTV survey footage will then be reviewed before final approval is issued. Where you consider that a build over agreement will be necessary for your HMO project, it is important to approach the water company as soon as possible to minimise any delays in the construction process and to keep your project on track.

66. Asbestos

You may be aware that asbestos has been used in the construction of commercial buildings for decades. It may however surprise you to know that it has also been used in the construction of some residential buildings right up until the year 2000! If you are not sure what asbestos is, it is a group of naturally occurring minerals, made of fine, durable, heat and chemical resistant fibres. It was commonly used in a range of building materials and products because of these very properties. Asbestos containing materials (ACM) are typically odourless, tasteless and are difficult to detect visually.

These properties make it problematic to determine the specific risks of asbestos exposure when seeking to carry out building and/or refurbishment works, particularly on older residential properties, which may not have been altered or modernised for several decades, for example, where properties become available on the market as a result of a probate sale.

Where Is Asbestos Likely To Be In A Residential Property?

In residential properties, asbestos can in found in numerous locations. Internally, this can be in items such as water tanks, pipe lagging, insulation, aertex ceilings, vinyl flooring, behind fireplaces, in toilet and cistern blocks and older fuse boxes. Externally, items such as gutters, downpipes, window panels, felts, outbuildings and garages can also be hiding asbestos containing materials.

Under the Health and Safety at Work Act 1974[136] (HASWA), in cases where you intend to carry out improvements or refurbishment works to a property and are proposing to bring

---

[136] https://www.legislation.gov.uk/ukpga/1974/37/contents.

HMO Property Set Up

builders or contractors into the property, you have the ultimate responsibility for all works being carried out, similar to the CDM Regulations. You must therefore inform any workers of the presence of any ACMs prior to the commencement of any works. This helps reduce the risks of any ACMs unwittingly being disturbed or damaged which could affect the health of those who are brought into contact with them.

What Should You Do If You Think There Is Asbestos In A Property?

Asbestos and ACMs are highly dangerous if disturbed and prolonged exposure can lead to conditions such as asbestosis or mesothelioma. The only safe way of identifying the presence (or absence) of suspected asbestos is to carry out laboratory tests on samples. The Health and Safety Executive (HSE) strongly encourages that trained and accredited professionals are employed to identify and either repair or remove ACMs where their presence is detected.

To do this, it is recommended an asbestos refurbishment survey (ARS) is undertaken where you consider there may be ACMs in a property. These surveys are typically both 'destructive' and 'intrusive', intended to identify the location and presence of asbestos in a property where works with the potential to disturb asbestos are due to be taking place (such as internal reconfigurations for a HMO use). Because of the destructive nature of the survey, in most circumstances you will probably not be able to commission a survey until after you have exchanged and completed on the property purchase – understandably, most owners and vendors would not be happy to have holes knocked in walls by a prospective purchaser! Any test samples collected are then taken for laboratory analysis. Following this, a report is compiled, highlighting the risks of exposure and measures for mitigation or removal where asbestos is confirmed. This report should then be provided to all contractors on the site to minimise the risks of exposure and included in the health and safety file for the project.

How Long Do Asbestos Refurbishment Surveys Take?

Usually, asbestos surveyors are able to work quickly in order to minimise any site disruption. Once areas of a property have been intrusively assessed, these areas must then be certified as being 'fit for reoccupation' before anyone else is allowed to enter the area after the survey has taken place, to help further minimise any risks of exposure. This could include a need for asbestos air testing during and on completion of the survey in cases where significant amounts of asbestos are uncovered.

If asbestos is found, you can use your own builder or contractor to remove the ACMs, provided they are suitably qualified to do so. They must also be able to dispose of it by proper means as it is classed as a 'hazardous waste' if it contains more than 0.1 percent asbestos and is therefore not able to be disposed of by conventional means. However, in many cases, asbestos surveyors are capable of removing and disposing of ACMs themselves, where instructed to do so. On completion of any works to remove or repair ACMs, an asbestos air survey may again be necessary to confirm the room or property is fit for re-occupation.

How Much Will An Asbestos Survey Cost?

Survey costs can vary, as they are normally based on the type of property and its construction, its age and condition (whether it is structurally sound or flood/fire-damaged, for example), the number of rooms to be surveyed and the anticipated number of samples required, as well as the nature

HMO Property Set Up

and extent of the refurbishments you are seeking to undertake. Depending on some of the above factors, you can expect to pay in the region of £500 – £800 for an asbestos refurbishment survey undertaken on a three-to-four-bedroom semi-detached house. Whilst it may seem like an extra expense, it is worthwhile factoring into your budget an asbestos refurbishment survey, particularly for properties built pre-2000, as it ensures that where there is the potential for ACMs to be found or exposed within a property during refurbishment works, those working on site as well as the potential future occupiers of the property will be kept safe, ultimately helping to protect you as the property owner or agent.

67. Speaking To Neighbours

Unless you are purchasing a house in the middle of nowhere (not ideal for most HMO properties), dealing with and speaking to neighbours is likely to become an inevitable part of the set up and long term management of your HMO. Where you have neighbours living next to or close to a property you are buying for use as a HMO, they are naturally going to want to understand what you are doing and may have concerns about noise, parking and the transient nature of different people coming and going who they do not recognise. As neighbours of the property, they have to live there, whereas you do not. It is therefore worthwhile remembering that having a good relationship with neighbours can make a big difference, not only during the refurbishment phase of a HMO project, but also once the property is ready for occupiers. Getting off 'on the wrong foot' with any neighbours can lead to issues and bad feeling; ultimately it can impact on whether tenants wish to stay in a property, or whether they want to leave as soon as their tenancy agreement ends if there is an 'unfriendly' vibe between them and any neighbours. These vibes can really drive tenants away and make it difficult to replace them!

I can recall one instance where a seemingly good relationship was soured when a builder let slip that the property being refurbished would become a HMO to a neighbour. Unfortunately, before the new owner knew about it and could speak to the neighbour to try and reassure them, a petition had been organised in the local neighbourhood against the proposal and a story decrying the project even appeared in the local newspaper, with ridiculous suggestions about the number of people to be 'crammed' into the property, how the

HMO Property Set Up

house would lead to an increase in local crime, reduction in property values and that there would be cars parked all over the street – all as a result of one six bedroom HMO!

Another matter to be aware of is that if you are considering a property which is within a cul-de-sac location, neighbours can often be quite 'defensive' against proposed HMO developments, particularly if the property to be converted is at the bottom of the cul-de-sac – so do try to tread carefully!

When Should You Speak With Neighbours?

As you progress through your HMO journey, you are likely to have to engage with neighbours at several different stages. Typically, this can be:

- When you first view the property/return to carry out a pre-refurbishment survey after having an offer accepted;

- If you are putting in a planning application;

- Serving a Party Wall notice (if applicable);

- When you begin refurbishment works;

- If any issues arise during refurbishment; and

- Where any issues arise after the property is occupied by tenants.

Viewing Stage

When viewing a property, if neighbours are around and you end up speaking with them, by all means introduce yourself,

HMO Property Set Up

but try to avoid telling them about your intentions for the dwelling at this stage. If pressed, you can say you are thinking about purchasing the property to use as a buy to let, as this is usually relatively uncontentious. Avoid mentioning that you intend for the property to be used a HMO as this could lead to anxiety and unnecessary concerns being raised by neighbours which could even result in the vendor refusing to sell the property to you for fear of upsetting their neighbours. It has happened before...!

Pre-planning For Extensions Or Alterations Stage

Once you have bought the property – or are close to exchanging and you decide you need to apply for planning permission for an extension or other alterations, it is worthwhile going to speak with neighbours about the proposal first, or if you cannot speak to them, writing a letter and including your contact details to they can discuss any queries. You might need to speak to them anyway at a later stage for agreement over works to a party wall. Again though, avoid mentioning the property will be a HMO at this stage. This is because the future use of the property is not relevant to any planning application you may be submitting and as neighbours will likely be consulted by the LPA for comments on an extension, for example, you'll want to keep their comments focused on what you are *actually* applying for planning permission to do (i.e. the extension only). If neighbours are submitting comments relating to the future use of the property as a HMO, this can simply raise unnecessary considerations for the LPA and detract from the proposal you have submitted.

I understand that some of you may have reservations about this approach and concealing the future use of the property as

HMO Property Set Up

a HMO. If so, try discussing your plans with any immediate neighbours and listen to the concerns they may want to raise about property being used as a HMO. When speaking with neighbours, reassure them of the high-quality accommodation and type of tenants you will be seeking to place in the property. To aid with discussions and help further reassure them, it can be worthwhile providing them with visuals, floorplans and photographs, as well as guiding them through the planning process if they are unfamiliar with it. If neighbours are aware of the standards you will be working to achieve and the type of tenants you are seeking to market the house to, this can often help alleviate concerns about the property being a HMO. A parking plan and proposed parking management strategy could also be useful in cases where on-street parking is limited.

Pre-refurbishment Stage

Assuming planning permission is granted for works to extend or alter your property (and even where you are just carrying out works under PD rights), I would always recommend approaching neighbours ahead of any refurbishment or extension works being commenced. This is also the stage at which you may need to speak with (certainly immediate) neighbours to agree any party wall works. Apologising in advance for any disruption which will be caused as a result of works will certainly go a long way with neighbours, especially if your builders are going to be making lots of noise or will need to park their vehicles in the road for several weeks whilst works are undertaken.

Always aim to be polite and courteous with neighbours – they are the ones who live in the street at the end of the day. Being accommodating of their comments and suggestions can go a

HMO Property Set Up

long way in building good relationships too, even in cases where you may not specifically agree with them.

Post-refurbishment Stage

Once works have been completed and you are getting ready to tenant your property, it may be a good idea to speak with your neighbours once again about how the property will be used, if they are not already aware it will be a HMO. If they have concerns about the use of the property as a HMO, there isn't really anything they can do to stop it, particularly if you have the correct licences and planning permissions in place (if Sui Generis or within an A4D area) but do try to take any concerns onboard.

To help overcome any concerns, I have known some landlords and HMO property developers to have given understanding neighbours small gifts and invited them around to see the finished house when refurbishment works have been completed. This has two benefits:

1. It shows your neighbours that you are open and willing to listen to their concerns, so if there are issues once the property has been let out, they are more likely to approach you rather than go straight to the local authority with an issue; and

2. It enables them to see the high standards of accommodation you are providing for your tenants, so any misconceptions about your HMO are addressed then and there.

HMO Property Set Up

Occupation Stage

On occupation of the property, if you or your agent regularly go there to carry out inspections of common areas or to work on any small maintenance jobs, it can present a good opportunity to catch up with neighbours and your tenants to see how things are going. If you have provided neighbours with your contact details, get in touch with them before your visit and let them know when you'll be around so they have the opportunity to talk to you. Be particularly mindful of common issues such as noise, on-street parking and refuse bins being left out on the pavement – these can often end up becoming 'major' concerns for some neighbours which can sour a relationship and lead to resentment. If there are any issues or concerns raised, these can be discussed and you can work to find ways to address them before they become 'major' issues.

Sui Generis Planning Permission

Where you set up a new property as a C4 HMO, it is a good idea to allow some time for it to 'bed' into the neighbourhood (usually between three and six months is a good amount of time), before applying for planning permission to change it into a larger Sui Generis HMO. This essentially allows time for any little 'niggles' to be ironed out and for neighbours to get used to how the property operates, as well as how you have dealt with any issues which may have arisen. If you have a seventh or eighth bedroom (or more!) which is not yet occupied in your property, before applying for planning permission to change the use of your C4 HMO into a Sui Generis HMO, it is worthwhile arranging a time to discuss your proposal with neighbours that you intend to open up one (or more) of the bedrooms in the property for further

HMO Property Set Up

occupation. Where you have created all your bedrooms as part of the overall refurbishment stage, you are not 'adding' more bedrooms to the property, you are simply unlocking the ones which are already there waiting!

If there have been no issues previously and you have been able to build a good relationship with neighbours, they should be reassured the property will still be managed and maintained effectively with the additional tenants. Should they raise concerns, try to work with neighbours to address these before applying for planning permission for a larger HMO. If they are generally supportive of the proposal, you could ask them to prepare and submit comments of support to the LPA.

In cases where you are unable to reach an agreement and neighbours have said they are likely to object, it is worth remembering that their comments on a planning application have to be related to 'material considerations' to count. Neighbours cannot simply say they do not like the idea of having a larger HMO in their street; there would have to be specific concerns around intensification of use, noise, levels of parking, waste management and amenity impacts, for example. Ultimately, the decision lies with the LPA, so if your HMO property is policy compliant and you can evidence it is well run, maintained and managed professionally, opening up additional rooms for occupation should not be contentious.

68. Reduced VAT

If you haven't previously carried out a development project, you may not be aware there is currently a beneficial VAT reduction which can help you to save a significant amount on the costs of undertaking works. This is known as 'VAT Notice 708 Buildings and Construction[137]'.

There are certain provisions which allow for 'qualifying' property conversions and building works to be either zero-rated or receive a five percent reduced rate of VAT. The zero-rating applies to the construction of a new building, designed as a dwelling and used solely for residential purposes, subject to meeting the qualifying criteria. For most HMO projects, these will involve the conversion of existing properties rather than new builds, so I won't go into any further detail on zero-rated works here. The five percent rate applies to materials and services related to a conversion project and to any repairs or construction works within the immediate vicinity of the building area, such as a garage.

The reduction applies to labour involved in building or refurbishing the property, any utility changes, such as the installation of heating, water, electricity and broadband, energy efficiency materials, security and drainage, the conversion of an existing outbuilding into a garage and the building or a driveway to said garage, for example. The reduction does not however extend to or apply to labour or goods which are not considered building materials (such as carpets and wood or laminate flooring, scaffolding, fitted wardrobes etc.). It is therefore imperative to ensure your

---

[137] https://www.gov.uk/guidance/buildings-and-construction-vat-notice-708#overview.

HMO Property Set Up

builder/contractor purchases all the project materials, rather than you purchasing the materials yourself and providing them for installation. If you were to do this, you would be charged at 20% VAT. Other services and activities are also exempt and are charged at the standard 20% rate. This includes paying architects, planning and surveyor's fees, skip and/or specialist tool hire, the erection and dismantling of any scaffolding and any landscaping activities.

The five percent rate also applies to the conversion of any property (i.e. commercial property, single dwellinghouse or another type of relevant residential building) into a HMO, subject to the following criteria:

- The property must not already contain any multiple occupancy dwellings prior to the conversion; and

- The property must only contain a multiple occupancy dwelling after the conversion process.

It is worthwhile noting that a certificate is often required to claim the five percent rate where the conversion of a property into a relevant residential building, or to renovation works on a residential building, which has been left empty for two years are proposed. In addition to the qualifying criteria, you will need to employ a VAT registered builder or contractor to undertake the refurbishment project. In their role, they must be comfortable with 'self-assessing' the project does indeed meet the criteria for a 'qualifying conversion'. Non-VAT registered builders or contractors would obviously not able to undertake this task. In cases where the builder or contractor

HMO Property Set Up

you wish to employ is quite a small outfit, they may not be aware of the VAT reduction.

As mentioned above, it is up to the builder/contractor to assess whether the project qualifies though and it would be their responsibility to pay any extra VAT and subsequent HMRC penalties and interest if the project is not considered to qualify by HMRC. As a result, some builders/contractors can understandably be reluctant or hesitant to agree or be overly cautious when assessing the VAT status of a refurbishment project, particularly if they are a small firm and have not done it before. Where they are not confident or comfortable in undertaking a 'self-assessment', you may end up having to unnecessarily pay the standard 20% rate, unless you find another builder/contractor who is more familiar with the process and happy to carry out the self-assessment.

Therefore, when discussing the reduced rate with builders/contractors, it may be worth putting them in touch with your accountant, who should be able to advise and reassure them of the process and why your project is capable of qualifying. This can be aided by providing builders and contractors with existing and proposed floorplans, any relevant planning permissions and any drawings or images of similar conversion projects you have undertaken or know of in the local area.

Where builders and contractors are VAT registered and they are happy to self-assess the project, they can then charge you the five percent VAT rate. This method works by the builder and/or contractor simply charging you five percent rather than 20% VAT when invoicing you for the project. The builder and/or contractor will then recover the VAT through the quarterly VAT return process. In cases where you intend to

HMO Property Set Up

use a builder or contractor who is new to the process, it may be helpful to incentivise them to self-assess your project by offering a small 'buffer' fund to bridge the gap between paying for items, such as bathroom suites and then receiving the VAT refund from HMRC. An example of this would be the purchase of three-bathroom suites costing £2,400+VAT by the builder or contractor, resulting in a total cost of £2,880. Your builder or contractor will then charge you £2,400+VAT at the five percent rate, which results in a total cost of £2,520.

Following this, your builder or contractor will then include these transactions in their next quarterly VAT return and will recover £120, where £480 VAT has been paid out to the bathroom supplier, less the £120 VAT you paid. This means you will have only paid five percent VAT on the bathroom suites and the main contractor has not been left carrying the expense.

Obviously, where you are seeking to spend a significant budget on refurbishing a property, this process can result in saving a large chunk on VAT. This can result in the difference between being able to provide your tenants with a *good* standard of finish or a *great* standard of finish, which could have an impact on how much they are willing to pay for the accommodation you are providing.

69. Sustainability And Energy Efficiency In HMOs

As you will likely already be aware, energy costs have risen sharply in recent years across the UK due to increased demand, limited supplies and a shortage of storage space for energy, coupled with the way in which wholesale energy is bought and sold. HMOs are notoriously power-hungry properties due to the number of people living in them, the number of appliances and typically high utility demands. Anything you can do to help improve their energy efficiency, reduce running costs and make them more sustainable will therefore help to keep money in both yours – and your tenant's pockets!

Sustainability and energy efficiency have both grown to become quite the buzzwords these days, but the importance of providing both sustainable and energy efficient accommodation cannot be ignored and is increasingly important for viability reasons, particularly where government guidance and legislation is constantly evolving in an effort to meet climate targets, amid the rising costs of energy. There is arguably a greater awareness of the impact of climate change now than ever before, meaning many tenants are equally more receptive to protecting the environment and wanting to live 'sustainably'. But what does sustainability actually mean?

Various definitions exist, but the basic premise is to meet our own current needs without compromising the ability of future generations to meet their own needs. Put simply, in property, being sustainable means using less energy and resources, taking account of the entire life cycle of a project and ongoing maintenance. What you do use, you should try to do so as efficiently as possible by utilising energy efficient appliances, heating systems and materials, whilst seeking to reduce energy loss and wastage as much as possible.

I have deliberately put this chapter before the refurbishment and furnishing chapters because starting out with sustainability and energy efficiency in mind can help steer your project towards more sustainable options from the offset. Not only this but creating and managing your HMOs so they are sustainable and energy efficient from the start can help save you money in the long run and increase profitability by ensuring your bills can remain as low as possible and could make your property more attractive to purchasers when you come to sell. It also means you may stay one step ahead of any additional legislative changes the government wishes to bring in, which could be costly to retrofit, such as works to improve the EPC of rental properties.

Incorporating sustainability and energy efficiency into the refurbishment and management plan for your HMO and marketing it as a sustainable and 'eco-friendly' property can really help you 'tap into' the cultural shift too. Making the most of those green credentials can help you find tenants who are increasingly aware of their carbon footprint and who are willing to pay for accommodation which is seen to be 'greener', as the findings of recent research reveals[138]. Grants are often available to landlords to help assist with making properties more energy efficient, so make sure to check out

---

[138] The survey, by LettingaProperty.com, found that 98% of renters would prefer to live in an energy-efficient home and 52% would be willing to pay an extra 10% to do so.

HMO Property Set Up

your local authority's Private Landlord webpage for details of these schemes.

How Can I Make My HMOs More Sustainable And Energy Efficient?

As a HMO property developer, you often have the ability to take poorly insulated, out-dated and older dwellings and turn them into energy efficient, warm, modern and comfortable properties which tenants will want to live in. This can be achieved through a combination of high-quality refurbishment and the use of smart technology. Coupled with energy efficient and eco-friendly property management techniques, this can help to contribute towards changing attitudes, tackling climate change and being energy efficient.

As will be discussed in Chapter 73, the Government are bringing in measures to improve the energy efficiency of all rented properties to help meet net-zero commitments by 2050, starting with requiring rented properties to achieve a minimum EPC rating of 'C' by 2028[139].

Energy Efficiency

There are a number of ways you can help to tackle the rising costs of energy bills and improve the energy efficiency of your properties which can help to reduce your refurbishment budget and long-term running costs – and enable you to meet the minimum EPC 'C' rating. If you have an existing HMO property already or you are scoping out your approach to converting an existing property into a new HMO which is as

---

[139] Previously the inception date for this was 2025: https://www.telegraph.co.uk/property/buy-to-let/landlords-get-five-years-hit-net-zero-targets/.

energy efficient as possible, it is initially worthwhile going around with an electrician or specialist energy assessor and getting their input on what can be done. Standard Assessment Procedure (SAP) calculations can be undertaken as well as the production of an energy statement, which can calculate the predicted energy efficiency of the property.

Once you have an idea of what needs to be carried out, including the type of materials to use (for insulation, heating and hot water, windows and doors, any renewables energy systems for example) and appliances to install (you can run these past your energy assessor), you can also look at other ways to save energy through the use of home automation systems and smart technology, such as Passive Infrared (PIR) sensors in hallways and communal spaces to ensure lights are off when rooms are empty, switching to or using LED bulbs throughout your property and fully utilising smart thermostats, digital Thermostatic Radiator Valves (TRVs) and heat controls which can detect when windows are open.

If you have existing HMOs, it is very important to understand the current power usage in your properties. Installing smart meters can help to track usage and work out peak hours of consumption, as well as when there are 'quite' periods throughout the day. For new HMOs it is worthwhile monitoring energy consumption closely for the first three to six months of full occupation, giving you a clear baseline of when demand is at its highest. Typically, you will find that first thing in the morning as tenants get ready for work and at the end of the day when tenants return from work are going to be where you will notice peak power consumption times. This of course depends on the type of tenants you have and their working practices/lifestyles.

HMO Property Set Up

'Zoning' the heating of bedrooms and other areas of a property with individual smart thermostats and TRVs can assist with reduce running costs during peak times. This enables you to monitor usage at an individual level and for tenants to simply heat their own room, rather than the entire house if they are working from home, whilst other tenants may be out, for example. If you are considering electric towel radiators in bathrooms or ensuites, fit them with scheduling controls so they are only on when tenants need them to be.

Other measures include providing minimum grade A+ energy efficient appliances, improving insulation throughout the property, installing a more efficient boiler and heating system, consider installing triple glazed windows with low emissivity (low-E) coated glass, which reflects heat back into a property. Shopping around for the best tariffs is of course another way to help reduce your costs.

Installing renewable energy technologies such as solar photovoltaic (PV) arrays, air source heat pumps (ASHP) and ground source heat pumps (GSHP) can also help with reducing running costs, although these are typically expensive to put in place initially, have long payback periods and particularly with solar PV arrays, will depend on the location and orientation of the property they are to be installed on. However, if you intend to hold a property for a long time, these measures can make the costs viable. If you are considering any of these technologies, make sure to speak to a qualified advisor.

Changing the attitudes of your tenants can also go a long way towards helping cut high energy usage. It can be beneficial to provide regular feedback to tenants on a monthly basis about how much energy has been used, the costs and good economic practice. You could even offer rent reduction incentives if your tenants help to reduce the amount of electricity or gas used. Conversely, if energy efficiency does not improve, don't be afraid to discuss rental increases to cover the additional utility costs. All conversations around rental increases should be backed up with clear evidence and should show they are not simply profit-driven exercises.

The rising costs of utilities are a major issue for HMO property developers, so taking steps to reduce these costs as much as possible must be a key part of any refurbishment programme or upgrading strategy.

Making Use Of What Already Exists In A Property

Taking a sustainable approach to HMO property development isn't all about new items though and you should seek to assess and reuse existing items within a property during the refurbishment phase of a project where you can.

Aim to avoid simply ripping everything out and disposing of it. Instead, think about whether you can reuse the existing flooring or kitchen cupboards. For example, would painting the kitchen cupboard doors and changing the handles provide you with the look you were after? Can the carpets be used in other rooms if you don't want them in the room they are in? Are there any items which could be upcycled and made into a feature? In cases where existing fixtures or fittings cannot be reused in your property, try selling them on or upcycling them for additional profit, rather than just dumping them in a skip.

Fixtures, Fittings And Furniture

When sourcing fixtures, fittings and furniture, think about where these items are coming from and what they are made

HMO Property Set Up

of. You can quite easily pick up second hand or reclaimed high-quality materials and items which look great and still have the 'wow' factor by simply doing a bit of research online. Additionally, think about what materials are used in the items themselves – are they recyclable or sustainably produced? Are they manufactured using energy efficient and sustainable practices? What packaging do the items come in and can this packaging be recycled?

Finally, think about the longevity of the items you will be purchasing. Remember, if you buy cheap, you may then pay twice! You want to avoid having to replace cheaper items every couple of months because they have worn out or broken. This will likely result in costing you more in the long term anyway through repeat purchases and be worse for the environment if these items are then not easily recyclable!

Recycling

Speaking of recycling, it is important to encourage your tenants to do their bit when living in your property. Try to initiate a sustainable management practice early on by communicating clearly with tenants about what you expect them to do from the beginning of their tenancy agreement. Providing suitable general waste and recycling bins is a must and can help reduce the impact of having more people living in a shared property. This is often a condition of your HMO licence anyway.

Sustainable Transport Options and Locations

As mentioned in Chapter 60, providing EVCPs are a good way of encouraging more sustainable transport options for your tenants, along with encouraging the use of bicycles through the provision of secure bicycle storage sheds and the

HMO Property Set Up

use of public transport over private cars. Whilst there has been considerable growth in working from home practices, location still plays a significant role in whether your property is considered to be 'sustainably located' and the attractiveness of this to tenants.

To ensure your property is attractive, remember to consider how close it is to employment centres, public transport nodes as well as other services, facilities and amenities in the area such as local shops, gyms, cinemas, pubs, bars and cafes. Being within easy walking or cycling distance can be very desirable for tenants and reduces your tenant's reliance on private cars, even if they are electric.

Sustainable Garden Spaces

As well as works inside of your property, carrying out works to the garden space to make it more sustainable can also be worthwhile (assuming you won't be using it for off-street parking). High quality outdoor amenity space has become increasingly sought after by tenants as a result of lockdown measures and the popularity of working from home[140]. The introduction of Biodiversity Net Gain (BNG) through the Environment Act 2021[141] requires all planning permissions in England, regardless of size, to deliver at least a ten percent biodiversity net gain. These measures are expected to come into effect in November 2023. This could mean BNG is required for applications such as change of use to a Sui Generis HMO to a householder application for a rear extension, although works carried out using PD rights will not

---

[140] https://www.rightmove.co.uk/news/articles/property-news/rightmove-survey-home-hunters-want-bigger-gardens/.
[141] https://www.legislation.gov.uk/ukpga/2021/30/contents.

HMO Property Set Up

need to demonstrate compliance. BNG is a measurable approach to increasing the overall biodiversity value of a development site. Whilst a HMO development is typically very small scale, increases in BNG can help with 'urban greening' by reducing air and noise pollution, reducing flood risks and surface water runoff and creating additional habitats for local wildlife. For larger proposals, for example, converting a former hotel or office building into a Sui Generis HMO, you may need the specialist input of an ecologist to help demonstrate BNG.

To help with achieving BNG on standard HMO conversions you could seek to create a visually appealing outdoor space by planting low maintenance native species shrubs, bushes and flowers to attract local wildlife. You could install decking or use permeable surfacing for a patio area to help reduce surface water flooding. This would also reduce the size of the lawn area which typically provides little to no habitat for pollinators, reducing the need for regular mowing and watering. Instead, you could set aside a 'wild garden' area or create wildflower planters to encourage pollinators and provide a habitat for insects. A gardener can then still maintain the garden space quickly and efficiently. To further encourage and help local wildlife, adding simple items such as bird and bat boxes, log piles, hedgehog holes in fencing and bee bricks can really make a difference.

In terms of garden furniture, sustainably produced garden furniture, such as tables and chairs or loungers can also be obtained for your tenants to make use of and you could consider purchasing good quality second hand items instead of buying new. Additionally, rainwater harvesting tubs can be installed to water the garden space or be used to help flush

HMO Property Set Up

toilets, for example. Depending on the type of tenants you are seeking to attract, a composter could be installed in the garden for food waste, although this would need to be carefully managed to avoid any pest-control and odour issues! A small allotment space where tenants could grow their own fruits and vegetables could also be worthwhile looking into, again depending on the type of tenants you are seeking to attract.

The inclusion of a green roof or sedum roof can be a creative way to provide BNG and could be installed as a feature on flat roof extensions or on other roof pitches, angled between 10 degrees and 20 degrees without a frame being required to prevent slipping. Green roofs or sedum roofs can be visually appealing, create natural habitats and increase biodiversity. They can even help to reduce the amount of energy needed for heating, as well as dampen the impact of any noise produced by tenants.

As the above demonstrates, there are several ways in which the sustainability and energy efficiency of your HMOs can be improved, as well as contributing positively to local wildlife and biodiversity.

70. Refurbishment

As you'd expect, there is a natural order and progression to the way in which the refurbishment of a property into a HMO should take place. This should be informed by a refurbishment schedule, setting out what works need to be carried out and when. The schedule should take account of any advice received from HMO licensing officers in relation to the design, layout, amenities and facilities to be provided. A schedule can also assist with estimating the length of time required for the refurbishment stage and consequently, the costs involved. You should therefore seek the input of an architect, principal designer and/or contractor and your build team to help draw up a comprehensive schedule, covering all aspects of the refurbishment and any build work to ensure nothing is missed. This should help the works to progress in the most logical and cost-effective manner.

Where you are undertaking a full refurbishment of the whole property, naturally the refurbishment schedule can become quite complex. It is therefore beneficial to break the project down into smaller phases and then into sub-phases. For example, the refurbishment of upstairs bedrooms could be broken down into individual rooms. This could then be broken down further into the tasks required within that room, based on the order they'd need to be done in. Obviously, you'd want to start with more intrusive works such as re-wiring and fitting new plug sockets, chasing in cables and pipework etc. before moving onto more cosmetic works like painting the walls and laying carpets! This method should help to minimising the overlapping of any works taking place too and therefore help to reduce your costs. Once you have

HMO Property Set Up

your refurbishment schedule in place and it has been agreed with your project/build team, the fun can begin!

<ins>Undertaking The Refurbishment</ins>

I would estimate that most of the properties you will be looking to purchase will be existing residential houses already. These are likely to still be occupied by the vendor or have only recently been vacated (for example through probate sales). Therefore, most properties are generally going to be in a reasonable condition to start with and have existing water and power connections. In rare cases where no power or water are provided, rectifying this must be one of the first actions undertaken so your build team can progress without delay.

For any properties purchased where they have been left empty for a while, if damp is present, this is another issue which must be addressed immediately. As the property will likely be empty, there is no better time than at the start of the refurbishment stage to rectify a damp problem. In addition, there's little to be gained from spending thousands on refurbishing a property if damp ruins the finish and leaves you liable for additional future works once the property is occupied. Damp issues could affect your ability to refinance the property until the issue is resolved too and may see a HMO licence withheld until the property can be safely occupied.

Assuming the property is weatherproof, free from damp and that all the utilities are already connected, unless there are fixtures or fittings you intend to keep, the next stage would be to empty the property and strip it back to bear walls and floors. This will help get the property ready for any rewiring, plumbing and other works involving drilling or the removal of

HMO Property Set Up

material from walls and floors. This is also the ideal stage to start carrying out any external building works, assuming planning permission has been granted to do so (or you do not need it). Make sure that any works being undertaken by your build team are in accordance with planning permission or the limitations of PD rights and will comply with the relevant approved documents for building regulations.

Whilst any external works are taking place, it is a good idea to organise for the cleaning, repair or replacement of any guttering and downpipes, as well as repainting, re-rendering or cladding the walls of the property. This will help to enhance the look of your property and give it a 'fresher' look. Works could also include upgrading the facias, soffits, parapets, barge boards and windows.

First Fixing Stage

Following the stripping out of the existing property and the building of any extension, you will enter the 'first fix' stage of the refurbishment, which comprises all the works needed to take a property from the basic 'foundations' to plastering the internal walls and ceiling. This includes constructing internal stud walls, floors and ceilings, where necessary. Interior linings (the surface finish and substrate of a wall) can also be made ready for plastering works. Once this has been undertaken, the first phase of electrical and plumbing works can commence.

On completion of the first fix, re-plastering can begin to cover any new walls or ceilings created, as well as to any existing or damaged walls or ceilings. Make sure the plaster is allowed to completely dry out before starting any further works. This can sometimes take a few days up to a week in some cases. If you

HMO Property Set Up

don't allow sufficient time for the plaster to dry, this can cause problems during the 'second fix' stage for the installation of any wood fixtures and fittings. Where you intend to lay any fixed flooring, such as tiles or solid wooded floors, it is a good idea to cover the entire room 'edge to edge' so any fitted furniture, kitchen base units or bathroom units can be installed on top, as can any skirting and architrave. This of course depends on whether you are seeking to retain any kitchen or bathroom units which may have already been in place.

Second Fixing Stage

Entering the 'second fix' stage of the refurbishment typically takes places after all the plastering has been completed. Electrical fixtures such as light fittings, switches, sockets, phone, TV and internet points are connected to the installed cables; sinks and baths are connected to pipework and boxed in, whilst doors are fitted into door frames, along with other skirting and architrave works. This stage also includes the fitting out of the kitchen and the installation of the boiler, its controls and any radiators so the heating system can be commissioned. As the second fix works are carried out closer to the end of a project, the attention to detail should be much higher to ensure a neat finish to the works is achieved.

Following these works, the refurbishment will be ready to enter the 'design, decorating and furnishing' phases (see Chapter 71). However, prior to commencing this stage, the property should be thoroughly cleaned and be 'dust free' before any painting or tiling can take place. Once decorating has been completed, blinds, curtains, shelving, carpets and laminate flooring can be installed. White goods for the kitchen can be also be fitted.

HMO Property Set Up

As the works progress, it is common for a number of minor issues to arise. It is important to get these issues dealt with as soon as you see them or are made aware of them as it is usually much easier to fix them whilst you have your built team there. Inevitably, there will be issues towards the end of the refurbishment process which may still need looking at. This is where it is important to inspect the property 'room by room' to identify any issues which will be added to a snagging list. Make sure to discuss these with your project/build team so the issues can be resolved before your contractors leave the site. On completion of the refurbishment (including any snagging), make sure to conduct a thorough deep clean of the property. You can then get the rooms ready for furniture and fixtures.

71. Designing, Decorating and Furnishing HMOs

The first thing to bear in mind when you are thinking about how to design, decorate and furnish (DDF) your HMO is that you won't be living there, so your personal tastes and preferences should not play a huge role in how the interior of the property will look. Instead, to help with designing the look of your HMO, try creating your ideal 'tenant profile' and think about what a prospective tenant will be looking for in a home. Think about what is likely to be important to them and what is not, for example – a desk in their room or home working facilities in communal areas, a lounge to relax in after work or a games room, a garden or a patio area? As part of creating your tenant profile, it helps to be clear on what age range are you try to attract, as well as their gender (should you have a preference – i.e. all female/male tenants or a mix), their employment background and level of income and their hobbies and interests and this will impact the way you go about 'DDF-ing' your property. For example, if you wanted to set up an eco-friendly HMO, it would make sense to refurbish it as such and then market it towards tenants who aspire to live in a property like that and wish to be with other like-minded people.

Make sure to think carefully about the design and furnishings of your HMOs interior. Good design and attention to detail make a real difference in helping your property to stand out from others in the area when it comes to marketing your rooms. It can even help with commanding higher rental amounts, along with retaining tenants once they are in your property, particularly if the standard of accommodation on offer elsewhere is not a high as yours.

HMO Property Set Up

When starting to think about design, carry out some research into current and popular trends by seeing what is already being advertised in your area on sites such as SpareRoom, OpenRent[142] and Ideal Flatmate[143]. Ask yourself what stands out to you, for both good and bad reasons and what catches your eye as you browse room listings? What seems to work well? Make a note of how quickly the adverts get taken down too as this will give you an indication of what is popular and in demand. If there are particularly creative styles or designs being used well, take note of them and try to emulate them in your HMO designs.

Rooms do need to be designed to suit their functional needs and to meet (or preferably exceed) minimum HMO licensing standards. They also need to be designed to be comfortable, appealing and feel 'homely'. You should aim to provide kitchens, lounges and other communal areas which are bright and airy spaces that are practical, well laid out and attractive. Think about good lighting when designing your rooms too. Not only can this change the perception of the space, but it can also influence people's moods as well as how they will use the space. A dark and dingy looking room is much less likely to attract a potential tenant than a bright and well-lit room, although a room which is too bright can also be off-putting and look too 'clinical', which may make it hard for people to relax and unwind in . Try to get the balance right with natural lighting and using a mixture of warm main central lights, desk or table lights and lamps as well as feature

---

[142] https://www.openrent.co.uk/.
[143] https://www.idealflatmate.co.uk/.

HMO Property Set Up

lighting over items such as dining tables, breakfast bars and kitchen areas.

Communal Rooms

In particular, kitchens should have plenty of natural and artificial lighting as well as practical worktop space, cupboard storage and space for communal dining, as per the relevant HMO licensing standards. If you have space for breakfast bars or kitchen islands, these features can provide a variety of versatile spaces for your tenants to make use of. Lounges and living rooms should be designed with comfort and relaxation in mind and along with the kitchen, should be seen as the 'hub' of the house where tenants can get together and socialise. The use of artificial lighting can be more muted in these rooms to promote a more relaxed feeling, like that of a trendy bar. This will help tenants to not only relax after a busy day of work but will help them to get along with one another and can even enable friendships to develop, which could lead to tenants staying longer in your property.

Where practical, a mix of sofas and seating areas with coffee tables can assist with making the place feel more relaxed, with a TV taking centre stage; creating the perfect set up for your tenants to kick back and watch the latest Netflix or Disney+ series.

Bedrooms

Bedrooms are no longer just places to sleep in HMOs anymore. They are often places of work or study and a private place for tenants to relax and hang out with their own circle of friends, so you should design them with these functions in mind – practical and comfortable spaces where tenants can work or study and unwind. Additionally, tenants often come

HMO Property Set Up

with lots of possessions and clothing, so make sure your rooms are fitted with lots of storage space too! Remember, it's not all about plain old magnolia walls these days – tenants often want 'Instagram-able' rooms and houses. Use this to your advantage – it can be a source of free advertising!

<u>Interior Designing And Layouts</u>

As with most things, designing and furnishing rooms is easy when you know how. The best way to do this is to create a basic floorplan either using online software, apps or on paper to try out different layouts and furniture combinations. This method allows you to create a 'virtual' room or house layout where you know the proposed design will work in advance and that it will provide your tenants with a great place they can use. When starting out, try to think about where the focal point of the room will be; for example the bed in a bedroom is likely to be the focal point, whilst the cooker or breakfast bar might be the focal point of the kitchen; similarly, the TV will likely be the main area of attention in the lounge. Once you have this 'layout' in your mind, you can build up the rest of the room from there. The design, colours, textures and furniture should all work together to enhance the room whilst keeping it functional. Try to avoid over-cluttering rooms with furniture though – that can deter tenants by making rooms look crowded and 'busy', especially where items are bulky.

Once you know what furniture works within the space and in what combination on paper, you can proceed with furnishing the property. It is worth choosing furniture that is going to be durable, long lasting and can easily be replaced. As I mentioned in Chapter 69, you should keep in mind the sustainability of the items you are sourcing. As a minimum,

HMO Property Set Up

you may want to think about providing the following items in your furnished HMO:

Items to be provided in a Furnished HMO
Kitchen crockery, cutlery, glasses and utensils relative to the number of tenants at full occupancy
Fridge Freezer
Cooker, hob and microwave
Kettle and toaster
Washing machine and tumble dryer
Refuse and recycling bins
Vacuum cleaner
Dining table/breakfast bar and chairs/benches
Curtains and/or blinds
Carpets and wood/laminate/tiled flooring
Lighting and lampshades
TV with Amazon Firestick or equivalent/games console
Sofas and armchairs
Coffee tables and side tables
Bed and mattress
Wardrobe
Chest of drawers and bedside drawers/table
Desk and chair

Table 71.1: Indicative items to be provided in a furnished HMO.

Decorative Items And 'Dressing Rooms'

Try to include decorative items that will complement your design scheme and the furniture you purchase as well, without looking like clutter. Decorative items can include smaller items such as small ornaments, coffee tables, potted plants (artificial may be preferable for longevity), shelves and shelving units, canvas prints and framed photographs or artworks, mirrors, lamps, lampshades, books and soft

HMO Property Set Up

furnishings such as pillows, cushions, blankets and rugs. Add your furniture and decorative items and then 'dress' each individual room in the property to make it look as attractive as possible – but remember not to over-crowd or clutter up rooms! You could look to 'theme' individual rooms for a really unique look and dressing these rooms will be an important part of this process, so it can be worthwhile spending some time placing items, making beds and creating a 'homely' and welcoming feel, rather than simply taking photos of a bare bed in an empty room. Use natural and artificial lighting to your advantage to make rooms like bright, fresh and inviting.

Either appoint a professional photographer or videographer to take plenty of photographs and video walkthroughs for marketing purposes – remember, the property will probably only likely look this fresh once, so make the most of the opportunity to show it off! If you decide to take photos or videos yourself, try to keep the camera as steady as possible and stay out of any mirrors, windows and other reflective surfaces – no tenant wants to see a shaky video of the property and their prospective landlord peering out from behind a camera in a reflection! When finalising your walkthrough videos, make sure to put them to some upbeat music and show off the best bits about your property. A professional looking video can make a big difference in how attractive your property is to prospective tenants.

HMO Property Set Up

Summary

In this section, I have covered a whole range of associated legislative and other considerations related to the setting up and refurbishment of a HMO and what you may need to be aware of as you go through this process to ensure you set up your HMOs properly and are in line with current (but often evolving) legislation.

This section has provided an overview of party walls and the processes involved in serving notice, as well as how to negotiate the legislation so that works can go ahead even if neighbours are uncooperative.

I have discussed restrictive covenants in more detail and explained how these may be varied or removed or indemnified against.

This section has considered bicycle and vehicle parking standards for HMOs, including electric vehicle charging points to help future-proof your HMO development, as well as discussed how to go about applying for a dropped kerb.

In addition, I have discussed the importance of construction design management and contracts to help ensure development or building projects are delivered, to protect you as the property owner.

Council Tax implications have been discussed, including the re-banding and re-valuation process and the adaptations to a property which can trigger this.

I have also covered a range of insurances which you may wish to consider which can protect not only yourself, but your property, its contents and your investment.

HMO Property Set Up

I have explained what build over agreements are and why they can be important if you are planning on extending, adding a conservatory or are going to be carrying out other building works which could interfere with existing pipework, as well as the approval processes involved.

I have identified common places where asbestos can be found in residential properties and the importance of having a thorough inspection carried out where building works could disturb asbestos.

How and when to approach neighbours and speak to them about your intentions for a property have also been discussed.

I have provided an explanation of how you can reduce your refurbishment budget through VAT reductions on qualifying building works.

Finally, the importance of sustainability in HMOs has been discussed, as well as how to go about conducting the refurbishment process, through to designing and furnishing your HMO property ready for occupation by tenants.

Part III

Section VII: Being A Landlord

In this final section, I will discuss some of the realities of being a landlord, including what you will need to do as a minimum to stay compliant and how software can be useful to help keep on top of these requirements.

"A house is made of bricks and mortar, but a home is made by the people who live there."

– M. K. Soni

72. Introduction To Being A Landlord

For those of your reading this who may not have prior experience of being a landlord, this chapter outlines some of the realities on that role, along with setting out how to make sure you are compliant with all the necessary requirements. If you are already a landlord, it will hopefully serve as a helpful reminder of your obligations.

In theory, being a HMO landlord sounds relatively straightforward, doesn't it? You provide a high-quality property and the rental income flows in from your tenants every month. Being a landlord can be incredibly rewarding, both financially and from a lifestyle point of view, but naturally it does require hard work, time and effort to do it successfully – not to mention having to keep up to date with all the regulatory and governmental changes! That is not to say being a landlord isn't worth it – it totally can be, if done correctly. Therefore, being organised, navigating the legislative requirements and staying up to date with this fast-paced sector is a key component for success.

Landlords – and in particular HMO landlords – often end up receiving an unfair and biased representation in the media. Even 'good' landlords can typically find themselves being wrongly judged or categorised as those who bend or completely break the rules, although with increasing legislation and Government regulation, it is become more difficult for those 'rough' types of landlords to let out sub-standard accommodation, which can only be a good thing in the long run. However, it can certainly seem like landlords in the private sector are being unfairly being targeted by the Government at times. In my experience though, the majority

HMO Property Set Up

of landlords I've come across are merely trying to make a living and genuinely want to deliver good quality accommodation for their tenants, as well as a comfortable lifestyle for themselves and their families. I don't see anything wrong with that.

If you've not previously had experience of being a landlord, the realities can be quite different from the images portrayed in the media. Property is not a passive investment and as a residential landlord, you will have to deal with all aspects of the letting market, frequent wear and tear, maintenance and refurbishment/replacement issues, rent arrears and void periods, disputes between tenants and occasionally disputes between tenants and yourself/letting agents, property damage (whether accidental or deliberate) and the complexities of the eviction process, to name a few.

As I've said before, property and in particular, letting property is a people business and whilst the setup process is a big part of that, the long-term property management, marketing for and retention of tenants is probably where most of your time will be spent. Being a landlord therefore becomes a business in itself and should be administered professionally as such. Even in cases where you decided to use a letting agent to do all the 'heavy lifting', the agent will still need to be in constant contact with you and you'll want to keep an eye on what they're doing to make sure they're carrying out their duties correctly and are managing your property as you want them to. Ultimately though, the responsibility for ensuring legislative compliance lies with you, so if a letting agent isn't doing what they're meant to, you could be liable for their failings.

HMO Property Set Up

At the end of the day, your tenants are your 'clients' and your reputation as a professional landlord is important to maintain if you want to keep your clients happy and retain their 'business' (i.e. have them living in your properties). If issues arise, you should act swiftly but reasonably to resolve them as best you can.

73. Certificates, Checks And Compliance

Keeping on top of your legal obligations as well as knowing you have the correct documentation, paperwork and certificates to hand if you are required to provide them can be a difficult task, but it is one you must master so you never have to worry about missing an important deadline and potentially ending up being non-compliant. As I've mentioned in various chapters throughout this book, the importance of good record keeping cannot be overestimated and where certificates and compliance is involved, this becomes an even more important factor in administering your business as a landlord – it is worthwhile remembering that ignorance is no defence!

Aside from renewing your HMO licence, typically every five years, there are a number of other important certificates and documents which need to be renewed, updated or reviewed, often on an annual basis and which should be provided to tenants at the start of their tenancies. I have therefore put together the following list of important certificates and documents you should be aware of. Please note though that this list isn't exhaustive and as with most things in the private rental sector, could be subject to change as legislation and the regulation of this sector continues to evolve.

Electrical Safety Standards Report

As a landlord, under the Electrical Safety Standards in the Private Rented Sector (England) Regulations 2020[144], you have a legal duty to ensure the electrical installations within your property are inspected at least every five years and that a suitably qualified person tests them to ensure the installations

---

[144] https://www.legislation.gov.uk/ukdsi/2020/9780111191934.

are safe and fit for purpose. These regulations came into force on 1st June 2020 and apply to all residential tenancies.

Typically, an Electrical Installation Condition Report (EICR) will need to be produced to assess the safety of the existing 'fixed' electrical installation within your property and the condition of these installations. The report includes wiring, consumer units, protective bonding, light fittings, switches and sockets. It also includes permanently connected equipment such as shower units and extractors. Following an inspection and testing, you may be required to provide a copy of the report to your tenants (existing, new and prospective) and the local authority, if requested, as well as retain a copy of the report to provide to any person(s) carrying out a future inspection. Existing tenants should receive this report within 28 days, whilst the local authority should be provided the report within seven days of a request being made.

In cases where remedial or further investigative work is identified as being necessary by the report, this should be completed within 28 days, unless specified otherwise. Written confirmation of the completion of any remedial works by a qualified electrician should then be provided to tenants and the local authority within 28 days. As the report is valid for five years, make a note of the expiry date and get in touch with an electrician at least three months before the report expires. This will give your plenty of time to arrange for a qualified electrician to come in and certify that the property's electrics are safe and provide time to carry out any remedial works needed or further investigations, as deemed necessary.

Portable Appliance Tests (PAT)

Portable appliance testing (PAT) is the term used to describe the examination of removable (i.e. not fixed) electrical

HMO Property Set Up

appliances and equipment to ensure they are safe to be used. The purpose of PAT is to minimise accidents and injuries caused by faulty items provided by the landlord, although there is no need to check a tenants' own appliances. The requirement for the testing of the landlord's appliances is set out in the Electricity at Work Regulations 1989[145], which states that any 'portable' electric equipment that has the potential to cause injury much be maintained in a safe condition. The regulations fail to specify what needs to be done, by whom and how frequently though. Typically for HMOs, local authorities will request that PAT is carried out on an annual basis often for HMO licensing purposes, although technically there is no legal requirement or obligation to do so.

Anyone carrying out PAT will need to be competent enough to do so, but it doesn't need to be done by a qualified electrician. Whoever does the testing will, however, need the correct equipment to carry out tests properly and be able to understand the results. The test usually involves a visual and electrical inspection. The visual inspection examines items for signs of damage and wear and confirmation that plugs bear the 'CE' mark (the manufacturers statement confirming the appliance meets European safety standards), whilst the electrical inspection uses a specialist device to detect defects and includes earth resistance and continuity and insulation resistance tests, polarity and safety-switch checks.

There is no legal requirement to label equipment which has been inspected or tested, nor is there a requirement to keep records, but it can be useful to do so as a monitoring tool and to demonstrate to the local authority that testing has been carried out if evidence is asked to be provided. There are a

---

[145] https://www.legislation.gov.uk/uksi/1989/635/contents/made.

HMO Property Set Up

number of useful online training courses which exist for PAT, enabling you to carry out your own annual inspections if you wish to, or you can usually find a local company or individual who does this in your area. Local landlord forums are typically a good place to ask for recommendations.

Gas Safety Checks

Under Regulation (36)(1) of the Gas Safety (Installation & Use) Regulations 1998[146], as a HMO landlord you have a responsibility to ensure all installed gas appliances, such as boilers, flues and cookers etc., are safe for tenants to use. A gas safety certificate must therefore be obtained on an annual basis, a copy of which must be provided to any prospective tenants before they move in – and to existing tenants once it has been renewed. If appliances are new, you should have them checked within 12 months of the installation date, although you can align the date of the annual gas safety check of a new appliance with the gas safety check on any other existing appliances in a property. This can only be applied once to each new appliances and the gas safety check can only be extended by a maximum of two months.

To obtain a gas safety certificate, all gas appliances in existing properties must be checked by a Gas Safe registered engineer who is able to undertake the necessary works, sign off on the appliances and issue the certificate. It is worth putting a reminder in your calendar a few weeks prior to the annual deadline so you have plenty of time to arrange for a qualified engineer to visit your property and so you can provide suitable notice to tenants that a gas safety inspection will be taking place.

---

[146] https://www.legislation.gov.uk/uksi/1998/2451/contents.

HMO Property Set Up

Carbon Monoxide Alarms

Carbon monoxide monitors are currently only required in rooms considered to be living accommodation and which contain an appliance that burns, or can burn solid fuel, such as coal or wood, but not near to boilers. The regulations do not stipulate what type of alarms (hardwired or battery powered) should be installed and require landlords to choose the most appropriate alarms for their properties, based on the needs of their building and their tenants, and that those alarms are compliant with British Standards BS 5839-6. Hard wired alarms will be more expensive to install, but you won't have to worry about batteries needing to be replaced. Where battery powered alarms are selected, alarms with 'sealed for life' batteries rather than alarms with replaceable batteries are considered to be the 'better' option.

As of 1st October 2022, the Smoke and Carbon Monoxide Alarm (Amendment) Regulations 2022[147] require all landlords of private and social housing to provide a carbon monoxide alarm in rooms where there is any type of fixed combustion appliance, such as a gas boiler. Additionally, landlords are required to ensure a smoke alarm is fitted on every floor of their property where a room is used wholly or partly as living accommodation. The regulations set out that landlords are obliged to check the alarms are in working order on the first day of a new tenancy, but it is recommended that alarms are tested regularly to ensure they remain in working order. In the event that smoke alarms and carbon monoxide alarms are faulty, landlord should ensure these are repaired or replaced as soon as possible.

---

[147] https://www.legislation.gov.uk/uksi/2022/707/contents/made

HMO Property Set Up

Fire Detection System (FDS)

Fire Safety is incredibly important in a HMO. The main regulation for fire safety in HMOs is set out in the Fire Safety Act 2021[148], which builds upon the Regulatory Reform (Fire Safety) Order 2005[149], requiring the person responsible for the accommodation (i.e. the landlord or their agent) to take all 'reasonable' steps to ensure the safety of the property and the people living within it. The type of fire safety system you have will depend on the size and layout of your property and any local HMO licensing requirements. LACORS guidance, referred to in Chapter 25, provides general guidelines for HMO properties, identifying that as a minimum you should have a heat detector in any kitchen areas and hard-wired and interlinked smoke alarms which sound on every floor of the property.

There is varying guidance on how often you should test your fire detection system. In some cases, larger, more 'complex' HMOs (seven or more persons) can be considered as being 'higher risk' properties, where more thorough management, frequent inspection and professional servicing of the fire detection system are required. This includes weekly fire alarm tests and visual checks, monthly emergency lighting tests and bi-annual fire alarm serving, all of which should be recorded in a log book. However, you may find that weekly fire alarm test can be excessive and potentially disruptive to tenants, so may want to consider doing this on a monthly basis instead.

As for smaller HMO (of up to six persons), these are typically seen as being 'lower risk' properties. These usually have simpler systems, although regular testing and checks are still

---

[148] https://www.legislation.gov.uk/ukpga/2021/24.
[149] https://www.legislation.gov.uk/uksi/2005/1541/contents.

HMO Property Set Up

necessary. As a minimum, it is recommended you should visually check and test smoke, other alarms and emergency lighting during routine visits, whilst annual alarm maintenance should be caried out in accordance with manufactures instructions. Annual emergency lighting maintenance should also be undertaken. This may be a requirement of your HMO licence. Again, all records of checks should be noted down.

In addition, any furnishings present within a property (except for carpets and curtains) need to comply with the Furniture and Furnishings (Fire) (Safety) Regulations 1988[150] (as amended). Most furniture in the UK usually already complies with these regulations, but it is something to keep in mind when looking for items, which should bear this label. The labels should not be removed from furniture.

Legionella Certificate/Risk Assessment

Legionnaires' Disease is a severe form of pneumonia which causes the lungs to become inflamed. In some circumstances it can be fatal. Legionella bacteria live in natural water sources, such as lakes, rivers and reservoirs, but can also be found in artificial water systems such as water tanks, pipework, taps and shower heads. Legionnaires disease can occur where legionella bacteria is able to grow in these domestic water systems and is then breathed in, in the form of water droplets.
Therefore, properly designing and maintaining the hot and cold-water system in your property will help reduce the risks, as well as controlling the conditions which allow legionella to grow by ensuring water is not able to stagnate.

---

[150] https://www.legislation.gov.uk/uksi/1988/1324/contents/made.

HMO Property Set Up

Whilst it is not a legal requirement for a landlord to produce a legionella water sample test certificate, a landlord can be fined or face a custodial sentence if a tenant were to fall ill or dies from contracting Legionnaires' disease and you are unable to prove you have taken 'reasonable steps' to prevent and control the risk. As a landlord, under the Health and Safety at Work Act 1974, you have a legal responsibility to ensure that the risk of exposure to legionella bacteria is controlled and minimised[151]. This can be undertaken through a Legionella Risk Assessment.

Legislation does not prescribe that a risk assessment is reviewed on an annual or even biannual basis. Instead, it is advised that an assessment is reviewed when there is reason to suspect it is no longer valid. This could be when a change in the use of the building occurs where the water system is located, a change in the water system itself, such as the installation of a new boiler, a change in the building, from being unoccupied to occupied and if there is a reported case of Legionnaires' disease. In addition, legislation does not stipulate who should carry out the risk assessment, other than they should be 'suitably informed' to a level that ensures tasks are carried out in a safe, technically competent manner.

As most domestic properties have simple water systems, this enables landlords to assess the risk themselves without needing to be trained or accredited; but where they do not feel competent, or inclined to do so, they can arrange for a water hygiene specialist to undertake the assessment on their behalf. If a specialist is brought in, the cost for a risk assessment will vary depending on the size and complexity of your property and its water systems. However, most landlords understand the risks of running hot and cold-water systems and can

---

[151] https://www.hse.gov.uk/legionnaires/what-you-must-do.htm.

HMO Property Set Up

implement inexpensive, straightforward and effective control measures to minimise the risk of a water system allowing Legionella to grow and spread.

A risk assessment will typically involve reviewing the current assessment and existing records (where available) and checking to see whether any remedial woks have been acted upon. A physical inspection should also take place with a specific focus on areas of your property where water is stored or where there is the potential for aerosols to be created. Following inspection, a report should then be prepared to assess the risk level of occupants. The report should include a description of both hot and cold-water systems and records of the water outlet temperature should be taken. The report should also note whether any water tanks are accessible, insulated and well covered to prevent contamination. Finally, the report should identify any areas of risk and suitable control steps. This could include noting whether showers and mixing valves are correctly installed and properly maintained and whether there is any redundant pipework in the property which needs to be altered or removed. Additionally, the report should include a procedure to ensure the water system is flushed, should the property be left unoccupied for an extended period of time.

Keeping the water system clean and treating water to limit the growth of the bacteria are suitable control steps. It is also advisable to inform tenants of any control methods in place which need to be maintained, such as not adjusting the temperature setting of the calorifier[152] (if accessible to tenants) and the regular cleaning of showerheads. A guidance note which sets out any control methods should be issued to

---

[152] An indirect or direct electrically heated water vessel that provides hot water in a domestic hot water (DHW) system.

each new tenant on entry. Once completed, this report and any previous reports should be kept safe as a record of what has been carried out. On top of assessments, appropriate checks of the water system can be made periodically, for example, when undertaking mandatory visits such as gas safety checks or routine maintenance callouts.

Energy Performance Certificate (EPC)

As mentioned in previous chapters, EPCs are important documents for both vendors and landlords. Since October 2008, legislation under the Energy Performance of Buildings Directive[153] has made it a requirement to market any standalone property over 50 square metres with a valid EPC. EPCs provide information on the property's energy use, typical energy costs and include recommendations on how to reduce energy usage further and increase efficiency. They are necessary documents for landlords to provide to tenants as part of the move in process. EPCs are issued following an inspection by an accredited inspector, usually a domestic energy assessor or energy advisor. Assessors will evaluate the property for its energy-efficiency and will look at:

- Walls and roof insulation;

- Windows;

- Boilers and heating systems;

- Lighting;

- Building dimensions;

---

[153] https://eur-lex.europa.eu/eli/dir/2010/31/oj.

HMO Property Set Up

- Property age; and

- Any renewable energy devices.

The property is then rated from 'A' to 'G', with 'A' being the most efficient and 'G' being the least. When an EPC certificate is issued, it provides the current rating and an indication of the potential rating, should you undertake changes to improve the energy efficiency of the property. To help, a list of suggested changes and improvements are included. These measures can typically involve the installation of loft insulation and cavity wall insulation, draught proofing doors and windows, insulating any pipes and tanks, reducing water usage, the installation of energy efficient glazing and the installation of low energy lighting.

Once issued, EPCs last for a ten years period, unless you carry out works to improve the energy efficiency of the property. In which case, you'd want to have the property reassessed to demonstrate the energy efficient measures you've taken and to ensure you achieve the minimum EPC rating for a lettable property. Where a certificate needs to be renewed for tenants in an existing property, landlords must provide tenants with at least 24 hour's written notice before an assessment can take place. Once issued, the new EPC must be provided to any existing and all new tenants entering the property going forwards. Without an EPC, your property cannot legally be rented out and you could be liable for a fine. Providing an EPC to all tenants when they move in is also important as currently under Section 21 of the Housing Act 1988, you won't be able to repossess your property using a Section 21 'no fault possession' notice without evidence of an EPC being issued.

HMO Property Set Up

Changing Legislation

As of 1st April 2018, the Domestic Minimum Energy Efficiency Standards (MEES) Regulations came into force, requiring rented properties to achieve a minimum EPC rating of 'E' or above. This was introduced for all new tenancies only, unless a valid exemption is in place. From 1st April 2020 the MEES regulations were updated again, extending the rule to apply to all tenancies, not just new ones, unless a valid exemption is also in place. Currently, therefore, if properties are let which do not meet the minimum 'E' rating (i.e. properties with 'F' and 'G' ratings), landlords could be issued with fines of up to £5,000 as the property should not legally be let out.

At the time of writing (May 2023), current government proposals seek to raise the minimum EPC rating to 'C' or above for all rental properties by 2025, although recent reports suggest this will be pushed back to 2028[154]. The regulations are due to be introduced for new tenancies only at first. This will be followed by all tenancies from 2028 (unless pushed back). The regulation changes are being proposed to make homes more energy-efficient and to help reduce carbon emissions as part of the Government's drive to achieve net-zero by 2050. The changes may also see fines for not having a valid EPC being increased from a maximum of £5,000 pr property to £30,000 from 2025 (unless pushed back). However, the upgrading of some properties to achieve a minimum 'C' rating may not be feasible for all properties, particularly older houses. The proposals largely fail to consider the reality of the existing housing stock, the affordability of the improvements required compared with the

---

[154] https://www.telegraph.co.uk/property/buy-to-let/landlords-get-five-years-hit-net-zero-targets/.

HMO Property Set Up

return on investment for landlords and the impact on existing tenants if they have to be moved out to allow for extensive refurbishment works to take place. The Government are recommending a 'fabric first' approach is taken to cover wall, loft and floor insulation upgrades, although this may only be practical if you are looking to set up a new HMO and can incorporate these changes into your initial refurbishment.

The energy performance investment is understood to be currently capped at £3,500[155] for landlords, including funding or grants provided by the government, local authorities or energy companies, but this is expected to be raised to £10,000 as the requirement to achieve a better EPC rating will mean greater levels of investment are needed. The Government is estimating the average cost to improve properties to reach the minimum EPC 'C' rating is around £4,700. If the suggested improvements exceed £3,500 you can apply for a high-cost exemption from the PRS Exemptions Register, which is then valid for five years; after this time, the exemption will cease and you will need to try to improve the property's EPC rating. If this still cannot be achieved, a further exemption may be registered. Landlords are therefore being urged to apply for a 'Green Homes Grant'[156] to help with upgrading the energy performance of properties.

In some ways, the drive to improve the energy efficiency of existing properties can be a 'blessing in disguise' for professional HMO landlords, as whilst costs may be added to the refurbishment process, landlords who are unwilling, or perhaps unable, to upgrade their properties to meet the minimum 'C' rating may look to exit the market, enabling an

---

[155] https://www.gov.uk/guidance/domestic-private-rented-property-minimum-energy-efficiency-standard-landlord-guidance.
[156] https://www.simpleenergyadvice.org.uk/.

HMO Property Set Up

opportunity for other landlords to pick up cheaper properties with lower EPC ratings and refurbish them to meet energy efficient requirements. Alternatively, focusing on newer build properties to invest in which already achieve minimum EPC 'C' ratings could be a cost-effective way forward.

Right To Rent

Legislation to limit access to the private rental property sector only to those with the lawful right to be in the UK was introduced through Sections 20 to 37 of the Immigration Act 2014[157]. As a landlord, it is your responsibility to ensure your tenants have the legal right to rent and live in this country, which involves checking the identity and UK immigration status for each prospective adult tenant. Checks on a person's status can be undertaken as part of the referencing process. The Government has introduced useful online guidance on checking whether someone has the right to rent your property[158]. In addition, the Government published updated guidance in March 2023[159].

A tenant has the right to rent if they are a British or Irish citizen; have indefinite leave to remain; have refugee status or humanitarian protection; have settled or pre-settled status under the EU settlement scheme; have permission to be in the UK on a work or student visa; or the Home Office has granted a time-limited right to rent.

---

[157] https://www.legislation.gov.uk/ukpga/2014/22/contents.
[158] https://www.gov.uk/check-tenant-right-to-rent-documents.
[159] https://www.gov.uk/government/publications/landlords-guide-to-right-to-rent-checks/landlords-guide-to-right-to-rent-checks-6-april-2022-accessible-version.

HMO Property Set Up

Failure to carry out these checks could result in you being issued with a fine and receiving a custodial sentence in some cases under Section 28 of the 2014 Immigration Act. If a tenant fails a pre-tenancy check, you cannot legally offer them a tenancy and it is your duty to inform the Home Office. You should be aware that it is possible for a tenant's right to rent to expire part way through a tenancy, so if you have any tenants in your property who may only have temporary permits, make sure to keep track of these expiry dates or you could again find yourself liable for a penalty.

How To Rent Guide

All landlords are required to present their tenants at the start of any tenancy with the latest copy of the Government's 'How to Rent' guide. This is a booklet which details a checklist for tenants when renting. The guide also provides advice to prospective and current tenants on the rental process in England and Wales, detailing their rights and responsibilities as well as the landlords' legal obligations. For landlords, the guide can be used as a checklist to keep on top of the latest legislation and what you are required to do to ensure your property is compliant. Additionally, it can help to educate some tenants who might not have rented before about the process, improving tenant-landlord relations. Unless you are happy printing the guide out for each tenant, sending them a direct link via email to the most up to date version of the guidance (currently March 2023[160]) is usually the most practical way to provide this guide. You should ask your tenant to sign to confirm they have received the guide so you have a written record of this.

---

[160] https://www.gov.uk/government/publications/how-to-rent.

HMO Property Set Up

As with EPCs, under Section 21 of the Housing Act 1988, you are currently unable to repossess your property using a Section 21 'no fault possession' notice if you fail to issue the most up to date guide at the start of all new tenancies. This, therefore, can have significant legal implications for you as a landlord. Any updates to the guide do not need to be provide to your tenants during their tenancy, provided you issued them with the most up to date guide at the time their tenancy began. However, you must provide the updated copy to them if their tenancy is renewed or if a statutory periodic tenancy is entered into at the end of a fixed term assured shorthold tenancy (AST).

Tenancy Deposit Schemes (TDS) And Prescribed Information

Most tenancies in HMOs are ASTs and as a landlord, you are required to register and protect your tenant's deposit, which should be no more than five weeks rent in total, in accordance with the Tenant Fees Act 2019[161]. Deposits should be held in a government-approved deposit protection scheme, such as the Tenancy Deposit Service or Deposit Protection Service within 30 days of the deposit being received by a landlord.

The TDS allows tenants to get their deposit back at the end of their fixed term tenancy, should they decide not to renew it. This is provided they have met the terms of their tenancy agreement, have not damaged their room or the property in any way and have paid their rent. Costs can be deducted if there is direct damage to the property, indirect damage due to tenant negligence, damaged or missing contents (such as furniture supplied by the landlord), returning the room in an unclean state, leaving unwanted belongings at the end of the tenancy and outstanding rental fees. However, costs cannot be

---

[161] https://www.legislation.gov.uk/ukpga/2019/4/contents

deducted for general maintenance and repair works as a result of 'fair wear and tear'. Landlords must return the tenant's deposit within ten days of agreeing how much should be paid back. In the event of a dispute arising between yourself and a tenant over the amount to be paid back, the TDS will continue to protect the deposit until any issues are resolved. In addition to registering the deposit within 30 days, landlords have a responsibility to provide tenants with 'Prescribed Information' within this 30-day period. Prescribed information is specific information relating to the tenancy agreement which commonly includes:

- The address of the rented property;

- The deposit amount;

- How the deposit is protected;

- The name and contact details of the TDS and the relevant dispute resolution service;

- The landlord's name and address (or letting agency's);

- The name and contact details of any third-party who's paid the deposit;

- Details of why some or all of the deposit may be kept by the landlord;

- How to apply to return the deposit;

- What to do if the landlord cannot be reached at the end of the AST agreement; and

- What to do in the event of a dispute.

HMO Property Set Up

You must give a tenant the opportunity to check and sign the Prescribed Information to confirm that its contents are correct, under the Housing (Tenancy Deposits) (Prescribed Information) Order 2007[162]. To cover yourself, it is worthwhile issuing a prescribed information acknowledgement form for your tenants to sign and return to you as written confirmation that they have been provided with the necessary details. Where a landlord fails to protect a tenant's deposit correctly, or does not issue the prescribed information, fines can be issued up to three times the amount of the deposit. Without following the correct procedure, it can also make life much more difficult in the event that a landlord wishes to end a tenancy before the fixed term expires as this currently prevents a Section 21 notice from being issued.

House Manuals

Whilst not a legal requirement, it is useful to provide a tenant with an information pack about the property in the form of a house book or manual to help them settle in and so they don't have to keep asking you or other tenants about how the house operates when they first move in and what is around them. This could either be a physical or digital book or file. As a guide, I would recommend providing the following information in your house manual:

---

[162] https://www.legislation.gov.uk/uksi/2007/797/introduction/made.

HMO Property Set Up

House Manual Contents
Welcome message
The WiFi details and password (obviously the most important!)
Landlord contact details (and availability) and who to contact in case of an emergency
House rules (which could include things such as not disturbing other tenants (quiet hours), washing up, bringing over friends/guests etc.)
Information about when recycling and refuse bins need to be taken out for collection and whether a rota system is in place
Parking provisions and whether a rota system is in place or details relating to on-street parking
Property specific fire safety information and emergency exits/egress routes
Setting and disabling an alarm (if one is installed)
Instructions for using the boiler and central heating (where appropriate)
Stopcock location
Appliance manuals for any items you have provided within the property (oven, microwave, washing machine, tumble dryer, dishwasher, coffee machine, TV etc.)
Minor maintenance tasks tenants can carry out (such as removing hair from plugholes to avoid blockages)
A list of local amenities and facilities nearby including pubs, cafes and takeaways, leisure centres, gyms and sports facilities, doctors' surgeries, dentists and the nearest hospital
A list of local transport details, such as bus and train timetables, cycle routes, local taxi firms and bicycle and car hire firms, public rights of way
Local attractions/sights of interest

Table 73.1: Typical House Manual content guidance.

HMO Property Set Up

Property Inventory Report

An inventory report is an important in-depth report setting out a schedule of the condition of your property and its contents. These reports are created for all types of rental property, listing the furniture, fixtures and fittings in every room, along with providing a detailed description of their condition. It is essential that a full and accurate inventory is conducted every time a tenant leaves and before a new one moves in, so you have a truthful record of the condition of a property, room and/or any furniture provided, in the event of a dispute arising. Without a report, a landlord may struggle to prove that theft or damage has occurred at the end of a tenant's occupation and it is likely that any partial claim against the full deposit amount held would not be successful.

Inventories typically comprise a written and photographic report of a properties condition, including walls, floors, windows and doors, as well as any appliances and furniture supplied. To avoid reports being 'too basic', sufficient detail needs to be provided with adequate descriptions of items and their condition. Reports should include all rooms (including any walk-in cupboards or hallway or walkway areas, for example) and property components, as well as provide suitable photographic or video evidence of rooms and their components, highlighting any cleaning, damage and maintenance issues. Once completed, the report should be issued to a tenant for them to comment on. They must sign to confirm they have received the report and accept that it is accurate and presents a true depiction of the condition of the property and its contents. Where this relates to rooms in a HMO, a tenant will only need to sign for the condition of the room they occupy and the communal areas.

HMO Property Set Up

Due to the nature of HMOs, it is common for a tenant's individual room to be inspected on a quarterly or six-monthly basis (also known as an interim inspection). If you have a tenant who wishes to renew their agreement, it is worthwhile undertaking a full inspection of their room and its contents to ensure that standards continue to be maintained. At the end of a tenancy agreement or prior to a tenancy being renewed, where damage (accidental or otherwise) is identified that was not previously included in the report and you and your tenant agree this needs to be addressed, estimates should be prepared for replacements or repair works. The tenant must be informed of these costs in writing, including the amount to be deducted from the original deposit amount.

In the event of a deposit dispute arising, this is where an inventory needs to be capable of standing up in a court of law, if necessary, so the property inventory report must be capable of providing quality information which confirms the landlord's claims.

Assured Shorthold Tenancies (ASTs)

Tenancy agreements are a way for landlords to grant a set of rights over a property or room for an often specified period of time. ASTs are essential for HMOs and should be prepared so they are legally correct, clearly setting out the expectations and obligations of both the landlord and the tenant and include the correct procedures to start, maintain and end the tenancy. ASTs should also serve as a reference throughout the agreement period, in the event of certain situations (for example, non-payment of rent).

As a minimum, ASTs should include the landlords name and address or the letting agent or your solicitor's address if you'd prefer not to provide your home address (although tenants can

HMO Property Set Up

legally put in a written request for this information under Section 1 of the Landlord and Tenant Act 1985[163]) so tenants know who to contact in the event they wish to serve notice to leave. The AST should provide the full address of the property and room number to be let, as well as the full name (or names, if a shared room) of who will be the tenant(s) occupying the room. It is standard to also include a phone number and email address for each tenant and their current address, as well as a post-tenancy address where they can be reached after they move out (typically a relative's address).

ASTs should set out clearly the amount of rent to be paid and how regularly it is to be paid (for example, on a weekly or monthly basis). It should also set out that rent should be paid in advance of each period to cover that month of occupancy, the payment method to be used and importantly whether the rent can be increased during the fixed term and how often it will be reviewed during the tenancy.

Typically, ASTs for HMOs are structured so that they grant rights of occupation for an initial fixed term of six months, although you could look at agreeing a 12-month term, with a break clause at six months. Currently, this enables either the tenant or the landlord to end the tenancy early by serving appropriate notice. The AST should therefore clearly specify the start and end date of the agreement. At present, once the initial term expires, unless renewed, the agreement moves directly onto a 'statutory periodic' basis. This means the agreement continues unchanged as is from period to period, where each period is the interval at which rent is paid. For most HMOs, rent is paid on a monthly basis, therefore, the 'period' is one month.

---

[163] https://www.legislation.gov.uk/ukpga/1985/70.

HMO Property Set Up

When a fixed term comes to an end, either the tenants can move out, the tenancy continues 'as is' on a statutory periodic basis, or the landlord and tenant can sign a new tenancy agreement, with either the same terms, or different ones, for another fixed period. Should the tenant wish to leave, there is a minimum notice period of one month for tenants, whilst as a landlord serving notice on a tenant, you typically need to provide a minimum of two months' notice. The notice period for both parties should be clearly set out in the AST for clarity. For an idea of what else an AST should include, the Government has provided a 'model agreement for a shorthold assured tenancy[164]', which you can use as a basic template for designing your own ASTs and which you can add your own specific clauses to. Before using your AST however, a solicitor should check this to ensure it is both legally compliant and fair.

Section 8 And Section 21 Notices

This next part is all to do with repossessing your property, in the event that you need to regain it from a tenant. However, where possible, it is always worth trying to resolve any disputes with your tenant before seeking repossession of their room, such as working with your tenant to manage any rental payments and arrears or agreeing to a rental repayment plan, or in the case of 'in-house' disputes, trying to get to the bottom of any issues with other members of the house. Should these measures fail, there are currently two ways of applying for possession in England; through either a 'Section 8' notice or through a 'Section 21' notice. These are known as such

---

[164] https://www.gov.uk/government/publications/model-agreement-for-a-shorthold-assured-tenancy.

HMO Property Set Up

because they operate under Section 8 and Section 21 of the Housing Act 1988[165].

The difference between the two is that, put simply, a Section 8 notice can be served if your tenant breaks the terms of their tenancy before it ends, whilst a Section 21 notice can be served on tenants after their fixed term tenancy ends or during a tenancy which has no fixed end date (a periodic tenancy). It is also known as a 'no fault' procedure, where the fixed term is ending and you simply wish to have the property back.

Section 8 Notices

Section 8 notices are served on a tenant by the landlord who wishes to regain possession of a property during the fixed term of an AST but can only be issued to a tenant who has breached the terms of their agreement and if certain circumstances have been met. There are currently 17 different grounds on which a landlord can seek possession, prior to the end of the fixed term tenancy, eight of which are mandatory and nine of which are discretionary. Not all of them are specific to the use of a property as a HMO, although most of the discretionary grounds are more likely to apply to HMO use.

Mandatory grounds include the landlord taking the property as their own home, becoming a mortgageable property (where the lender wants to repossess the property or the mortgagee wants to dispose of the property with vacant possession), becoming a holiday let, becoming a property tied to an educational institution, housing for a minister of religion, for refurbishment purposes, following the death of a tenant, following the conviction of a tenant for a serious offence,

---

[165] https://www.legislation.gov.uk/ukpga/1988/50/contents.

HMO Property Set Up

notice being served on the landlord by the Secretary of State in respect of illegal immigrant and for a tenant being in two months of rent arrears.

Discretionary grounds include alternative accommodation, any rent arrears, regular failure to pay rent, breach of tenancy agreement, neglect of property, anti-social behaviour, domestic violence, poor treatment of furnishings, the rental agreement being tied to employment (i.e. the tenant is employed by the landlord and has now left that employment) and false statements.

Prior to serving notice, it is worthwhile seeking legal advice to understand where you stand. Sending a tenant reminder letters that they are in breach of their tenancy agreement every seven, 14 and 21 days is a good idea too as it provides the tenant with an opportunity to deal with any issues or rectify the situation before matters are taken further. If they still fail to deal with the issues, then the issuing of a Section 8 notice won't come as a surprise.

To start the process, you will need to serve a Section 8 notice on the tenant using 'Form 3' (notice seeking possession of a property let on an assured tenancy or an assured agricultural occupancy[166]), which sets out your intentions to seek possession and the grounds on which possession is sought. The notice period you give your tenant will depend on the reason(s) why possession is sought. Some grounds require a minimum two months' notice, whilst others only require two weeks' notice. Effectively, this is the expiry date after which court proceedings can begin. The notice gives the tenant a further opportunity to rectify the issue(s) before it gets to the

---

[166] Available from https://www.gov.uk/guidance/assured-tenancy-forms.

HMO Property Set Up

court stage. The notice can be given directly to the tenant, put through the door of their room or posted to them. The tenant must sign and return a copy of the notice the landlord. It is a good idea to keep a record of the date and method of service as well as details of any witnesses who can vouch that notice was provided.

If you find your tenant fails to leave by the expiry date set out in the notice, you can apply to a court for a possession order to evict your tenant. This can be started on the day following the date cited on the Section 8 form, which is the date the notice is deemed to be 'served'. Issuing a Section 8 notice on a tenant, however, does not guarantee an 'easy ride' to repossession and you may have to wait several months just to get a court date. When you get to court, there is no guarantee that you will be granted a possession order either. This typically depends on what grounds for possession are listed and the strength of your argument. The evidence is closely scrutinised by the court and factors such as hardship and extenuating circumstances suffered by the tenant are taken into account.

Where a court is satisfied that the landlord is entitled to take possession on one or more of the 17 grounds, then a possession order will be granted. This can take effect within 14 days, although can be extended up to six weeks in some circumstances. If the possession order fails to motivate the tenant to move on, you can return to court and obtain instructions for bailiffs to evict the tenant. You will of course be liable for the courts fee and any bailiff fees, if necessary. On the designated 'eviction day', in addition to bailiffs, in some instances police may also need to be involved to ensure the tenant vacates the property and does cause a breach of the peace.

HMO Property Set Up

Section 21 Notices

Currently, Section 21 notices (Form 6A: for a no fault possession notice on an assured shorthold tenancy[167]) are notices which can be served at the end of an AST agreement or when a tenancy becomes 'periodic' and is the first step taken by a landlord wishing to repossess their property where no fault or breach of the tenancy agreement has occurred by the tenant. They are often known as 'no fault possession notices' because of this and are generally a very straightforward way for landlords to repossess a property, provided the procedure is followed and completed correctly. It is worth bearing in mind however that Section 21 notices cannot be served within the first six months of an AST.

In order for landlords to regain possession of their property, it is essential the correct legal process is followed at all stages of the tenancy. Failure to do so can result in a number of problems which can prove costly and result in delaying the repossession of a property or room. It is therefore advisable to seek legal advice before commencing the process. In order to be able to serve a valid Section 21 notice, you will need to have provided the following items to your tenants at the start of their agreement:

- A valid AST agreement

- The latest version of the 'How to Rent' guide;

- An up-to-date Energy Performance Certificate;

- Gas Safety Certificate;

---

[167] https://www.gov.uk/guidance/assured-tenancy-forms.

HMO Property Set Up

- Register their deposit correctly (within 30 days of receiving it) and provide details of the tenancy deposit scheme;

- Provide the necessary Prescribed Information within the 30-day period of receiving the tenant's deposit; and

- Where the property is a HMO, you must have an appropriate and up to date HMO licence.

When serving notice, it is worth double checking that your tenants name and address are accurate and match those in the tenancy agreement. You will need to give your tenant at least two months' notice, even if the agreement is out of the fixed term and is now 'periodic' and specify a moved-out date where you will take the property or room back. Of course, if the tenant is happy to move out before this date, that is not a problem. You can serve notice either by post (First Class enables it to be deemed 'served' on the second business day from posting), email (if the tenancy agreement allows it and your tenant has voluntarily provided their email address) or in person (where it is deemed to be served on the date of delivery if before 16:30 on a weekday. Once notice has been served and acknowledged in writing by the tenants (certificate of posting, date stamped photos if hand delivered and delivery and read receipts if by email), make sure to keep accurate records, including ensuring all exchanges are signed for by the tenant and yourself.

If on the day where the tenant is supposed to have vacated the property by comes and goes and the tenant is still there you can use the 'accelerated possession procedure' by applying to the courts to legally remove the tenant. You will need to

HMO Property Set Up

complete a form[168] and send it to your local court with all relevant information and documents and pay a fee. On the court date, you don't have to attend yourself and the court will typically grant the 'possession order', providing you have followed the correct processes, provided all the necessary information to your tenant and where your tenant does not offer any defence.

In cases where your tenant still fails to leave after the granting of a possession order you will need to return to court and ask the bailiffs to evict them. Again, as with the Section 8 process, you will be liable for their fees and will have to wait for a date when they are available. On the eviction date, you or a representative will need to attend the property with the bailiffs. If the tenant is still there, the bailiffs will remove them and allow you to change the locks.

Emerging Legislation

The Government issued a pledge in the White Paper 'A Fairer Private Rented Sector[169]' as part of the emerging Renters Reform Bill[170], which builds on the Levelling Up White Paper and sets out the Government's plans to fundamentally reform the PRS and 'level up' housing quality. This has resulted in the Renters Reform Bill, which was first read in the House of Commons on 17th May 2023 and is currently being debated. As part of the reforms, the Government is seeking to abolish Section 21 no-fault evictions to replacement them with an amended version of the Section 8 Grounds for Possession to

---

[168] https://www.gov.uk/evicting-tenants/accelerated-possession-orders.

[169] https://www.gov.uk/government/publications/a-fairer-private-rented-sector/a-fairer-private-rented-sector.

[170] Expected to be debated and voted on in the late autumn of 2023.

HMO Property Set Up

provide a 'modern tenancy system' and a more secure tenancy structure, coupled with a 'powerful' new Private Renters Ombudsman so that disputes between tenants and landlords can be settled quickly and cost effectively without going to court. The aim is to ensure a tenancy will only end if the tenant ends it or if the landlord has a valid ground for possession. The aim is to *"empower tenants to challenge poor practice and reduce the costs associated with unexpected moves."*

The reforming of the Grounds for Possession are meant to ensure landlords have an *"effective means of gaining possession of their properties when necessary"*. As part of this, the Government is proposing to *"expediate landlords' ability to evict tenants who disrupt neighbourhoods through antisocial behaviour and introduce new grounds for persistent arrears and the sale of property."* Landlords will however only be able to evict a tenant in 'reasonable circumstances', to be defined in law, which will be at the discretion of a judge. The Government considers that by removing Section 21, this will *"level the playing field between landlord and tenant, empowering tenants to challenge poor practice and unjustified rent increases, as well as incentivising landlords to engage and resolve issues. With a single tenancy structure, both parties will better understand their rights and responsibilities"*.

As part of the proposals, the Government is seeking to move all tenants on an assured tenancy or ASTs onto a single system of periodic tenancies to provide greater security for tenants whilst retaining important flexibility offered by private rented accommodation. The changes are proposed to enable tenants to leave poor quality properties without remaining liable for the rent or to move more easily when their circumstances change, for example to take up a new job

HMO Property Set Up

opportunity. Tenants will need to provide two months' notice when leaving a tenancy, ensuring landlords can 'recoup the costs of finding a tenant and avoid lengthy void periods'. Further, through the reforms, the Government has set out that the system must work for responsible landlords, letting agents and communities, where landlords who maintain good letting practices and standards are a valued part of the housing market and must be able to regain possession of their properties when necessary. The reforms aim to introduce comprehensive, fair and efficient grounds which strike a balance between protecting tenants' securities and landlords' rights to manage their property.

In addition, measures are proposed to end the use of rent review clauses *"preventing tenants being locked into automatic rent increases that are vague or may not reflect changes in the market price"* and restricting rent increases to once per year in a move to help combat the rising costs of living. Other measures include minimum housing standards for the PRS by widening the application of the 'Decent Homes Standard[171]', which currently only applies to the social housing sector. It is not clear how this will interact with HMO licensing legislation at this stage.

Another measure the reforms seek to bring in is a digital 'Property Portal' to *"provide a single 'front door' to help landlords understand, and demonstrate compliance with their legal requirements."* The Government considers that *"too often tenants find out too late that they are renting a substandard property from landlords who wilfully fail to*

---

[171] Explained in the 'Fairer Private Rented Sector White Paper' as homes which are "free from the most serious health and safety hazards, such as fall risks, fire risks, or carbon monoxide poisoning."

HMO Property Set Up

comply, and councils don't know who to track down when serious issues arise". It notes that the portal will *"support good landlords to demonstrate regulatory compliance and to attract prospective tenants."* The nature and extent of the portal is yet to be determined but could include a system where landlords and agents are required to meet minimum standards before properties can be let out. Again, how this is intended to interact with existing HMO licensing standards is unclear. The introduction of the reforms may also see landlords and agents be legally required to register their properties on the portal. Local authorities may be empowered to take enforcement action against landlords who fail to join the portal or register their properties as well. Other measures include tenant's being given the legal right to request to keep a pet in their home, which a landlord cannot 'unreasonably' refuse. How this will work in a HMO setting remains unclear.

It is currently estimated that the Bill will receive Royal Assent in the late autumn of 2023 once it has been passed by both House of Parliament. It will then become the Renters (Reform) Act. Following this, it is expected that the Act will apply to all new tenancies (apart from Section 21) at least six months after receiving Royal Assent (summer/autumn of 2024). After 12 months from Royal Assent (summer/autumn 2025), the Act will be applicable to all existing tenancies which will transition onto the new system, meaning Section 21 will cease to apply. It is not known what form these new measures will take following debates, but they are clearly on the horizon, so make sure to keep yourself up to date as matters evolve. The Bill could result in more landlords seeking to leave the PRS, reducing the supply of rental properties, however, this could present an opportunity for landlords remaining in the PRS to pick up other's portfolios and help serve the demand for quality rented accommodation.

74. General Data Protection Regulations

Since leaving the EU, the United Kingdom General Data Protection Regulations (UK-GDPR) and an amended version of the Data Protection Act 2018[172] became the UK's data privacy law which governs the processing of personal data from individuals within the UK. These regulations took effect from 31st January 2020.

The regulations can often be a point of confusion for some landlords who aren't sure what their obligations are. To help with interpreting them, I have simplified the key requirements, although for your reading pleasure, further details can be found on the Information Commissioners Office (ICO)[173] website. The purpose of GDPR is to give individuals full control over how their personal data is handled, including rights to be forgotten, the right to alter data and the right to transfer data. In cases where a tenant no longer wishes for you to hold their information, they can decide to update it, transfer it to a 'competitor' or request for it to be deleted permanently. As a landlord, it is your legal responsibility to comply with a tenant's request.

There are four main steps involved in complying with GDPR. These are: a) registering with the ICO; b) preparing a data audit; c) obtaining a GDPR compliant landlord privacy policy; and d) the handling and protection of data collected.

In cases where you are required to store, use or delete a tenant's personal information, such as their name and contact

---

[172] https://www.legislation.gov.uk/ukpga/2018/12/contents.
[173] https://ico.org.uk/for-organisations/guide-to-data-protection/guide-to-the-general-data-protection-regulation-gdpr/.

details using an electronic device, then you need to be registered to do so with the ICO, for which a small annual fee is required. A registration self-assessment form is available online which can help you decided if you need to register[174].

The regulations set out that you must 'audit' the information you collect and hold, decide under what lawful basis the information is being processed and document this. As part of your audit, this should involve looking at what personal information will be held; whether or not it is 'sensitive' personal information; the method by which this information is held; who it is shared with; how long it is held for and how it can be removed. To further comply with GDPR, you'll need to document your 'processing activities'. This should list categories of people you 'process' data for. As a landlord, 'processing activities' are considered to be where you have:

- Enquiring tenants;

- Prospective tenants;

- Actual tenants; and

- Former tenants.

To process this personal information, you must have a lawful basis to do so. It is your responsibility to keep your tenant's data safe and secure and for it to only be used for lawful purposes. For landlords, this typically involves where there is:

---

[174] https://ico.org.uk/for-organisations/data-protection-fee/self-assessment/.

HMO Property Set Up

- A legitimate interest: as a landlord, you will use people's data in a way they would reasonably expect for it to be used and there is a reasonable justification for the processing of that information for a commercial purpose;

- A contractual fulfilment: personal data may be used to fulfil a contract;

- A legal requirement: as a landlord, you may be required to process data for right to rent checks, referencing checks, or for tenancy deposit services; and

- Consent: as a landlord, you may speak to housing benefits officers in some circumstances.

Following the undertaking of an audit and understanding the lawful basis you are allowed to collect and process the information under, you are obliged to inform tenants of how you will use their information. A GDPR complaint Landlord Privacy Policy should be prepared and issued to your tenants (and any other relevant parties). This should be provided at the time of collecting any personal information from them and should identify how their personal information is collected, held, used and how long it is retained for. Tenants do have the right to be sent any information you hold about them as well so you should have a procedure in place to allow for this to happen and know how to respond to such a request. A written record of your tenant's consent should be kept on file. This could be in the form of a signed document (physical or digital), email or text message.

HMO Property Set Up

All data collected must be kept safe. Physical data, such as paperwork, external hard drives and USB sticks should be securely locked away, whilst digital data devices, such as computers, laptops, mobile phones and cloud storage should be password protected. Fingerprint and facial recognition software can be useful tools and act as an added layer of security for personal data protection. As part of being a responsible landlord, you should keep each tenant's data organised and delete anything you are not required to keep. As mentioned, tenants do have the 'right to be forgotten', where a request can be made to remove all information you hold about them, unless you are required to retain that information for legal purposes.

HMO Property Set Up

75. Property And Tenant Management Software

As the previous sections have demonstrated, being a landlord certainly isn't always an easy job, so it is worthwhile trying to make your life as simple and as organised as possible. Whilst you may be pretty adept with a spreadsheet, there are now various property management and landlord/tenant software packages out there to help you save both time and money in administering your business and managing tenants. Some are more focused on the tenancy side of matters, whilst others are more focused on the financial management of your properties and organisation of paperwork/certification.

Proper management of HMOs is especially key due to the additional numbers of tenants involved – you could easily find yourself having to juggle multiple mortgages, inspections, certificates and over 30+ individual tenancy agreements spread across five, six or more HMO properties, for example. Therefore, anything you can do to help keep track of all the paperwork and legislative requirements, along with tracing payments and other important financials will really help you build and maintain a successful and profitable HMO business – as well as help keep your sanity!

In this next part of the chapter, I'll go through a couple of the available packages currently out there, in no particular order.

GoTenant

In my opinion, GoTenant[175] is a particularly useful paid-for tool, providing both property and tenant management features.

---

[175] https://gotenant.co.uk/.

HMO Property Set Up

In terms of property, it allows you to track rents for all your properties and add notes to follow up with people who might need chasing. The software also helps you monitor the performance of all your properties and comes with training videos, a customer help desk, live chat and face-to-face training courses, helping you to quickly and efficiently set up and optimise your property portfolio.

As for tenant management, it enables you to create your own professional looking website to help market your property, see all your bookings as well as your availability to conduct viewings. It features surveys which help with automatically 'pre-qualifying' prospective tenants to see whether they would be suitable to rent a room. If a tenant passes the qualification criteria and then wishes to view the property, the software can send email confirmations and text reminders to them ahead of a visit to help ensure you don't waste your time with any 'no-shows'.

The software allows you to put together AST agreements and provide all the relevant safety certificates and the latest Right to Rent information to tenants for them to sign electronically, minimising the time you spend on paperwork and helping you with systemising your approach. You can set up reminders across your property portfolio for all property safety certificates so these can be renewed in good time, ensuring you remain compliant.

The software enables you to store all your documents and email conversations in an easy and accessible way, so correspondence relating to specific tenants and properties can be found without hassle. Another benefit is that it allows you to produce personalised documents and email templates to send to your tenants.

HMO Property Set Up

In terms of ongoing maintenance, there is the ability to log any reported issues, provide general household updates and give tenants access to their documents and information. Any outstanding actions can be quickly flagged, followed up on and resolved.

As for rent, payment management and accounting, the software integrates with Xero for live bank feeds and allows you to see which of your tenants have paid and those who have not, notifying you by email if tenants are overdue on their rent. It is also capable of creating recurring invoices for your tenants.

COHO

Next on my list there is COHO[176], which is, in my opinion, another great paid-for platform which helps to manage shared living properties and housemates in one property management software platform. COHO allows landlords and property managers to oversee HMO finances by tracking portfolio income, expenses and fees and to generate tenant and landlord settlement statement and profitability reports.

For prospective new tenants, the platform provides a useful 'onboarding' process which provides flexible application forms to suite individual circumstances using pre-set mandatory and optional questions, in addition to your own questions and automatic calculations of pro rata rental amounts to create rent schedules. Applicants are also able to acknowledge compliance documents as they go through the process and can eSign documents online to confirm the tenancy agreement. Completed forms are then stored securely.

---

[176] https://coho.life/?&NR=1.

HMO Property Set Up

There is even a 'move-in' monies calculator and a way to take holding fees to reserve rooms.

For existing tenants, there is an easy to use tenant messaging platform which enables landlords to keep all relevant property and tenant messages in one place and allows for maintenance issues to be reported, managed and tracked. This allows you to see any open and outstanding issues across your portfolio and for individual tenants, or whole households to be kept up to date with the progress of resolving any issues flagged, from first logging to completion.

To keep up to date with all compliance issues, regulations and legislation, the platform allows landlords and property managers to store and share important documents, obtain renewal and notification reminders, either on login or via email alert which can be set in advance to suit your requirements and log an audit trail. Confirmation of tenants acknowledging receipt of important documents is also provided. If tenants fail to acknowledge an important document or certificate, this is flagged to you and you can then take action to ensure they acknowledge it, giving you peace of mind should a dispute ever arise.

For the marketing of your rooms, a marketing profile can be put together which pushes listings to SpareRoom and Facebook Maketplace and enables you to advertise on COHOs platform itself. Once your advert is live, the platform allows you to view leads from multiple sources, as well as managing viewing bookings by inviting prospective tenants to viewings or dismissing leads.

When you are ready to propose a viewing date, you can select a date and it is automatically added to your viewings calendar.

HMO Property Set Up

Dates can then be accepted or rejected by the applicant. All viewing requests are tracked and logged as conversations so you can keep up to date with who is interested in your rooms, enabling a single conversation to go from lead, to viewing to tenant.

LendLord

Thirdly, another useful property management system in my opinion is Lendlord[177]. The core functionality of this platform is free and allows you to efficiently manage all your property and tenancy details and relevant data securely, track your income and expenditure on each property, generate downloadable reports and create a payment schedule for your tenants.

Alerts can be set up to let you know when payments have been made and when they are overdue so you can track your monthly income and expenses with ease. The software enables you to input the dates of any mortgage product or insurance expiry dates, EPC, gas safety, EICR, tenancy agreements and other important dates you need to keep on top of to help ensure your property portfolio runs smoothly. Additionally, you can also store important documents relating to your properties, such as certificates or invoices and receipts for works carried out, as well as tenancy agreements.

Ongoing KPIs and insights into how your portfolio is performing are available too. This lets you see an individual property's key metrics such as ROI, LTV, yield, P&L and more, such as where potential savings could be made.

---

[177] https://www.lendlord.io/.

HMO Property Set Up

Other functionality includes current and long-term portfolio evaluation and stress testing, mortgage and tax insights and deal analysis for other property deals.

Summary

In addition to the above three software packages, there are loads of other software packages available for you to find and try, some paid for and some free and all with slightly different levels of functionality. However, you may find you are perfectly happy using a simple spreadsheet to manage your tenants and properties – if that is the case, then feel free to carry on!

However, if you are looking to systemise your property portfolio by using tenant and property management software, whichever option you choose, try to find one which is easy for you to use, suits your needs and allows you to make more efficient use of your time. Some paid-for platforms offer free trials to allow you to get used to the way the software works, so do explore these options too. When set up correctly, this type of software can really help give you peace of mind that your HMO property portfolio – or any other rental property you set up – is running as smoothly as possible.

76. Keeping Up To Date

The regulations and legislation concerning HMOs and the PRS in general are constantly evolving and being updated at both national and local levels, as has been explained in previous chapters. The PRS always appears to be under some kind of scrutiny, be that in the media or from the Government. Legislative changes are frequently being talked about, which could impact on what landlords and property developers are required to do, if, and, or when any proposed measures are brought in.

Because of the evolving nature of the PRS and with different legislative and regulatory requirements often overlapping, it can sometimes feel difficult to keep track of the changes being proposed and to stay one step ahead of any incoming changes. Remember though that by embracing change, you also embrace opportunities. Whilst some changes may result in regulatory or legislative 'challenges' being implemented, these can actually benefit some landlords and property developers as others may seek to exist the PRS, increasing demand for rental accommodation and reducing your direct competition.

To help stay abreast of changes there are a few simple steps you can take to ensure you remain up to date, such as:

- Signing up to receive local plan updates from the LPA;

- Become a member of a national landlord association, such as the NRLA[178];

---

[178] https://www.nrla.org.uk/.

HMO Property Set Up

- Join any local landlord forums (either private or Council-led);

- Keep in regular contact with your HMO licensing team;

- Make use of the free advice and guidance available on the following websites and forums:

    o Property Tribes[179]

    o HMO Hub[180]

    o Property Hub[181]

    o Landlord Zone[182]

    o OpenRent Community[183]

    o Property Investment Project[184] and

    o Nearly Legal[185].

You can also use the power of social media (at your discretion, as not all advice posted is reliable or accurate) and join various HMO and Landlord groups on Facebook or LinkedIn to keep in touch with important updates. It is also

---

[179] https://www.propertytribes.com/.
[180] https://www.hmohub.co.uk/.
[181] https://propertyhub.net/.
[182] https://www.landlordzone.co.uk/.
[183] https://community.openrent.co.uk/.
[184] https://www.propertyinvestmentproject.co.uk/.
[185] https://nearlylegal.co.uk/.

HMO Property Set Up

worthwhile following other landlords and HMO property developers on Instagram to pick up tips and see what they're doing regarding trending themes and how the rooms of their properties are decorated and fitted out – some can be quite inspirational!

HMO Property Set Up

Summary

In this final section, I have briefly discussed the realities of being a landlord, including providing an explanation of the certificates, checks and other requirements you will need to ensure you are compliant with relevant guidance and legislation, including GDPR, as well as outlining how property and tenant management software can help assist you in staying organised.

I have also provided some guidance on how you can keep up to date as a landlord so you can always be prepared in the event of any legislative or regulatory changes which could affect the way in which your HMO property business operates.

Conclusion And Final Thoughts

And that brings us to the end of our journey – but perhaps just the start of yours! At this point, I'd like to say a huge 'thank you' for taking the time to read my book. I have spent a great deal of time researching and putting together its contents into what I hope is an interesting, informative and comprehensive guide. My hope is that you are now armed with the essential knowledge you will need to give you the confidence to take those first steps into setting up a HMO correctly and that by using the information in this book, you will be able to maintain a successful and profitable HMO property business. For those of you reading who may already have HMO properties, I hope the information has either served as a reminder for you or has helped to 'plug' any gaps in your knowledge that you may not have been aware of previously or given you inspiration to try something different.

Overall, my hope is that this knowledge will help motivate you and provide you with the drive towards successfully achieving your goals and objectives. But this is just the start – there is no substitute for experience. Take this opportunity to invest in yourself (or continue investing in yourself) from a personal and professional point of view and put the steps covered in this book into practice by investing in your future. You'll certainly learn more from taking action and 'doing something' than any book can teach you, no matter how comprehensive!

HMO property development (and other property development strategies for that matter) is an exciting and satisfying business and when set up correctly, can ensure you are able to generate high, reliable and secure long-term returns in a relatively low-risk way. Remember, there will of course be times when the path towards success appears challenging but try not to get too 'bogged down'. In these times, focus on the reasons why you wish to become a HMO property developer, your goals and objectives and your business plan. These will provide you with a solid foundation to continue onwards in tougher times and will ensure you are able to take the necessary actions towards success.

Throughout the journey, don't forget to keep learning and developing yourself so you can pass that knowledge and experience onto others who may just to setting out themselves.

Stay In Touch

It would be great to connect with you via social media. Please feel free to get in touch with me to discuss anything HMO property related, or just for a general chat about property:

LinkedIn: hmo-property-setup

Facebook: @hmopropertysetup

Thanks again for reading – and best of luck with your future endeavours in the world of HMOs! I'd be delighted to hear how you get on.

Printed in Great Britain
by Amazon